Second Edition

 POINTS OF DEPARTURE

A Collection of Contemporary Essays

• Michelle J. Brazier •

Rutgers University

Houghton Mifflin Company
Boston   New York

Custom Publishing Editor: Dee Renfrow
Custom Publishing Production Manager: Tina Kozik
Custom Publishing Project Coordinator: Anisha Sandhu

Cover Designer: Majel Peters
Cover Art: Transportation, A Pictorial Archive from Nineteenth-Century Sources/Jim
Harter/Dover Publications

Printed in the United States of America.

ISBN: 978-0-618-63689-1
ISBN: 0-618-63689-7
N-04843

    4 5 6 7 8 9 – BMP – 07

Houghton Mifflin
     Custom Publishing

222 Berkeley Street • Boston, MA 02116

Address all correspondence and order information to the above address.

Contents

Introduction

Beyond the Text Message

Reading practices have changed dramatically in the past fifteen years. Just imagine, when your instructors were undergraduates, some as recently as the 1990s, college students rarely carried cell phones, many didn't know what email was, let alone how to use it, modems were external, and instant messaging was only used by the computer savvy crowd. Students got most of their news from the papers and network TV. Now, you're more likely to log on to your preferred website or check your cell phone to see what is going on in the world. Advances in technology have changed our way of reading, and not just *where* we read or *what* we read, but *how* we read. Innovation in print technology is nothing new, of course. It began with the printing press over five hundred years ago, and has recently brought us blogging, personal online journalism. As we adapt to the quicker pace of life, we are all perfecting the text-message, a kind of written speech that serves efficiency and direct communication, but not necessarily complexity or nuance.

And yet, the world becomes more complex every day, and the power and prevalence of the text-message has not replaced our need to communicate and understand this complexity through reading and writing. You may have done this kind of reading and writing only in school, unless you are an avid reader or writer. But even if you don't consider yourself an active reader, the truth is that you're reading all the time. You're just not reading extended pieces of prose, the kind of writing that invites you to process complex ideas, develop your own ideas, and fashion a response of equal complexity and depth. Learning to read and write with complexity are two privileges and responsibilities of being a college student, and the need for these skills doesn't end when you receive your diploma. In your professional lives, regardless of your career, this is the kind of reading and writing future employers and employees will expect of you as a college graduate.

With this collection of essays, you'll be reading beyond the text message, beyond the text bytes of daily life. It's our greatest hope that in the process of simply reading these essays, you'll find that reading beyond the text message, finding your own position, and articulating your own response in writing can be a rewarding experience, an enjoyable initiation into the reading practices of the literate public. This collection is designed for you as a way to begin that initiation. It's also designed for your instructors, as a way to connect with you through reading and writing about contemporary issues that affect us all. Each essay in this collection is for you a point of access into the university and the world beyond, and a point departure as you write your way into the on-going conversation.

Reading in the University, Reading in the World

In the university, you will observe, and soon participate in, two kinds of conversations: first, conversations in which members of specific departments, or disciplines, communicate with one another using their professional vocabularies, and share the unique insights that their own discipline has laid claim to; and second, conversations in which individuals across the university use a common vocabulary to discuss issues that mutually affect their disciplines. The first kind of conversation privileges those who have already adopted the vocabulary, or learned the discourse, of a discipline; for example, two physicians can talk to one another about a disease in great depth because their shared vocabulary can accommodate details that a typical patient's vocabulary cannot. Because of a shared vocabulary, those physicians may be able to communicate some of that knowledge to a biologist, or chemist, or even engineer. But the depth of a doctor's knowledge is useless to a patient who has not learned that vocabulary, unless the doctor can translate it into a language that is understandable and clear.

That is why the second kind of conversation is of interest to me when teaching reading and writing. If we want to introduce you to the scholarship of the university, and you enter college needing to practice or improve your reading skills, enhance your vocabulary, and become more confident with your writing skills, then it's in your best interest and that of your instructors to begin communicating with each other through essays that use a common language. You will learn a specialized vocabulary, the discourse of your discipline, upon choosing your major or entering a professional school. This anthology will not teach you the technical language of the biochemist, the political scientist, the theologian, the physician, or the literary critic. But in designing this book, we were interested in initiating conversations about issues of importance to these specialists. We believe that composition courses, at their best, can teach you to read and write at the college level by using essays that open up topics of importance to the entire university community, and by using language that invites you in, rather than language that makes you feel excluded at the outset. And we see these cross-curricular conversations within the university as the jumping-off place for conversations in and about the world around us.

As a result, this collection is not a typical composition rhetoric or introduction to writing within an English department. You will notice that the table of contents is not organized in units by topic, or style of writing, as is common in composition readers. Instead, it is decidedly cross-disciplinary, without announcing at the outset the differences between these disciplines. We hope you will discover in college where and how these disciplines overlap, to discover where inter-disciplinary conversations can emerge, and we believe that the writing composition classroom is an ideal place to begin. We encourage you and your instructors to create the cross-curricular connections between these essays that are most compelling to you. For example, you might begin the course reading about factory farming and animal rights, and wind your way through a consideration of how life on Mars could affect our idea of God; reality TV and American democracy; racial profiling and civil liberties; the global market of soccer; and end with chaos theory in the business world. We invite you to read and write across these essays, and across the categories in which we could place them, and we've selected essays that allow you specifically to do this kind of work, to introduce you to the possibilities of thinking "connectively" within and beyond your composition classroom.

To help you begin making these kinds of connections, most of the essays in this collection, even those by recognized scholars and experts in traditionally academic fields, are written for popular or mainstream publications. Included are essays by physicist Paul Davies, anthropologist Jane Goodall, and sociologist Arlie Russell Hochschild; socio-political journalists Andrew Sullivan and Katha Pollitt; writers Barbara Kingsolver and Adam Gopnik; cognitive psychologist Steven Pinker; and philosopher Alain de Botton, among many from other fields. I've brought these authors together in one table of contents to create the kinds of cross-curricular conversations that have potential to thrive in a university setting, but are easily lost in the translation between departments or professional schools. Many of these authors move seamlessly in their careers between university communities or research centers and the general public. We might even call some of them public intellectuals. For example, for more than forty years, Jane Goodall has communicated her deep knowledge of anthropology, through her study of the chimpanzees of Gombe in Africa, to people all over the world. In her essay, "In the Forests of Gombe," she considers her scientific work in the context of a personal loss, and explores the connections between anthropology, religion, and spirituality in nature. In her chapter on capitalism and the family, Arlie Russell

Hochschild shows us how an individual decision to go to a shopping mall may be part of a much larger economic and social structure. In addition to being scholars, these two authors, and many others in this collection, are experienced in writing to communicate with a broad audience; that is, they have written essays, opinion pieces, and articles for newspapers and popular journals in the course of their academic careers.

All of these essays are written for an audience of readers who want to learn about an issue, figure out their own position, and then join the discussion. That's one reason they are so readable, and so enjoyable. They are written for the literate public. That is what you are becoming a part of as a college student, regardless of your major or your intended career. And your semesters in college composition classes are the first steps toward joining this literate public. We would like you to regard your time spent using this collection as practice in the art and skill of reading; to learn that, with discipline and commitment, reading well can be valuable to your overall education *and* pleasurable along the way; and that even at college age—as adults—you can shape the way you think and learn by regarding reading as both a point of departure for your own writing, and as a useful project in and of itself. We want to give you practice with reading, make you excited about reading, and we have done our best to choose essays that you will find interesting and relevant.

Working with This Collection

You may have heard the expression, "Practice makes perfect." Most people accept this as true with activities that take visible effort, like sports or music. Most people also understand that practice alone really isn't enough; it also takes a good coach and the resources to back you up. You will only become a great basketball player by practicing consistently over the years, and finding the right coach for motivation and technique. Having a good pair of shoes also helps. You will only become a concert violinist by practicing several hours a day for many years, and finding the right violin teacher for guidance and support. You don't need a Stradivarius to be a fine violinist, but with enough practice you can certainly appreciate one. The same goes with reading and writing. The more time and effort you invest in both, with the right resources, and the right guidance, the better you will become at both—and the more enjoyable reading and writing will become for you. Your instructor will provide the guidance; this collection and a good dictionary are your current set of resources. It's up to you to put in the time and effort, to practice.

Prepare yourself for this kind of practice, and try to think of it as an opportunity. You will be reading a great deal over the course of your semester. We do not expect you to absorb in a few months what you might have been absorbing over ten years of consistent, dedicated reading. But we can expect that within one semester, your reading skills will improve dramatically when focused on longer essays that demand reading concentration over time. Unlike many composition readers in which essays may be as short as two or three pages, the essays in this collection range from 8 to 20 pages, every one a complete book chapter or article. We have included no excerpts in this collection, in part because of our commitment to longer texts, and in part because we want to give you examples of complete works, in content and structure. We ask nothing less from you than to produce papers that are complete, thoughtful, well-constructed responses to the essays in this collection.

We have chosen essays that are examples of what we want you to produce in writing, and what we hope you will learn to value—in their vocabulary and clear sentences, assertion of a position and project, paragraph structure and development, and investment in contemporary issues. Every essay presents a critical, and often creative, assessment of a contemporary issue that will be familiar to some of you, unfamiliar to others, but of relevance to all. The essays are accessible because they use language you have probably been practicing in speech throughout your education, but have not explored deeply in reading, or yet managed to translate into writing of your own. On the surface, these essays are no more difficult than the reading we would hope accessible to all high school graduates. In order to produce an equally critical and creative response in writing, however, you will have to learn to read actively, to think "connectively," and to develop your own position, not unlike what the authors themselves have done. Consider John Waterbury's essay, "Hate Your Policies, Love Your Institutions," in which he describes both the long-standing and current conflicts between the United States and the Muslim Middle East. Waterbury makes his position clear: he believes that American institutions, educational institutions in particular, can help to improve U.S.-foreign relations by influencing the debate on global terrorism; but he recognizes the challenges to making this a reality through higher education alone. In his essay, Waterbury presents opposing points of view—those he does not accept—with *integrity*, demonstrating one productive way to disagree with other people in writing, especially people whose positions are reasonable despite differences of opinion.

Many essays in this collection, like Waterbury's, highlight the kinds of positions we are asking you to take in response to our assignment questions. They also present the kinds of overall projects you can aspire to in your own writing. You'll notice that many are written from the first person. They demonstrate individuals working through information they've gathered, in an effort to come to some understanding regarding a complex issue or problem: for example, Lisa Belkin, Michael Pollan, and Lauren Slater tackle the controversial topics of genetic engineering, animal rights, and radical plastic surgery by working through multiple conflicting positions; David Brooks, Fenton Johnson, and Lewis Lapham discuss how historical contexts can influence our thinking on suburban development, marriage, and American identity politics; and V.S. Naipaul, Lenore Look, and Michael Kamber each describe a slice-of-life experience in a foreign culture that can only be understood upon reflection at home. All of these authors explore a small part of the world's complexity. This is the kind of writing we are asking you to do, and that we believe will help you to become more intuitive about articulating your own position in response to anything you might read. We want you to begin recognizing how writers can address many sides of a complicated problem, carve out their own positions, assert their own projects, and still keep the complexity alive, instead of closing it down with a simple, but truthfully inadequate, solution.

How can we encourage these kinds of reading and writing practices in a world of text messaging? Not simply by helping you read. But by helping you *want to read*. That's my main goal with this collection, and the primary impulse behind the selection of these essays. I hope you sense that as you read them. I hope they open up your interests in the contemporary issues, problems and opportunities that you are inheriting even today. I hope that, with practice, you begin to experience the value of reading beyond the text message. Finally, I hope you can imagine these essays as useful points of departure in your own writing: from discovering within them a reason to want to read, to discovering within yourself a host of reasons to want to write.

Michelle

The Made-to-Order Savior
Lisa Belkin

Points of Access

1. Imagine how you would feel if you learned that you had been conceived and born so that someone in your family could be treated for a life-threatening disease. Would it change your feeling of being valued in your family? How? Freewrite for 15 minutes.

2. How might you feel if you learned that one of your siblings had been conceived in order to save your life? Would it change how you thought of your sibling? How?

3. What kind of sacrifice is too great to save one person's life? Is there such a thing? Can you think of a situation where medical technology should *not* be used to save someone's life?

Henry Strongin Goldberg was the first to arrive in Minneapolis. His parents decorated his room on the fourth floor of the Fairview-University Medical Center with his inflatable Batman chair, two Michael Jordan posters, a Fisher-Price basketball hoop and a punching bag hanging from the curtain rod over the bed. They took turns sleeping (or not) in his room for more than a month. It was too risky for his little brother to visit, but there was a playground across the courtyard, and if Henry, who was 4, stood at the window and Jack, who was 3, climbed to the top of the slide, the boys could wave to each other.

Henry had lost his hair by the time 6-year-old Molly Nash moved in down the hall on the bone-marrow transplant unit. Soon she, too, was bald. The two children had always looked alike, just as all children with this type of Fanconi anemia look alike, with their small faces and small eyes and bodies that are tiny for their age. The "Fanconi face" is one more reminder of the claim of the disease. Over time, Fanconi children also come to sound alike, with a deep, mechanical note in their voices, the result of the androgens they take to keep the illness at bay. Once their scalps were bare, Henry and Molly looked nearly identical. But there was one invisible difference between them—a difference that could mean everything.

These two families, the Strongin-Goldbergs and the Nashes, had raced time, death, threats of government intervention and (although they cringe to admit it) each other, to make medical history. The best chance to save a Fanconi child is a bone-marrow transplant from a perfectly matched sibling donor. Many Fanconi parents have conceived second children to save their first, hoping that luck would bring them a match. These two couples became the first in the world not to count on luck. Using in-vitro fertilization, then using even newer technology to pick and choose from the resulting embryos, they each spent years trying to have a baby whose marrow was guaranteed to be an ideal genetic fit.

One family would succeed and one would fail. One child would receive a transplant from a perfectly matched newborn brother and the other from a less well-matched stranger. One would have an excellent chance of survival; the fate of the other was not as clear. Their parents, now friends, would find themselves together in the tiny lounge at the end of the transplant hall, waiting for the new cells to take root, sharing pizza and a pain that only they could understand.

When the rest of the world learned about the baby born to be a donor, there were questions. Is it wrong to breed a child for "spare parts"? ethicists asked. If we can screen an embryo for tissue type, won't we one day screen for eye color or intelligence? There was talk in the news media of "Frankenstein medicine" and threats by Congress to ban embryo research, which had made this technique possible.

It is the kind of talk heard with every scientific breakthrough, from the first heart transplant to the first cloned sheep. We talk like this because we are both exhilarated and terrified by what we can do, and we wonder, with each step, whether we have gone too far. But though society may ask, "How could you?" the only question patients and families ask is, "How could we not?"

Which is why there is virtually no medical technology yet invented that has not been used. It is human nature to do everything to save a life and just as human to agonize over everything we do. The story of Molly and Henry is the story of groundbreaking science. It is also the story of last-ditch gambles on unproven theories, of laboratory technique cobbled from instinct and desperation, of a determined researcher who sacrificed his job and more trying to help and of a frantic drive through a hurricane to deliver cells on time. In other words, it is simply the story of what it now takes, in the 21st century, to save one child.

* * *

Back at the beginning, it was Molly who arrived first. She was born on July 4, 1994, at Rose Medical Center in Denver, and from the start it was clear that something was terribly wrong. She was missing both thumbs, and her right arm was 30 percent shorter than her left. Her parents, Lisa and Jack, saw her, but could not hold her, before she was whisked off to the ICU, where doctors would eventually find two separate malformations of her heart. (She was also deaf in one ear, but that would not be known until later.) Lisa, wide awake and distraught at 4 a.m. in the maternity ward, made a phone call to the nearby university hospital where she worked as a neonatal ICU nurse caring for babies just like this one, and asked a friend to bring her the book of malformations. Flipping from page to page, she landed on a photo of a Fanconi face and saw in it the face of her newborn daughter.

Named for the Swiss physician who first identified it in 1927, Fanconi anemia causes bone marrow failure, eventually resulting in leukemia and other forms of cancer. Until very recently, children with Molly's form of FA rarely lived past the age of 6, the age Molly is right now. Fanconi is a recessive disorder, which means both parents must pass along one copy of the mutated gene in order for a child to develop the disease. Among the general population, one of every 200 people has a Fanconi mutation. Every ethnic group carries its own genetic baggage, however, and among Ashkenazi Jews like the Nashes and Strongin-Goldbergs, the incidence is 1 in 89, meaning that if both parents are Ashkenazi Jews the chance of having an affected baby is 1 in 32,000. But Lisa, with all her medical training, had never heard of the disease, and Jack, a Denver hotel manager, certainly had not, either.

The holes in Molly's heart closed by themselves, but her other problems remained. She failed to eat, she failed to grow and she was always sick. She had already been through three major surgeries by Oct. 25, 1995, when Henry Strongin Goldberg entered the world at the George Washington University Hospital in Washington. Doctors had warned his parents that he would be quite small, but Laurie Strongin and Allen Goldberg were not worriers, because life had never given them anything to worry about. "Our family history," Laurie says wistfully, "was blue, sunny skies."

Henry was born with an extra thumb on his right hand and a serious heart defect that would require surgery to fix. His parents were devastated, but within days the prognosis worsened. "Fanconi anemia," Laurie wrote in her journal. "If only it was just the heart and thumb. Please take me back a minute ago and make me feel lucky that is it only the heart and the thumb. Fanconi anemia. Rare. Fatal. Henry."

Laurie had spent her career working for nonprofit organizations; Allen had spent his in the computer industry. Both in their early 30's, they were new to parenting and to Fanconi anemia, but they both knew how to navigate a medical database, and within days they found Arleen Auerbach, a researcher at Rockefeller University in New York and the keeper of the Fanconi patient registry in the United States and Canada, a list that contains about 800 names. Although Molly's parents and Henry's parents still knew nothing of each other, the Nashes had found Auerbach, too, because all Fanconi children eventually find their way to her cluttered Manhattan office.

The rarer the disease, the more it needs a single champion, someone to keep the lists, track the trends, follow the research of others while relentlessly pursuing his or her own. Arleen Auerbach is that person for Fanconi anemia—a sweet, grandmotherly type at the core but with sharp outer edges, armor born of years spent delivering bad news.

She had little but bad news for the Nashes and the Strongin-Goldbergs when they first called. Of the eight separate genes that can mutate and cause Fanconi anemia, Molly and Henry both had Type C, which bares its teeth early and kills often. Had these children been born as recently as 1982, Auerbach explained, there would have been no possible treatment. Bone-marrow transplants—obliterating the faulty immune system and then replacing it with a donated one—used to be fatal for Fanconi patients, because their cells were fragile and crumbled during the chemotherapy and radiation that cleared the way for the actual transplant.

Then, in 1982, doctors in France found that if Fanconi patients were given a significantly lower dose of the chemotherapy drug Cytoxan they could survive. The chances of their survival were increased even further if the donor was a sibling who was a perfect match. The reason for this is found in a web of six proteins that together are known as human leukocyte antigen, or HLA, which is the radar by which bodies recognize what is "self" and what is "intruder." HLA is key to the immune system, and since a bone-marrow transplant is a replacement of the immune system, the HLA of the donor must be as close as possible to that of the recipient, or the new immune system can reject its new container, a life-threatening condition known as graft-versus-host disease.

Over the years it was discovered that the rate of success for sibling transplants was even higher if the sibling was a newborn, because then the transplanted cells could come from "cord blood" taken from the umbilical cord and placenta at birth. These are purer, concentrated, undifferentiated cells, meaning that they are less likely to reject their new body. Back in 1995, when Auerbach first spoke to the Nashes and the Strongin-Goldbergs, the survival odds of a sibling cord-blood transplant were 85 percent, while the odds of a nonrelated bone-marrow transplant were 30 percent and the odds of a nonrelated transplant for patients with Henry and Molly's particular mutation were close to zero.

If there was one thing working in their favor, Auerbach told them, it was that their children's disease was diagnosed so early in life. Fanconi anemia is rare, and few doctors have ever seen a case, which means the condition is often missed or mistaken for something else. Auerbach has seen too many children with this same Fanconi mutation whose blood fails, with little prior warning, at age 5. Those parents don't have time to do the only thing there is to do, the one thing the Nashes and Strongin-Goldbergs could do—have a baby.

Ten weeks into a pregnancy, Auerbach explained, a chorionic villus sampling test can determine whether the fetus is healthy and if it is a compatible donor. Couples regularly abort when they learn that the unborn child has Fanconi, Auerbach says; having seen the devastation wrought by the disease on one of their children, they refuse to allow it to claim another. Few couples abort, however, when they learn that the baby is healthy but not a donor. "Only three that I know of terminated for that reason," she says. "They were getting older, their child was getting sicker and they were running out of time." Far more common, she says, is for couples to keep having children, as many as time will allow, praying that one will be a match.

Timing a child's transplant means playing a stomach-churning game of chicken with leukemia. The younger a patient is when undergoing a transplant, the better the outcome, because the body is stronger and has suffered fewer infections. On the other hand, the longer the transplant can be delayed, the greater the odds of conceiving a sibling donor, and the better the chance that transplant technology will have improved. The risk of waiting is that every Fanconi patient will develop leukemia, and once that happens a transplant is all but impossible. "You want to wait as long as you can," Auerbach says, "but not so long that it's too late."

*   *   *

Good doctors learn from their patients, and so it was when Dr. John Wagner answered his telephone one afternoon seven years ago. A lanky, easygoing man, Wagner is scientific director of clinical research in the Marrow Transplant Program at the University of Minnesota, and he says he believes he has performed more bone-marrow transplants on Fanconi children than any other doctor in the country. The caller who set him thinking, however, was not the parent of a Fanconi patient, but rather the father of a toddler with thalassemia, another rare blood disease. The man was calling to inquire about a sibling cord-blood transplant. "You have another child who is a match?" Wagner asked. "No," came the reply. "But we will."

The father went on to explain that he and his wife were using a relatively new technique known as pre-implantation genetic diagnosis, or PGD, to guarantee that their next child would be free of thalassemia. PGD is an outgrowth of in-vitro fertilization; sperm and egg are united in a petri dish, and when the blastocyst (it is still technically too small to be called an embryo) reaches the eight-cell stage, it is biopsied (meaning one of those cells is removed and screened). Only blastocysts found to be healthy are returned to the womb. Then the waiting game begins—more than two months until it is possible to know if the fetus is a transplant match, then an agonizing choice if it is not. Why, the caller wondered, can't the donor-compatibility tests be done before the embryos are implanted?

Wagner was intrigued by the possibility. Why use PGD just as prevention, he wondered, when it could be used as treatment? Why not, in effect, write a prescription that says "one healthy baby who is going to be a perfect donor"?

Wagner called Mark Hughes, who pioneered the technique and who was working with this family. Hughes is known as a brilliant researcher, simultaneously passionate and wary, a scientist and physician who chose the field of genetics because it combined the intellectual rigor of the lab with the emotional connection to flesh-and-blood patients. In 1994, at about the time he first spoke to Wagner, Hughes was recruited to work at the National Institutes of Health and also as director of Georgetown University's Institute for Molecular and Human Genetics, where his salary was paid in part by the NIH In other words, much of his research was supported by the government. At that time he was also a member of a federal advisory committee that developed guidelines for the type of single-cell embryo analysis that was central to PGD. But no sooner had those guidelines been developed than Congress banned all federal financing of embryo research, and Hughes was forced to continue his research with private funds only.

Under the current Bush administration there is talk of banning all embryo research, even work supported by private funds. For that reason—and for reasons that will become clearer as this tale unfolds—Hughes has developed a healthy distrust of the limelight and refused to be interviewed for this story. As Wagner and Auerbach tell it, Hughes had certainly thought of the possibility of using PGD to determine HLA type long before Wagner called, but he had several concerns.

The ones that weighed heaviest were ethical. It could be argued that using PGD to eliminate embryos with disease helps the patient—in this case, the embryo, the biopsied organism—by insuring that it is not born into a life of thalassemia or cystic fibrosis or Duchenne muscular dystrophy or any of the other agonizing illnesses for which Hughes was screening. Using the same technique to select for a compatible donor, however, does not help the "patient" whose cells are being tested. "It helps the family," says Arleen Auerbach, "and it helps the sibling with Fanconi, but it does not help the embryo."

What Wagner proposed, therefore, would be stepping into new territory. If society gives its blessing to the use of one child to save another, then what would prevent couples from someday going through with the process but aborting when the pregnancy was far enough along that the cord blood could be retrieved? Or what would prevent couples whose child needed a new kidney from waiting until the fetal kidney was large enough, then terminating the pregnancy and salvaging the organs? What would stop those same couples from waiting until the child was born and subjecting it to surgery to remove one kidney? Once the technology exists, who decides how to use it?

Ethicists think in terms of a slippery slope. But is the potential for abuse in some circumstances reason not to pursue research that can be lifesaving under the right circumstances? Unlike donating a kidney, or even donating bone marrow, donating cord blood involves negligible harm to the newborn donor. The stem cells are collected at birth, directly from the placenta, not from the baby. That is one reason why Wagner argued that HLA testing is ethically defensible. A second reason, he said, was that it is indefensible not to try.

"I'm here as the patient's advocate," he says, meaning Molly and Henry and all the other children in need of transplants. "It's my obligation to push the envelope because I see how bad the other side can be. I see the results of a sibling transplant; they're the easiest transplant to do. And then I walk into the room of the patient who had an unrelated donor, I see that their skin is sloughing off, the mucous membranes are peeling off and they have blood pouring out of their mouths. You cannot imagine anything so horrible in your entire life, and you're thinking, I did this—because there was nothing else available for me to do."

That was apparently what Hughes's gut told him, too, and he agreed to try to develop a lab procedure to screen HLA at the single-cell level. His participation came with certain conditions. First, that the mother must be younger than 35, because younger women produce more eggs, increasing the odds of a healthy match. Second, that he would work only with families who carried a specific subset of the Type C mutation, known as IVS4, because it is the most common. And, last of all, the child being created must be wanted. Only families who had expressed a wish for more children would be approached for this procedure. Hughes did not want to create a baby who was nothing but a donor.

Arleen Auerbach immediately thought of two couples who were the right age, fit the specific genetic profile and who had always planned to have a houseful of children. Her first phone call was to Lisa and Jack Nash in Denver. Without a moment's hesitation, they said yes. Her second call was to Laurie Strongin and Allen Goldberg in Washington.

"If I told you that you could potentially go into a pregnancy knowing that your baby was healthy and a genetic match for Henry, would you be interested?" she asked.

Two hours earlier, Laurie had taken a home pregnancy test. It was positive. If early test results were negative for Fanconi she would carry to term, she answered, even if the baby were not the right HLA type to save Henry's life.

Henry was only 5 months old. His heart surgery had gone smoothly, he was happy and looked deceptively healthy. Fate seemed to be on his side. "If this baby's not a match, we'll try it your way in nine months," Laurie remembers telling Auerbach. "We still thought," she says, "that we had a lot of time."

*   *   *

Henry became a big brother in December 1995. Jack Strongin Goldberg was free of Fanconi and was not even a carrier of the disease, so there was no chance that he might pass it on to his own children. His HLA, however, was as unlike Henry's as a biological brother's could possibly be. Laurie and Allen admit that they were briefly disappointed when they heard this last piece of news, three months into the pregnancy. Then they brushed off their psyches and called Mark Hughes, telling him they would be ready to try PGD at the start of the following year.

As baby Jack was being born, Lisa Nash was undergoing the shots and monitoring that are part of in-vitro fertilization. Theirs would be a very difficult case, Hughes had told them. Of the cluster of genes that together determine HLA type, science, at the time, could look at only three. As it happened, Lisa and Jack's patterns were almost identical on those three genes, making it nearly impossible to sort hers from his. That genetic quirk, he warned, could lead to the wrong results. The science to fix this didn't exist yet, he said, and he was figuring it all out as they spoke.

Hughes was also struggling with other problems, ones that had nothing to do with the Nashes' DNA. On the day that Lisa's eggs were retrieved by laparoscopy and fertilized in a dish, the headline in *The Washington Post* read: "NIH Severs Ties With Researcher Who Experimented on Embryos." Hughes had been accused of using federal funds for embryo research, in violation of the Congressional ban. Hughes denied that government money was used for that portion of his work and argued that in any case his research was not even on embryos since all that ever arrived in his lab was DNA extracted from a biopsied cell.

Lisa Nash did not become pregnant.

Mark Hughes resigned from his positions with N.I.H. and Georgetown University rather than agree to stop his research.

The turn of events was devastating for Hughes. He was out of a job and forced to uproot his two young sons and his wife, who was fighting a battle of her own, against breast cancer. Those close to him say he talked of quitting medicine entirely, so frustrated and angry was he that the rug had been pulled out from under him.

The turn of events was also devastating for the Nashes. "We called him two, three times a week," Jack Nash remembers, and as he speaks a frantic note creeps into his voice. "But he wouldn't return our calls. Months went by, then a year." Over those months they learned that Hughes was moving halfway across the country to a new, privately financed lab where he could continue his work. Then they learned that Hughes's wife was critically ill, that her cancer had spread, that the prognosis was grim. The one thing they did not learn was when and if their quest to save Molly might begin again.

They now understand that science solves the simplest equation first, then moves on to the more difficult ones; their complicated genetic makeup meant their case had to wait. Added to that was the fact that the initial decoding of their DNA had been done at Hughes's former lab in Washington, and he no longer had access to the data. They now also understand that Hughes was in this to save lives, and that having to come to the phone and say that he couldn't, that he didn't know how to match an HLA type for Molly, was more than he could bear. But at the time they didn't understand. At the time they were angry.

"When we manage to speak to him he says we have to give him a few more months to get the lab set up," Jack says. "Meanwhile Molly's counts are dropping and he's the only one who can do this, and he won't help."

*   *   *

Life for a chronically ill child is a jumble of numbers. The average platelet count in a healthy child: 150,000 to 450,000. The lowest that platelets are allowed to drop before Dr. Wagner urges a transplant: 40,000. Where Henry's platelets hovered when Jack was born: 100,000. The cost of each in-vitro cycle: $11,000. The amount paid by insurance: officially, $0, because the in-vitro fertilization was not being done to treat infertility, nor was it being done to directly treat Henry. The amount the Strongin-Goldbergs raised for Fanconi anemia research at the fund-raiser they held on Henry's first birthday: $67,500. The odds of a blastocyst being healthy: 3 in 4. The odds of a blastocyst being a match: 1 in 4. The odds of a blastocyst being a match and also being healthy, and of Laurie becoming pregnant and delivering before Henry had to have a transplant: God only knows.

Since the day Henry's FA was diagnosed, life for Laurie and Allen was filtered through these numbers, through the lens of Fanconi anemia. "Every ensuing pregnancy," she wrote in her journal after baby Jack was born, "will be marred by the fact that the little baby in my belly could have a fatal disease. Every job that Allen and I consider has to offer medical insurance without excluding pre-existing conditions and with compassion and flexibility. Every relationship has to offer quiet understanding of our travails accompanied by the capacity to give without expecting too much in return."

While Mark Hughes worked to set up his new lab at Wayne State University School of Medicine, near Detroit, the Nashes and the Strongin-Goldbergs were at home, waiting in two very different ways. A crisis can strip a family down to its skeleton of strengths and faults, peeling the niceties away and revealing the bare core of who they are. Henry's parents, for instance, effervescent, embracing and fiercely optimistic from the start, became more so as the clock ran out. They took on Hughes's problems as their own, bonding with him deeply, knowing that they needed him to bond back if they were to save Henry. Molly's parents, in turn, are determined and intense, and they did not waste emotional energy that might be spent protecting their daughter. They were demanding of Hughes, but no more demanding than they were of themselves or of anyone else who could help Molly.

Until the spring of 1997, the two families had still not met. In May of that year, when Hughes was promising both of them that he would be able to resume work soon, a retreat for Fanconi families was held near Portland, Me. The Strongin-Goldbergs went there determined to meet the anonymous couple Arleen Auerbach had mentioned—the couple who had already tried HLA screening with Hughes. Armed with two facts—that the couple had a daughter, and that they lived in Colorado—the Strongin-Goldbergs skimmed the directory and found a family who fit that description.

When Laurie Strongin shook Lisa Nash's hand for the first time she felt an instant bond with the only other mother in the world whose life paralleled her own. Lisa was more reserved. Up to that moment she hadn't realized that the elusive Hughes was working with a second family. Six months later, however, by the time of Laurie's initial in-vitro attempt, the women had paddled past their opening awkwardness and were close telephone friends. When Henry, now 2, talked about his future, he spoke in gradations: first he would be "better," then "super better," then "super-duper better." When all this was over, Lisa and Laurie promised each other, when their children were both "super-duper better," the two families would travel to Disneyworld to celebrate.

In January 1998, when Hughes was finally ready for them, Laurie took the train up to New York City for her appointment with Dr. Zev Rosenwaks, the baby-making guru at the in-vitro fertilization clinic at New York Weill Cornell Medical Center. Henry's platelet count was 71,000 that morning. Eighteen days later, after 18 shots of Lupron, a brutal migraine, hot sweats and cold chills, Laurie's body refused to cooperate, and the in-vitro fertilization process for that cycle had to be abandoned. That week Henry's platelet count dropped to 31,000, its lowest level up to that point.

Doctors often suggest that in-vitro fertilization patients wait a month or more between attempts, but Laurie didn't have a month, and in early February she was in New York again. This time the numbers were on her side. She produced 24 eggs, and 21 of them were mature enough to be fertilized. Statistically that meant six should be perfect matches for Henry, and three or four of those six should also be disease free.

Sixteen blastocysts survived the biopsy. Allen refused to entrust the cells to anyone, so he flew them to Detroit himself. At the airport he handed his Styrofoam hope chest to a waiting Mark Hughes, then got on the next plane back to New York. The following evening, Laurie was at the Rosenwaks clinic ready for the re-implantation when word came from Hughes. Of the 16 blastocysts tested, 2 were absolutely perfect matches to Henry. Both those matches had Fanconi anemia.

"I'm struggling to come to terms with how much pain I can withstand," Laurie wrote in her journal. She and Allen shared that pain long-distance with the Nashes, who still had not heard when and if Hughes would begin to work with them again. Jack and Lisa were supportive, but also envious and confused. "Were they the family of choice because he liked them better?" Jack remembers wondering. "Is this personal? Does he have something against us, and he's taking that out on Molly? Things like that definitely go through your mind."

The Nashes sent frantic e-mail messages to Hughes, telling him what he already knew—that Molly's counts were dropping and that they were running out of time. In August 1998, when Molly's platelet count had fallen to 30,000, they received his answer. He couldn't help them, he wrote in an e-mail message. Their case was too complicated, both genetically and politically. The genetic analysis he'd so painstakingly done on them belonged to the NIH. "We tried to get the lab at Georgetown to help us, since they were key in our being able to do this for you the first time around," Hughes wrote. The lab has been ordered by the "Catholic administration" of the university "not to get involved 'in any way.'"

Hughes continued: "Go ahead without us. You are anxious, and we understand that very well. But I cannot make this work today and I don't know when I will be able to do so. I am sorry. Science sucks sometimes."

Reeling, Lisa and Jack called Laurie and Allen, who were about to begin their third in-vitro cycle—one that would produce 26 eggs, 24 of which were mature and 21 of which would fertilize. Of those, three would be perfect, healthy matches for Henry. The Strongin-Goldbergs would not share these details with the Nashes because they had come to understand that other people's good news is sometimes too difficult to hear.

*   *   *

Taking Mark Hughes's advice, the Nashes did go on without him. They'd decided to jump into a cross-your-fingers pregnancy when they learned, almost by accident, of a private clinic in Chicago that had been quietly doing PGD for nearly 10 years, though never for Fanconi anemia. This news was "like opening a door," say the Nashes, who had not realized that other labs in the country besides Hughes's were providing PGD. If this Chicago lab could test for cystic fibrosis and Tay-Sachs, they wondered, why not Fanconi? And if it had the equipment to screen DNA for disease, why not also screen for HLA?

Lisa and Jack brought Molly along on their trip to the Reproductive Genetics Institute, on the theory that doctors couldn't say no with their adorable but ashen-cheeked child in the room. Her platelets were half what they had been a month earlier. She was weak and tired. They could not have walked into a more receptive office. A year earlier, Charles Strom, then the head of the institute's genetics lab, had heard Mark Hughes speak at a genetics meeting about his attempts to screen DNA for an anonymous couple who were trying to have a child who would be a cord-blood match. "It was like a revelation to me," says Strom, a broad, genial bear of a man now at Quest Diagnostics in California, who could, at that time, perform PGD for 35 diseases but had never thought of HLA screening. "This is what pre-implantation genetics should be about."

A few in the audience expressed their disapproval, he remembers, fearing that this was a step on the road to eugenics. Strom, on the other hand, was enthusiastic. "I stood up and said I thought this was great," he says. "I'm trained not just as a geneticist, but as a pediatrician, and I was tired of watching kids die. I thought this would be the future, and from then on, I was basically waiting for someone to ask me to do it." So when the very same "anonymous" couple arrived and asked, Strom said yes.

He immediately discovered what Hughes had struggled with for years—the "nightmare" caused by the near-identical patterns in the HLA portion of Jack and Lisa's DNA. But he and his team tried something new—they looked farther down the strand, beyond the three known genes, to a spot where it was easier to differentiate one parent from the other. This increased the risk of being wrong, but Molly's blood counts were dropping, and they did not have time to waste. "This isn't what we want to do, but it will probably work," Strom told the Nashes two months after they first met.

It is one thing to screen embryos; it is another to become pregnant, and adding HLA screening to Fanconi anemia screening lowers the odds even more. Only 1 in 6 blastocysts is likely to be both healthy and a matched donor, and that one might not be the quality that the reproductive endocrinologist would have chosen under ideal circumstances. Lisa spent all of 1999 trying to defy those odds. In January she produced 12 eggs, 2 of which were healthy matches; she became pregnant, then miscarried. In June she produced only four eggs, one of which was a match but did not result in a pregnancy. In September she produced eight eggs, six of which had Fanconi anemia; the single healthy match was implanted, but again, her pregnancy test was negative.

In October the Nash family traveled to Minneapolis for Molly's twice-yearly checkup with Dr. Wagner. Her platelets were down to 10,000. In every measurable way she was failing, and she needed a bone-marrow transplant. "You have to stop," Wagner told her parents. It was time to proceed with a transplant from a nonrelated donor. "There comes a point where I have to say: 'It's over. You've done it. You've done the best you could.'"

He began to search for a donor. Lisa and Jack went ahead with the in vitro that had been scheduled for December. "I couldn't hear the word no," Lisa says. "'No' meant Molly could die."

Because they knew it was the last try, and because they needed to feel certain that they had done the best they could, the Nashes insisted on one change of procedure for this final try. It troubled them that Lisa was producing so few eggs per cycle, and they wondered if a different in-vitro fertilization clinic might do better. They approached Dr. William Schoolcraft, an infertility doctor in Colorado known for pushing the envelope. He changed Lisa's hormone regimen and in December 1999 retrieved 24 eggs from her ovaries. For two days the Nashes fantasized about twins and even triplets. Then Strom called to say that there was only one match.

It all came down to one embryo that, statistically, had less than a 30 percent chance of taking hold and staying put. "All it takes is one, all it takes is one," Lisa reminded herself as she drove to Dr. Schoolcraft's office nine days later for a pregnancy test. Minutes after she left, her cell phone rang.

"You're pregnant," said the nurse on the other end.

It was too soon, however, for a happy ending. And indeed, seven weeks into the pregnancy Lisa had just gotten out of the shower when deep red blood began flowing down her legs. The drive to Schoolcraft's office was a blur, but the memory of the picture on the ultrasound screen is vividly clear: a large gap where the placenta had separated from the uterine wall, and the flub-dub pulses of a tiny, living, beating heart.

Lisa went home and went to bed. She was permitted to get up three or four times a day to use the bathroom and once a week for an appointment with Schoolcraft, nothing more. Every time she stood up she began to bleed. Molly, too weak to really play, was on her own manner of bed rest, and mother and daughter spent entire days lying upstairs together.

In March, Molly's blood tests showed signs of pre-leukemia. Wagner sent more data to the national bone-marrow bank, escalating his search for an unrelated donor. In April, Molly's platelets fell to 3,000. She began to need blood transfusions but fought whoever tried to insert the needle; one particularly rocky weekend Strom flew to Denver from a business meeting in Los Angeles, because he was the only one Molly would permit to start the IV. April became May; May turned to June. Along the way, Lisa asked her doctors what could be done should she spontaneously lose the baby. They began to discuss whether stem cells could be harvested from a fetal liver. And all the while, Lisa was still bleeding—clawing her way through the pregnancy, trying to hold onto her baby while holding off her daughter's transplant.

*   *   *

Back when the Nashes were deciding whether to go ahead with Molly's transplant or try somehow to wait until summer, the Strongin-Goldbergs were making their own impossible choice: whether or not to give up. Their optimism back in August 1998, when they had three healthy embryos, had long since faded. That in-vitro attempt did not result in a pregnancy. Neither did attempt No.4, in November, when 30 eggs failed to provide a single healthy match.

Attempt No.5, in February 1999, was almost more than they could bear. Laurie produced 17 eggs and was waiting to be summoned to the clinic when she received another call instead. Allen had taken to scanning the Detroit newspapers online, knowing that Mark Hughes's wife was dying, but not wanting to pester his friend. The morning of Laurie's retrieval, Allen found the news he'd been dreading in the obituary section. Laurie's ovaries were past the point of no return, so Rosenwaks went ahead with the retrieval and fertilization without any idea who would screen the blastocysts. "I couldn't imagine doing this without our friend on the other end and didn't even know if it was possible," Laurie wrote.

But saving Henry had come to mean as much to Hughes as to Laurie and Allen. The researcher had watched his own life nearly destroyed in defense of this work, and he promised he would be there. Fourteen blastocysts survived the biopsy, and on the morning of Feb. 11, 1999, just a few days after Hughes's wife's death, Allen loaded his Styrofoam box with vials and dry ice and boarded the 11:10 a.m. flight to Detroit. He took the container to the lab, where he was moved to tears to find a large picture of his own son hanging on the wall. Underneath it was the question, "Can we help save Henry's life?"

Allen was certain that this attempt would work. There was bittersweet poetry in the timing: death preceding life and preventing death. But when Hughes called the Strongin-Goldbergs in New York, his news was not the stuff of poetry. There was only one match. It did not result in a pregnancy.

Attempt No.6 took place in June 1999. Twenty-eight eggs, two healthy matches. No pregnancy. Attempt No.7 came in the middle of Hurricane Floyd. Allen drove his Styrofoam box through the eye of the storm—1,200 miles in 26 hours—and delivered the cells, alive, at 2 a.m. Laurie became pregnant, then miscarried.

Their eighth try took place in February 2000. Laurie was in New York, at the clinic, the morning that Allen raced Henry to the hospital with pneumonia so serious doctors warned it could kill him. Laurie agonized over whether to come home (canceling the in-vitro cycle) or stay where she was. If she left, she was certain Henry would die, because he would have lost this chance for a sibling donor. If she stayed, then she was equally certain that Henry would die—of pneumonia, in a Georgetown hospital, without his mother.

She stayed. Henry received two blood transfusions and was pumped full of three intravenous antibiotics. Laurie produced 21 eggs and only one implantable match. "I did not get pregnant," she says, "and I still haven't recovered from the experience."

As the Strongin-Goldbergs dragged themselves from one attempt to the next, the technology of bone-marrow transplants was changing. Specifically, Wagner was testing a new method of removing T-cells from donor blood. T-cells are the ones that recognize the host as foreign, leading to graft-versus-host disease. Simultaneously, Wagner was using fludarabine, an immunosuppressant that appears to encourage the new cells to engraft, or take root. Based on a tiny sample of patients, Wagner's best guess was that these adjustments to the protocol showed promise, apparently increasing the odds of surviving an unrelated bone-marrow transplant from 30 percent to 50 percent in a Fanconi anemia patient. This was still far lower than the 85 percent odds of a sibling cord-blood transplant, but better than it had been before.

Laurie went through one last, disappointing in-vitro cycle, then she and Allen grabbed those new 50-50 odds. Wagner warned that it was time to stop, and they knew, from looking at Henry, that he was probably right. Henry had had two platelet and two red-cell transfusions in the past two months, and he had been on Anadrol, a steriod to boost his blood counts, for two and a half years. There comes a point at which a child is too sick for a transplant, and Henry, like Molly, was all but there. In two and a half years of desperate trying, Laurie had 353 injections, produced 198 eggs and had no successful pregnancy. During the same time period, Henry's platelets fell from a high of 103,000 to a low of 10,000.

"We gave it all we had," Laurie wrote when her last pregnancy test was negative and the family was leaving for Minneapolis, for Henry's transplant. "We worked with the world's best doctors. We hoped. We believed. We were brave. We persevered. And despite all that it didn't work. I am left with my belief system intact. I believe in love and science. Nothing more, nothing less."

*   *   *

A bone-marrow transplant is a medical resurrection. First doctors all but kill a patient; then they bring him back to life. Treacherous and risky, in the end it all comes down to one squishy plastic bag of pale brown liquid which could easily be mistaken for rusty water from a tap. Henry's bag of marrow was collected from an anonymous donor somewhere in the United States on the morning of July 6, 2000, and was flown to the Fairview-University Medical Center, arriving in Room 5 of the bone-marrow transplant floor around dinnertime. A nurse came in with a Polaroid, snapped a few pictures, then added the bag to Henry's leafy IV tree. There was no blaring of trumpets, no rolling of drums. From 8:15 to 8:30 Central Daylight Time, the fluid dripped soundlessly.

Molly Nash's bag was collected with more drama. Lisa's pregnancy had managed to hold. For months Molly's baby brother had been trying to arrive prematurely, and now that he was due, he didn't seem eager to arrive at all. By the evening of Aug. 29, Lisa had been in labor for 52 hours, insisting she be allowed to continue because she knew that more cord blood could be collected during a vaginal birth. Finally, when it looked as if the baby was in distress, he was delivered by C-section. Dr. Strom—his godfather—collected the cord blood. Lisa cradled both the newborn Adam and the warm intravenous bag in her arms.

"God created Adam in his image," Lisa says, explaining how she chose her son's name. "Adam was the first. And from Adam—from his rib, which is full of marrow—God created woman, which is fitting because God used our Adam to give Molly a second chance at life."

When he was 9 days old, Adam flew with his parents and his sister to Minneapolis. Molly settled into the room down from Henry's for the standard four-month stay—a surreal time when it seems as if every child in the world is having a bone-marrow transplant, because every child that you see is. Molly went through all that

Henry had gone through a month before her, and yet everything was different. She had a higher chance of engraftment and a far lower chance of rejection. Her parents were rubbed emotionally raw watching her suffer in order to live. But then they looked at Henry, whose parents feared he was showing early signs of graft-versus-host disease—something Molly would almost certainly never get. They looked beyond Henry, too, at the eight patients who died in the bone-marrow transplant unit during Molly's endless summer.

In the end, Molly's life was saved. That is the Nashes' answer to people who question their right to manipulate nature. Their right springs from the difference between 30 percent and 85 percent; the difference between Molly and Henry. That is also their answer to those who would urge the government to ban all embryo research because it harms unborn children. The research, they say, saves children like Molly.

"We did what we needed to do to keep our daughter from dying," Lisa Nash says. "That is what any parent would do. Isn't this what parents are supposed to do? How can anything be wrong with that?"

Yes, ethicists say, it is exactly what any parent would do, and that is why it is troubling. Parents are being asked to make a choice not only on behalf of their living child, but also on behalf of their unborn child, and that can be an impossible position when the choices get hard. If Molly were closer to death, for instance, would her parents have terminated the pregnancy and used stem cells from Adam's fetal liver to save her?

"We know people will do anything to save their child," says Jeffrey Kahn, an ethicist at the University of Minnesota, where there was much debate about the decisions of the transplant team at the hospital next door. "Now we are learning what 'anything' really means."

Susan M. Wolf, a professor of law and medicine at the University of Minnesota, says she believes that this case is emblematic of the whole of reproductive technology, which she describes as "a multibillion dollar industry based solely on consumer demand." While it might seem logical in each isolated case to let the parents decide, all those single choices add up to a hodgepodge of technology scattered throughout private clinics and laboratories, with no one authorized to say no.

Wagner and Strom agree. They say they do not believe that they, or any other individual doctor, should have the responsibility of sorting through this thicket alone. "As the technology progresses," Strom says, "I see the possibility that someone will come to us and say: 'While you're screening for Tay-Sachs, how about making sure he's not going to have heart disease, too? And while you're at it, why not check for the gene that predisposes him to lupus or makes him immune to HIV?'"

"It has the potential to be abused," agrees Wagner. But the response to that potential, he warns, should not be to ban the research or suspend federal financing of the procedure. "It's not going to go away," he says. "We can't put our heads in the sand and say it doesn't exist. I have a stack of requests this high from all over the world, couples asking if they can come use this technology."

Compounding the problems caused by the current ban on federal financing, he says, is the accompanying lack of federal rules. "It's all been forced into the private sector," he says, "where there are no controls. There should be controls. There should be limits. It is up to us, as a society, to decide what they are."

*   *   *

Since her transplant, Molly Nash has gone back to school. More accurately, school has started to come to her, but her visiting teacher has to wear a mask during lessons. Her ballet teacher comes for in-home classes, too, and Molly twirls and pliés and giggles. Her hair is beginning to grow back. Instead of taking 44 pills every day she only takes 10. She is still fed through a stomach tube that her mother hooks up four times a day, and she doesn't have much of an appetite, which is characteristic of Fanconi anemia. The transplant did not cure her of that disease; it merely erased her risk of developing imminent leukemia. She is still likely to suffer Fanconi's other complications, particularly cancers of the mouth and neck. But those will not show themselves for many years, and, her mother says, "maybe they will have a cure by then."

Henry Strongin Goldberg has been ill almost since the day he left the hospital in Minnesota. While Molly's platelet count is 381,000, Henry's is 15,000. He spent months looking yellow and feeling miserable, moaning instead of talking, the result of a near fatal liver infection that is common in transplant patients because of the drugs they are given to suppress their immune system.

In January, for the first time in his tortured life, his parents were struck full force by the thought that he was dying. "All I can think about," Allen said then, "is how much I'll miss him."

Since then, things have gotten even worse. Allen lost his job at an Internet start-up in January, and although he is now working again, the family has burned through its savings. Laurie, who takes home $600 every other week, has spent months sleepwalking through work, hanging on partly out of a need to have one foot tenuously in the real world but also because Henry needed health insurance. Henry's liver slowly improved, but he then began to lose weight at an alarming rate—20 percent of his body weight within weeks—and his skin began to disintegrate, turning red, scaly and raw. Several painful skin biopsies were inconclusive, suggesting that this was either an allergy to a medication or a sign of graft-versus-host disease.

While Henry was at the clinic having his skin examined, one doctor noticed that he was dragging his left leg when he walked. Two weeks later his left side became so weak that he could not lift himself to a sitting position in bed. He was rushed back to Minneapolis, where a scan showed a mass of unknown origin in his brain. Doctors operated but were unable to determine the cause. Whatever it was, it may have spread to his chest. Just last week, Henry was rushed to the hospital again—his sixth hospitalization in the past 12 weeks—where doctors found lesions in his lungs.

Of the 21 Fanconi patients who have received transplants within the past two years at Fairview under the new drug protocol that gave the Strongin-Goldbergs so much hope, 13 have survived so far. Of those, Henry is in the greatest danger. The first anniversary of his transplant is this coming Friday, a milestone that no longer seems like a victory.

What might have been another red-letter day will come in October, when the Nashes and the Strongin-Goldbergs had planned to meet in Disneyworld. The Strongin-Goldbergs will not be there. After years of technology and intervention, Laurie became pregnant the old-fashioned way, and her baby is due this fall. Tests show him to be a healthy boy who is not an HLA match for Henry.

Reading Comprehension—Points of Engagement

1. Look up the word "ethics" in your dictionary or online. Using your understanding of that definition, explain in your own words the ethical dilemma Belkin outlines in her essay. Who or what is at stake? Refer to two passages in the text to show how you know.

2. According to Belkin, the doctors she interviewed agree that the technology used to create a viable donor for a child with Fanconi anemia could be abused, but that the related research should not be banned. Name two potentials for abuse mentioned in the essay. Do you think the research should be banned? Why or why not?

3. At the end of the essay the two children profiled—Molly and Henry—end up with very different prognoses. Do an online search for both of them to find out what has happened since Belkin's essay was published. What factors were involved in their respective fates? Do those factors suggest how society might approach questions of medical ethics?

Assignment Questions—Points of Departure

1. In "The Made-to-Order Savior " Lisa Belkin describes controversial medical technology that enables parents to conceive a child genetically configured to be a bone marrow donor for another child. She cites critics who question the right of these parents to "manipulate nature." Use Belkin's discussion to consider another text that also addresses this idea of tampering with nature, such as Lauren Slater's "Dr. Daedalus," Andrew Sullivan's "The He Hormone," or Barbara Kingsolver's "A Fist in the Eye of God." What do these authors have to say about when or when not to let nature take its course? Write a paper in which you engage with their projects, and suggest an answer of your own to that difficult question.

2. On page 7 Belkin refers to the slippery slope argument, or the "potential for abuse in some circumstances" of medical technology. Read another text in which the slippery slope argument figures in the discussion, such as John Waterbury's "Hate Your Policies, Love Your Institutions," or Lauren Slater's "Dr. Daedalus." Use the two texts together to explore the slippery slope idea and the challenges of creating social policy to balance the potential for good against the potential for misuse.

3. On page 16 Belkin quotes parent Laurie Strongin who says, "I believe in love and science. Nothing more, nothing less," while Lisa Nash says, "God used our Adam to give Molly [her daughter] a second chance at life." How are these two parental responses to adversity different? Now consider another text such as Jane Goodall's "In the Forests of Gombe," Paul Davies's, "E.T. and God," or Susan Blackmore's "The Ultimate Memeplex" or "Strange Creatures," that specifically addresses the idea of scientific versus spiritual, or religious, thinking. How might these different belief systems, and the potential conflicts that arise between them, influence the discussion of medical ethics? Your project for this paper is to reconsider the dilemmas and decisions made by the Strongin and Nash families by using your insight on religious and scientific thinking from one of these other essays.

Strange Creatures
Susan Blackmore

Points of Access

1. What have you learned about genetics from your biology classes? How do genes replicate? Why do some genetic traits survive, while others die off?

2. Think about something—an idea, a fashion, or an object—that you used to think was really cool, but no longer is. Why did you think that something was 'cool' in the first place? How did you find out about it? Why do you think it's not cool any more? Did someone tell you, or did you decide gradually on your own?

3. What do you think it is that makes humans different from other animals? What ideas have you heard? What do *you* believe?

We humans are strange creatures. There is no doubt that our bodies evolved by natural selection just as other animals' did. Yet we differ from all other creatures in many ways. For a start we speak. We believe ourselves to be the most intelligent species on the planet. We are extraordinarily widespread and extremely versatile in our ways of making a living. We wage wars, believe in religions, bury our dead and get embarrassed about sex. We watch television, drive cars and eat ice cream. We have had such a devastating impact upon the ecosystems of our planet that we appear to be in danger of destroying everything on which our lives depend. One of the problems of being a human is that it is rather hard to look at humans with an unprejudiced eye.

On the one hand, we are obviously animals comparable with any others. We have lungs, hearts and brains made of living cells; we eat and breathe and reproduce. Darwin's theory of evolution by natural selection can successfully explain how we, along with the rest of life on this planet, came to be here, and why we all share so many characteristics. On the other hand, we behave quite differently from other animals. Now that biology has so successfully explained much of our similarity with other creatures we need to ask the opposite question. What makes us so different? Could it be our superior intelligence, our consciousness, our language, or what?

A common answer is that we are simply more intelligent than any other species. Yet the notion of intelligence is extremely slippery, with interminable arguments about how to define it, how to measure it, and to what extent it is inherited. Research in artificial intelligence (AI) has provided some nice surprises for those who thought they knew what makes human intelligence so special.

In the early days of AI, researchers thought that if they could teach a computer to play chess they would have reproduced one of the highest forms of human intelligence. In those days the idea that a computer could ever play well, let alone beat a Grand Master, was unthinkable. Yet now most home computers come with passable chess programmes already installed, and in 1997 the program *Deep Blue* beat World Champion Garry Kasparov, ending unquestioned human supremacy at the game. Computers may not play chess in the same way as humans, but their success shows how wrong we can be about intelligence. Clearly, what we thought were human beings' most special capabilities may not be.

Quite the opposite goes for some apparently quite unintelligent things like cleaning the house, digging the garden or making a cup of tea. Time and again AI researchers have tried to build robots to carry out such tasks and been defeated. The first problem is that the tasks all require vision. There is a popular (though possibly apocryphal) story about Marvin Minsky at MIT (the Massachusetts Institute of Technology) that he once gave his graduate students the problem of vision as a summer project. Decades later the problem of computer vision is still just that—a problem. We humans can see so effortlessly that we cannot begin to imagine how complex the process has to be. And in any case, this kind of intelligence cannot distinguish us from other animals because they can see too.

If intelligence does not provide simple answers perhaps consciousness might. Many people believe that human consciousness is unique and is responsible for making us human. Yet scientists cannot even define the term 'consciousness'. Everyone knows what their own consciousness is like but they cannot share that knowledge with anyone else. This troublesome fact—the subjectivity of consciousness—may explain why for most of this century the whole topic of consciousness was more or less banned from scientific discussion. Now at last it has become fashionable again, but scientists and philosophers cannot even agree on what an explanation of consciousness would look like. Some say that the 'Hard Problem' of subjectivity is quite different from any other scientific problem and needs a totally new kind of solution, while others are sure that when we fully understand brain function and behaviour the problem of consciousness will have disappeared.

Some people believe in the existence of a human soul or spirit that transcends the physical brain and explains human uniqueness. With the decline in religious belief fewer and fewer people intellectually accept that view, yet most of us continue to think of ourselves as a little conscious 'me' inside our brain; a 'me' who sees the world, makes the decisions, directs the actions and has responsibility for them.

As we shall see later, this view has to be wrong. Whatever the brain is doing it does not seem to need help from an extra, magical self. Various parts of the brain carry on their tasks independently of each other and countless different things are always going on at once. We may feel as though there is a central place inside our heads into which the sensations come and from which we consciously make the decisions. Yet this place simply does not exist. Clearly, something is very wrong with our ordinary view of our conscious selves. From this confused viewpoint we cannot say with certainty that other animals are not conscious, nor that consciousness is what makes us unique. So what does?

What Makes Us Different?

The thesis of this book is that what makes us different is our ability to imitate.

Imitation comes naturally to us humans. Have you ever sat and blinked, or waved, or 'goo gooed', or even just smiled, at a baby? What happens? Very often they blink too, or wave, or smile back at you. We do it so easily, even as an infant. We copy each other all the time. Like seeing, it comes so effortlessly that we hardly think about it. We certainly do not think of it as being something very clever. Yet, as we shall see, it is fantastically clever.

Certainly, other animals do not take naturally to it. Blink, or wave, or smile at your dog or cat and what happens? She might purr, wag her tail, twitch, or walk away, but you can be pretty sure she will not imitate you. You can teach a cat, or rat, to beg neatly for its food by progressively rewarding it, but you cannot teach it by demonstrating the trick yourself—nor can another cat or rat. Years of detailed research on animal imitation has led to the conclusion that it is extremely rare. Though we may think of mother cats as teaching their kittens to hunt, or groom, or use the cat door, they do not do it by demonstration or imitation. Parent birds 'teach' their babies to fly more by pushing them out of the nest and giving them the chance to try it than by demonstrating the required skills for them to copy.

There is a special appeal to stories of animals copying human behaviour, and pet owners are fond of such tales. I read on the Internet about a cat who learned to flush the toilet and soon taught a second cat the same trick. Now the two of them sit together on the cistern flushing away. A more reliable anecdote was told by Diana Reiss, a psychologist at Rutgers University. She works with bottlenose dolphins, who are known to be able to copy vocal sounds and artificial whistles, as well as simple actions (Bauer and Johnson 1994; Reiss and McCowan 1993). She trained the dolphins by giving them fish as a reward and also by a 'time out' procedure for punishment. If they did the wrong thing she would walk away from the water's edge and wait for one minute before returning to the pool. One day she threw a fish to one of the dolphins but had accidentally left on some spiky bits of fin. Immediately the dolphin turned, swam away, and waited for a minute at the other side of the pool.

That story touched me because I could not help thinking of the dolphins as *understanding* the action, as having intelligence and consciousness and intentionality like ours. But we cannot even define these things, let alone be sure that the dolphin was using them in this apparent act of reciprocation. What we can see is that it imitated Dr. Reiss in an appropriate way. We are so oblivious to the cleverness of imitation that we do not even notice how rare it is in other animals and how often we do it ourselves.

Perhaps more telling is that we do not have separate words for radically different kinds of learning. We use the same word 'learning' for simple association or 'classical conditioning' (which almost all animals can do), for learning by trial and error or 'operant conditioning' (which many animals can do), and for learning by imitation (which almost none can do). I want to argue that the supreme ease with which we are capable of imitation, has blinded us to this simple fact—that *imitation* is what makes us special.

Imitation and the Meme

When you imitate someone else, something is passed on. This 'something' can then be passed on again, and again, and so take on a life of its own. We might call this thing an idea, an instruction, a behaviour, a piece of information . . . but if we are going to study it we shall need to give it a name.

Fortunately, there is a name. It is the 'meme'.

The term 'meme' first appeared in 1976, in Richard Dawkins's best-selling book *The Selfish Gene*. In that book Dawkins, an Oxford zoologist, popularised the increasingly influential view that evolution is best understood in terms of the competition between genes. Earlier in the twentieth century, biologists had blithely talked about evolution occurring for the 'good of the species' without worrying about the exact mechanisms involved, but in the 1960s serious problems with this view began to be recognised (Williams 1966). For example, if a group of organisms all act for the good of the group then one individual who does not can easily exploit the rest. He will then leave more descendants who in turn do not act for the group, and the group benefit will be lost. On the more modern 'gene's eye view', evolution may *appear* to proceed in the interests of the individual, or for the good of the species, but in fact it is all driven by the competition between genes. This new viewpoint provided a much more powerful understanding of evolution and has come to be known as 'selfish-gene theory'.

We must be absolutely clear about what 'selfish' means in this context. It does not mean genes *for* selfishness. Such genes would incline their carriers to act selfishly and that is something quite different. The term 'selfish' here means that the genes act only for themselves; their only interest is their own replication; all they want is to be passed on to the next generation. Of course, genes do not 'want' or have aims or intentions in the same way as people do; they are only chemical instructions that can be copied. So when I say they 'want', or are 'selfish' I am using a shorthand, but this shorthand is necessary to avoid lengthy explanations. It will not lead us astray if we remember that genes either *are* or *are not* successful at getting passed on into the next generation. So the shorthand 'genes want *x*' can always be spelled out as 'genes that do *x* are more likely to be passed on'. This is the only power they have—replicator power. And it is in this sense that they are selfish.

Dawkins also introduced the important distinction between 'replicators' and their 'vehicles'. A replicator is anything of which copies are made, including 'active replicators' whose nature affects the chances of their being copied again. A vehicle is the entity that interacts with the environment, which is why Hull (1988*a*) prefers the term 'interactors' for a similar idea. Vehicles or interactors carry the replicators around inside them and protect them. The original replicator was presumably a simple self-copying molecule in the primeval soup, but our most familiar replicator now is DNA. Its vehicles are organisms and groups of organisms that interact with each other as they live out their lives in the seas or the air, the forests or fields. Genes are the selfish replicators that drive the evolution of the biological world here on earth but Dawkins believes there is a more fundamental principle at work. He suggested that wherever it arises, anywhere in the universe, 'all life evolves by the differential survival of replicating entities' (1976, p. 192). This is the foundation for the idea of Universal Darwinism; the application of Darwinian thinking way beyond the confines of biological evolution.

At the very end of the book he asked an obvious, if provocative, question. Are there any other replicators on our planet? The answer, he claimed, is 'Yes'. Staring us in the face, although still drifting clumsily about in its primeval soup of culture, is another replicator—a unit of imitation.

> We need a name for the new replicator, a noun that conveys the idea of a unit of cultural transmission, or a unit of *imitation*. 'Mimeme' comes from a suitable Greek root, but I want a monosyllable that sounds a bit like 'gene'. I hope my classicist friends will forgive me if I abbreviate mimeme to meme.

As examples, he suggested tunes, ideas, catch-phrases, clothes fashions, ways of making pots or of building arches'. He mentioned scientific ideas that catch on and propagate themselves around the world by jumping from brain to brain. He wrote about religions as groups of memes with a high survival value, infecting whole societies with belief in a God or an afterlife. He talked about fashions in dress or diet, and about ceremonies, customs and technologies—all of which are spread by one person copying another. Memes are stored in human brains (or books or inventions) and passed on by imitation.

In a few pages, Dawkins laid the foundations for understanding the evolution of memes. He discussed their propagation by jumping from brain to brain, likened them to parasites infecting a host, treated them as physically realised living structures, and showed how mutually assisting memes will gang together in groups just as genes do. Most importantly, he treated the meme as a replicator in its own right. He complained that many of his colleagues seemed unable to accept the idea that memes would spread for their own benefit, independently of any benefit to the genes. 'In the last analysis they wish always to go back to "biological advantage"' to answer questions about human behaviour. Yes, he agreed, we got our brains for biological (genetic) reasons but now we have them a new replicator has been unleashed. 'Once this new evolution begins, it will in no necessary sense be subservient to the old' (Dawkins 1976, pp. 193–4). In other words, memetic evolution can now take off without regard to its effects on the genes.

If Dawkins is right then human life is permeated through and through with memes and their consequences. Everything you have learned by imitation from someone else is a meme. But we must be clear what is meant by the word 'imitation', because our whole understanding of memetics depends on it. Dawkins said that memes jump from 'brain to brain via a process which, in the broad sense, can be called imitation' (1976, p. 192). I will also use the term 'imitation' in the broad sense. So if, for example, a friend tells you a story and you remember the gist and pass it on to someone else then that counts as imitation. You have not precisely imitated your friend's every action and word, but something (the gist of the story) has been copied from her to you and then on to someone else. This is the 'broad sense' in which we must understand the term 'imitation'. If in doubt, remember that something must have been copied.

Everything that is passed from person to person in this way is a meme. This includes all the words in your vocabulary, the stories you know, the skills and habits you have picked up from others and the games you like to play. It includes the songs you sing and the rules you obey. So, for example, whenever you drive on the left (or the right), eat curry with lager or pizza and coke, whistle the theme tune from *Neighbours* or even shake hands, you are dealing in memes. Each of these memes has evolved in its own unique way with its own history, but each of them is using your behaviour to get itself copied.

Take the song 'Happy Birthday to You'. Millions of people—probably thousands of millions of people the world over—know this tune. Indeed, I only have to write down those four words to have a pretty good idea that you may soon start humming it to yourself. Those words affect you, probably quite without any conscious intention on your part, by stirring up a memory you already possess. And where did that come from? Like millions of other people you have acquired it by imitation. Something, some kind of information, some kind of instruction, has become lodged in all those brains so that now we all do the same thing at birthday parties. That something is what we call the meme.

Memes spread themselves around indiscriminately without regard to whether they are useful, neutral, or positively harmful to us. A brilliant new scientific idea, or a technological invention, may spread because of its usefulness. A song like Jingle Bells may spread because it sounds OK, though it is not seriously useful and can definitely get on your nerves. But some memes are positively harmful—like chain letters and pyramid selling, new methods of fraud and false doctrines, ineffective slimming diets and dangerous medical 'cures'. Of course, the memes do not care; they are selfish like genes and will simply spread if they can.

Remember that the same shorthand applies to memes as to genes. We can say that memes are 'selfish', that they 'do not care', that they 'want' to propagate themselves, and so on, when all we mean is that successful memes are the ones that get copied and spread, while unsuccessful ones do not. This is the sense in which memes 'want' to get copied, 'want' you to pass them on and 'do not care' what that means to you or your genes.

This is the power behind the idea of memes. To start to think memetically we have to make a giant flip in our minds just as biologists had to do when taking on the idea of the selfish gene. Instead of thinking of our ideas as our own creations, and as working for us, we have to think of them as autonomous selfish memes, working only to get themselves copied. We humans, because of our powers of imitation, have become just the physical 'hosts' needed for the memes to get around. This is how the world looks from a 'meme's eye view'.

Meme Fear

This is a scary idea indeed. And perhaps that is why the word 'meme' is so often written with inverted commas around it, as though to apologise for using it. I have even seen eminent lecturers raise both hands and tweak them above their ears when forced to say 'meme' out loud. Gradually, the word has become more generally known, and has even been added to the *Oxford English Dictionary*. There are discussion groups and a *Journal of Memetics* on the Internet, and the idea almost seems to have acquired a cult following in cyberspace. But in academia it has not yet been so successful. A perusal of some of the best recent books on human origins, the evolution of language and evolutionary psychology shows that the word does not appear at all in most of them ('meme' is not in the indexes of Barkow *et al.* 1992; Diamond 1997; Dunbar 1996; Mithen 1996; Pinker 1994; Mark Ridley 1996; Tudge 1995; Wills 1993; Wright 1994). The idea of memes seems extremely relevant to these disciplines, and I want to argue that it is time for us to take on board the notion of a second replicator at work in human life and evolution.

One of the problems with the idea of memes is that it strikes at our deepest assumptions about who we are and why we are here. This is always happening in science. Before Copernicus and Galileo, people believed they lived at the centre of the universe in a world created especially for them by God. Gradually, we had to accept not only that the sun does not revolve around the earth, but that we live on some minor little planet in an ordinary galaxy in a vast universe of other galaxies.

A hundred and forty years ago Darwin's theory of evolution by natural selection provided the first plausible mechanism for evolution without a designer. People's view of their own origin changed from the biblical story of special creation in the image of God, to an animal descended from an apelike ancestor—a vast leap indeed, and one that led to much ridicule and fanatical opposition to Darwin. Still—we have all coped with that leap and come to accept that we are animals created by evolution. However, if memetics is valid, we will have to make another vast leap in accepting a similar evolutionary mechanism for the origin of our minds and our selves.

*   *   *

What will determine whether the theory of memes is worth having or not? Although philosophers of science argue over what makes a scientific theory valid, there are at least two commonly agreed criteria, and I will use these in judging memetics. First, a theory must be able to explain things better than its rival theories; more economically or more comprehensively. And second, it must lead to testable predictions that turn out to be correct. Ideally, those predictions should be unexpected ones—things that no one would have looked for if they were not starting from a theory of memetics.

My aim in this book is to show that many aspects of human nature are explained far better by a theory of memetics than by any rival theory yet available. The theory starts only with one simple mechanism—the competition between memes to get into human brains and be passed on again. From this, it gives rise to explanations for such diverse phenomena as the evolution of the enormous human brain, the origins of language, our tendency to talk and think too much, human altruism, and the evolution of the Internet. Looked at through the new lens of the memes, human beings look quite different.

Is the new way better? It seems obviously so to me, but I expect that many people will disagree. This is where the predictions come in. I shall try to be as clear as I can in deriving predictions and showing how they follow from mimetic theory. I may speculate and even, at times, leap wildly beyond the evidence, but as long as the speculations can be tested then they can be helpful. In the end, the success or failure of these predictions will decide whether memes are just a meaningless metaphor or the grand new unifying theory we need to understand human nature.

Reading Comprehension—Points of Engagement

1. What is a meme? Point to two passages in Blackmore's essay to support your answer.

2. What relationship do memes have with genes?

3. How do memes replicate? Be specific. Give two examples: one from Blackmore's essay, and one of your own.

Assignment Questions—Points of Departure

1. In this chapter of her book, *The Meme Machine*, Blackmore offers a theory of what differentiates humans from other animals: the meme. In her essay, "Dr. Daedalus," Lauren Slater discusses some of the implications of blurring species divisions. She suggests that by altering our physical selves to emulate something more animal, our brains, and possibly even our souls, become somehow more animal as well. What do *you* think? Your project in this paper is to answer that question while referring to relevant passages in both Slater and Blackmore's essays. Does altering

ourselves physically make any difference to the one thing, memes, that Blackmore claims ultimately differentiates us from animals?

2. Is there a God in the Meme Machine? Can we understand everything using scientific reasoning, the logic of the finite mind, or is there a superordinate power? If so, what is it? Your project is to answer those questions while engaging with the ideas of Susan Blackmore and Jane Goodall. What are their respective positions in response to these questions? Do you agree more with Blackmore or with Goodall? Do you think that Goodall's God might be a parable for understanding memes, or do you think the two must be kept separate? Why?

3. What is gender? In your opinion, is it closer to a meme or a gene? Does it matter whether it is one or the other? What are the repercussions for thinking of gender as an 'artifact' or consequence of human society, rather than a result of biology? Do you see Andrew Sullivan's discussion of masculinity in "The He Hormone," or Katha Pollitt's discussion of feminism in "Marooned on Gilligan's Island," as a construct of memetics or genetics?

The Ultimate Memeplex
Susan Blackmore

Points of Access

1. What do you think your 'self' is? Where does it come from, and how do you define it? Is it real and constant, or does it change depending on your environment?

2. What do you think drives you to make certain choices in life? Why do you think you are influenced to act in some ways, but not in others?

3. Do you believe in God? If so, why do you believe? If not, why not? Have you ever doubted or changed your position on whether you believed in God? Did that doubt come from within you or from some influence outside of you?

'We, alone on earth, can rebel against the tyranny of the selfish replicators'. So ends Dawkins's book *The Selfish Gene* in which the whole idea of memes began. But who is this 'we'? That is the question I want to ask now. The 'ultimate memeplex' of my title is no science fiction futuristic invention, but our own familiar self.

Think for a moment about yourself. I mean the 'real you', the inner self, that bit of yourself that really feels those heartfelt emotions, the bit of you that once (or many times) fell in love, the you that is conscious and that cares, thinks, works hard, believes, dreams and imagines; I mean who you really are. Unless you have thought about this a good deal you probably jump to many conclusions about your self—that it has some kind of continuity and persists through your life, that it is the centre of your consciousness, has memories, holds beliefs and makes the important decisions of your life.

Now I want to ask some simple questions about this 'real you'. They are: What am I? Where am I? What do I do?

What Am I?

You may be one of the large majority who believes in the existence of a soul or spirit. Ethnographic studies show that most cultures include notions of a soul or spirit, nearly half believing that the soul can separate from the body (Sheils 1978). Surveys show that in the United States 88 per cent believe in a human soul, and in Europe 61 per cent, figures in line with high levels of belief in God, life after death, and supernatural phenomena (Gallup and Newport 1991; Humphrey 1995). Presumably, people assume that the soul is their inner self or 'real me' and will survive when their body dies.

There is a long history of philosophers and scientists trying to make sense of such a view. In the seventeenth century, the French philosopher René Descartes took a wonderfully skeptical view of the world, doubting every belief and opinion he had. He decided to treat everything as though it were absolutely false 'until I have encountered something which is certain or at least, if I can do nothing else, until I have learned with certainty that there is nothing certain in the world.' (Descartes 1641, p. 102). Amidst all his doubts, he concluded that he could not doubt that he was thinking. Thus he came to his famous 'Cogito ergo sum'—I think therefore I am—and to what is now known, after him, as 'Cartesian dualism': the idea that that thinking stuff is different from physical, or extended, stuff. Our bodies may be a machine of sorts but 'we' are something else.

Dualism is tempting but false. For a start no such separate stuff can be found. If it could be found it would become part of the physical world and so not be a separate stuff at all. On the other hand if it cannot, in principle, be found by any physical measures then it is impossible to see how it could do its job of controlling the brain. How would immaterial mind and material body interact? Like Descartes' 'thinking stuff', souls, spirits and other self-like entities seem powerless to do what is demanded of them.

Nevertheless, a few scientists have developed dualist theories. The philosopher Sir Karl Popper and neuroscientist Sir John Eccles (1977) suggest that the self controls its brain by intervening at the synapses (or chemical junctions) between neurons. Yet as our understanding grows of how neurons and synapses work there is less and less need for a ghost to control the machine. Mathematician Roger Penrose (1994) and anaesthetist Stuart Hameroff (1994) suggest that consciousness operates at a quantum level in the tiny microtubules inside the membranes of neurons. Yet their proposal just replaces one mystery with another. As the philosopher Patricia Churchland (1998, p. 121) observes 'Pixie dust in the synapses is about as explanatorily powerful as quantum coherence in the microtubules'. These attempts to find a self that lurks in the gaps in our understanding just do not help, and few scientists or philosophers are convinced by them.

The opposite extreme is to identify the self with the whole brain, or whole body. This might seem appealing. After all, when you talk about Simon you mean him—the whole body, the entire person. So why not say the same of yourself? Because this does not get at the problem we are struggling with—that it feels as though there is someone inside who is consciously making the decisions. You can point to your body and say 'that is me' but you do not really mean it. Let us try a thought experiment. Imagine for a moment that you are given a choice (and you cannot say neither). Either you will have your body completely swapped for another body and keep your inner conscious self, or you will have your inner self swapped for another unspecified self and keep the body. Which will it be?

Of course, this is both practically and conceptually daft. Unless we can identify this inner self the experiment could not be done, and even then it implies a further self to do the choosing. However, the point is this. I bet you did make a choice and I bet you chose to keep your inner self. However daft the notion is, we seem to have it, and have it bad. We think of ourselves as something separate from our brains and bodies. This is what needs explaining, and so far we are not getting on very well.

This problem applies to any scientific theory that leaves the sense of self out of the picture. The most thorough-going reductionist view of this kind is what Nobel laureate Francis Crick calls 'The Astonishing Hypothesis':

> The Astonishing Hypothesis is that 'You', your joys and your sorrows, your memories and your ambitions, your sense of personal identity and free will, are in fact no more than the behavior of a vast assembly of nerve cells and their associated molecules. As Lewis Carroll's Alice might have phrased it: 'You're nothing but a pack of neurons' (Crick 1994, p. 3).

There are at least two problems with this. First, you do not feel like a pack of neurons. So what the theory needs, and does not provide, is an explanation of how a pack of neurons comes to believe that it is actually an independent conscious self. Second, the theory does not say *which* neurons. It cannot be all neurons because 'I' am not consciously aware of most of what goes on in my brain; 'I' do not identify with the neurons that control glucose levels in my blood or the fine movements that keep me sitting up straight. On the other hand if you try to identify 'self' neurons you are doomed to trouble. All neurons look much the same under the microscope and all of them are doing something all the time regardless of what 'I' am doing. Crick is working on the theory that neurons bound together by simultaneous firing at 40 cycles per second form the basis for visual awareness, but this is not the same as a theory of a conscious self.

Note that this theory is more reductionist than many others. Crick not only assumes that you are utterly dependent upon the actions of nerve cells—most neuroscientists assume that—but that you are *nothing but* the pack of neurons. Other scientists assume that new phenomena may emerge from simpler ones, and cannot be understood by understanding the underlying neurons and their connections. For example, we cannot understand human intentions, motivations, or emotions just by observing the behaviour and connections of neurons, any more than we can understand the activity of a desktop computer by looking at its chips and circuits. On this more common view the intentions depend completely on the neurons (just as the computation depends completely on the chips in the computer) but to understand them we must work at an appropriate level of explanation. But what is the appropriate level of explanation for the self? The behaviour of neurons seems to miss it.

Another approach is to identify the self with memory or personality. Victorian spiritualists believed that 'human personality' was the essence of the self and could survive physical death (Myers 1903). However, personality is nowadays understood not as a separate entity but as a fairly consistent way of behaving that makes one person identifiably different from another. This way of behaving reflects the kind of brain we were born with and our lifetime's experiences. It cannot be separated from our brain and body any more than our memories can. The more we learn about personality and memory the more obvious it is that they are functions of a living brain and inseparable from it. In an important sense you are your memories and personality—at least, you would not be the same person without them—but they are not things, or properties of a separate self. They are complex functions of neural organisation.

A final way of looking at the self is as a social construction. If I asked you who you are, you might answer with your name, your job, your relationship to other people (I'm Sally's mum or Daniel's daughter), or your reason for being where you are (I'm the cleaner, Adam invited me). All of these self-descriptions come out of your mastery of language, your interactions with other people, and the world of discourse in which you live. They are all useful in certain circumstances, but they do not describe the sort of 'inner self' we were looking for. They describe no persistent conscious entity. They are just labels for an ever-changing social creature. They depend on where you are and who you are with. We can find out a lot about how such constructions are created—indeed social psychologists do just that—but we do not find a conscious self this way. The inner 'me' seems to be mighty elusive.

Where Am I?

You probably feel as though 'you' are located somewhere behind your eyes, looking out. This seems to be the most commonly imagined perspective, though others include the top of the head, the heart, or even in the neck, and there are apparently cultural differences in this imagined position. The location may change with what you are doing, and you may even be able to move it around at will. Blind people report feeling themselves in their fingertips when reading Braille, or in their long white cane when walking. Drivers sometimes inhabit the edges of their cars and wince if something passes too close. So is there anything actually at this imagined spot? Presumably not in the case of the stick or the car, but it still feels as though there is a self in there somewhere. Where, then, should we look for the self?

The most obvious place to look is in the brain. Drugs that affect the brain affect our sense of self, and damage to various areas of the brain can destroy or change it. Stimulating the brain with electrodes can produce changes in body image, feelings of shrinking or expanding, or sensations of floating and flying. Yet we do not feel as though we are inside a warm, wet, and pulsating organ. In a lurid thought experiment Dennett (1978) imagines his brain being removed to a vat in a life-support lab while his body roams around as usual, connected to his body as intricately as it ever was before, but by radio links instead of nerves. Now where would Dennett feel he was? As long as he could see and hear, he would feel as though he was wherever his eyes and ears were. He would not fancy himself to be inside the vat. Of course, we cannot do the experiment to check his intuitions, but it suggests the disturbing conclusion that Dennett would still imagine he was living in there, somewhere behind his eyes, even if the skull were empty and his brain were controlling things from the vat.

If we look inside the brain we do not see a self. To the naked eye a human brain looks like a lump of rather solid porridge with a convoluted shiny surface and various areas of paler or darker grey; it is hard to believe that all our thinking goes on in there. Only with high magnification and the techniques of modern neuroscience can we find out that it contains about a hundred billion neurons or nerve cells. The neurons are connected up in fantastically complex ways and, by virtue of these connections, store and process the information that controls our behaviour. However, there is no centre of action where a self might reside. There is no one place into which all the inputs go, and from which all the instructions get sent out. This is an important point, and deeply disturbing. We feel as though we are a central observer and controller of what goes on, but there is no place for this central controller to live.

Let us consider what happens when you perform a simple task. For example, find a letter 'p' on this page and then point to it. What has gone on? It may feel as though you have decided to find a 'p' (or not if you could not be bothered), searched the next few lines, found one, and then commanded your finger to move into position and touch it. The role of the self seems obvious, 'you' decided to act (or not), 'you' moved your finger and so on.

From an information-processing point of view the role of the 'you' is not at all obvious. Light enters the eye and is focused on a layer of light-sensitive cells. The output from these goes into four layers of cells in the retina which extract edges and brightness discontinuities, enhance differences across boundaries, change the coding of colour information from a three-receptor system to one based on pairs of opposites, and throw away a great deal of unnecessary detail. The part-digested information is then compressed and passed along the optic nerve into the thalamus inside the brain. Here, different types of information about the image are separately processed and the results passed on to other parts of the visual cortex at the back of the brain. As the information passes through it is at some times and places coded like a map, with neighbouring positions corresponding to neighbouring locations in the world, but, at other times and places, as more abstract information about shape, movement or texture. Throughout the system there are numerous things going on at once.

From the visual cortex, outputs go off to other parts of the brain, for example, those dealing with language, reading, speech, object recognition and memory. Since you know how to read, a search identifies a letter 'p'. Some of the information goes to the motor cortex which co-ordinates action. From here a movement such as pointing with your finger, will be pre-processed and then coordinated with visual feedback as it happens, so that the finger ends up in line with the 'p'.

The details of this do not matter. The important point is that the description that neuroscientists are building up of the way the brain works leaves no room for a central self. There is no single line in to a central place, nor a single line out; the whole system is massively parallel. In this description there is no need for a 'you' who decided to find the 'p' (or not) and who started the finger moving. The whole action inexorably created itself, given this book with its instruction, and your brain and body.

You might think that there is still room for a central self as some kind of informational or abstract centre rather than an actual place. There are several theories of this kind, such as Baars's (1997) global workspace theory. The workspace is like a theatre with a bright spotlight on the stage; the events in the bright spot are the only ones 'in consciousness'. But this is only a metaphor and can be a misleading one. If there is any sense to the idea of a spotlight, it is that at any time some information is being attended to—or actively processed—while other information is not. However, this focus of activity changes continuously with the complex demands of the task we are performing. If there is a spotlight, it is one that switches on and off all over the place and can shine in several places at once; if there is a global workspace it is not located in any particular place. It cannot tell us where 'I' am.

The theatre metaphor may do more harm than good to our thinking about self and consciousness. Dennett (1991) argues that although most theorists now reject Cartesian dualism, they still secretly believe in what he calls the 'Cartesian Theatre'. They still imagine that somewhere inside our heads is a place where 'it all comes together'; where consciousness happens and we see our mental images projected on a mental screen; where we make our decisions and initiate actions; where we agonise about life, love, and meaning. The Cartesian Theatre does not exist. When sensory information comes into the brain it does not go to an inner screen where a little self is watching it. If it did, the little self would have to have little eyes and another inner screen, and so on. According to Dennett, the brain produces 'multiple drafts' of what is happening as the information flows through its parallel networks. One of these drafts comes to be the verbal story we tell ourselves, which includes the idea that there is an author of the story, or a user of the brain's virtual machine. Dennett calls this the 'benign user illusion'. So maybe this is all we are; a centre of narrative gravity; a story about a persisting self who does things, feels things and makes decisions; a benign user illusion. And illusions do not have locations.

What Do I Do?

Hold out your arm in front of you and then, whenever you feel like it, spontaneously and of your own free will, flex your wrist. You might like to do this a few times, making sure you do it as consciously and spontaneously as you can. You will probably experience some kind of inner dialogue or decision process in which you hold back from doing anything, and then decide to act. Now ask yourself, what began the process that led to the action? Was it you?

This task formed the basis of some fascinating experiments carried out by the neurosurgeon Benjamin Libet (1985). His subjects had electrodes on their wrists to pick up the action, and electrodes on their scalps to measure brain waves, and they watched a revolving spot on a clock face. As well as spontaneously flexing their wrists they were asked to note exactly where the spot was when they decided to act. Libet was therefore timing three things: the start of the action, the moment of the decision to act, and the start of a particular brain wave pattern called a readiness potential. This pattern is seen just before any complex action, and is associated with the brain planning the series of movements to be carried out. The question was, which would come first, the decision to act or the readiness potential?

If you are a dualist you may think that the decision to act must come first. In fact what Libet found was that the readiness potential began about 550 milliseconds (just over half a second) before the action, and the decision to act about 200 milliseconds (about one-fifth of a second) before the action. In other words, the decision to act was not the starting point—a finding that can seem a little threatening to our sense of self. There was much controversy over his results and many criticisms of the experiments, but given all I have said above, his results were only to be expected. There is no separate self jumping into the synapses and starting things off. My brain does not need me.

So what does my self do? Surely it must at least be the centre of my awareness; the thing that receives impressions as I go about my life? Not necessarily. This false view is just part of Dennett's illusory Cartesian Theatre. You can think about this either logically, or from the point of view of your own experience. We have already considered the logic; so now let us try to introspect carefully. Sit down comfortably and look at something uninteresting. Now concentrate on feeling the sensations from your body and on hearing what is going on around you. Stay like that long enough to get used to it and then ask yourself some questions. Where is that sound? Is it inside my head or over there? If it's over there, then what is hearing it? Can I be conscious of the thing that is hearing it? If so, am I separate from that thing as well?

You can make up your own questions. The general idea is an old one, and has been used in many meditation traditions over the millennia. Staring determinedly into your own experience does not reveal a solid world observed by a persisting self but simply a stream of ever-changing experience, with no obvious separation between observed and observer. The eighteenth-century Scottish philosopher David Hume explained that whenever he entered most intimately into himself he always stumbled upon some particular perception—of heat or cold or pain or pleasure. He could never catch *himself* without a perception, nor observe anything but the perception. He concluded that the self was no more than a 'bundle of sensations' (Hume 1739–40). The very natural idea that 'I' hear the sounds, feel the sensations, or see the world may be false.

Another series of experiments by Libet (1981) adds an interesting twist to the argument. Conscious sensory impressions can be induced by stimulating the brain, but only when it is continuously stimulated for about half a second. It is as though consciousness takes some time to build up. This would lead to the odd idea that our conscious appreciation of the world lags behind the events, but because of a process Libet calls 'subjective antedating' we never realise it is lagging behind. The story we tell ourselves puts events in order. Further experiments showed that with short stimuli (too short to induce conscious sensation) people could nevertheless guess correctly whether they were being stimulated or not (Libet *et al.* 1991). In other words they could make correct responses without awareness. Again the implication is that consciousness does not direct the action. Conscious awareness comes all right, but not in time. The hand is removed from the flame before we consciously feel the pain. We have whacked the tennis ball back before we can be conscious of it coming towards us. We have avoided the puddle before we were conscious of its existence. Consciousness follows on later. Yet we still feel that 'I' consciously did these things.

Something else we think we do is to believe things. Because of our beliefs we argue vehemently over dinner that President Clinton really could not have done it, that the Israelis ought (or ought not) to have built those homes, that private education ought to be abolished, or that all drugs should be legalised. We are so convinced of our belief in God that we will argue for hours (or perhaps even go to war or lay down our life for Him). We are so convinced by the alternative therapy that helped *me* that we force its claims on all our friends. But what does it mean to say that I believe? It sounds as though there must be a self in there who has things called beliefs, but from another perspective there is only a person arguing, a brain processing the information, memes being copied or not. We cannot actually find either the beliefs or the self who believes.

The same can be said of memory. We speak as though the self pulls up memories at will from its personal store. We conveniently ignore the fact that memories are ever-changing mental constructions, that often we fail to remember accurately, that some memories come unbidden and that we often use complex memories with no conscious awareness at all. It is more accurate to say that we are just human beings doing complex things that need memory and who then construct a story about a self who does the remembering.

In this, and many other ways, we seem to have an enormous desire to describe ourselves (falsely) as a self in control of 'our' lives. The British psychologist Guy Claxton suggests that what we take for self control is just a more or less successful attempt at prediction. Much of the time our predictions about what we will do next are reasonably accurate and we can get away with saying 'I did this' or 'I intended to do that'. When they go wrong we just bluff. And we use some truly outrageous tricks to maintain the illusion.

> I meant to keep my cool but I just couldn't. I'm supposed not to eat pork but I forgot. I'd decided on an early night but somehow here we are in Piccadilly Circus at four a.m. with silly hats and a bottle of wine . . . If all else fails—and this is a truly audacious sleight of hand—we can reinterpret our failure of control as an actual success! 'I changed my mind,' we say (Claxton 1986, p. 59).

Claxton concludes that consciousness is 'a mechanism for constructing dubious stories whose purpose is to defend a superfluous and inaccurate sense of self' (1994, p. 150). Our error is to think of the self as separate, persistent, and autonomous. Like Dennett, Claxton thinks that the self is really only a *story* about a self. The inner self who does things is an illusion.

The Function of a Self

Where have we got to in this brief exploration of the nature of self and consciousness? I can summarise by comparing two major kinds of theory about the self. On the one hand are what we might call 'real self' theories. They treat the self as a persistent entity that lasts a lifetime, is separate from the brain and from the world around, has memories and beliefs, initiates actions, experiences the world, and makes decisions. On the other hand are what we might call 'illusory self' theories. They liken the self to a bundle of thoughts, sensations, and experiences tied together by a common history (Hume 1739–40; Parfit 1987), or a series of pearls on a string (Strawson 1997). On these theories, the illusion of continuity and separateness is provided by a story the brain tells, or a fantasy it weaves.

Everyday experience, ordinary speech and 'common sense' are all in favour of the 'real self', while logic and evidence (and more disciplined experience) are on the side of the 'illusory self'. I prefer logic and evidence and therefore prefer to accept some version of the idea that the continuous, persistent and autonomous self is an illusion. I am just a story about a me who is writing a book. When the word 'I' appears in this book, it is a convention that both you and I understand, but it does not refer to a persistent, conscious, inner being behind the words.

Now, having accepted that, a new question arises. Why do we humans tell this story? If no persistent conscious self exists, why do people believe it does? How is it that people routinely live their lives as a lie?

The most obvious kind of explanation to try is that having a sense of self benefits the replication of our genes. Crook (1980) argues that self-consciousness arose from using Machiavellian Intelligence and reciprocal altruism, with its need for balancing the trust and distrust of others. In a rather dualistic version of a similar theory Humphrey (1986) suggests that consciousness is like an inner eye observing the brain. As primates developed ever more complex social structures, their survival began to depend on more sophisticated ways of predicting and outwitting others' behaviour. In this, he argues, *Homo psychologicus* would win out. Imagine a male who wanted to steal a mate from his rival or get more than his fair share of a kill. Predicting what the rival would do next would help, and one way to predict what others will do is to observe your own inner processes. These and other theories suggest that a complex social life makes it necessary to have a sense of self, to tot up scores in reciprocation, and to develop what psychologists now call a 'theory of mind'—that is, the understanding that other people have intentions, beliefs, and points of view.

However, this does not explain why our theory of mind is so wrong. Surely one could understand one's own behaviour without creating the idea of a separate and persistent self when it does not exist. Crook and Humphrey jump from the idea that early hominids might have benefited genetically by having an accurate model of their own behaviour to the idea that they would therefore acquire the idea of a separate self. Our self, the self we are trying to understand, is not just a model of how our own body—and by inference other bodies—is likely to behave, but a false story about an inner self who believes things, does things, wants things and persists throughout life.

Self-deception can have benefits. According to Trivers' (1985) theory of adaptive self-deception, hiding intentions from oneself may be the best way to hide them from others, and so deceive them. However, this theory does not help in the use of inventing a central self. Dennett (1991) describes us as adopting 'the intentional stance'; that is, we behave 'as if' other people (and sometimes animals, plants, toys and computers) have intentions, desires, beliefs, and so on. He argues that this metaphor of agency is a practical necessity of life; it gives us new and useful tools for thinking with. The problem is, it seems to me, that we apply this intentional stance too thoroughly to ourselves—we fall too deeply into the 'benign user illusion'. We do not say to ourselves 'it's *as if* I have intentions, beliefs and desires' but 'I really do'. I am left wondering how we get from the evolutionary advantage of having a theory of mind, or the practical advantage of adopting the intentional stance, to living our lives as a lie, protecting our ideas, convincing others of our beliefs, and caring so much about an inner self who does not exist.

Perhaps we create and protect a complex self because it makes us happy. But does it? Acquiring money, admiration, and fame gives some kind of happiness, but it is typically brief. Happiness has been found to depend more on having a life that matches your skills to what you are doing than to having a rich lifestyle. The Chicago psychologist Mihaly Csikszentmihalyi (1990) studied the fulfilling experience of 'flow' that artists describe when they lose themselves in their work. 'Flow' comes to children playing games, people deep in conversation, people skiing or mountain climbing, playing golf or making love. These all entail the same sense of happiness through loss of self-consciousness.

What makes *you* happy? Or consider the reverse: What makes *you* unhappy? Probably it is things like disappointment, fear of the future, worry about loved ones, not having enough money, people not liking you, living too stressful a life, and so on. Many of these things are only relevant to a creature that has self-awareness and the idea of a self as the owner of experience. Other animals can show disappointment, as when food does not arrive when they expect it, but they cannot have the deep disappointment of not getting a job, the fear of being thought stupid, or the misery of thinking someone they care about does not like them. We construct many of our miseries out of the idea of a persistent self that we desperately want to be loved, successful, admired, right about everything, and happy.

According to many traditions this false sense of self is precisely the root of all suffering. This idea is probably clearest in Buddhism with the doctrine of *anatta* or no self. This does not mean that there is no body, nor that there is literally no self at all, but that the self is a temporary construction, an idea or story about a self. In a famous speech, the Buddha told the monks 'actions do exist, and also their consequences, but the person that acts does not' (Parfit 1987). He taught that because we have the wrong idea about our self, we think that we will be happy if we gain more material things, or status or power. In fact it is wanting some things and being averse to others that makes us unhappy. If only we could realise our true nature then we would be free of suffering because we would know there is no 'me' to suffer.

Now we can see the difference between Dennett's view and the Buddhist one. Both understand the self to be some kind of story or illusion, but for Dennett it is a 'benign user illusion' and even a life-enhancing illusion, while for the Buddhist it is the root of human suffering. Either way it is an untruth. There is no doubt that having a clear sense of identity, a positive self-image and good self-esteem are associated with psychological health, but this is all about comparing a positive sense of self with a negative one. When we ask what good is done by having a sense of self at all, the answer is not obvious.

The Selfplex

Memetics provides a new way of looking at the self. The self is a vast memeplex—perhaps the most insidious and pervasive memeplex of all. I shall call it the 'selfplex'. The selfplex permeates all our experience and all our thinking so that we are unable to see it clearly for what it is—a bunch of memes. It comes about because our brains provide the ideal machinery on which to construct it, and our society provides the selective environment in which it thrives.

As we have seen, memplexes are groups of memes that come together for mutual advantage. The memes inside a memeplex survive better as part of the group than they would on their own. Once they have got together they form a self-organising, self-protecting structure that welcomes and protects other memes that are compatible with the group, and repels memes that are not. In a purely informational sense a memeplex can be imagined as having a kind of boundary or filter that divides it from the outside world. We have already considered how religions, cults, and ideologies work as memeplexes; we can now consider how the selfplex works.

Imagine two memes. The first concerns some esoteric points of astrology: that the fire element in Leo indicates vitality and power, while Mars in the first house indicates an aggressive personality, and transits of Mars should be ignored unless the aspect is a conjunction. The other meme is a personal belief—'I believe that the fire element in Leo . . .' Which meme will fare better in the competition to get into as many brains, books and television programmes as possible? The second will. A piece of information on its own may be passed on if it is relevant to a particular conversation, or useful for some purpose, but it is just as likely to be forgotten. On the other hand, people will press their beliefs and opinions on other people for no very good reason at all and, on occasion, fight very hard to convince others about them.

Take another example: the idea of sex differences in ability. As an abstract idea (or isolated meme) this is unlikely to be a winner. But get it into the form 'I believe that boys and girls are equally good at everything' and it suddenly has the enormous weight of 'self' behind it. 'I' will fight for this idea as though I were being threatened. I might argue with friends, write opinion pieces, or even go on marches. The meme is safe inside the haven of 'self', even in the face of evidence against it. 'My' ideas are protected by the behaviour they induce.

This suggests that memes can gain an advantage by becoming associated with a person's self concept. It does not matter how they do this—whether by raising strong emotions, by being especially compatible with memes already in place, or by providing a sense of power or attractiveness—they will fare better than other memes. These successful memes will more often be passed on, we will all come across them and so we, too, will get infected with self-enhancing memes. In this way our selfplexes are all strengthened.

Note that we do not have to agree with or like the memes we pass on, but only to engage with them in some way. Whether it's eating pasta, watching *The Simpsons,* or listening to jazz, the memes are passed on not just in eating the food or playing the music but in statements such as 'I like . . .' 'I hate . . .' 'I can't stand . . .' Pyper concludes that 'Dawkins himself has become a "survival machine" for the bible, a "meme nest" for its dispersed memes which may induce readers who would otherwise leave their bibles unread to go back to the text' (Pyper 1998, pp. 86–7). Presumably, Dawkins did not intend to encourage religious memes in this way but his powerful response to religion has had that effect. Memes that provoke no response fare poorly, while those that provide emotional arguments can induce their carrier to pass them on. By acquiring the status of a personal belief a meme gets a big advantage. Ideas that can get inside a self—that is, become 'my' ideas, or 'my' opinions, are winners.

Then there are possessions. Some other animals, without memes, might be said to have possessions: a robin owns the territory he guards, a powerful male owns his harem of females, and a lioness owns her kill. Human possessions can serve similar functions, such as enhancing personal status and providing a genetic advantage. But we should not overlook a big difference, that our possessions seem to belong to the mythical 'I', not just to the body it supposedly inhabits. Think of something you own and care about, something you would be sorry to lose, and ask yourself who or what actually owns it. Is it sufficient to say that your body does? Or are you tempted to think that it is the inner conscious you who owns it? I am. I realise, with some dismay, that I am partly defined by my house and garden, my bicycle, my thousands of books, my computer, and my favorite pictures. I am not just a living creature, but all these things as well; and they are things that would not exist without memes and would not matter without 'me'.

An interesting consequence of all this is that beliefs, opinions, possessions and personal preferences all bolster the idea that there is a believer or owner behind them. The more you take sides, get involved, argue your case, protect your possessions, and have strong opinions, the more you strengthen the false idea that there is not only a person (body and brain) talking, but an inner self with esoteric things called beliefs. The self is a great protector of memes, and the more complex the memetic society in which a person lives, the more memes there are fighting to get inside the protection of the self.

As the number of memes we all come across increases, so there are more and more chances for memes to provoke strong reactions and get passed on again. The stakes are thereby raised, and memes must become ever more provocative to compete. The consequence is that stress levels increase as we are bombarded by memes that have successfully provoked other people. We acquire more and more knowledge, opinions, and beliefs of our own, and in the process become more and more convinced that there is a real self at the centre of it all.

There is no 'I' who 'holds' the opinions. There is a body that says 'I believe in being nice to people', and a body that is (or is not) nice to people. There is a brain that can store knowledge of astrology and the tendency to talk about it, but there is not *in addition* a self who 'has' the belief. There is a biological creature who eats yogurt every day but there is not *in addition* a self inside who loves yogurt. As the memosphere becomes more and more complicated, selves follow suit. To function in our society we are all expected to hold opinions on science, politics, the weather, and relationships; to hold a job, bring up a family, read the paper, and enjoy our leisure time. With constant memetic bombardment our lives and our selves become more and more stressful and complicated. But this is a 'Red Queen' process. No one benefits because everyone has to keep running just to stay in the same place. I wonder just how much memetic pressure selfplexes can take before they blow apart, become unstable, or divide into fragments. The unhappiness, desperation, and psychological ill-health of many modern people may reveal just this. Today's psychotherapy is a kind of memetic engineering, but it is not based on sound memetic principles. That is something for the future.

In conclusion, the selfplex is successful not because it is true or good or beautiful; nor because it helps our genes; nor because it makes us happy. It is successful because the memes that get inside it persuade us (those poor overstretched physical systems) to work for their propagation. What a clever trick. That is, I suggest, why we all live our lives as a lie, and sometimes a desperately unhappy and confused lie. The memes have made us do it—because a 'self' aids in their replication.

Reading Comprehension—Points of Engagement

1. What is a memeplex? Construct a definition in your own words based on Blackmore's chapter.

2. What are the two "major kinds of theory" about the self in Blackmore's essay? Explain each separately. Which does Blackmore subscribe to? Why? Quote her in support of your answer.

3. Which memes, according to Blackmore, will be "winners"? Why? How are these "winner" memes related to our "selfplexes"? Refer to pages 42–45, and give several examples to help explain your answers.

Assignment Questions—Points of Departure

1. In his essay, "Control Artist," Steven Johnson describes a pure-bred emergent system as "a meshwork of autonomous agents following simple rules and mutually influencing each other's behavior" (180). How are these "emergent systems" related to Susan Blackmore's description of memeplexes? What attributes do they share? How are they different? How do human beings fit into these kinds of systems? Do we have agency—power to affect our own destinies—or are we just responding to one another in a vast emergent system?

2. Consider the memeplexes at work in the essays by David Brooks, Adam Gopnik, Lewis Lapham, or Arlie Russell Hochschild. What are those memeplexes? How do Brooks, Gopnik, Lapham, or Hochschild feel about them? Do they propose any response to the memeplexes you've identified? Do you agree with their positions? Why or why not?

3. What do memes have to do with the business of sports? Reread Franklin Foer's essay, "Soccer vs. McWorld," with Blackmore's theory of memes in mind. In his essay, Foer observes a resurgence of local clubs and traits, even when faced with the overwhelming economic and cultural power of globalism. Is this trend be a product of memetics? What do you think Foer would say? Blackmore? You? Does Foer's essay demonstrate the rise of the individual over the power of memes, or has the 'local' memeplex simply proven stronger than the 'global' memeplex because it seems to provide more of an advantage to the host?

On Habit
Alain de Botton

Points of Access

1. Why do you think people go away on vacation? Write down five reasons that you can think of. What are you able to do, and to see, on vacation that it is impossible to do at home?

2. What can cause you to act differently from the way you normally act? Do you think that your physical environment causes you to act in certain ways? Can changing your physical environment cause changes in your behavior? Can you change your behavior without changing your physical environment, or is it often too difficult to do so?

3. Look at some familiar object in your room. Try to write half a page describing it. Think of this description as trying to paint the object with words. Do you notice things about it that you had not before? What makes this experience different from the way you usually experience this object? Has your attitude towards the object changed after looking at it in so much detail?

1.

I returned to London from Barbados to find that the city had stubbornly refused to change. I had seen azure skies and giant sea anemones, I had slept in a raffia bungalow and eaten a kingfish, I had swum beside baby turtles and read in the shade of coconut trees. But the home town was unimpressed. It was still raining. The park was still a pond, and the skies funereal. When we are in a good mood and it is sunny, it is tempting to impute a connection between what happens inside and outside of us, but the appearance of London on my return was a reminder of the indifference of the world to any of the events unfolding in the lives of its inhabitants. I felt despair to be home. I felt there could be few worse places on earth than the one I had been fated to spend my existence in.

2.

> The sole cause of man's unhappiness is that he does not know how to stay quietly in his room.
>
> Pascal, *Pensées,* 136

3.

From 1799 to 1804, Alexander von Humboldt undertook a journey around South America, later entitling the account of what he had seen *Journey to the Equinoctial Regions of the New Continent.*

Nine years earlier, in the spring of 1790, a twenty-seven-year-old Frenchman, Xavier de Maistre, undertook a journey around his bedroom, later entitling the account of what he had seen *Journey around My Bedroom.* Gratified by his experiences, in 1798, De Maistre undertook a second journey. This time, he travelled by night and ventured out as far as the window-ledge, later entitling his account *Nocturnal Expedition around My Bedroom.*

Two approaches to travel: *Journey to the Equinoctial Regions of the New Continent, Journey around My Bedroom.* The first required ten mules, thirty pieces of luggage, four interpreters, a chronometer, a sextant, two telescopes, a Borda theodolite, a barometer, a compass, a hygrometer, letters of introduction from the King of Spain and a gun. The second, a pair of pink and blue cotton pyjamas.

Xavier de Maistre was born in 1763 in the picturesque town of Chambéry at the foot of the French Alps. He was of an intense, romantic nature, was fond of reading, especially Montaigne, Pascal and Rousseau, and of paintings, especially Dutch and French domestic scenes. At the age of twenty-three, De Maistre became fascinated by aeronautics. Etienne Montgolfier had, three years before, achieved international renown by constructing a balloon that flew for eight minutes above the royal palace at Versailles, bearing as passengers a sheep called Montauciel (Climb-to-the-sky), a duck and a rooster. De Maistre and a friend fashioned a pair of giant wings out of paper and wire and planned to fly to America. They did not succeed. Two years later De Maistre secured himself a place in a hot air balloon and spent a few moments floating above Chambéry before the machine crashed into a pine forest.

Then in 1790, while he was living in a modest room at the top of an apartment building in Turin, De Maistre pioneered a mode of travel that was to make his name: room-travel.

Introducing *Journey around My Bedroom,* Xavier's brother, the political theorist Joseph de Maistre, emphasized that it was not Xavier's intention to cast aspersions on the heroic deeds of the great travellers of the past: 'Magellan, Drake, Anson and Cook'. Magellan had discovered a western route to the Spice Islands around the southern tip of South America, Drake had circumnavigated the globe, Anson had produced accurate sea charts of the Philippines, and Cook had confirmed the existence of a southern continent. 'They were no doubt remarkable men,' wrote Joseph; it was just that his brother had discovered a way of travelling that might be infinitely more practical for those neither as brave nor as wealthy as they.

'Millions of people who, before me, had never dared to travel, others who had not been able to travel and still more who had not even thought of travelling will now be able to follow my example,' explained Xavier as he prepared for his journey. 'The most indolent beings won't have any more reason to hesitate before setting off to find pleasures that will cost them neither money nor effort.' He particularly recommended room-travel to the poor and to those afraid of storms, robberies and high cliffs.

4.

Unfortunately, De Maistre's own pioneering journey, rather like his flying machine, did not fly very far.

The story begins well. De Maistre locks his door and changes into his pink and blue pyjamas. Without the need for luggage, he travels to the sofa, the largest piece of furniture in the room. His journey having shaken him from his usual lethargy, he looks at it through fresh eyes and rediscovers some of its qualities. He admires the elegance of its feet and remembers the pleasant hours he has spent cradled in its cushions, dreaming of love and advancement in his career. From his sofa, De Maistre spies his bed. Once again, from a traveller's vantage point, he learns to appreciate this complex piece of furniture. He feels grateful for the nights he has spent in it and takes pride that his sheets almost match his pyjamas. 'I advise every man who can to get himself pink and white bedlinen,' he writes, for these are colours to induce calm and pleasant reveries in the fragile sleeper.

But thereafter De Maistre may be accused of losing sight of the overall purpose of his endeavour. He becomes mired in long and wearing digressions about his dog, Rosinne, his sweetheart, Jenny, and his faithful servant, Joannetti. Travellers in search of a specific report on room-travel risk closing *Journey around My Bedroom* feeling a little betrayed.

And yet De Maistre's work springs from a profound and suggestive insight that the pleasure we derive from journeys is perhaps dependent more on the mindset with which we travel than on the destination we travel to. If only we could apply a travelling mindset to our own locales, we might find these places becoming no less interesting than the high mountain passes and butterfly-filled jungles of Humboldt's South America.

What, then, is a travelling mindset? Receptivity might be said to be its chief characteristic. We approach new places with humility. We carry with us no rigid ideas about what is interesting. We irritate locals because we stand on traffic islands and in narrow streets and admire what they take to be strange small details. We risk getting run over because we are intrigued by the roof of a government building or an inscription on a wall. We find a supermarket or hairdresser's unusually fascinating. We dwell at length on the layout of a menu or the clothes of the presenters on the evening news. We are alive to the layers of history beneath the present and take notes and photographs.

Home, on the other hand, finds us more settled in our expectations. We feel assured that we have discovered everything interesting about a neighbourhood, primarily by virtue of having lived there a long time. It seems inconceivable that there could be anything new to find in a place which we have been living in for a decade or more. We have become habituated and therefore blind.

De Maistre tried to shake us from our passivity. In his second volume of room-travel, *Nocturnal Expedition around My Bedroom*, he went to his window and looked up at the night sky. Its beauty made him frustrated that such ordinary scenes were not more generally appreciated: 'How few people are right now taking delight in this sublime spectacle which the sky lays on uselessly for dozing humanity! What would it cost those who are out for a walk or crowding out of the theatre, to look up for a moment and admire the brilliant constellations which gleam above their heads?' The reason they weren't looking was that they had never done so before. They had fallen into the habit of considering their universe to be boring—and it had duly fallen into line with their expectations.

5.

I attempted to travel around my bedroom, but it was so small, with barely enough space for a bed, that I concluded that the De Maistrean message might prove more rewarding if it was applied to the neighbourhood as a whole.

So on a clear March day, at around three in the afternoon, several weeks after my return home from Barbados, I set out on a De Maistrean journey around Hammersmith.

It felt peculiar to be outside in the middle of the day with no particular goal in mind. A woman and two small blond children were walking along the main road, which was lined with a variety of shops and restaurants. A double-decker bus had stopped to pick up passengers opposite a small park. A giant billboard was advertising gravy. I walked along this particular road almost every day to reach my Underground station and was unused to considering it as anything other than a means to my end. Information that assisted me in my goal attracted my attention, what did not was judged irrelevant. I was therefore sensitive to the number of people on the pavement, for they might interrupt my path, whereas their faces and expressions were invisible to me, as invisible as the shapes of the buildings or the activity in the shops.

It had not always been thus. When I had first moved to the area, my attention had been less jealously focused. I had at that time not settled so firmly on the goal of reaching the Underground quickly.

On entering a new space, our sensitivity is directed towards a number of elements, which we gradually reduce in line with the function we find for the space. Of the 4,000 things there might be to see and reflect on in a street, we end up actively aware of only a few: the number of humans in our path, the amount of traffic and the likelihood of rain. A bus, which we might at first have viewed aesthetically or mechanically or as a springboard to thoughts about communities within cities, becomes simply a box to move us as rapidly as possible across an area which might as well not exist, so unconnected is it to our primary goal, outside of which all is darkness, all is invisible.

I had imposed a grid of interests on the street, which left no space for blond children and gravy adverts and paving stones and the colours of shop fronts and the expressions of businesspeople and pensioners. The power of my primary goal had drained me of the will to reflect on the layout of the park or on the unusual mixture of Georgian, Victorian and Edwardian architecture along a single block. My walks along the street had been excised of any attentiveness to beauty, of any associative thoughts, any sense of wonder or gratitude, any philosophical digressions sparked by visual elements. And in its place, there was simply an insistent call to reach the Underground posthaste.

However, following De Maistre, I tried to reverse the process of habituation, to disassociate my surroundings from the uses I had found for them until then. I forced myself to obey a peculiar kind of mental command: to look around me as though I had never been in this place before. And slowly, my travels began to bear fruit.

Under the command to consider everything as of potential interest, objects released latent layers of value. A row of shops which I had known as one large, undifferentiated reddish block acquired an architectural identity. There were Georgian pillars around one flower shop, and late Victorian Gothic-style gargoyles on top of the butcher's. A restaurant became filled with diners rather than shapes. In a glass-fronted office block, I noticed some people gesticulating in a boardroom on the first floor. Someone was drawing a pie chart on an overhead projector. At the same time, just across the road from the office, a man was pouring out new slabs of concrete for the pavement and carefully shaping their corners. I got on a bus and, rather than slipping at once into private concerns, tried to connect imaginatively with other passengers. I could hear a conversation in the row ahead of me. Someone in an office somewhere, a person quite high up in the hierarchy apparently, didn't understand. They complained of how inefficient others were, but never reflected on what they might have been doing to increase that inefficiency. I thought of the multiplicity of lives going on at the same time at different levels in a city. I thought of the similarities of complaints—always selfishness, always blindness—and the old psychological truth that what we complain of in others, others will complain of in us.

The neighbourhood did not just acquire people and defined buildings, it also began to collect ideas. I reflected on the new wealth that was spreading into the areas. I tried to think why I liked railway arches so much, and why the motorway that cut across the skyline.

It seemed an advantage to be travelling alone. Our responses to the world are crucially moulded by whom we are with, we temper our curiosity to fit in with the expectations of others. They may have a particular vision of who we are and hence subtly prevent certain sides of us from emerging: 'I hadn't thought of you as someone who was interested in flyovers,' they might intimidatingly suggest. Being closely observed by a companion can inhibit us from observing others, we become taken up with adjusting ourselves to the companion's questions and remarks, we have to make ourselves seem more normal than is good for our curiosity. But I had no such concerns, alone in Hammersmith in mid-afternoon. I had the freedom to act a little weirdly. I sketched the window of a hardware shop and word-painted the flyover.

6.

De Maistre was not only a room-traveller. He was also a great traveller in the classic sense. He journeyed to Italy and Russia, he spent a winter with the royalist armies in the Alps and fought a Russian campaign in the Caucasus.

In an autobiographical note written in 1801 in South America, Alexander von Humboldt had written of his motives for travelling: 'I was spurred on by an uncertain longing to be transported from a boring daily life to a marvellous world.' It was this dichotomy, 'boring daily life' pitted against 'marvellous world', that De Maistre had tried to redraw with greater subtlety. He would not have told Humboldt that South America was dull, he would merely have urged him to consider that his native Berlin might have something to offer too.

Eight decades later, Nietzsche, who had read and admired De Maistre (and spent much time in his room), picked up on the thought:

> When we observe how some people know how to manage their experiences—their insignificant, everyday experiences—so that they become an arable soil that bears fruit three times a year, while others—and how many there are!—are driven through surging waves of destiny, the most multifarious currents of the times and the nations, and yet always remain on top, bobbing like a cork, then we are in the end tempted to divide mankind into a minority (a minimality) of those who know how to make much of little, and a majority of those who know how to make little of much.

We meet people who have crossed deserts, floated on icecaps and cut their way through jungles—and yet in whose souls we would search in vain for evidence of what they have witnessed. Dressed in pink and blue pyjamas, satisfied within the confines of his own bedroom, Xavier de Maistre was gently nudging us to try, before taking off for distant hemispheres, to notice what we have already seen.

Reading Comprehension—Points of Engagement

1. On page 51 de Botton claims that he had imposed a "grid of interests" on the suburb, Hammersmith, where he lives. Explain, in your own words, what it means to impose a grid of interests on something. Is it possible that such a view of the world could be positive, or is it only ever negative way, as de Botton sees it?

2. In the first paragraph of his essay, de Botton expresses a feeling of discontent, of malaise (if you don't know what this word means, look it up). By the end of the essay, he says something quite different: he seems to be cured of his restlessness, and viewing his world in quite a different way. How do you think he cured himself? Give two quotations from the essay, and explain what you think they show.

3. Give two reasons from de Botton as to why traveling around your bedroom, or around your town, is a good idea. Why is it better than embarking on a von Humboldt-style journey? Why is it not the same? Provide evidence from the text.

Assignment Questions—Points of Departure

1. While de Botton discusses our reactions to physical spaces, the same thinking can be applied to our interactions with people and with ideas. Think about what may help people, or cause people, to change their perspectives or the way they interact with the world. Is being confronted with new places, objects, or people the only way we can cause a change in our attitudes, or are there other ways? Answer this question using de Botton and one other essay by Jane Goodall, V.S. Naipaul, or Jeanette Winterson.

2. Like Alain de Botton and Xavier de Maistre in "On Habit," the families in Arlie Russell Hochschild's "From the Frying Pan into the Fire" pay a lot of attention to, and are deeply affected by, aspects of their environments. Is it ever possible to notice too much? To be *too* sensitive and reactive to the world around us? What are the consequences if we are? Can 'stimulation' from your environment influence your behavior and your character in negative or distressing ways, or is it all, ultimately, to the good? Your project for this paper is to propose your own answers to these questions in conversation with the essays by de Botton and Hochschild.

3. Alain de Botton demonstrates in his essay that it is sometimes easier to look outside the normal to see something exciting, rather than making the effort within the boundaries of the everyday, or "quotidian." He claims, however, that the latter can be just as rewarding as the former. In this essay, consider whether Dr. Rosen, in Lauren Slater's "Dr. Daedalus," is actually maximizing the potential he sees in humans, or trying to compensate for human inadequacies by blurring species lines? In trying to change humans fundamentally, is he looking in the wrong place for inspiration? Is blurring species boundaries looking in the wrong place for stimulation and interest? Is Rosen a visionary like von Humboldt or one like de Maistre?

Our Sprawling, Supersize Utopia
David Brooks

Points of Access

1. Did you grow up in the suburbs? What are some of the most obvious physical characteristics of the suburbs? Make a list. Have you ever thought about why the suburbs look the way they do? Any ideas?

2. What qualities and values do you associate with suburban areas? How do they relate to your ideas about being American or living in America?

3. In your history classes, you've probably read about "the pursuit of happiness" being a fundamental American right. How have you seen people create their own "happiness" in this country? Are there any downsides to the pursuit of happiness? What might they be?

We're living in the age of the great dispersal. Americans continue to move from the Northeast and Midwest to the South and West. But the truly historic migration is from the inner suburbs to the outer suburbs, to the suburbs of suburbia. From New Hampshire down to Georgia, across Texas to Arizona and up through California, you now have the booming exurban sprawls that have broken free of the gravitational pull of the cities and now float in a new space far beyond them. For example, the population of metropolitan Pittsburgh has declined by 8 percent since 1980, but as people spread out, the amount of developed land in the Pittsburgh area increased by nearly 43 percent. The population of Atlanta increased by 22,000 during the 90's, but the expanding suburbs grew by 2.1 million.

The geography of work has been turned upside down. Jobs used to be concentrated in downtowns. But the suburbs now account for more rental office space than the cities in most of the major metro areas of the country except Chicago and New York. In the Bay Area in California, suburban Santa Clara County alone has five times as many of the region's larger public companies as San Francisco. Ninety percent of the office space built in America by the end of the 1990's was built in suburbia, much of it in far-flung office parks stretched along the Interstates.

These new spaces are huge and hugely attractive to millions of people. Mesa, Ariz., a suburb of Phoenix, now has a larger population than Minneapolis, St. Louis or Cincinnati. It's as if Zeus came down and started plopping vast developments in the middle of farmland and the desert overnight. Boom! A master planned community. Boom! A big-box mall. Boom! A rec center and 4,000 soccer fields. The food courts come and the people follow. How many times in American history have 300,000-person communities materialized practically out of nothing?

In these new, exploding suburbs, the geography, the very landscape of life, is new and unparalleled. In the first place, there are no centers, no recognizable borders to shape a sense of geographic identity. Throughout human history, most people have lived around some definable place—a tribal ring, an oasis, a river junction, a port, a town square. But in exurbia, each individual has his or her own polycentric nodes—the school, the church and the office park. Life is different in ways big and small. When the New Jersey Devils won the Stanley Cup, they had their victory parade in a parking lot; no downtown street is central to the team's fans. Robert Lang, a demographer at Virginia Tech, compares these new sprawling exurbs to the dark matter in the universe: stuff that is very hard to define but somehow accounts for more mass than all the planets, stars and moons put together.

We are having a hard time understanding the cultural implications of this new landscape because when it comes to suburbia, our imaginations are motionless. Many of us still live with the suburban stereotypes laid down by the first wave of suburban critics—that the suburbs are dull, white-bread kind of places where Ozzie and Harriet families go to raise their kids. But there are no people so conformist as those who fault the supposed conformity of the suburbs. They regurgitate the same critiques decade after decade, regardless of the suburban reality flowering around them.

The reality is that modern suburbia is merely the latest iteration of the American dream. Far from being dull, artificial and spiritually vacuous, today's suburbs are the products of the same religious longings and the same deep tensions that produced the American identity from the start. The complex faith of Jonathan Edwards, the propelling ambition of Benjamin Franklin, the dark, meritocratic fatalism of Lincoln—all these inheritances have shaped the outer suburbs.

At the same time the suburbs were sprawling, they were getting more complicated and more interesting, and they were going quietly berserk. When you move through suburbia—from the old inner-ring suburbs out through the most distant exurbs—you see the most unexpected things: lesbian dentists, Iranian McMansions, Korean megachurches, outlaw-biker subdevelopments, Orthodox shtetls with Hasidic families walking past strip malls on their way to shul. When you actually live in suburbia, you see that radically different cultural zones are emerging, usually within a few miles of one another and in places that are as architecturally interesting as a piece of aluminum siding. That's because in the age of the great dispersal, it becomes much easier to search out and congregate with people who are basically like yourself. People are less tied down to a factory, a mine or a harbor. They have more choice over which sort of neighborhood to live in. Society becomes more segmented, and everything that was once hierarchical turns granular.

You don't have to travel very far in America to see radically different sorts of people, most of whom know very little about the communities and subcultures just down the highway. For example, if you are driving across the northern band of the country—especially in Vermont, Massachusetts, Wisconsin or Oregon—you are likely to stumble across a crunchy suburb. These are places with meat-free food co-ops, pottery galleries, sandal shops (because people with progressive politics have a strange penchant for toe exhibitionism). Not many people in these places know much about the for-profit sector of the economy, but they do build wonderful all-wood playgrounds for their kids, who tend to have names like Milo and Mandela. You know you're in a crunchy suburb because you see the anti-lawns, which declare just how fervently crunchy suburbanites reject the soul-destroying standards of conventional success. Anti-lawns look like regular lawns with eating disorders. Some are bare patches of dirt, others are scraggly spreads of ragged, weedlike vegetation, the horticultural version of a grunge rocker's face.

Then a few miles away, you might find yourself in an entirely different cultural zone, in an upscale suburban town center packed with restaurants—one of those communities that perform the neat trick of being clearly suburban while still making it nearly impossible to park. The people here tend to be lawyers, doctors and professors, and they drive around in Volvos, Audis and Saabs because it is socially acceptable to buy a luxury car as long as it comes from a country hostile to U.S. foreign policy.

Here you can find your Trader Joe's grocery stores, where all the cashiers look as if they are on loan from Amnesty International and all the snack food is especially designed for kids who come home from school screaming, "Mom, I want a snack that will prevent colorectal cancer!" Here you've got newly renovated Arts and Crafts seven-bedroom homes whose owners have developed views on beveled granite; no dinner party in this clique has gone all the way to dessert without a conversational phase on the merits and demerits of Corian countertops. Bathroom tile is their cocaine: instead of white powder, they blow their life savings on handcrafted Italian wall covering from Waterworks.

You travel a few miles from these upscale enclaves, and suddenly you're in yet another cultural milieu. You're in one of the suburban light-industry zones, and you start noting small Asian groceries offering live tilapia fish and premade bibimbap dishes. You see Indian video rental outlets with movies straight from Bollywood. You notice a Japanese bookstore, newspaper boxes offering The Korea Central Daily News and hair salons offering DynaSky phone cards to Peru.

One out of every nine people in America was born in a foreign country. Immigrants used to settle in cities and then migrate out, but now many head straight for suburbia, so today you see little Taiwanese girls in the figure skating clinics, Ukrainian boys learning to pitch and hints of cholo culture spreading across Nevada. People here develop their own customs and patterns that grow up largely unnoticed by the general culture. You go to a scraggly playing field on a Saturday morning, and there is a crowd of Nigerians playing soccer. You show up the next day and it is all Mexicans kicking a ball around. No lifestyle magazine is geared to the people who live in these immigrant-heavy wholesale warehouse zones.

You drive farther out, and suddenly you're lost in the shapeless, mostly middle-class expanse of exurbia. (The inner-ring suburbs tend to have tremendous income inequality.) Those who live out here are very likely living in the cultural shadow of golf. It's not so much the game of golf that influences manners and morals; it's the Zen-like golf ideal. The perfect human being, defined by golf, is competitive and success-oriented, yet calm and neat while casually dressed. Everything he owns looks as if it is made of titanium, from his driver to his BlackBerry to his wife's Wonderbra. He has achieved mastery over the great dragons: hurry, anxiety and disorder.

His DVD collection is organized, as is his walk-in closet. His car is clean and vacuumed. His frequently dialed numbers are programmed into his phone, and his rate plan is well tailored to his needs. His casual slacks are well pressed, and he is so calm and together that next to him, Dick Cheney looks bipolar. The new suburbs appeal to him because everything is fresh and neat. The philosopher George Santayana once suggested that Americans don't solve problems; we just leave them behind. The exurbanite has left behind that exorbitant mortgage, that long commute, all those weird people who watch "My Daughter Is a Slut" on daytime TV talk shows. He has come to be surrounded by regular, friendly people who do not scoff at his daughter's competitive cheerleading obsession and whose wardrobes are as Lands' End-dependent as his is.

Exurban places have one ideal that soars above all others: ample parking. You can drive diagonally across acres of empty parking spaces on your way from Bed, Bath & Beyond to Linens 'n Things. These parking lots are so big that you could recreate the Battle of Gettysburg in the middle and nobody would notice at the stores on either end. Off on one side, partly obscured by the curvature of the earth, you will see a sneaker warehouse big enough to qualify for membership in the United Nations, and then at the other end there will be a Home Depot. Still, shoppers measure their suburban manliness by how close they can park to the Best Buy. So if a normal healthy American sees a family about to pull out of one of those treasured close-in spots just next to the maternity ones, he will put on his blinker and wait for the departing family to load up its minivan and apparently read a few chapters of "Ulysses" before it finally pulls out and lets him slide in.

*   *   *

You look out across this landscape, with its sprawling diversity of suburban types, and sometimes you can't help considering the possibility that we Americans may not be the most profound people on earth. You look out across the suburban landscape that is the essence of modern America, and you see the culture of Slurp & Gulps, McDonald's, Disney, breast enlargements and "The Bachelor." You see a country that gave us Prozac and Viagra, paper party hats, pinball machines, commercial jingles, expensive orthodontia and Monster Truck rallies. You see a trashy consumer culture that has perfected parade floats, corporate-sponsorship deals, low-slung jeans and frosted Cocoa Puffs; a culture that finds its quintessential means of self-expression through bumper stickers ("Rehab Is for Quitters").

Indeed, over the past half century, there has been an endless flow of novels, movies, anti-sprawl tracts, essays and pop songs all lamenting the shallow conformity of suburban life. If you scan these documents all at once, or even if, like the average person, you absorb them over the course of a lifetime, you find their depictions congeal into the same sorry scene. Suburban America as a comfortable but somewhat vacuous realm of unreality: consumerist, wasteful, complacent, materialistic and self-absorbed.

Disneyfied Americans, in this view, have become too concerned with small and vulgar pleasures, pointless one-upmanship. Their lives are distracted by a buzz of trivial images, by relentless hurry instead of contemplation, information rather than wisdom and a profusion of unsatisfying lifestyle choices. Modern suburban Americans, it is argued, rarely sink to the level of depravity—they are too tepid for that—but they don't achieve the highest virtues or the most demanding excellences.

These criticisms don't get suburbia right. They don't get America right. The criticisms tend to come enshrouded in predictions of decline or cultural catastrophe. Yet somehow imperial decline never comes, and the social catastrophe never materializes. American standards of living surpassed those in Europe around 1740. For more than

260 years, in other words, Americans have been rich, money-mad, vulgar, materialistic and complacent people. And yet somehow America became and continues to be the most powerful nation on earth and the most productive. Religion flourishes. Universities flourish. Crime rates drop, teen pregnancy declines, teen-suicide rates fall, along with divorce rates. Despite all the problems that plague this country, social healing takes place. If we're so great, can we really be that shallow?

Nor do the standard critiques of suburbia really solve the mystery of motivation— the inability of many Americans to sit still, even when they sincerely want to simplify their lives. Americans are the hardest-working people on earth. The average American works 350 hours a year—nearly 10 weeks—more than the average Western European. Americans switch jobs more frequently than people from other nations. The average job tenure in the U.S. is 6.8 years, compared with more than a decade in France, Germany and Japan. What propels Americans to live so feverishly, even against their own self-interest? What energy source accounts for all this?

Finally, the critiques don't explain the dispersion. They don't explain why so many millions of Americans throw themselves into the unknown every year. In 2002, about 14.2 percent of Americans relocated. Compare that with the 4 percent of Dutch and Germans and the 8 percent of Britons who move in a typical year. According to one survey, only slightly more than a quarter of American teenagers expect to live in their hometowns as adults.

What sort of longing causes people to pick up and head out for the horizon? Why do people uproot their families from California, New York, Ohio and elsewhere and move into new developments in Arizona or Nevada or North Carolina, imagining their kids at high schools that haven't even been built yet, picturing themselves with new friends they haven't yet met, fantasizing about touch-football games on lawns that haven't been seeded? Millions of people every year leap out into the void, heading out to communities that don't exist, to office parks that are not yet finished, to places where everything is new. This mysterious longing is the root of the great dispersal.

* * *

To grasp that longing, you have to take seriously the central cliché of American life: the American dream. Albert Einstein once said that imagination is more important than knowledge, and when you actually look at modern mainstream America, you see what a huge role fantasy plays even in the seemingly dullest areas of life. The suburbs themselves are conservative utopias, where people go because they imagine orderly and perfect lives can be led there. This is the nation of Hollywood, Las Vegas, professional wrestling, Elvis impersonators, Penthouse letters, computer gamers, grown men in

LeBron James basketball jerseys, faith healers and the whole range of ampersand magazines (Town & Country, Food & Wine) that display perfect parties, perfect homes, perfect vacations and perfect lives.

This is the land of Rainforest Café theme restaurants, Ralph Lauren WASP-fantasy fashions, Civil War re-enactors, gated communities with names like Sherwood Forest and vehicles with names like Yukon, Durango, Expedition and Mustang, as if their accountant-owners were going to chase down some cattle rustlers on the way to the Piggly Wiggly. This is the land in which people dream of the most Walter Mitty-esque personal transformations as a result of the low-carb diet, cosmetic surgery or their move to the Sun Belt.

Americans—seemingly bland, ordinary Americans—often have a remarkably tenuous grip on reality. Under the seeming superficiality of suburban American life, there is an imaginative fire that animates Americans and propels us to work so hard, move so much and leap so wantonly.

Ralph Waldo Emerson once wrote that those who "complain of the flatness of American life have no perception of its destiny. They are not Americans." They don't see that "here is man in the garden of Eden; here, the Genesis and the Exodus." And here, he concluded fervently, will come the final Revelation. Emerson was expressing the eschatological longing that is the essence of the American identity: the assumption that some culminating happiness is possible here, that history can be brought to a close here.

The historian Sacvan Bercovitch has observed that the United States is the example par excellence of a nation formed by collective fantasy. Despite all the claims that American culture is materialist and pragmatic, what is striking about this country is how material things are shot through with enchantment.

America, after all, was born in a frenzy of imagination. For the first European settlers and for all the subsequent immigrants, the new continent begs to be fantasized about. The early settlers were aware of and almost oppressed by the obvious potential of the land. They saw the possibility of plenty everywhere, yet at the start they lived in harsh conditions. Their lives took on a slingshot shape—they had to pull back in order to someday shoot forward. Through the temporary hardships they dwelt imaginatively in the grandeur that would inevitably mark their future.

This future-minded mentality deepened decade after decade, century after century. Each time the early settlers pushed West, they found what was to them virgin land, and they perceived it as paradise. Fantasy about the future lured them. Guides who led and sometimes exploited the 19th-century pioneers were shocked by how little the trekkers often knew about the surroundings they had thrown themselves into, or what would be involved in their new lives. As so often happens in American history, as happens every day in the newly sprawling areas, people leapt before they really looked.

Americans found themselves drawn to places where the possibilities seemed boundless and where there was no history. Francis Parkman, the great 19th-century historian, wrote of his youthful self, "His thoughts were always in the forest, whose features possessed his waking and sleeping dreams, filling him with vague cravings impossible to satisfy."

Our minds are still with Parkman's in the forest. Our imagination still tricks us into undertaking grand projects—starting a business, writing a book, raising a family, moving to a new place—by enchanting us with visions of future joys. When these tasks turn out to be more difficult than we dreamed, the necessary exertions bring out new skills and abilities and make us better than we planned on being.

And so we see the distinctive American mentality, which explains the westward crossing as much as the suburban sprawl and the frenzied dot-com-style enthusiasms. It is the Paradise Spell: the tendency to see the present from the vantage point of the future. It starts with imagination—the ability to fantasize about what some imminent happiness will look like. Then the future-minded person leaps rashly toward that gauzy image. He or she is subtly more attached to the glorious future than to the temporary and unsatisfactory present. Time isn't pushed from the remembered past to the felt present to the mysterious future. It is pulled by the golden future from the unsatisfactory present and away from the dim past.

There's a James Fenimore Cooper novel called "The Pioneers," in which a developer takes his cousin on a tour of the city he is building. He describes the broad streets, the rows of houses. But all she sees is a barren forest. He's astonished she can't see it, so real is it in his mind already.

Mentality matters, and sometimes mentality is all that matters. The cognitive strands established early in American history and through its period of explosive growth—the sense that some ultimate fulfillment will be realized here, that final happiness can be created here, that the United States has a unique mission to redeem the world—are still woven into the fabric of everyday life. The old impulses, fevers and fantasies still play themselves out amid the BlackBerries, the Hummers, the closet organizers and the travel-team softball leagues.

Suburban America is a bourgeois place, but unlike some other bourgeois places, it is also a transcendent place infused with everyday utopianism. That's why you meet so many boring-looking people who see themselves on some technological frontier, dreaming of this innovation or that management technique that will elevate the world—and half the time their enthusiasms, crazes and fads seem ludicrous to others and even to them, in retrospect.

We members of this suburban empire still find ourselves veering off into world crises, roaring into battle with visions of progressive virtue on our side and retrograde evil on the other, waging moralistic crusades others do not understand, pushing our movie, TV and rock-star fantasies onto an ambivalent and sometimes horrified globe.

This doesn't mean all Americans, or even all suburban Americans, think alike, simply that there is a prevailing current to national life that you feel when you come here from other places with other currents. Some nations are bound, in all their diversity, by a common creation myth, a tale of how they came into being. Americans are bound, in all our diversity, by a fruition myth.

Born in abundance, inspired by opportunity, nurtured in imagination, spiritualized by a sense of God's blessing and call and realized in ordinary life day by day, this Paradise Spell is the controlling ideology of national life. Just out of reach, just beyond the next ridge, just in the farther-out suburb or with the next entrepreneurial scheme, just with the next diet plan or credit card purchase, the next true love or political hero, the next summer home or all-terrain vehicle, the next meditation technique or motivational seminar; just with the right schools, the right moral revival, the right beer and the right set of buddies; just with the next technology or after the next shopping spree—there is this spot you can get to where all tensions will melt, all time pressures will be relieved and happiness can be realized.

This Paradise Spell is at the root of our tendency to work so hard, consume so feverishly, to move so much. It inspires our illimitable faith in education, our frequent born-again experiences. It explains why, alone among developed nations, we have shaped our welfare system to encourage opportunity at the expense of support and security; and why, more than people in comparable nations, we wreck our families and move on. It is the call that makes us heedless of the past, disrespectful toward traditions, short on contemplation, wasteful in our use of the things around us, impious toward restraints, but consumed by hope, driven ineluctably to improve, fervently optimistic, relentlessly aspiring, spiritually alert and, in this period of human history, the irresistible and discombobulating locomotive of the world.

Reading Comprehension—Points of Engagement

1. David Brooks claims that a "mysterious longing is the root of the great dispersal" from cities to suburbs (60). What mystery does Brooks describe in the paragraphs around that line? How would you characterize this "mysterious longing"?

2. What is the "Paradise Spell"? How is it related to the American ideal of "the pursuit of happiness"? Use two separate passages from Brooks's essay to explain your answers.

3. Brooks points out that suburbanites "search out and congregate with people who are basically like" themselves. In doing so "society becomes more segmented, and everything that was once hierarchical turns granular" (57). What do you think he means by that last statement? How does that statement capture the significance of "cultural zones" in suburbia?

Assignment Questions—Points of Departure

1. David Brooks argues that Americans "sprawl" because they imagine possibilities and happiness, and they travel around in pursuit of them. What "pursuits of happiness" are described in the travels of V.S. Naipaul, Lenore Look, the narrator of Jeanette Winterson's story, or of the young men in Michael Kamber's essay? What roles do imagination and fantasy play in them? Does "happiness" result, and how do you know?

2. Brooks's ideas about the "Paradise Spell" and "myth of fruition" go a long way in describing what motivates the suburban lifestyle, and hit on common, shared American ideas. Using Brooks and Susan Blackmore, Alain de Botton, Jack Hitt, Fenton Johnson, or Lewis Lapham, describe how the American "myth of fruition" puts a "spell" on what we see in our surroundings. How is perception (the information we take in) related to perspective (the way that we see that information) in these essays? Have you fallen under the Paradise Spell? In what ways?

3. Brooks notes that our suburbs have "no centers, no recognizable borders to shape a sense of geographic identity" (56). What happens when we lose that sense of geographic identity? How do we make up for it in other ways? If "geographic identity" is not currently offered through town centers and borders, then where does it come from? Using David Brooks and either Michael Kamber, Arlie Russell Hochschild, V.S. Naipaul, John Waterbury, or Francine Prose, your project is to discuss how geography, or its substitute, is related to identity. Would these authors agree with David Brooks's premise and position in his essay? Do you?

E.T. and God
Paul Davies

Points of Access

1. Do you think intelligent life exists elsewhere in the universe? What has lead you to this belief? What would constitute "intelligence" in life forms not from Earth?

2. Based on your answer to the first question above, how has your religious or spiritual affiliation influenced your view on extraterrestrial life? How has your education affected your understanding of this issue?

3. If you could contact and communicate with a life form on another planet, what would you express about humanity here on Earth? What would you ask this being? How would such an interaction affect your belief system?

The recent discovery of abundant water on Mars, albeit in the form of permafrost, has raised hopes for finding traces of life there. The Red Planet has long been a favorite location for those speculating about extraterrestrial life, especially since the 1890s, when H. G. Wells wrote *The War of the Worlds* and the American astronomer Percival Lowell claimed that he could see artificial canals etched into the planet's parched surface. Today, of course, scientists expect to find no more than simple bacteria dwelling deep underground, if even that. Still, the discovery of just a single bacterium somewhere beyond Earth would force us to revise our understanding of who we are and where we fit into the cosmic scheme of things, throwing us into a deep spiritual identity crisis that would be every bit as dramatic as the one Copernicus brought about in the early 1500s, when he asserted that Earth was not at the center of the universe.

Whether or not we are alone is one of the great existential questions that confronts us today. Probably because of the high emotional stakes, the search for life beyond Earth is deeply fascinating to the public. Opinion polls and website hits indicate strong support for and interest in space missions that are linked even obliquely to this search. Perceiving the public's interest, NASA has reconfigured its research strategy and founded the NASA Astrobiology Institute, dedicated to the study of life in the cosmos. At the top of the agenda, naturally, is the race to find life elsewhere in the solar system.

Researchers have long focused on Mars in their search for extraterrestrial life because of its relative proximity. But twenty-five years ago, as a result of the 1976 *Viking* mission, many of them became discouraged. A pair of spacecraft had passed through the planet's extremely thin atmosphere, touched down on the surface, and found it to be a freeze-dried desert drenched with deadly ultraviolet rays. The spacecraft, equipped with robotic arms, scooped up Martian dirt so that it could be examined for signs of biological activity. The results of the analysis were inconclusive but generally negative, and hopes faded for finding even simple microbes on the surface of Mars.

The outlook today is more optimistic. Several probes are scheduled to visit Mars in the coming months, and all will be searching for signs of life. This renewed interest is due in part to the discovery of organisms living in some remarkably hostile environments on Earth (which opens up the possibility of life on Mars in places the *Viking* probes didn't examine), and in part to better information about the planet's ancient history. Scientists now believe that Mars once had a much thicker atmosphere, higher temperatures, rivers, floods, and extensive volcanic activity—all conditions considered favorable to the emergence of life.

The prospects for finding living organisms on Mars remain slim, of course, but even traces of past life would represent a discovery of unprecedented scientific value. Before any sweeping philosophical or theological conclusions could be drawn, however, it would be necessary to determine whether this life was the product of a second genesis— that is, whether its origin was independent of life on Earth. Earth and Mars are known to trade material in the form of rocks blasted from the planets' surfaces by the violent impacts of asteroids and comets. Microbes could have hitched a ride on this detritus, raising the possibility that life started on Earth and was transferred to Mars, or vice versa. If traces of past life were discovered on Mars but found to be identical to some form of terrestrial life, transportation by ejected rocks would be the most plausible explanation, and we would still lack evidence that life had started from scratch in two separate locations.

*   *   *

The significance of this point is crucial. In his theory of evolution Charles Darwin provided a persuasive account of how life evolved over billions of years, but he pointedly omitted any explanation of how life got started in the first place. "One might as well think of origin of matter," he wrote in a letter to a friend. A century and a half later, scientists still have little understanding of how the first living thing came to be.

Some scientists believe that life on Earth is a freak accident of chemistry, and as such must be unique. Because even the simplest known microbe is breathtakingly complex, they argue, the chances that one formed by blind molecular shuffling are infinitesimal; the probability that the process would occur twice, in separate locations, is virtually negligible. The French biochemist and Nobel laureate Jacques Monod was a firm believer in this view. "Man at last knows he is alone in the unfeeling immensity of the universe, out of which he has emerged only by chance," he wrote in 1971. He used this bleak assessment as a springboard to argue for atheism and the absurdity and pointlessness of existence. As Monod saw it, we are merely chemical extras in a majestic but impersonal cosmic drama—an irrelevant, unintended sideshow.

But suppose that's not what happened. Many scientists believe that life is not a freakish phenomenon (the odds of life's starting by chance, the British cosmologist Fred Hoyle once suggested, are comparable to the odds of a whirlwind's blowing through a junkyard and assembling a functioning Boeing 747) but instead is written into the laws of nature. "The universe must in some sense have known we were coming," the physicist Freeman Dyson famously observed. No one can say precisely in what sense the universe might be pregnant with life, or how the general expectancy Dyson spoke of might translate into specific physical processes at the molecular level. Perhaps matter and energy always get fast-tracked along the road to life by what's often called "self-organization." Or perhaps the power of Darwinian evolution is somehow harnessed at a pre-biotic molecular stage. Or maybe some efficient and as yet unidentified physical process (quantum mechanics?) sets the gears in motion, with organic life as we know it taking over the essential machinery at a later stage. Under any of these scenarios life becomes a fundamental rather than an incidental product of nature. In 1994, reflecting on this same point, another Nobel laureate, the Belgian biochemist Christian de Duve, wrote, "I view this universe not as a 'cosmic joke,' but as a meaningful entity—made in such a way as to generate life and mind, bound to give birth to thinking beings able to discern truth, apprehend beauty, feel love, yearn after goodness, define evil, experience mystery."

Absent from these accounts is any mention of miracles. Ascribing the origin of life to a divine miracle not only is anathema to scientists but also is theologically suspect. The term "God of the gaps" was coined to deride the notion that God can be invoked as an explanation whenever scientists have gaps in their understanding. The trouble with invoking God in this way is that as science advances, the gaps close, and God gets progressively squeezed out of the story of nature. Theologians long ago accepted that they would forever be fighting a rearguard battle if they tried to challenge science on its own ground. Using the formation of life to prove the existence of God is a tactic that risks instant demolition should someone succeed in making life in a test tube. And the idea that God acts in fits and starts, moving atoms around on odd occasions in competition with natural forces, is a decidedly uninspiring image of the Grand Architect.

The theological battle line in relation to the formation of life is not, therefore, between the natural and the miraculous but between sheer chance and lawlike certitude. Atheists tend to take the first side, and theists line up behind the second; but these divisions are general and by no means absolute. It's perfectly possible to be an atheist and believe that life is built ingeniously into the nature of the universe. It's also possible to be a theist and suppose that God engineered just one planet with life, with or without the help of miracles.

*   *   *

Though the discovery of microbes on Mars or elsewhere would ignite a passionate theological debate, the truly difficult issues surround the prospect of advanced alien beings in possession of intelligence and technology. Most scientists don't think that such beings exist, but for forty years a dedicated band of astronomers has been sweeping the skies with radio telescopes in hopes of finding a message from a civilization elsewhere in the galaxy. Their project is known as *SETI (Search for Extraterrestrial Intelligence)*.

Because our solar system is relatively young compared with the universe overall, any alien civilization the SETI researchers might discover is likely to be much older, and presumably wiser, than ours. Indeed, it might have achieved our level of science and technology millions or even billions of years ago. Just contemplating the possibility of such advanced extraterrestrials appears to raise additional uncomfortable questions for religion.

The world's main faiths were all founded in the pre-scientific era, when Earth was widely believed to be at the center of the universe and humankind at the pinnacle of creation. As scientific discoveries have piled up over the past 500 years, our status has been incrementally diminished. First Earth was shown to be just one planet of several orbiting the Sun. Then the solar system itself was relegated to the outer suburbs of the galaxy, and the Sun classified as an insignificant dwarf star among billions. The theory of evolution proposed that human beings occupied just a small branch on a complex evolutionary tree. This pattern continued into the twentieth century, when the supremacy of our much vaunted intelligence came under threat. Computers began to outsmart us. Now genetic engineering has raised the specter of designer babies with superintellects that leave ours far behind. And we must consider the uncomfortable possibility that in astrobiological terms, God's children may be galactic also-rans.

Theologians are used to putting a brave face on such developments. Over the centuries the Christian church, for example, has time and again been forced to accommodate new scientific facts that challenge existing doctrine. But these accommodations have usually been made reluctantly and very belatedly. Only recently, for example, did the Pope acknowledge that Darwinian evolution is more than just a theory. If SETI succeeds, theologians will not have the luxury of decades of careful deliberation to assess the significance of the discovery. The impact will be instant.

The discovery of alien superbeings might not be so corrosive to religion if human beings could still claim special spiritual status. After all, religion is concerned primarily with people's relationship to God, rather than with their biological or intellectual qualities. It is possible to imagine alien beings who are smarter and wiser than we are but who are spiritually inferior, or just plain evil. However, it is more likely that any civilization that had surpassed us scientifically would have improved on our level of moral development, too. One may even speculate that an advanced alien society would sooner or later find some way to genetically eliminate evil behavior, resulting in a race of saintly beings.

Suppose, then, that E.T. is far ahead of us not only scientifically and technologically but spiritually, too. Where does that leave mankind's presumed special relationship with God? This conundrum poses a particular difficulty for Christians, because of the unique nature of the Incarnation. Of all the world's major religions, Christianity is the most species-specific. Jesus Christ was *humanity's* savior and redeemer. He did not die for the dolphins or the gorillas, and certainly not for the proverbial little green men. But what of deeply spiritual aliens? Are they not to be saved? Can we contemplate a universe that contains perhaps a trillion worlds of saintly beings, but in which the only beings eligible for salvation inhabit a planet where murder, rape, and other evils remain rife?

Those few Christian theologians who have addressed this thorny issue divide into two camps. Some posit multiple incarnations and even multiple crucifixions—God taking on little green flesh to save little green men, as a prominent Anglican minister once told me. But most are appalled by this idea or find it ludicrous. After all, in the Christian view of the world, Jesus was God's *only* son. Would God have the same person born, killed, and resurrected in endless succession on planet after planet? This scenario was lampooned as long ago as 1794, by Thomas Paine. "The Son of God," he wrote in *The Age of Reason*, "and sometimes God himself, would have nothing else to do than to travel from world to world, in an endless succession of death, with scarcely a momentary interval of life." Paine went on to argue that Christianity was simply incompatible with the existence of extraterrestrial beings, writing, "He who thinks he believes in both has thought but little of either."

Catholics tend to regard the idea of multiple incarnations as verging on heresy, not because of its somewhat comic aspect but because it would seem to automate an act that is supposed to be God's singular gift. "God chose a very specific way to redeem human beings," writes George Coyne, a Jesuit priest and the director of the Vatican Observatory, whose own research includes astrobiology. "He sent his only son, Jesus, to them, and Jesus gave up his life so that human beings would be saved from their sin. Did God do this for extraterrestrials? . . . The theological implications about God are getting ever more serious."

Paul Tillich, one of the few prominent Protestant theologians to give serious consideration to the issue of alien beings, took a more positive view. "Man cannot claim to occupy the only possible place for incarnation," he wrote. The Lutheran theologian Ted Peters, of the Center for Theology and the Natural Sciences, in Berkeley, California, has made a special study of the impact on religious faith of belief in extraterrestrials. In discussing the tradition of debate on this topic, he writes, "Christian theologians have routinely found ways to address the issue of Jesus Christ as God incarnate and to conceive of God's creative power and saving power exerted in other worlds." Peters believes that Christianity is robust enough and flexible enough to accommodate the discovery of extraterrestrial intelligence, or ETI. One theologian who is emphatically not afraid of that challenge is Robert Russell, also of the Center for Theology and the Natural Sciences. "As we await 'first contact,' " he has written, "pursuing these kinds of questions and reflections will be immensely valuable."

Clearly, there is considerable diversity—one might even say muddle—on this topic in theological circles. Ernan McMullin, a professor emeritus of philosophy at Notre Dame University, affirms that the central difficulty stems from Christianity's roots in a pre-scientific cosmology. "It was easier to accept the idea of God's becoming man," he has written, "when humans and their abode both held a unique place in the universe." He acknowledges that Christians especially face a stark predicament in relation to ETI, but feels that Thomas Paine and his like-minded successors have presented the problem too simplistically. Pointing out that concepts such as original sin, incarnation, and salvation are open to a variety of interpretations, McMullin concludes that there is also widespread divergence among Christians on the correct response to the ETI challenge. On the matter of multiple incarnations he writes, "Their answers could range . . . from 'yes, certainly' to 'certainly not.' My own preference would be a cautious 'maybe.' "

Even for those Christians who dismiss the idea of multiple incarnations there is an interesting fallback position: perhaps the course of evolution has an element of directionality, with humanlike beings the inevitable end product. Even if *Homo sapiens* as such may not be the unique focus of God's attention, the broader class of all humanlike beings in the universe might be. This is the basic idea espoused by the philosopher Michael Ruse, an ardent Darwinian and an agnostic sympathetic to Christianity. He sees the incremental progress of natural evolution as God's chosen mode of creation, and the history of life as a ladder that leads inexorably from microbes to man.

Most biologists regard a "progressive evolution," with human beings its implied preordained goal, as preposterous. Stephen Jay Gould once described the very notion as "noxious." After all, the essence of Darwinism is that nature is blind. It cannot look ahead. Random chance is the driving force of evolution, and randomness by definition has no directionality. Gould insisted that if the evolutionary tape were replayed, the result would be very different from what we now observe. Probably life would never get beyond microbes next time around.

But some respected biologists disagree sharply with Gould on this point. Christian de Duve does not deny that the fine details of evolutionary history depend on happenstance, but he believes that the broad thrust of evolutionary change is somehow innately predetermined—that plants and animals were almost destined to emerge amid a general advance in complexity. Another Darwinian biologist, Simon Conway Morris, of Cambridge University, makes his own case for a "ladder of progress," invoking the phenomenon of convergent evolution—the tendency of similar-looking organisms to evolve independently in similar ecological niches. For example, the Tasmanian tiger (now extinct) played the role of the big cat in Australia even though, as a marsupial, it was genetically far removed from placental mammals. Like Ruse, Conway Morris maintains that the "humanlike niche" is likely to be filled on other planets that have advanced life. He even goes so far as to argue that extraterrestrials would have a humanoid form. It is not a great leap from this conclusion to the belief that extraterrestrials would sin, have consciences, struggle with ethical questions, and fear death.

The theological difficulties posed by the possibility of advanced alien beings are less acute for Judaism and Islam. Muslims, at least, are prepared for ETI: the Koran states explicitly, "And among His Signs is the creation of the heavens and the earth, and the living creatures that He has scattered through them." Nevertheless, both religions stress the specialness of human beings—and, indeed, of specific, well-defined groups who have been received into the faith. Could an alien become a Jew or a Muslim? Does the concept even make sense? Among the major religious communities, Buddhists and Hindus would seem to be the least threatened by the prospect of advanced aliens, owing to their pluralistic concept of God and their traditionally much grander vision of the cosmos.

Among the world's minority religions, some would positively welcome the discovery of intelligent aliens. The Ralians, a Canada-based cult recently propelled to fame by its claim to have cloned a human being, believe that the cult's leader, Ral, a French former journalist originally named Claude Vorilhon, received revelations from aliens who briefly transported him inside a flying saucer in 1973. Other fringe religious organizations with an extraterrestrial message include the ill-fated Heaven's Gate cult and many UFO groups. Their adherents share a belief that aliens are located further up not only the evolutionary ladder but also the spiritual ladder, and can therefore help us draw closer to God and salvation. It is easy to dismiss such beliefs as insignificant to serious theological debate, but if evidence for alien beings were suddenly to appear, these cults might achieve overnight prominence while established religions floundered in doctrinal bewilderment.

Ironically, SETI is often accused of being a quasi-religious quest. But Jill Tarter, the director of the SETI Institute's Center for SETI Research, in Mountain View, California, has no truck with religion and is contemptuous of the theological gymnastics with which religious scholars accommodate the possibility of extraterrestrials. "God is our own invention," she has written. "If we're going to survive or turn into a long-lived technological civilization, organized religion needs to be outgrown. If we get a message [from an alien civilization] and it's secular in nature, I think that says that they have no organized religion—that they've outgrown it." Tarter's dismissal is rather naive, however. Though many religious movements have come and gone throughout history, some sort of spirituality seems to be part of human nature. Even atheistic scientists profess to experience what Albert Einstein called a "cosmic religious feeling" when contemplating the awesome majesty of the universe.

Would advanced alien beings share this spiritual dimension, even though they might long ago have "outgrown" established religion? Steven Dick, a science historian at the U.S. Naval Observatory, believes they would. Dick is an expert on the history of speculation about extraterrestrial life, and he suggests that mankind's spirituality would be greatly expanded and enriched by contact with an alien civilization. However, he envisages that our present concept of God would probably require a wholesale transformation. Dick has outlined what he calls a new "cosmotheology," in which human spirituality is placed in a full cosmological and astrobiological context. "As we learn more about our place in the universe," he has written, "and as we physically move away from our home planet, our cosmic consciousness will only increase." Dick proposes abandoning the transcendent God of monotheistic religion in favor of what he calls a "natural God"—a superbeing located within the universe and within nature. "With due respect for present religious traditions whose history stretches back nearly four millennia," he suggests, "the natural God of cosmic evolution and the biological universe, not the supernatural God of the ancient Near East, may be the God of the next millennium."

Some form of natural God was also proposed by Fred Hoyle, in a provocative book titled *The Intelligent Universe*. Hoyle drew on his work in astronomy and quantum physics to sketch the notion of a "superintellect"—a being who had, as Hoyle liked to say, "monkeyed with physics," adjusting the properties of the various fundamental particles and forces of nature so that carbon-based organisms could thrive and spread across the galaxy. Hoyle even suggested that this cosmic engineer might communicate with us by manipulating quantum processes in the brain. Most scientists shrug off Hoyle's speculations, but his ideas do show how far beyond traditional religious doctrine some people feel they need to go when they contemplate the possibility of advanced life forms beyond Earth.

* * *

Though in some ways the prospect of discovering extraterrestrial life undermines established religions, it is not all bad news for them. Astrobiology has also led to a surprising resurgence of the so-called "design argument" for the existence of God. The original design argument, as articulated by William Paley in the eighteenth century, was that living organisms' intricate adaptation to their environments pointed to the providential hand of a benign Creator. Darwin demolished the argument by showing how evolution driven by random mutation and natural selection could mimic design. Now a revamped design argument has emerged that fully embraces the Darwinian account of evolution and focuses instead on the origin of life. (I must stress that I am not referring here to what has recently become known as the Intelligent Design movement, which relies on an element of the miraculous.) If life is found to be widespread in the universe, the new design argument goes, then it must emerge rather easily from nonliving chemical mixtures, and thus the laws of nature must be cunningly contrived to unleash this remarkable and very special state of matter, which itself is a conduit to an even more remarkable and special state: mind. This sort of exquisite bio-friendliness would represent an extraordinary and unexpected bonus among nature's inventory of principles—one that could be interpreted by those of a religious persuasion as evidence of God's ingenuity and foresight. In this version of cosmic design, God acts not by direct intervention but by creating appropriate natural laws that guarantee the emergence of life and mind in cosmic abundance. The universe, in other words, is one in which there are no miracles except the miracle of nature itself.

The E.T. debate has only just begun, but a useful starting point is simply to acknowledge that the discovery of extraterrestrial life would not have to be theologically devastating. The revamped design argument offers a vision of nature distinctly inspiring to the spiritually inclined—certainly more so than that of a cosmos sterile everywhere but on a single planet. History is instructive in this regard. Four hundred years ago Giordano Bruno was burned at the stake by the Church in Rome for, among other things, espousing the notion of a plurality of inhabited worlds. To those whose theological outlook depended on a conception of Earth and its life forms as a singular miracle, the very notion of extraterrestrial life proved deeply threatening. But today the possibility of extraterrestrial life is anything but spiritually threatening. The more one accepts the formation of life as a natural process (that is, the more deeply embedded one believes it is in the overall cosmic scheme), the more ingenious and contrived (dare one say "designed"?) the universe appears to be.

Reading Comprehension—Points of Engagement

1. What does Davies mean when he writes, "The trouble with invoking God in this way is that as science advances, the gaps close, and God gets progressively squeezed out of the story of nature" (68)? Which of the scientists or theologians offer a possible solution to this spiritual conundrum? What are the solutions?

2. Davies says that the debate concerning alien life and existence of God is not drawn "between the natural and the miraculous, but between sheer chance and lawlike certitude" (68). What is the main difference between these two positions? Does this move the discussion out of the realm of religion and into empirical science? If so, how? If not, explain.

3. Define the following terms in your own words, but be able to point to passages in the essay that support your explanation: cosmotheology, progressive evolution, multiple incarnations, and design argument.

Assignment Questions—Points of Departure

1. How could Alain de Botton's observations in "On Habit" help us to integrate the many possibilities opened up by the discovery of life elsewhere in the universe? Write a paper in which you consider the challenges to both religion and science in Paul Davies's essay in light of the philosophy towards perception and life in de Botton's essay.

2. Davies claims that religion is pre-scientific and this fact complicates any modern belief in extraterrestrial life. Jane Goodall and Barbara Kingsolver, in "A Fist in the Eye of God," both describe a world in which science and religion need not be incompatible. Can all three authors be correct about the relationship between science and religion? What do you think is compromised by scientists and theologians as they try to reconcile these two ways of thinking about the world around us? Can we believe in both E.T. and God?

3. Paul Davies, Susan Blackmore, and Steven Johnson are all interested in how the "laws of nature" function in other contexts: Davies explores how scientific discovery might affect religious beliefs, Susan Blackmore proposes a "cultural gene" called the "meme," and Steven Johnson explores how emergent behavior operates in computer programming. Write a paper in which you consider how Davies and either Blackmore or Steven Johnson use scientific knowledge for different projects. For example, what roles do "self-organization" (Davies 67) and "complexity" (Davies 71) play in each of their essays? Where does evolution fit into their discussions? Natural selection? Is anyone, or anything, controlling things "from the edges" (Steven Johnson 185)? What other scientific theories do both essays reference? How and why are they helpful to each author's project?

4. According to Paul Davies's essay, who will be the "God of the next millennium" (73)? How would other authors in this collection respond to that question? How would you? Write a paper in which you propose your own answer to this question using essays by Davies and one or two of the following authors: Lisa Belkin, Susan Blackmore, David Brooks, Adam Gopnik, Arlie Russell Hochschild, Francine Prose, Lauren Slater or Barbara Kingsolver.

Soccer vs. McWorld
Franklin Foer

Points of Access

1. Despite its relatively low status in the United States, soccer is the world's most popular sport, with leagues that cover entire continents and more fans globally than any other sport. How much do you know about soccer? What images does it conjure up in your mind? Could it ever, do you think, be on par with baseball, football, and basketball in terms of popularity and national significance in the United States? Why, or why not?

2. Look up the word "parochial" in your dictionary or online, and write down the definition. Now look up the word "globalism" in your dictionary or online, and write down the definition. How are these two words related? Which describes more closely the way you view the world around you? Why?

3. Assess the various benefits and drawbacks of coming into another culture from the outside. What might a visitor be looking for in coming to a foreign place? How are visitors beneficial to a local community? How are they detrimental? When coming into a culture from outside, especially into somewhere bigger and more powerful, what strategies can the non-indigenous visitor use to succeed in the local culture?

Two omens of apocalypse, or perhaps global salvation: During the 2002 World Cup, the English midfielder David Beckham, famed bender of the ball, styled his hair in a mohawk. Almost instantly, Japanese adolescents appeared with tread marks on their shorn heads; professional women, according to the Japanese newsmagazine *Shukan Jitsuwa,* even trimmed their pubic hair in homage. A bit further west, in Bangkok, Thailand, the monks of the Pariwas Buddhist temple placed a Beckham statuette in a spot reserved for figures of minor deities.

It should surprise no one that this London cockney has replaced basketball icon Michael Jordan as the world's most transcendent celebrity athlete. After all, more than basketball or even the World Bank and the International Monetary Fund, soccer is the most globalized institution on the planet.

Soccer began to outgrow its national borders early in the post-World War II era. While statesman Robert Schuman was daydreaming about a common European market and government, European soccer clubs actually moved toward union. The most successful clubs started competing against one another in regular transnational tournaments, such as the events now known as Champions League and the Union of European Football Associations (UEFA) Cup. These tournaments were a fan's dream: the chance to see Juventus of Turin play Bayern Munich one week and FC Barcelona the next. But more important, they were an owner's dream: blockbuster fixtures that brought unprecedented gate receipts and an enormous infusion of television revenue. This transnational idea was such a good one that Latin America, Africa, and Asia quickly created their own knockoffs.

Once competition globalized, the hunt for labor resources quickly followed. Club owners scoured the planet for superstars that they could buy on the cheap. Spanish teams shopped for talent in former colonies such as Argentina and Uruguay. Argentina plundered the leagues of poorer neighbors such as Paraguay. At first, this move toward an international market inspired a backlash. Politicians and sportswriters fretted that the influx from abroad would quash the development of young local talent. In Spain, for example, dictator Francisco Franco prohibited the importation of foreign players. Brazil's government declared Pelé a national treasure in 1961 and legally forbade his sale to a foreign team. But these stabs at nationalist economics could not ultimately stave off the seductive benefits of cheap, skilled labor from abroad. And, after a while, the foreign stars were needed to compete at the highest levels of European soccer. The game evolved to the point where an English club might field a team without any Englishmen.

By the 1990s, capital frictionlessly flowed across borders in the global soccer economy. European clubs not only posted scouts throughout the developing world, they also bought teams there. Ajax of Amsterdam acquired substantial shares of outfits in Cape Town and Ghana. Newcastle United began using China's Dalian Shide Football Club as a feeder. The biggest clubs started to think of themselves as multinational conglomerates. Organizations such as Manchester United and Real Madrid acquired a full portfolio of cable stations, restaurants, and mega-stores, catering to audiences as far away as Kuala Lumpur and Shanghai. Even with last year's dull markets, Manchester United's pretax profits for the 12 months ending on July 31, 2003, exceeded $65 million.

It is ironic, then, that soccer, for all its one-worldist features, doesn't evince the power of the new order as much as expose its limits. Manchester United and Real Madrid may embrace the ethos of globalization by accumulating wealth and diminishing national sovereignty. But a tangle of intensely local loyalties, identities, tensions, economies, and corruption endures—in some cases, not despite globalization, but because of it.

England, Half English?

During Franco's rule, the clubs Athletic Bilbao and Real Sociedad were the only venues where Basque people could express their cultural pride without winding up in jail. In English industrial towns such as Coventry and Derby, soccer clubs ballasted together communities amid oppressive dinginess. It wasn't just that many clubs had deep cultural roots. Each nation evolved its own particular style of play—the Italian doctrine of *catenaccio* (or defensive lockdown), Brazilian samba soccer, and so on. In part, these were easy clichés. But to anyone who watched World Cups, they were also undeniably true clichés.

Three years ago, England, birthplace of the beautiful game, handed over its national team to a Swedish manager named Sven Goran Eriksson. It is difficult to convey just how shocked English fans felt. For much of the nation's soccer history, beloved, quintessentially English characters had run the team. These "lads," typically ex-players, often turned a blind eye when their squads drank lager on the eve of big games, and forgave men for lack of training so long as they spilled their guts on the field. For all their inspirational power, though, these English managers tended to lack tactical acumen. They recycled stodgy formations that encouraged the same, ineffectual mode of attack—a long ball kicked over the midfield to a lone attacker, a style that perfectly reflected stereotypes about stiff-upper-lip English resoluteness. Their lack of creativity was evident in the national trophy case. Despite England's singular place in the game's history, it has won a lone World Cup (in 1966, as the tournament's host team), and not a single European championship.

The English Football Association installed Eriksson to remedy this sorry situation. He seemed precisely the character for the job. The Swede, a reader of Tibetan verse, exudes cosmopolitanism. During his celebrated career, he has managed clubs in Lisbon, Genoa, and Rome. Whereas the English managers had tended to wear tracksuits, Eriksson dresses in impeccable Italian threads and wears a pair of tiny, chic spectacles. He speaks in far more complete and far more elegant English sentences than any of his predecessors.

Never before had a man from across the channel coached England. This break with precedent wasn't just grist for pub trivia. Throughout the post-imperial decades,

Britain has worried that the continent would encroach on its distinctive way of life—a repeat of the Norman and German assaults on the island. Now, that debate echoed on the populist pages of London's tabloids. A *Daily Mail* headline argued, "We've Sold Our Birthright down the Fjord." Gordon Taylor, the head of the English players' associ-

---

Fair Trade Soccer

Fans across cultures argue that soccer used to be a lot fairer. A middling team, fueled by gritty players and loyal fans, could emerge from nowhere to hoist the championship trophy. What's more, these underdog teams often hailed from smaller cities, without massive stadiums or deep-pocketed owners.

That level playing field, some fear, has disappeared entirely. With their global chains of superstores and vast array of television deals, the big clubs have become wealthier, not just in absolute terms, but relative to the poorer clubs. Sales from Ronaldo and Beckham's replica jerseys bring Real Madrid more income in a month than many clubs make in a year, so it's no surprise that Real so frequently rolls over its poorer foes in the Spanish game. Indeed, the results of domestic competition are virtually preordained. Manchester United or Arsenal of London has won 10 of the last 11 English Premier League titles. If you support an Italian team other than Juventus or AC Milan, you wake up every morning with a depressingly accurate sense of how the final league table will ultimately shake out.

Such lamentations, which sound a lot like the left's critiques of global free trade, are hard to resist. They have an aura of romance. But they simply don't withstand close examination. The richest clubs have always dominated their leagues. They might not be the same rich clubs; neither Liverpool nor Atlético Madrid nor Borussia Moenchengladbach dominates as they once did. Even so, the ruling elite of European and Latin American soccer has been extraordinarily constant over time. Teams like Juventus and Manchester United only fall from their thrones for brief and historically insignificant spells.

Globalization has actually added a measure of mobility to the system. Foreign investors have created new powerhouses overnight. Chelsea, funded by Russian oil money, looks poised to break the monopoly in English soccer. Parmalat has used money from its international sale of dairy products to rocket clubs in Italy and Brazil to success. Of course, it is possible to overstate the glory of the new soccer order. A few years ago, a Swedish parliamentarian named Lars Gustafson nominated the game for a Noble Peace Prize, unleashing a fury of ridicule. And his critics have a point. Soccer doesn't deserve a prize for peace. It deserves one for economics.

ation spluttered, "I think it's a betrayal of our heritage." Some of these reactions can be chalked up to xenophobia. But the matter is psychologically deeper than that. English fans loved their old managers because they were such authentic representatives of the country, in all their faults and glories.

But the Eriksson era has taken an entirely unexpected direction: The new coach has practiced a caricature of old-fashioned, gritty English football. His system depends on goonish performances from relatively no-name defensive midfielders. Goals come from long passes to the fleet-footed forward Michael Owen. Every time Eriksson abandons the classic English formula, he gets in trouble.

Why hasn't Eriksson been able to remake English soccer in his suave continental image? The answer has to do with the deeply ingrained culture of the game. From a very early age, English players learn certain virtues—hard tackling, reckless winning of contested balls—and not others, such as fancy dribbling or short passing. Remaking these instincts isn't possible in a few seasons, let alone a few training sessions, of Swedish coaching.

The Eriksson story is archetypal. Portugal handed its squad over to a Brazilian; the Polish national team fronted a Nigerian striker who starred for a club in Greece; one of Japan's best players, Alessandro Santos (a.k.a. Alex), was born and raised in Brazil. None of these foreigners has succeeded in transforming the style and culture of national soccer teams. When Eriksson succumbed to Englishness, he upended one of the great clichés of the antiglobalization movement: that a consequence of free markets is Hollywood, Nike, and KFC steamrolling indigenous cultures. It is ironic that the defenders of indigenous cultures so often underestimate their formidable ability to withstand the market's assault.

Corruption 1, Investors 0

While globalization's critics have overestimated the market's destruction of local cultures, so too have its proponents. Take Brazil, for instance. How could a country with so many natural resources be so poor? How could a country with so much foreign investment remain so stymied?

Based on the stylishness of Brazil's most recent World Cup triumph in 2002—Edmilson springing backwards, catapult-like, into a poster-quality bicycle kick; Ronaldo scoring in-stride with a poke of the toe—outside observers would have no conception of the crisis in the national passion. But then, study the team's roster, and a pattern emerges. Between appearances for the national team, Edmilson contributes his stunts to a club in Lyon, France. The 27-year-old Ronaldo, now with Real Madrid, hasn't played professionally in Brazil since he was 17. Of the 23 players who wore their country's radioactive yellow jerseys in the 2002 World Cup, only 12 currently play in their home country. An estimated 5,000 Brazilians have contracts with foreign teams. While pumping out the world's greatest players, Brazil's sport couldn't be in a sorrier state. Only a handful of clubs operates anywhere in the vicinity of the black. Signs of decay are visible everywhere. Attending games in some of the country's most storied stadiums, buying their most expensive tickets, fans find themselves worrying about splinters and rusty nails protruding from the rotting wooden seats. Thousands more fans attend the average soccer game in Columbus, Ohio, and Dallas, Texas, than in the top flight of the Brazilian league.

Global capital was supposed to provide an easy fix. Foreign investors promised, implicitly at least, to wipe away the practices of corrupt elites who ran the Brazilian game and replace them with the ethic of professionalism, the science of modern marketing, and a concern for the balance sheet. In 1999, a Dallas-based investment fund called Hicks, Muse, Tate & Furst sunk tens of millions of dollars into the São Paulo club Corinthians and Cruzeiro of Belo Horizonte. ISL, a Swiss marketing company, acquired a share of the famed soccer club Flamengo in Rio de Janeiro. A few years earlier, the Italian food giant Parmalat took over Palmeiras of São Paulo. "Capitalism is winning out against the feudal attitudes that have prevailed in the sport for too long," crowed Juca Kfouri, Brazil's most venerable soccer journalist, at the height of the foreign influx. Kfouri predicted that soccer would generate 4 percent of Brazil's gross domestic product in just a few years.

Less than three years after the foreign investors arrived triumphantly in Brazil, they left in disgrace. At Corinthians, fans held demonstrations against Hicks Muse, protesting its failure to build a modern stadium. At Flamengo, ISL collapsed into bankruptcy. Foreign capital didn't turn Brazilian soccer into a commercial force like the National Basketball Association. In fact, by all objective measures, the game is now in worse shape than it was five years ago.

Why was the era of foreign investment such a debacle? The answer has to do with the men who ran the Brazilian game, perfect avatars of Latin American populism—corrupt, charismatic, and sly. When the foreign investors arrived in Brazil, they had no choice but to deal with these *cartolas*, or "top hats." But then the predictable happened. The *cartolas* siphoned funds into accounts in Bahamas and built themselves homes in Florida, expenditures documented in a congressional investigation. After they took the foreign investors' cash, the *cartolas* turned on their partners. When I visited Eurico

Miranda, the president of the Rio de Janeiro club Vasco da Gama, he complained how the foreign investors brought in guys "who barely speak Portuguese." He condemned the foreign investors for selling star players to hated crosstown rivals—previously an unthinkable act. Miranda's genius was that he made these antiglobalization arguments only after he allegedly robbed his foreign investors blind. A culture of corruption, as it turns out, is not any easier to remedy in soccer than it is elsewhere in the global economy. People have an attachment to their populist leaders and politicians, not just because of their cult of personality and their ability to deliver goods. They like them because the populists paint themselves as defenders of the community against the relentless onslaught of outsiders. It's going to take more than Dallas-based pension funds and Wharton business school graduates to sweep them away.

Winning The Peace

Local hostilities, even outright racism, ought to be the easiest sort of legacy for global soccer to erase. When people have a self-interested reason for getting along, they are supposed to put aside their ancient grudges and do business. But there's a massive hole in this argument: Glasgow, Scotland.

Glasgow has two teams, or rather, existential enemies. Celtic represents Irish Catholics. Its songs blame the British for the potato famine, and its games have historically provided fertile territory for Irish Republican Army (IRA) recruiters. Across town, there is Rangers, the club of Tory unionism. Banners in the stadium trumpet the Ulster Defense Forces and other Northern Irish protestant paramilitaries. Before games, fans—including respectable lawyers and businessmen—shout a song with the charming line, "We're up to our knees in Fenian blood." They sing about William of Orange, "King Billy," and his masterminding of the Protestant triumph in 1690 at the Battle of the Boyne. Until 1989, Rangers consciously forbade the hiring of Catholic players. Crosstown rivalries are, of course, a staple of sports, but the Celtic-Rangers rivalry represents something more than the enmity of proximity. It is the unfinished fight over the Protestant Reformation.

The Celtic and Rangers organizations desperately want to embrace the ethos of globalism, to convert themselves into mass entertainment conglomerates. They've done everything possible to move beyond the relatively small Scottish market—sending clothing catalogs to the Scottish and Irish diasporas in North America, and campaigning to join the bigger, better, wealthier English league.

But the Celtic and Rangers clubs don't try too hard to eliminate bigotry. Rangers, for example, continues to sell Orange jerseys. It plays songs on the stadium loudspeaker that it knows will provoke anti-Catholic lyrics. The club blares Tina Turner's "Simply the Best," which culminates in 40,000 fans screaming "Fuck the Pope!" Celtic, for its part, flies the Irish tricolor above its stadium. At Glasgow's Ibrox Park, I've watched Protestants celebrate a goal, egged on by former team captain Lorenzo Amoruso, a long-haired Italian with the look of a 1980s model. He applauds the fans. Flailing his arms, he urges them to sing their anti-Catholic songs louder. The irony is obvious: Amoruso is Catholic. Since the late 1990s, Rangers has routinely fielded more Catholics than Celtic. Its players have come from Georgia, Argentina, Germany, Norway, Portugal, and Holland, because money can buy no better ones. But ethnic hatred, it seems, makes good business sense. In fact, from the start of their rivalry, Celtic and Rangers have been nicknamed the "Old Firm," because they're seen as colluding to profit from their mutual hatreds. Even in the global market, they attract more fans because their supporters crave ethnic identification—to join a fight on behalf of their tribe.

There are plenty of economic causes for illiberal hatreds—unemployment, competition for scarce jobs, inadequate social safety nets—but none of those material conditions is especially widespread in Glasgow. Discrimination has faded. The city's unemployment problem is no better or worse than the rest of Britain. Glasgow has kept alive its tribalism, despite the logic of history, because it provides a kind of pornographic pleasure. Thousands of fans arrive each week from across the whole of Britain, in ferries from Belfast and buses from London, all aching to partake in a few hours of hate-filled tribalism. Once they release this bile from their system, they can return to their comfortable houses and good jobs.

If there were any place one would expect this sort of hostility to get messy, it would be Chelsea. During the 1980s, the club was the outfit most associated with English hooliganism. Its fans joined the xenophobic British National Party and merged with violent racist gangs like the notorious Combat 18. There are famous stories of Chelsea fans visiting Auschwitz, where they would walk around delivering *Sieg Heil* salutes to the tourists and try to climb inside the ovens. When the Holocaust denier David Irving went on trial for libel in 2001, the hooligan group Chelsea Headhunters provided security for his rallies.

Like a college alumni association, older, retired Chelsea hooligans make a point of sticking together. They stay in touch through an online message board, where they exchange war stories and debate the fortunes of their beloved club. The board makes a

Want to Know More?

Much of the literature on soccer veers from the vacuous to the absurdly academic. There are, however, some worthy exceptions. *Financial Times* columnist Simon Kuper charts the sport's intersection with politics through witty travelogue in *Football Against the Enemy* (London: Orion, 1994). Uruguayan novelist Eduardo H. Galeano provides a less journalistic, more poetic rendering of the same subject in *Soccer in the Sun and Shadow* (New York: Verso, 1998).

In addition to these tours through the global game, several excellent case studies are available. David Winner's *Brilliant Orange: The Neurotic Genius of Dutch Football* (London: Bloomsbury, 2000) finds the aesthetic underpinnings for the national style in art, architecture, and politics. *Offside: Soccer and American Exceptionalism* (Princeton: Princeton University Press, 2001) by Andrei S. Markovits and Steven L. Hellerman explores why the United States has sat on the periphery of this most globalized phenomenon. Alex Bellos uses the game as an anthropological vehicle for understanding Brazilian race, class, and corruption in *Futebol: The Brazilian Way of Life* (New York: Bloomsbury, 2002). And Bill Murray covers the history of the Celtic and Rangers clubs in *The Old Firm: Sectarianism, Sport, and Society in Scotland* (Atlantic Highlands: Humanities Press, 1984).

Several top journalists and leading publications examine the political economy of soccer. The London-based columnist Gabriele Marcotti writes the "Inside World Soccer" column for *Sports Illustrated* and contributes to various European publications. See Franklin Foer's "Glooooooooooo-balism!" (*Slate,* February 12, 2001) for perspectives on soccer and globalization. Argentina's monthly *El Gráfico* remains one of Latin America's top soccer publications, while the lively English monthly *Four Four Two* usually contains at least one lengthy story on the social significance of a crosstown rivalry, a band of hooligans, or some other unexpected aspect of the beautiful game.

Foreign Policy coverage of the intersection of culture, politics, and economics includes Joshua Fishman's "The New Linguistic Order" (Winter 1998–99), Theodore C. Bestor's "How Sushi Went Global" (November/December 2000), Mario Vargas Llosa's "The Culture of Liberty" (January/February 2001), Alberto Fuguet's "Magical Neoliberalism" (July/August 2001), Douglas McGray's "Japan's Gross National Cool" (May/June 2002), and Kym Anderson's "Wine's New World" (May/June 2003).

For links to relevant Web sites, access to the *FP* Archive, and a comprehensive index of related *Foreign Policy* articles, go to www.foreignpolicy.com

point of declaring, "WELCOME TO THE CHELSEA HOOLIGANS FORUM, FOR CHELSEA AND LOYAL FANS. PLEASE DON'T LEAVE RACIST MESSAGES AND DON'T USE THIS BOARD TO ARRANGE VIOLENCE." The warning is intended to inoculate the site against any exceptionally offensive posts, but it doesn't exactly deter the anti-Semitism. Almost immediately after oil baron Roman Abramovich, the second richest man in Russia, and a Jew, bought Chelsea, a guy calling himself West Ken Ken referred to Abramovich as a "yid," and moaned, "I like the money but the star of David will be flying down the [Stamford] bridge soon. "

However, as the Abramovich era began and the new owner spent more than $150 million stocking his new team, the complaints became less apparent. And then, when Chelsea jumped to the top of the English Premier League table, the anti-Semitism vanished altogether.

Chelsea, it seems, has discovered the only effective palliative for the vestiges of localism—not global cash or global talent, but victory.

Reading Comprehension—Points of Engagement

1. According to Foer, what should we *expect* the result of soccer's globalization to be, in terms of nationalism and patriotism? What, according to him, is the *reality*? Why does he think this happened? Cite two passages of his essay to support your answers.

2. Consider the case of Brazilian soccer presented by Foer. How has the Brazilian soccer scene suffered under the globalization of soccer? Has it gained anything? What has changed? How does Foer feel about the situation with the Brazilian team? How do you know?

3. Consider the title of Franklin Foer's essay, "Soccer vs. McWorld." What do you think the "McWorld" part of his title means? What does it have to do with soccer?

Assignment Questions—Points of Departure

1. In "Soccer vs. McWorld" Franklin Foer explores the conflict between globalism and parochialism in soccer. In "Hate Your Policies, Love Your Institutions," John Waterbury discusses the differences in world opinion about American foreign policy and American educational institutions. For this paper, your project is to consider the roles of *education* and of *sports* in drawing people together or pulling

them apart. Do you think education or sports are a more effective means of promoting communication and harmony amongst different nationalities? Why? How do sports and education function differently in these two essays? In what ways are they similar? What can one do that the other can't? Propose your own answers to these questions using the essays by Foer and Waterbury.

2. Is it a natural human response to divide ourselves up into small groups with clearly defined commonalities within the groups and oppositions between the groups? What incentives are there to resist forces of universalism and to seek power and autonomy through differentiating ourselves from other groups? *Is* there power in it, or is it ultimately destructive? Your project in this paper is to answer these questions using Franklin Foer and one or two of the following: David Brooks, Fenton Johnson, Michael Kamber, Lewis Lapham, Katha Pollitt, Francine Prose, V.S. Naipaul, or John Waterbury.

3. Look up the words "xenophobia" and "parochialism" in your dictionary or online. Now consider the following quotation from Franklin Foer's essay: "Ethnic hatred makes good business sense . . . it provides a kind of pornographic pleasure" (100). How does this quotation strike you? Do you agree with it? Considering the observations of David Brooks, John Waterbury, or Lewis Lapham regarding American identity, what might be done to address the problems of xenophobia and parochialism? Write an essay where you discuss connections between Foer's theory of the backlash—via parochialism—against globalism in soccer, and the image of America, and Americans, which the other authors defend.

The Theory of Thin Slices:
How a Little Bit of Knowledge Goes a Long Way
Malcolm Gladwell

Points of Access

1. Have you ever found yourself doing something without knowing why? You may be conscious of what you're doing, but you cannot explain in retrospect why you did it. What do you think is going on in your head at the time? Freewrite for 15 minutes about what you think happens in your own head when you're *not* consciously thinking. It may either be when you're asleep or when you just are not paying attention to what you're thinking or doing, when you're not being conscious, or when you're not self-aware.

2. Think about the various ways you communicate with people. The most obvious is talking, but how else do you communicate with friends, family, and strangers on the street? Make a list of the ways you communicate *without* talking. Then think about the relationship between verbal language and the items on your list. What can you communicate in words that you cannot communicate any other ways? What are the limitations of words alone that these other ways enhance? After you make your list, freewrite for 10-15 minutes about the relationship between verbal language and other ways you can communicate your feelings.

3. Think about your dorm room or your bedroom at home, and then imagine that you are somebody else looking at your room for the first time. How would your room look to a stranger? What would that person learn about you by looking only at your stuff? Pretend that you are that person, and describe the room and the person they would think you were based on your living space. What can, and can't, a stranger learn by looking at your belongings?

Some years ago, a young couple came to the University of Washington to visit the laboratory of a psychologist named John Gottman. They were in their twenties, blond and blue-eyed with stylishly tousled haircuts and funky glasses. Later, some of the people who worked in the lab would say they were the kind of couple that is easy to like—intelligent and attractive and funny in a droll, ironic kind of way—and that much is immediately obvious from the videotape Gottman made of their visit. The husband, whom I'll call Bill, had an endearingly playful manner. His wife, Susan, had a sharp, deadpan wit.

They were led into a small room on the second floor of the nondescript two-story building that housed Gottman's operations, and they sat down about five feet apart on two office chairs mounted on raised platforms. They both had electrodes and sensors clipped to their fingers and ears, which measured things like their heart rate, how much they were sweating, and the temperature of their skin. Under their chairs, a "jiggle-o-meter" on the platform measured how much each of them moved around. Two video cameras, one aimed at each person, recorded everything they said and did. For fifteen minutes, they were left alone with the cameras rolling, with instructions to discuss any topic from their marriage that had become a point of contention. For Bill and Sue it was their dog. They lived in a small apartment and had just gotten a very large puppy. Bill didn't like the dog; Sue did. For fifteen minutes, they discussed what they ought to do about it.

The videotape of Bill and Sue's discussion seems, at least at first, to be a random sample of a very ordinary kind of conversation that couples have all the time. No one gets angry. There are no scenes, no breakdowns, no epiphanies. "I'm just not a dog person" is how Bill starts things off, in a perfectly reasonable tone of voice. He complains a little bit—but about the dog, not about Susan. She complains, too, but there are also moments when they simply forget that they are supposed to be arguing. When the subject of whether the dog smells comes up, for example, Bill and Sue banter back and forth happily, both with a half smile on their lips.

> Sue: Sweetie! She's not smelly . . .
> Bill: Did you smell her today?
> Sue: I smelled her. She smelled good. I petted her, and my hands didn't stink or feel oily. Your hands have never smelled oily.
> Bill: Yes, sir.
> Sue: I've never let my dog get oily.
> Bill: Yes, sir. She's a dog.
> Sue: My dog has never gotten oily. You'd better be careful.
> Bill: No, you'd better be careful.
> Sue: No, you'd better be careful. . . . Don't call my dog oily, boy.

I. The Love Lab

How much do you think can be learned about Sue and Bill's marriage by watching that fifteen-minute videotape? Can we tell if their relationship is healthy or unhealthy? I suspect that most of us would say that Bill and Sue's dog talk doesn't tell us much. It's much too short. Marriages are buffeted by more important things, like money and sex and children and jobs and in-laws, in constantly changing combinations. Sometimes couples are very happy together. Some days they fight. Sometimes they feel as though they could almost kill each other, but then they go on vacation and come back sounding like newlyweds. In order to "know" a couple, we feel as though we have to observe them over many weeks and months and see them in every state—happy, tired, angry, irritated, delighted, having a nervous breakdown, and so on—and not just in the relaxed and chatty mode that Bill and Sue seemed to be in. To make an accurate prediction about something as serious as the future of a marriage—indeed, to make a prediction of any sort—it seems that we would have to gather a lot of information and in as many different contexts as possible.

But John Gottman has proven that we don't have to do that at all. Since the 1980s, Gottman has brought more than three thousand married couples—just like Bill and Sue—into that small room in his "love lab" near the University of Washington campus. Each couple has been videotaped, and the results have been analyzed according to something Gottman dubbed SPAFF (for specific affect), a coding system that has twenty separate categories corresponding to every conceivable emotion that a married couple might express during a conversation. Disgust, for example, is 1, contempt is 2, anger is 7, defensiveness is 10, whining is 11, sadness is 12, stonewalling is 13, neutral is 14, and so on. Gottman has taught his staff how to read every emotional nuance in people's facial expressions and how to interpret seemingly ambiguous bits of dialogue. When they watch a marriage videotape, they assign a SPAFF code to every second of the couple's interaction, so that a fifteen-minute conflict discussion ends up being translated into a row of eighteen hundred numbers—nine hundred for the husband and nine hundred for the wife. The notation "7, 7, 14, 10, 11, 11," for instance, means that in one six-second stretch, one member of the couple was briefly angry, then neutral, had a moment of defensiveness, and then began whining. Then the data from the electrodes and sensors is factored in, so that the coders know, for example, when the husband's or the wife's heart was pounding or when his or her temperature was rising or when either of them was jiggling in his or her seat, and all of that information is fed into a complex equation.

On the basis of those calculations, Gottman has proven something remarkable. If he analyzes an hour of a husband and wife talking, he can predict with 95 percent accuracy whether that couple will still be married fifteen years later. If he watches a couple for fifteen minutes, his success rate is around 90 percent. Recently, a professor who works with Gottman named Sybil Carrère, who was playing around with some of the videotapes, trying to design a new study, discovered that if they looked at only *three minutes* of a couple talking, they could still predict with fairly impressive accuracy who was going to get divorced and who was going to make it. The truth of a marriage can be understood in a much shorter time than anyone ever imagined.

John Gottman is a middle-aged man with owl-like eyes, silvery hair, and a neatly trimmed beard. He is short and very charming, and when he talks about something that excites him—which is nearly all the time—his eyes light up and open even wider. During the Vietnam War, he was a conscientious objector, and there is still something of the '60s hippie about him, like the Mao cap he sometimes wears over his braided yarmulke. He is a psychologist by training, but he also studied mathematics at MIT, and the rigor and precision of mathematics clearly moves him as much as anything else. When I met Gottman, he had just published his most ambitious book, a dense five-hundred-page treatise called *The Mathematics of Divorce,* and he attempted to give me a sense of his argument, scribbling equations and impromptu graphs on a paper napkin until my head began to swim.

Gottman may seem to be an odd example in a book about the thoughts and decisions that bubble up from our unconscious. There's nothing instinctive about his approach. He's not making snap judgments. He's sitting down with his computer and painstakingly analyzing videotapes, second by second. His work is a classic example of conscious and deliberate thinking. But Gottman, it turns out, can teach us a great deal about a critical part of rapid cognition known as thin-slicing. "Thin-slicing" refers to the ability of our unconscious to find patterns in situations and behavior based on very narrow slices of experience. When Evelyn Harrison looked at the kouros and blurted out, "I'm sorry to hear that," she was thin-slicing; so were the Iowa gamblers when they had a stress reaction to the red decks after just ten cards.

Thin-slicing is part of what makes the unconscious so dazzling. But it's also what we find most problematic about rapid cognition. How is it possible to gather the necessary information for a sophisticated judgment in such a short time? The answer is that when our unconscious engages in thin-slicing, what we are doing is an automated, accelerated unconscious version of what Gottman does with his videotapes and equations. Can a marriage really be understood in one sitting? Yes it can, and so can lots of other seemingly complex situations. What Gottman has done is to show us how.

2. Marriage and Morse Code

I watched the videotape of Bill and Sue with Amber Tabares, a graduate student in Gottman's lab who is a trained SPAFF coder. We sat in the same room that Bill and Sue used, watching their interaction on a monitor. The conversation began with Bill. He liked their old dog, he said. He just didn't like their new dog. He didn't speak angrily or with any hostility. It seemed like he genuinely just wanted to explain his feelings.

If we listened closely, Tabares pointed out, it was clear that Bill was being very defensive. In the language of SPAFF, he was cross-complaining and engaging in "yes-but" tactics—appearing to agree but then taking it back. Bill was coded as defensive, as it turned out, for forty of the first sixty-six seconds of their conversation. As for Sue, while Bill was talking, on more than one occasion she rolled her eyes very quickly, which is a classic sign of contempt. Bill then began to talk about his objection to the pen where the dog lives. Sue replied by closing her eyes and then assuming a patronizing lecturing voice. Bill went on to say that he didn't want a fence in the living room. Sue said, "I don't want to argue about that," and rolled her eyes—another indication of contempt. "Look at that," Tabares said. "More contempt. We've barely started and we've seen him be defensive for almost the whole time, and she has rolled her eyes several times."

At no time as the conversation continued did either of them show any overt signs of hostility. Only subtle things popped up for a second or two, prompting Tabares to stop the tape and point them out. Some couples, when they fight, *fight*. But these two were a lot less obvious. Bill complained that the dog cut into their social life, since they always had to come home early for fear of what the dog might do to their apartment. Sue responded that that wasn't true, arguing, "If she's going to chew anything, she's going to do it in the first fifteen minutes that we're gone." Bill seemed to agree with that. He nodded lightly and said, "Yeah, I know," and then added, "I'm not saying it's rational. I just don't want to have a dog."

Tabares pointed at the videotape. "He started out with 'Yeah, I know.' But it's a yes-but. Even though he started to validate her, he went on to say that he didn't like the dog. He's really being defensive. I kept thinking, He's so nice. He's doing all this validation. But then I realized he was doing the yes-but. It's easy to be fooled by them."

Bill went on: "I'm getting way better. You've got to admit it. I'm better this week than last week, and the week before and the week before."

Tabares jumped in again. "In one study, we were watching newlyweds, and what often happened with the couples who ended up in divorce is that when one partner would ask for credit, the other spouse wouldn't give it. And with the happier couples, the spouse would hear it and say, 'You're right.' That stood out. When you nod and say 'uh-huh' or 'yeah,' you are doing that as a sign of support, and here she never does it, not once in the entire session, which none of us had realized until we did the coding.

"It's weird," she went on. "You don't get the sense that they are an unhappy couple when they come in. And when they were finished, they were instructed to watch their own discussion, and they thought the whole thing was hilarious. They seem fine, in a way. But I don't know. They haven't been married that long. They're still in the glowy phase. But the fact is that she's completely inflexible. They are arguing about dogs, but it's really about how whenever they have a disagreement, she's completely inflexible. It's one of those things that could cause a lot of long-term harm. I wonder if they'll hit the seven-year wall. Is there enough positive emotion there? Because what seems positive isn't actually positive at all."

What was Tabares looking for in the couple? On a technical level, she was measuring the amount of positive and negative emotion, because one of Gottman's findings is that for a marriage to survive, the ratio of positive to negative emotion in a given encounter has to be at least five to one. On a simpler level, though, what Tabares was looking for in that short discussion was a pattern in Bill and Sue's marriage, because a central argument in Gottman's work is that all marriages have a distinctive pattern, a kind of marital DNA, that surfaces in any kind of meaningful interaction. This is why Gottman asks couples to tell the story of how they met, because he has found that when a husband and wife recount the most important episode in their relationship, that pattern shows up right away.

"It's so easy to tell," Gottman says. "I just looked at this tape yesterday. The woman says, 'We met at a ski weekend, and he was there with a bunch of his friends, and I kind of liked him and we made a date to be together. But then he drank too much, and he went home and went to sleep, and I was waiting for him for three hours. I woke him up, and I said I don't appreciate being treated this way. You're really not a nice person. And he said, yeah, hey, I really had a lot to drink.'" There was a troubling pattern in their first interaction, and the sad truth was that that pattern persisted throughout their relationship. "It's not that hard," Gottman went on. "When I first started doing these interviews, I thought maybe we were getting these people on a crappy day. But the prediction levels are just so high, and if you do it again, you get the same pattern over and over again."

One way to understand what Gottman is saying about marriages is to use the analogy of what people in the world of Morse code call a fist. Morse code is made up of dots and dashes, each of which has its own prescribed length. But no one ever replicates those prescribed lengths perfectly. When operators send a message—particularly using the old manual machines known as the straight key or the bug—they vary the spacing or stretch out the dots and dashes or combine dots and dashes and spaces in a particular rhythm. Morse code is like speech. Everyone has a different voice.

In the Second World War, the British assembled thousands of so-called interceptors—mostly women—whose job it was to tune in every day and night to the radio broadcasts of the various divisions of the German military. The Germans were, of course, broadcasting in code, so—at least in the early part of the war—the British couldn't understand *what* was being said. But that didn't necessarily matter, because before long, just by listening to the cadence of the transmission, the interceptors began to pick up on the individual fists of the German operators, and by doing so, they knew something nearly as important, which was *who* was doing the sending. "If you listened to the same call signs over a certain period, you would begin to recognize that there were, say, three or four different operators in that unit, working on a shift system, each with his own characteristics," says Nigel West, a British military historian. "And invariably, quite apart from the text, there would be the preambles, and the illicit exchanges. How are you today? How's the girlfriend? What's the weather like in Munich? So you fill out a little card, on which you write down all that kind of information, and pretty soon you have a kind of relationship with that person."

The interceptors came up with descriptions of the fists and styles of the operators they were following. They assigned them names and assembled elaborate profiles of their personalities. After they identified the person who was sending the message, the interceptors would then locate their signal. So now they knew something more. They knew who was *where.* West goes on: "The interceptors had such a good handle on the transmitting characteristics of the German radio operators that they could literally follow them around Europe—wherever they were. That was extraordinarily valuable in constructing an order of battle, which is a diagram of what the individual military units in the field are doing and what their location is. If a particular radio operator was with a particular unit and transmitting from Florence, and then three weeks later you recognized that same operator, only this time he was in Linz, then you could assume that that particular unit had moved from northern Italy to the eastern front. Or you would know that a particular operator was with a tank repair unit and he always came up on the air every day at twelve o'clock. But now, after a big battle, he's coming up at twelve, four in the afternoon, and seven in the evening, so you can assume that unit has a lot of work going on. And in a moment of crisis, when someone very high up asks, 'Can you really be absolutely certain that this particular Luftwaffe *Fliegerkorps* [German air force squadron] is outside of Tobruk and not in Italy?' you can answer, 'Yes, that was Oscar, we are absolutely sure.' "

The key thing about fists is that they emerge naturally. Radio operators don't deliberately try to sound distinctive. They simply end up sounding distinctive, because some part of their personality appears to express itself automatically and unconsciously in the way they work the Morse code keys. The other thing about a fist is that it reveals itself in even the smallest sample of Morse code. We have to listen to only a few characters to pick out an individual's pattern. It doesn't change or disappear for stretches or show up only in certain words or phrases. That's why the British interceptors could listen to just a few bursts and say, with absolute certainty, "It's Oscar, which means that yes, his unit is now definitely outside of Tobruk." An operator's fist is stable.

What Gottman is saying is that a relationship between two people has a fist as well: a distinctive signature that arises naturally and automatically. That is why a marriage can be read and decoded so easily, because some key part of human activity—whether it is something as simple as pounding out a Morse code message or as complex as being married to someone—has an identifiable and stable pattern. Predicting divorce, like tracking Morse Code operators, is pattern recognition.

"People are in one of two states in a relationship," Gottman went on. "The first is what I call positive sentiment override, where positive emotion overrides irritability. It's like a buffer. Their spouse will do something bad, and they'll say, 'Oh, he's just in a crummy mood.' Or they can be in negative sentiment override, so that even a relatively neutral thing that a partner says gets perceived as negative. In the negative sentiment override state, people draw lasting conclusions about each other. If their spouse does something positive, it's a selfish person doing a positive thing. It's really hard to change those states, and those states determine whether when one party tries to repair things, the other party sees that as repair or hostile manipulation. For example, I'm talking with my wife, and she says, 'Will you shut up and let me finish?' In positive sentiment override, I say, 'Sorry, go ahead.' I'm not very happy, but I recognize the repair. In negative sentiment override, I say, 'To hell with you, I'm not getting a chance to finish either. You're such a bitch, you remind me of your mother.' "

As he was talking, Gottman drew a graph on a piece of paper that looked a lot like a chart of the ups and downs of the stock market over the course of a typical day. What he does, he explains, is track the ups and downs of a couple's level of positive and negative emotion, and he's found that it doesn't take very long to figure out which way the line on the graph is going. "Some go up, some go down," he says. "But once they start going down, toward negative emotion, ninety-four percent will continue going down. They start on a bad course and they can't correct it. I don't think of this as just a slice in time. It's an indication of how they view their whole relationship."

3. The Importance of Contempt

Let's dig a little deeper into the secret of Gottman's success rate. Gottman has discovered that marriages have distinctive signatures, and we can find that signature by collecting very detailed emotional information from the interaction of a couple. But there's something else that is very interesting about Gottman's system, and that is the way in which he manages to simplify the task of prediction. I hadn't realized how much of an issue this was until I tried thin-slicing couples myself. I got one of Gottman's tapes, which had on it ten three-minute clips of different couples talking. Half the couples, I was told, split up at some point in the fifteen years after their discussion was filmed. Half were still together. Could I guess which was which? I was pretty confident I could. But I was wrong. I was terrible at it. I answered five correctly, which is to say that I would have done just as well by flipping a coin.

My difficulty arose from the fact that the clips were utterly overwhelming. The husband would say something guarded. The wife would respond quietly. Some fleeting emotion would flash across her face. He would start to say something and then stop. She would scowl. He would laugh. Someone would mutter something. Someone would frown. I would rewind the tape and look at it again, and I would get still more information. I'd see a little trace of a smile, or I'd pick up on a slight change in tone. It was all too much. In my head, I was frantically trying to determine the ratios of positive emotion to negative emotion. But what counted as positive, and what counted as negative? I knew from Susan and Bill that a lot of what looked positive was actually negative. And I also knew that there were no fewer than twenty separate emotional states on the SPAFF chart. Have you ever tried to keep track of twenty different emotions simultaneously? Now, granted, I'm not a marriage counselor. But that same tape has been given to almost two hundred marital therapists, marital researchers, pastoral counselors, and graduate students in clinical psychology, as well as newlyweds, people who were recently divorced, and people who have been happily married for a long time—in other words, almost two hundred people who know a good deal more about marriage than I do—and none of them was any better than I was. The group as a whole guessed right 53.8 percent of the time, which is just above chance. The fact that there was a pattern didn't much matter. There were so many other things going on so quickly in those three minutes that we couldn't find the pattern.

Gottman, however, doesn't have this problem. He's gotten so good at thin-slicing marriages that he says he can be in a restaurant and eavesdrop on the couple one table over and get a pretty good sense of whether they need to start thinking about hiring lawyers and dividing up custody of the children. How does he do it? He has figured out that he doesn't need to pay attention to everything that happens. I was overwhelmed by the task of counting negativity, because everywhere I looked, I saw negative emotions. Gottman is far more selective. He has found that he can find out much of what he needs to know just by focusing on what he calls the Four Horsemen: defensiveness, stonewalling, criticism, and contempt. Even within the Four Horsemen, in fact, there is one emotion that he considers the most important of all: contempt. If Gottman observes one or both partners in a marriage showing contempt toward the other, he considers it the single most important sign that the marriage is in trouble.

"You would think that criticism would be the worst," Gottman says, "because criticism is a global condemnation of a person's character. Yet contempt is qualitatively different from criticism. With criticism I might say to my wife, 'You never listen, you are really selfish and insensitive.' Well, she's going to respond defensively to that. That's not very good for our problem solving and interaction. But if I speak from a superior plane, that's far more damaging, and contempt is any statement made from a higher level. A lot of the time it's an insult: 'You are a bitch. You're scum.' It's trying to put that person on a lower plane than you. It's hierarchical."

Gottman has found, in fact, that the presence of contempt in a marriage can even predict such things as how many colds a husband or a wife gets; in other words, having someone you love express contempt toward you is so stressful that it begins to affect the functioning of your immune system. "Contempt is closely related to disgust, and what disgust and contempt are about is completely rejecting and excluding someone from the community. The big gender difference with negative emotions is that women are more critical, and men are more likely to stonewall. We find that women start talking about a problem, the men get irritated and turn away, and the women get more critical, and it becomes a circle. But there isn't any gender difference when it comes to contempt. Not at all." Contempt is special. If you can measure contempt, then all of a sudden you don't need to know every detail of the couple's relationship.

I think that this is the way that our unconscious works. When we leap to a decision or have a hunch, our unconscious is doing what John Gottman does. It's sifting through the situation in front of us, throwing out all that is irrelevant while we zero in on what really matters. And the truth is that our unconscious is really good at this, to the point where thin-slicing often delivers a better answer than more deliberate and exhaustive ways of thinking.

4. The Secrets of the Bedroom

Imagine that you are considering me for a job. You've seen my résumé and think I have the necessary credentials. But you want to know whether I am the right fit for your organization. Am I a hard worker? Am I honest? Am I open to new ideas? In order to answer those questions about my personality, your boss gives you two options. The first is to meet with me twice a week for a year—to have lunch or dinner or go to a movie with me—to the point where you become one of my closest friends. (Your boss is quite demanding.) The second option is to drop by my house when I'm not there and spend half an hour or so looking around. Which would you choose?

The seemingly obvious answer is that you should take the first option: the thick slice. The more time you spend with me and the more information you gather, the better off you are. Right? I hope by now that you are at least a little bit skeptical of that approach. Sure enough, as the psychologist Samuel Gosling has shown, judging people's personalities is a really good example of how surprisingly effective thin-slicing can be.

Gosling began his experiment by doing a personality workup on eighty college students. For this, he used what is called the Big Five Inventory, a highly respected, multi-item questionnaire that measures people across five dimensions:

1. Extraversion. Are you sociable or retiring? Fun-loving or reserved?
2. Agreeableness. Are you trusting or suspicious? Helpful or uncooperative?
3. Conscientiousness. Are you organized or disorganized? Self-disciplined or weak willed?
4. Emotional stability. Are you worried or calm? Insecure or secure?
5. Openness to new experiences. Are you imaginative or down-to-earth? Independent or conforming?

Then Gosling had close friends of those eighty students fill out the same questionnaire.

When our friends rank us on the Big Five, Gosling wanted to know, how closely do they come to the truth? The answer is, not surprisingly, that our friends can describe us fairly accurately. They have a thick slice of experience with us, and that translates to a real sense of who we are. Then Gosling repeated the process, but this time he didn't call on close friends. He used total strangers who had never even met the students they were judging. All they saw were their dorm rooms. He gave his raters clipboards and told them they had fifteen minutes to look around and answer a series of very basic questions about the occupant of the room: On a scale of 1 to 5, does the inhabitant of this room seem to be the kind of person who is talkative? Tends to find fault with others? Does a thorough job? Is original? Is reserved? Is helpful and unselfish with others? And so on. "I was trying to study everyday impressions," Gosling says. "So I was quite careful not to tell my subjects what to do. I just said, 'Here is your questionnaire. Go into the room and drink it in.' I was just trying to look at intuitive judgment processes."

How did they do? The dorm room observers weren't nearly as good as friends in measuring extraversion. If you want to know how animated and talkative and outgoing someone is, clearly, you have to meet him or her in person. The friends also did slightly better than the dorm room visitors at accurately estimating agreeableness—how helpful and trusting someone is. I think that also makes sense. But on the remaining three traits of the Big Five, the strangers with the clipboards came out on top. They were more accurate at measuring conscientiousness, and they were much more accurate at predicting both the students' emotional stability and their openness to new experiences. On balance, then, the strangers ended up doing a much better job. What this suggests is that it is quite possible for people who have never met us and who have spent only twenty minutes thinking about us to come to a better understanding of who we are than people who have known us for years. Forget the endless "getting to know" meetings and lunches, then. If you want to get a good idea of whether I'd make a good employee, drop by my house one day and take a look around.

If you are like most people, I imagine that you find Gosling's conclusions quite incredible. But the truth is that they shouldn't be, not after the lessons of John Gottman. This is just another example of thin-slicing. The observers were looking at the students' most personal belongings, and our personal belongings contain a wealth of very telling information. Gosling says, for example, that a person's bedroom gives three kinds of clues to his or her personality. There are, first of all, identity claims, which are deliberate expressions about how we would like to be seen by the world: a framed copy of a magna cum laude degree from Harvard, for example. Then there is behavioral residue, which is defined as the inadvertent clues we leave behind: dirty laundry on the floor, for instance, or an alphabetized CD collection. Finally, there are thoughts and feelings regulators, which are changes we make to our most personal spaces to affect the way we feel when we inhabit them: a scented candle in the corner, for example, or a pile of artfully placed decorative pillows on the bed. If you see alphabetized CDs, a Harvard diploma on the wall, incense on a side table, and laundry neatly stacked in a hamper, you *know* certain aspects about that individual's personality instantly, in a way that you may not be able to grasp if all you ever do is spend time with him or her directly. Anyone who has ever scanned the bookshelves of a new girlfriend or boyfriend—or peeked inside his or her medicine cabinet—understands this implicitly: you can learn as much—or more—from one glance at a private space as you can from hours of exposure to a public face.

Just as important, though, is the information you *don't* have when you look through someone's belongings. What you avoid when you don't meet someone face-to-face are all the confusing and complicated and ultimately irrelevant pieces of information that can serve to screw up your judgment. Most of us have difficulty believing that a 275-pound football lineman could have a lively and discerning intellect. We just can't get past the stereotype of the dumb jock. But if all we saw of that person was his bookshelf or the art on his walls, we wouldn't have that same problem.

What people say about themselves can also be very confusing, for the simple reason that most of us aren't very objective about ourselves. That's why, when we measure personality, we don't just ask people point-blank what they think they are like. We give them a questionnaire, like the Big Five Inventory, carefully designed to elicit telling responses. That's also why Gottman doesn't waste any time asking husbands and wives point-blank questions about the state of their marriage. They might lie or feel awkward or, more important, they might not *know* the truth. They may be so deeply mired—or so happily ensconced—in their relationship that they have no perspective on how it works. "Couples simply aren't aware of how they sound," says Sybil Carrère. "They have this discussion, which we videotape and then play back to them. In one of the studies we did recently, we interviewed couples about what they learned from the study, and a remarkable number of them—I would say a majority of them—said they were surprised to find either what they looked like during the conflict discussion or what they communicated during the conflict discussion. We had one woman whom we thought of as extremely emotional, but she said that she had no idea that she was so emotional. She said that she thought she was stoic and gave nothing away. A lot of people are like that. They think they are more forthcoming than they actually are, or more negative than they actually are. It was only when they were watching the tape that they realized they were wrong about what they were communicating."

If couples aren't aware of how they sound, how much value can there be in asking them direct questions? Not much, and this is why Gottman has couples talk about something involving their marriage—like their pets—without being *about* their marriage. He looks closely at indirect measures of how the couple is doing: the telling traces of emotion that flit across one person's face; the hint of stress picked up in the sweat glands of the palm; a sudden surge in heart rate; a subtle tone that creeps into an exchange. Gottman comes at the issue sideways, which, he has found, can be a lot quicker and a more efficient path to the truth than coming at it head-on.

What those observers of dorm rooms were doing was simply a layperson's version of John Gottman's analysis. They were looking for the "fist" of those college students. They gave themselves fifteen minutes to drink things in and get a hunch about the person. They came at the question sideways, using the indirect evidence of the students' dorm rooms, and their decision-making process was simplified: they weren't distracted at all by the kind of confusing, irrelevant information that comes from a face-to-face encounter. They thin-sliced. And what happened? The same thing that happened with Gottman: those people with the clipboards were *really good* at making predictions.

5. Listening to Doctors

Let's take the concept of thin-slicing one step further. Imagine you work for an insurance company that sells doctors medical malpractice protection. Your boss asks you to figure out for accounting reasons who, among all the physicians covered by the company, is most likely to be sued. Once again, you are given two choices. The first is to examine the physicians' training and credentials and then analyze their records to see how many errors they've made over the past few years. The other option is to listen in on very brief snippets of conversation between each doctor and his or her patients.

By now you are expecting me to say the second option is the best one. You're right, and here's why. Believe it or not, the risk of being sued for malpractice has very little to do with how many mistakes a doctor makes. Analyses of malpractice lawsuits show that there are highly skilled doctors who get sued a lot and doctors who make lots of mistakes and never get sued. At the same time, the overwhelming number of people who suffer an injury due to the negligence of a doctor never file a malpractice suit at all. In other words, patients don't file lawsuits because they've been harmed by shoddy medical care. Patients file lawsuits because they've been harmed by shoddy medical care and *something else* happens to them.

What is that something else? It's how they were treated, on a personal level, by their doctor. What comes up again and again in malpractice cases is that patients say they were rushed or ignored or treated poorly. "People just don't sue doctors they like," is how Alice Burkin, a leading medical malpractice lawyer, puts it. "In all the years I've been in this business, I've never had a potential client walk in and say, 'I really like this doctor, and I feel terrible about doing it, but I want to sue him.' We've had people come in saying they want to sue some specialist, and we'll say, 'We don't think that doctor was negligent. We think it's your primary care doctor who was at fault.' And the client will say, 'I don't care what she did. I love her, and I'm not suing her.'"

Burkin once had a client who had a breast tumor that wasn't spotted until it had metastasized, and she wanted to sue her internist for the delayed diagnosis. In fact, it was her radiologist who was potentially at fault. But the client was adamant. She wanted to sue the internist. "In our first meeting, she told me she hated this doctor because she never took the time to talk to her and never asked about her other symptoms," Burkin said. " 'She never looked at me as a whole person,' the patient told us. . . . When a patient has a bad medical result, the doctor has to take the time to explain what happened, and to answer the patient's questions—to treat him like a human being. The doctors who don't are the ones who get sued." It isn't necessary, then, to know much about how a surgeon operates in order to know his likelihood of being sued. What you need to understand is the relationship between that doctor and his patients.

Recently the medical researcher Wendy Levinson recorded hundreds of conversations between a group of physicians and their patients. Roughly half of the doctors had never been sued. The other half had been sued at least twice, and Levinson found that just on the basis of those conversations, she could find clear differences between the two groups. The surgeons who had never been sued spent more than three minutes longer with each patient than those who had been sued did (18.3 minutes versus 15 minutes).

They were more likely to make "orienting" comments, such as "First I'll examine you, and then we will talk the problem over" or "I will leave time for your questions"— which help patients get a sense of what the visit is supposed to accomplish and when they ought to ask questions. They were more likely to engage in active listening, saying such things as "Go on, tell me more about that," and they were far more likely to laugh and be funny during the visit. Interestingly, there was no difference in the amount or quality of information they gave their patients; they didn't provide more details about medication or the patient's condition. The difference was entirely in *how* they talked to their patients.

It's possible, in fact, to take this analysis even further. The psychologist Nalini Ambady listened to Levinson's tapes, zeroing in on the conversations that had been recorded between just surgeons and their patients. For each surgeon, she picked two patient conversations. Then, from each conversation, she selected two ten-second clips of the doctor talking, so her slice was a total of forty seconds. Finally, she "content-filtered" the slices, which means she removed the high-frequency sounds from speech that enable us to recognize individual words. What's left after content-filtering is a kind of garble that preserves intonation, pitch, and rhythm but erases content. Using that slice—and that slice alone—Ambady did a Gottman-style analysis. She had judges rate the slices of garble for such qualities as warmth, hostility, dominance, and anxiousness, and she found that by using only those ratings, she could predict which surgeons got sued and which ones didn't.

Ambady says that she and her colleagues were "totally stunned by the results," and it's not hard to understand why. The judges knew nothing about the skill level of the surgeons. They didn't know how experienced they were, what kind of training they had, or what kind of procedures they tended to do. They didn't even know *what* the doctors were saying to their patients. All they were using for their prediction was their analysis of the surgeon's tone of voice. In fact, it was even more basic than that: if the surgeon's voice was judged to sound dominant, the surgeon tended to be in the sued group. If the voice sounded less dominant and more concerned, the surgeon tended to be in the non-sued group. Could there be a thinner slice? Malpractice sounds like one of those infinitely complicated and multidimensional problems. But in the end it comes down to a matter of respect, and the simplest way that respect is communicated is through tone of voice, and the most corrosive tone of voice that a doctor can assume is a dominant tone. Did Ambady need to sample the entire history of a patient and doctor to pick up on that tone? No, because a medical consultation is a lot like one of Gottman's conflict discussions or a student's dorm room. It's one of those situations where the signature comes through loud and clear.

Next time you meet a doctor, and you sit down in his office and he starts to talk, if you have the sense that he isn't listening to you, that he's talking down to you, and that he isn't treating you with respect, *listen to that feeling.* You have thin-sliced him and found him wanting.

6. The Power of the Glance

Thin-slicing is not an exotic gift. It is a central part of what it means to be human. We thin-slice whenever we meet a new person or have to make sense of something quickly or encounter a novel situation. We thin-slice because we have to, and we come to rely on that ability because there are lots of hidden fists out there, lots of situations where careful attention to the details of a very thin slice, even for no more than a second or two, can tell us an awful lot.

It is striking, for instance, how many different professions and disciplines have a word to describe the particular gift of reading deeply into the narrowest slivers of experience. In basketball, the player who can take in and comprehend all that is happening around him or her is said to have "court sense." In the military, brilliant generals are said to possess "coup d'oeil"—which, translated from the French, means "power of the glance": the ability to immediately see and make sense of the battlefield. Napoleon had coup d'oeil. So did Patton. The ornithologist David Sibley says that in Cape May, New Jersey, he once spotted a bird in flight from two hundred yards away and knew, instantly, that it was a ruff, a rare sandpiper. He had never seen a ruff in flight before; nor was the moment long enough for him to make a careful identification. But he was able to capture what bird-watchers call the bird's "giss"—its essence—and that was enough.

"Most of bird identification is based on a sort of subjective impression—the way a bird moves and little instantaneous appearances at different angles and sequences of different appearances, and as it turns its head and as it flies and as it turns around, you see sequences of different shapes and angles," Sibley says. "All that combines to create a unique impression of a bird that can't really be taken apart and described in words. When it comes down to being in the field and looking at a bird, you don't take the time to analyze it and say it shows this, this, and this; therefore it must be this species. It's more natural and instinctive. After a lot of practice, you look at the bird, and it triggers little switches in your brain. It *looks* right. You know what it is at a glance."

The Hollywood producer Brian Grazer, who has produced many of the biggest hit movies of the past twenty years, uses almost exactly the same language to describe the first time he met the actor Tom Hanks. It was in 1983. Hanks was then a virtual unknown. All he had done was the now (justly) forgotten TV show called *Bosom Buddies.* "He came in and read for the movie *Splash,* and right there, in the moment, I can tell you just what I saw," Grazer says. In that first instant, he *knew* Hanks was special. "We read hundreds of people for that part, and other people were funnier than him. But they weren't as likable as him. I felt like I could live inside of him. I felt like his problems were problems I could relate to. You know, in order to make somebody laugh, you have to be interesting, and in order to be interesting, you have to do things that are mean. Comedy comes out of anger, and interesting comes out of angry; otherwise there is no conflict. But he was able to be mean and you forgave him, and you have to be able to forgive somebody, because at the end of the day, you still have to be with him, even after he's dumped the girl or made some choices that you don't agree with. All of this wasn't thought out in words at the time. It was an intuitive conclusion that only later I could deconstruct."

My guess is that many of you have the same impression of Tom Hanks. If I asked you what he was like, you would say that he is decent and trustworthy and down-to-earth and funny. But you don't know him. You're not friends with him. You've only seen him in the movies, playing a wide range of different characters. Nonetheless, you've managed to extract something very meaningful about him from those thin slices of experience, and that impression has a powerful effect on how you experience Tom

Hanks's movies. "Everybody said that they couldn't see Tom Hanks as an astronaut," Grazer says of his decision to cast Hanks in the hit movie *Apollo 13*. "Well, I didn't know whether Tom Hanks was an astronaut. But I saw this as a movie about a space-craft in jeopardy. And who does the world want to get back the most? Who does America want to save? Tom Hanks. We don't want to see him die. We like him too much."

If we couldn't thin-slice—if you really had to know someone for months and months to get at their true selves—then *Apollo 13* would be robbed of its drama and *Splash* would not be funny. And if we could not make sense of complicated situations in a flash, basketball would be chaotic, and bird-watchers would be helpless. Not long ago, a group of psychologists reworked the divorce prediction test that I found so over-whelming. They took a number of Gottman's couples videos and showed them to non-experts—only this time, they provided the raters with a little help. They gave them a list of emotions to look for. They broke the tapes into thirty-second segments and allowed everyone to look at each segment twice, once to focus on the man and once to focus on the woman. And what happened? This time around, the observers' ratings predicted with better than 80 percent accuracy which marriages were going to make it. That's not quite as good as Gottman. But it's pretty impressive—and that shouldn't come as a surprise. We're old hands at thin-slicing.

Reading Comprehension—Points of Engagement

1. What is the theory of "thin-slicing"? Look on page 92 for your answer. Define it in your own words and using 1 or 2 short quotations from Gladwell's essay. Then explain why Gladwell finds the theory of thin-slicing interesting and useful. Construct your response as a full, coherent, and textually engaged paragraph.

2. What is a "fist" in the context of Gladwell's essay? Look on pages 94–96 for your answer. Explain the original meaning of the term "fist" in this context, and then explain Gladwell's application of it in this chapter. Be sure to describe Gottman's role in Gladwell's insight and use of this term.

3. What are the Four Horsemen according to John Gottman? Why are they important? What is the most important emotion for Gottman's success at thin-slicing relation-ships? Why?

4. Describe Samuel Gosling's college dorm room experiment. What does it show? Why is it important to Gladwell?

Assignment Questions—Points of Departure

1. Malcolm Gladwell bases much of this chapter on the theories and work of John Gottman. A psychologist by training, Gottman observes couples—in this case, heterosexual couples—in brief conversations, and then makes predictions about how men and women will relate to one another over time, including the longevity of their relationships. In other words, he has found through his research that women and men respond in gendered ways. How does this square with the research done by Arlie Russell Hochschild, or the observations of Katha Pollitt, Andrew Sullivan, or Fenton Johnson? Do these authors think gender matters in relationships? In what ways? What other factors contribute to the way we relate to one another? Are they more, or less, powerful than gender in determining our behavior? Why? How do you know? Use Gladwell and one of these other essays to form a project about how, and whether, gender affects our relationships with one another, how we act and how we react.

2. In your many years of schooling, you have probably been conscious of *what* you were learning, but have you ever thought about *how* you were learning? Gladwell suggests that we "thin-slice," that we make certain observations and decisions, without thinking at all. How and what else do we learn without thinking? How much of what we think we control is really an amazing human form of autopilot? Your project for this paper will be to consider these questions, and to propose answers based upon your own experience and your understanding of essays by Gladwell and one of the following other authors: Susan Blackmore, Alain de Botton, Adam Gopnik, Steven Johnson, Steven Pinker, Francine Prose, or Jeanette Winterson.

3. Consider the following claim Gladwell makes about thin-slicing and human nature: "Thin-slicing is not an exotic gift. It is a central part of what it means to be human" (104). What does Gladwell mean by this? Does he make a compelling case for his theory and this claim? Why or why not? What else might constitute a "central part of what it means to be human" and how might that affect your understanding, and acceptance, of Gladwell's theory of thin slices? Your project for this paper is to reconsider Gladwell's claim about thin-slicing in light of the observations made by Susan Blackmore, Paul Davies, Steven Johnson, Steven Pinker, Katha Pollitt, Lauren Slater, or Andrew Sullivan. What do these authors have to say about "what it means to be human"? Can they offer insight about when thin-slicing might *not* work? Use their ideas to test Gladwell's theory about our human tendency to thin-slice.

In the Forests of Gombe
Jane Goodall

Points of Access

1. How would you define the "natural world"? Do you think most people have a relationship to the natural world? Should they? Do you have such a relationship? Explain.

2. What does the word "sacred" mean to you? What in your life would you describe using that word or idea?

3. Have you ever struggled with the conflict between scientific ideas and religious belief? Discuss what prompted the conflict and how, or if, you tried to resolve it.

I was taught, as a scientist, to think logically and empirically, rather than intuitively or spiritually. When I was at Cambridge University in the early 1960s most of the scientists and science students working in the Department of Zoology, so far as I could tell, were agnostic or even atheist. Those who believed in a god kept it hidden from their peers.

Fortunately, by the time I got to Cambridge I was twenty-seven years old and my beliefs had already been molded so that I was not influenced by these opinions. I believed in the spiritual power that, as a Christian, I called God. But as I grew older and learned about different faiths I came to believe that there was, after all, but One God with different names: Allah, Tao, the Creator, and so on. God, for me, was the Great Spirit in Whom "we live and move and have our being." There have been times during my life when this belief wavered, when I questioned—even denied—the existence of God. At such times I felt there can be no underlying meaning to the emergence of life on earth.

Still, for me those periods have been relatively rare, triggered by a variety of circumstances. One was when my second husband died of cancer. I was grieving, suffering, and angry. Angry at God, at fate—the unjustness of it all. For a time I rejected God, and the world seemed a bleak place.

It was in the forests of Gombe that I sought healing after Derek's death. Gradually during my visits, my bruised and battered spirit found solace. In the forest, death is not hidden—or only accidentally, by the fallen leaves. It is all around you all the time, a part of the endless cycle of life. Chimpanzees are born, they grow older, they get sick, and they die. And always there are the young ones to carry on the life of the species. Time spent in the forest, following and watching and simply being with the chimpanzees, has always sustained the inner core of my being. And it did not fail me then.

One day, among all the days, I remember most of all. It was May 1981 and I had finally made it to Gombe after a six-week tour in America—six weeks of fund-raising dinners, conferences, meetings, and lobbying for various chimpanzee issues. I was exhausted and longed for the peace of the forest. I wanted nothing more than to be with the chimpanzees, renewing my acquaintance with my old friends, getting my climbing legs back again, relishing the sights, sounds, and smells of the forest. I was glad to be away from Dar es Salaam, with all its sad associations—the house that Derek and I had shared, the palm trees we had bought and planted together, the rooms we had lived in together, the Indian Ocean in which Derek, handicapped on land, had found freedom swimming among his beloved coral reefs.

Back in Gombe. It was early in the morning and I sat on the steps of my house by the lakeshore. It was very still. Suspended over the horizon, where the mountains of the Congo fringed Lake Tanganyika, was the last quarter of the waning moon and her path danced and sparkled toward me across the gently moving water. After enjoying a banana and a cup of coffee, I was off, climbing up the steep slopes behind my house.

In the faint light from the moon reflected by the dew-laden grass, it was not difficult to find my way up the mountain. It was quiet, utterly peaceful. Five minutes later I heard the rustling of leaves overhead. I looked up and saw the branches moving against the lightening sky. The chimps had awakened. It was Fifi and her offspring, Freud, Frodo, and little Fanni. I followed when they moved off up the slope, Fanni riding on her mother's back like a diminutive jockey. Presently they climbed into a tall fig tree and began to feed. I heard the occasional soft thuds as skins and seeds of figs fell to the ground.

For several hours we moved leisurely from one food tree to the next, gradually climbing higher and higher. On an open grassy ridge the chimps climbed into a massive mbula tree, where Fifi, replete from the morning's feasting, made a large comfortable nest high above me. She dozed through a midday siesta, little Fanni asleep in her arms, Frodo and Freud playing nearby. I felt very much in tune with the chimpanzees, for I was spending time with them not to observe, but simply because I needed their company, undemanding and free of pity. From where I sat I could look out over the Kasakela Valley. Just below me to the west was the peak. From that same vantage point I had learned so much in the early days, sitting and watching while, gradually, the chimpanzees had lost their fear of the strange white ape who had invaded their world. I recaptured some of my long-ago feelings—the excitement of discovering, of seeing things unknown to Western eyes, and the serenity that had come from living, day after day, as a part of the natural world. A world that dwarfs yet somehow enhances human emotions.

As I reflected on these things I had been only partly conscious of the approach of a storm. Suddenly, I realized that it was no longer growling in the distance but was right above. The sky was dark, almost black, and the rain clouds had obliterated the higher peaks. With the growing darkness came the stillness, the hush that so often precedes a tropical downpour. Only the rumbling of the thunder, moving closer and closer, broke this stillness; the thunder and the rustling movements of the chimpanzees. All at once came a blinding flash of lightning, followed, a split second later, by an incredibly loud clap of thunder that seemed almost to shake the solid rock before it rumbled on, bouncing from peak to peak. Then the dark and heavy clouds let loose such torrential rain that sky and earth seemed joined by moving water. I sat under a palm whose fronds, for a while, provided some shelter. Fifi sat hunched over, protecting her infant; Frodo pressed close against them in the nest; Freud sat with rounded back on a nearby branch. As the rain poured endlessly down, my palm fronds no longer provided shelter and I got wetter and wetter. I began to feel first chilly, and then, as a cold wind sprang up, freezing; soon, turned in on myself, I lost all track of time. I and the chimpanzees formed a unit of silent, patient, and uncomplaining endurance.

It must have been an hour or more before the rain began to ease as the heart of the storm swept away to the south. At four-thirty the chimps climbed down, and we moved off through the dripping vegetation, back down the mountainside. Presently we arrived on a grassy ridge overlooking the lake. I heard sounds of greeting as Fifi and her family joined Melissa and hers. They all climbed into a low tree to feed on fresh young leaves. I moved to a place where I could stand and watch as they enjoyed their last meal of the day. Down below, the lake was still dark and angry with white flecks where the waves broke, and rain clouds remained black in the south. To the north the sky was clear with only wisps of gray clouds still lingering. In the soft sunlight, the chimpanzees' black coats were shot with coppery brown, the branches on which they sat were wet and dark as ebony, the young leaves a pale but brilliant green. And behind was the backcloth of the indigo sky where lightning flickered and distant thunder growled and rumbled.

Lost in awe at the beauty around me, I must have slipped into a state of heightened awareness. It is hard—impossible, really—to put into words the moment of truth that suddenly came upon me then. It seemed to me, as I struggled afterward to recall the experience, that *self* was utterly absent: I and the chimpanzees, the earth and trees and air, seemed to merge, to become one with the spirit power of life itself. The air was filled with a feathered symphony, the evensong of birds. I heard new frequencies in their music and

also in the singing insects' voices—notes so high and sweet I was amazed. Never had I
been so intensely aware of the shape, the color of the individual leaves, the varied patterns
of the veins that made each one unique. Scents were clear as well, easily identifiable: fer-
menting overripe fruit; waterlogged earth; cold, wet bark; the damp odor of chimpanzee
hair and, yes, my own too. I sensed a new presence, then saw a bushbuck, quietly brows-
ing upwind, his spiraled horns gleaming and chestnut coat dark with rain.

Suddenly a distant chorus of pant-hoots elicited a reply from Fifi. As though wak-
ening from some vivid dream I was back in the everyday world, cold, yet intensely
alive. When the chimpanzees left, I stayed in that place—it seemed a most sacred
place—scribbling some notes, trying to describe what, so briefly, I had experienced.

Eventually I wandered back along the forest trail and scrambled down behind my
house to the beach. Later, as I sat by my little fire, cooking my dinner of beans, tomatoes
and an egg, I was still lost in the wonder of my experience. Yes, I thought, there are many
windows through which we humans, searching for meaning, can look out into the world
around us. There are those carved out by Western science, their panes polished by a succession of brilliant minds. Through them we can see ever farther, ever more clearly, into
areas which until recently were beyond human knowledge. Through such a scientific
window I had been taught to observe the chimpanzees. For more than twenty-five years I
had sought, through careful recording and critical analysis, to piece together their complex social behavior, to understand the workings of their minds. And this had not only
helped us to better understand their place in nature but also helped us to understand a little
better some aspects of our own human behavior, our own place in the natural world.

Yet there are other windows through which we humans can look out into the world
around us, windows through which the mystics and the holy men of the East, and the
founders of the great world religions, have gazed as they searched for the meaning and
purpose of our life on earth, not only in the wondrous beauty of the world, but also in
its darkness and ugliness. And those Masters contemplated the truths that they saw, not
with their minds only but with their hearts and souls also. From those revelations came
the spiritual essence of the great scriptures, the holy books, and the most beautiful mys-
tic poems and writings. That afternoon it had been as though an unseen hand had drawn
back a curtain and, for the briefest moment, I had seen through such a window.

*   *   *

How sad that so many people seem to think that science and religion are mutually exclusive. Science has used modern technology and modern techniques to uncover so much
about the formation and the development of life-forms on Planet Earth and about the solar

system of which our little world is but a minute part. Alas, all of these amazing discoveries have led to a belief that every wonder of the natural world and of the universe—indeed, of infinity and time—can, in the end, be understood through the logic and the reasoning of a finite mind. And so, for many, science has taken the place of religion. It was not some intangible God who created the universe, they argue, it was the Big Bang. Physics, chemistry, and evolutionary biology can explain the start of the universe and the appearance and progress of life on earth, they say. To believe in God, in the human soul, and in life after death is simply a desperate and foolish attempt to give meaning to our lives.

But not all scientists believe thus. There are quantum physicists who have concluded that the concept of God is not, after all, merely wishful thinking. There are those exploring the human brain who feel that no matter how much they discover about this extraordinary structure it will never add up to a complete understanding of the human mind—that the whole is, after all, greater than the sum of its parts. The Big Bang theory is yet another example of the incredible, the awe-inspiring ability of the human mind to learn about seemingly unknowable phenomena in the beginning of time. Time as we know it, or think we know it. But what about before time? And what about beyond space? I remember so well how those questions had driven me to distraction when I was a child.

I lay flat on my back and looked up into the darkening sky. I thought about the young man I had met during the six-week tour I had finished before my return to Gombe. He had a holiday job working as a bellhop in the big hotel where I was staying in Dallas, Texas. It was prom night, and I wandered down to watch the young girls in their beautiful evening gowns, their escorts elegant in their tuxedos. As I stood there, thinking about the future—theirs, mine, the world's—I heard a diffident voice:

"Excuse me, Doctor—aren't you Jane Goodall?" The bellhop was very young, very fresh-faced. But he looked worried—partly because he felt that he should not be disturbing me, but partly, it transpired, because his mind was indeed troubled. He had a question to ask me. So we went and sat on some back stairs, away from the glittering groups and hand-holding couples.

He had watched all my documentaries, read my books. He was fascinated, and he thought that what I did was great. But I talked about evolution. Did I believe in God? If so, how did that square with evolution? Had we really descended from chimpanzees?

And so I tried to answer him as truthfully as I could, to explain my own beliefs. I told him that no one thought humans had descended from chimpanzees. I explained that I did believe in Darwinian evolution and told him of my time at Olduvai, when I had held the remains of extinct creatures in my hands. That I had traced, in the museum, the various stages of the evolution of, say, a horse: from a rabbit-sized creature that gradually, over thousands of years, changed, became better and better adapted to its environment and eventually was transformed into the modern horse. I told him I believed that millions of years ago there had been a primitive, apelike, humanlike creature, one branch of which had gone on to become the chimpanzee, another branch of which had eventually led to us.

"But that doesn't mean I don't believe in God," I said. And I told him something of my beliefs, and those of my family. I told him that I had always thought that the biblical description of God creating the world in seven days might well have been an attempt to explain evolution in a parable. In that case, each of the days would have been several million years.

"And then, perhaps, God saw that a living being had evolved that was suitable for His purpose. *Homo sapiens* had the brain, the mind, the potential. Perhaps," I said, "that was when God breathed the Spirit into the first Man and the first Woman and filled them with the Holy Ghost."

The bellhop was looking considerably less worried. "Yes, I see," he said. "That could be right. That does seem to make sense."

I ended by telling him that it honestly didn't matter how we humans got to be the way we are, whether evolution or special creation was responsible. What mattered and mattered desperately was our future development. How should the mind that can contemplate God relate to our fellow beings, the other life-forms of the world? What is our human responsibility? And what, ultimately, is our human destiny? Were we going to go on destroying God's creation, fighting each other, hurting the other creatures of His planet? Or were we going to find ways to live in greater harmony with each other and with the natural world? That, I told him, was what was important. Not only for the future of the human species, but also for him, personally. When we finally parted his eyes were clear and untroubled, and he was smiling.

* * *

Thinking about that brief encounter, I smiled too, there on the beach at Gombe. A wind sprang up and it grew chilly. I left the bright stars and went inside to bed. I knew that while I would always grieve Derek's passing, I could cope with my grieving. That afternoon, in a flash of "outsight" I had known timelessness and quiet ecstasy, sensed a truth of which mainstream science is merely a small fraction. And I knew that the revelation would be with me for the rest of my life, imperfectly remembered yet always within. A source of strength on which I could draw when life seemed harsh or cruel or desperate. The forest, and the spiritual power that was so real in it, had given me the "peace that passeth understanding."

Reading Comprehension—Points of Engagement

1. Why did Jane Goodall go to the forest? How would you describe her relationship with the chimpanzees? Refer to two passages from her essay in your answers.

2. How does Goodall describe her moment of truth on page 111? What do you think she means when she says, "*self* was utterly absent"?

3. Why does Goodall tell us about her encounter with the bellhop? What questions do they discuss? What are Goodall's answers? Do you find them persuasive? Why or why not?

Assignment Questions—Points of Departure

1. Goodall writes, "There are many windows through which we humans, searching for meaning, can look out into the world around us?" (112). What are the different windows she is referring to? Consider another text written by a scientist, such as Paul Davies, Susan Blackmore, or Barbara Kingsolver, and use it to reconsider this idea of different windows. Which windows are these authors using? What can you learn about Goodall's idea by examining the ways other scientists view their work and the world?

2. Goodall tells the bellhop that she believes in both Darwinian evolution and God, two ideas that are often understood in opposition, or conflict, with each other. Consider first how Goodall reconciles these two disparate beliefs, then how another author, such as Lisa Belkin, Paul Davies, Fenton Johnson, Katha Pollitt, Lauren Slater, or Andrew Sullivan addresses conflicting ideals. How do these other authors present conflict differently from Goodall? What do you learn about the process of analyzing ideas that complicate one another?

3. Goodall asks how we are "going to find ways to live in greater harmony with ourselves and the natural world" (114). Explore the possibility of achieving Goodall's notion of harmony, using another author who addresses the relationship between humanity and nature, such as Barbara Kingsolver, Alain de Botton, Michael Pollan, David Brooks, or Andrew Sullivan.

Bumping Into Mr. Ravioli
Adam Gopnik

My daughter, Olivia, who just turned three, has an imaginary friend whose name is Charlie Ravioli. Olivia is growing up in Manhattan, and so Charlie Ravioli has a lot of local traits: he lives in an apartment "on Madison and Lexington," he dines on grilled chicken, fruit, and water, and, having reached the age of seven and a half, he feels, or is thought, "old." But the most peculiarly local thing about Olivia's imaginary playmate is this: he is always too busy to play with her. She holds her toy cell phone up to her ear, and we hear her talk into it: "Ravioli? It's Olivia . . . It's Olivia. Come and play? OK. Call me. Bye." Then she snaps it shut and shakes her head. "I always get his machine," she says. Or she will say, "I spoke to Ravioli today." "Did you have fun?" my wife and I ask. "No. He was busy working. On a television," (leaving it up in the air if he repairs electronic devices or has his own talk show).

On a good day, she "bumps into" her invisible friend and they go to a coffee shop. "I bumped into Charlie Ravioli," she announces at dinner (after a day when, of course, she stayed home, played, had a nap, had lunch, paid a visit to the Central Park Zoo, and then had another nap). "We had coffee, but then he had to run." She sighs, sometimes, at her inability to make their schedules mesh, but she accepts it as inevitable, just the way life is. "I bumped into Charlie Ravioli today," she says. "He was working." Then she adds brightly, "But we hopped into a taxi." What happened then? we ask. "We grabbed lunch," she says.

It seemed obvious that Ravioli was a romantic figure of the big exotic life that went on outside her little limited life of parks and playgrounds—drawn, in particular, from a nearly perfect, mynah bird—like imitation of the words she hears her mother use when she talks about *her* day with *her* friends. ("How was your day?" Sighing: "Oh, you know. I tried to make a date with Meg, but I couldn't find her, so I left a message on her machine. Then I bumped into Emily after that meeting I had in SoHo, and we had coffee and then she had to run, but by then Meg had reached me on my cell and we arranged . . .") I was concerned, though, that Charlie Ravioli might also be the sign of some "trauma," some loneliness in Olivia's life reflected in imaginary form. "It seems odd to have an imaginary playmate who's always too busy to play with you," Martha, my wife, said to me. "Shouldn't your imaginary playmate be someone you tell secrets to and, I don't know, sing songs with? It shouldn't be someone who's always *hopping* into taxis."

We thought, at first, that her older brother, Luke, might be the original of Charlie Ravioli. (For one thing, he is also seven and a half, though we were fairly sure that this age was merely Olivia's marker for As Old as Man Can Be.) He is too busy to play with her much anymore. He has become a true New York child, with the schedule of a cabinet secretary: chess club on Monday, T-ball on Tuesday, tournament on Saturday, play dates and after-school conferences to fill in the gaps. But Olivia, though she counts days, does not yet really have days. She has *a* day, and into this day she has introduced the figure of Charlie Ravioli—in order, it dawned on us, to insist that she does have days, because she is too harried to share them, that she does have an independent social life, by virtue of being too busy to have one.

Yet Charlie Ravioli was becoming so constant and oddly discouraging a companion—"He canceled lunch. Again," Olivia would say—that we thought we ought to look into it. One of my sisters is a developmental psychologist who specializes in close scientific studies of what goes on inside the heads of one- and two- and three-year-olds. Though she grew up in the nervy East, she lives in California now, where she grows basil in her garden and jars her own organic marmalades. I e-mailed this sister for help with the Ravioli issue—how concerned should we be?—and she sent me back an e-mail, along with an attachment, and, after several failed cell-phone connections, we at last spoke on a land line.

It turned out that there is a recent book on this very subject by the psychologist Marjorie Taylor, called *Imaginary Companions and the Children Who Create Them,* and my sister had just written a review of it. She insisted that Charlie Ravioli was nothing to be worried about. Olivia was right on target, in fact. Most under-sevens (sixty-three percent, to be scientific) have an invisible friend, and children create their imaginary playmates not out of trauma but out of a serene sense of the possibilities of fiction—sometimes as figures of pure fantasy, sometimes, as Olivia had done, as observations of grown-up manners, assembled in tranquillity and given a name. I learned about the invisible companions Taylor studied: Baintor, who is invisible because he lives in the light; Station Pheta, who hunts sea anemones on the beach. Charlie Ravioli seemed pavement-bound by comparison.

"An imaginary playmate isn't any kind of trauma marker," my sister said. "It's just the opposite: it's a sign that the child is now confident enough to begin to understand how to organize her experience into stories." The significant thing about imaginary friends, she went on, is that the kids know they're fictional. In an instant message on AOL, she summed it up: "The children with invisible friends often interrupted the interviewer to remind her, with a certain note of concern for her sanity, that these characters were, after all, just pretend."

I also learned that some children, as they get older, turn out to possess what child psychologists call a "paracosm." A paracosm is a society thought up by a child—an invented universe with a distinctive language, geography, and history. (The Brontës invented a couple of paracosms when they were children.) Not all children who have an imaginary friend invent a paracosm, but the two might, I think, be related. Like a lonely ambassador from Alpha Centauri in a fifties sci-fi movie who, misunderstood by paranoid Earth scientists, cannot bring the life-saving news from his planet, perhaps the invisible friend also gets an indifferent or hostile response, and then we never find out about the beautiful paracosm he comes from.

"Don't worry about it," my sister said in a late-night phone call. "Knowing something's made up while thinking that it matters is what all fiction insists on. She's putting a name on a series of manners."

"But he seems so real to her," I objected.

"Of course he is. I mean, who's more real to you, Becky Sharp or Gandalf or the guy down the hall? Giving a manner a name makes it real."

I paused. "I grasp that it's normal for her to have an imaginary friend." I said, "but have you ever heard of an imaginary friend who's too busy to play with you?"

She thought about it "No," she said. "I'm sure that doesn't occur anywhere in the research literature. That sounds *completely* New York." And then she hung up.

* * *

The real question, I saw, was not "Why this friend?" but "Why this fiction?" Why, as Olivia had seen so clearly, are grownups in New York so busy, and so obsessed with the language of busyness that it dominates their conversation? Why are New Yorkers always bumping into Charlie Ravioli and grabbing lunch, instead of sitting down with him and exchanging intimacies, as friends should, as people do in Paris and Rome? Why is busyness the stuff our children make their invisible friends from, as country children make theirs from light and sand?

This seems like an odd question. New Yorkers are busy for obvious reasons: they have husbands and wives and careers and children, they have the Gauguin show to see and their personal trainers and accountants to visit. But the more I think about this, the more I think it is—well, a lot of Ravioli. We are instructed to believe that we are busier because we have to work harder to be more productive, but everybody knows that busyness and productivity have a dubious, arm's-length relationship. Most of our struggle in New York, in fact, is to be less busy in order to do more work.

Constant, exhausting, no-time-to meet-your-friends Charlie Ravioli-style busyness arrived as an affliction in modern life long after the other parts of bourgeois city manners did. Business long predates busyness. In the seventeenth and eighteenth centuries, when bourgeois people were building the institutions of bourgeois life, they seem never to have complained that they were too busy—or, if they did, they left no record of it. Samuel Pepys, who had a navy to refloat and a burned London to rebuild, often uses the word "busy" but never complains of busyness. For him, the word "busy" is a synonym for "happy," not for "stressed." Not once in his diary does Pepys cancel lunch or struggle to fit someone in for coffee at four-thirty. Pepys works, makes love, and goes to bed, but he does not bump and he does not have to run. Ben Franklin, a half century later, boasts of his industriousness, but he, too, never complains about being busy, and always has time to publish a newspaper or come up with a maxim or swim the ocean or invent the lightning rod.

Until sometime in the middle of the nineteenth century, in fact, the normal affliction of the bourgeois was not busyness at all but its apparent opposite: boredom. It has even been argued that the grid of streets and cafés and small engagements in the nineteenth-century city—the whole of social life—was designed self-consciously as an escape from that numbing boredom. (Working people weren't bored, of course, but they were engaged in labor, not work. They were too busy to be busy.) Baudelaire, basically, was so bored that he had to get drunk and run out onto the boulevard in the hope of bumping into somebody.

Turn to the last third of the nineteenth century and the beginning of the twentieth, though, and suddenly everybody is busy, and everybody is complaining about it. Pepys, master of His Majesty's Navy, may never have complained of busyness, but Virginia

Woolf, mistress of motionless lull, is continually complaining about how she spends her days racing across London from square to square, just like—well, like Charlie Ravioli. Ronald Firbank is wrung out by his social obligations; Proust is constantly rescheduling rendezvous and apologizing for being overstretched. Henry James, with nothing particular to do save live, complains of being too busy all the time. He could not shake the world of obligation, he said, and he wrote a strange and beautiful story, "The Great Good Place," which begins with an exhausting flood of correspondence, telegrams, and manuscripts that drive the protagonist nearly mad.

What changed? That James story helps supply the key. It was trains and telegrams. The railroads ended isolation, and packed the metropolis with people whose work was defined by a complicated network of social obligations. Pepys's network in 1669 London was, despite his official position, relatively small compared even with that of a minor aesthete like Firbank, two centuries later. Pepys had more time to make love because he had fewer friends to answer.

If the train crowded our streets, the telegram crowded our minds. It introduced something into the world which remains with us today: a whole new class of communications that are defined as incomplete in advance of their delivery. A letter, though it may enjoin a response, is meant to be complete in itself. Neither the Apostle Paul nor Horace Walpole ever ends an epistle with "Give me a call and let's discuss." By contrast, it is in the nature of the telegram to be a skeletal version of another thing—a communication that opens more than it closes. The nineteenth-century telegram came with those busy threatening words "Letter follows."

Every device that has evolved from the telegram shares the same character. E-mails end with a suggestion for a phone call ("Anyway, let's meet and/or talk soon"), faxes with a request for an e-mail, answering-machine messages with a request for a fax. All are devices of perpetually suspended communication. My wife recalls a moment last fall when she got a telephone message from a friend asking her to check her e-mail apropos a phone call she needed to make vis-a-vis a fax they had both received asking for more information about a bed they were thinking of buying from Ireland online and having sent to America by Federal Express—a grand slam of incomplete communication.

In most of the Western world outside New York, the press of trains and of telegraphic communication was alleviated by those other two great transformers: the car and the television. While the train and the telegram (and their love children, subways and commuter trains and e-mail) pushed people together, the car and the television pulled people apart—taking them out to the suburbs and sitting them down in front of a solo spectacle. New York, though, almost uniquely, got hit by a double dose of the first two technologies, and a very limited dose of the second two. Car life—car obsessions, car-defined habits—is more absent here than almost anywhere else in the country, while television, though obviously present, is less fatally prevalent here. New York is still a subject of television, and we compare *Sex and the City* to sex and the city; they are not yet quite the same. Here two grids of business remain dominant: the nineteenth- and early-twentieth-century grid of bump and run, and the late-twentieth- and early-twenty-first-century postmodern grid of virtual call and echo. Busyness is felt so intently here because we are both crowded and overloaded. We exit the apartment into a still dense nineteenth-century grid of street corners and restaurants full of people, and come home to the late-twentieth-century grid of faxes and e-mails and overwhelming incompleteness.

We walk across the Park on a Sunday morning and bump into our friend the baker and our old acquaintance from graduate school (what the hell is she doing now?) and someone we have been avoiding for three weeks. They all invite us for brunch, and we would love to, but we are too . . . busy. We bump into Charlie Ravioli, and grab a coffee with him—and come home to find three e-mails and a message on our cell phone from him, wondering where we are. The crowding of our space has been reinforced by a crowding of our time, and the only way to protect ourselves is to build structures of perpetual deferral: I'll see you next week, let's talk soon. We build rhetorical baffles around our lives to keep the crowding out, only to find that we have let nobody we love in.

Like Charlie Ravioli, we hop into taxis and leave messages on answering machines to avoid our acquaintances, and find that we keep missing our friends. I have one intimate who lives just across the Park from me, whom I e-mail often, and whom I am fortunate to see two or three times a year. We are always . . . busy. He has become my Charlie Ravioli, my invisible friend. I am sure that he misses me—just as Charlie Ravioli, I realized, must tell his other friends that he is sorry he does not see Olivia more often.

*   *   *

Once I sensed the nature of his predicament, I began to feel more sympathetic toward Charlie Ravioli. I got to know him better, too. We learned more about what Ravioli did in the brief breathing spaces in his busy life when he could sit down with Olivia and dish. "Ravioli read your book," Olivia announced, for instance, one night at dinner. "He didn't like it much." We also found out that Ravioli had joined a gym, that he was going to the beach in the summer, but he was too busy, and that he was working on a "show." ("It isn't a very good show," she added candidly.) Charlie Ravioli, in other words, was just another New Yorker: fit, opinionated, and trying to break into show business.

I think we would have learned to live happily with Charlie Ravioli had it not been for the appearance of Laurie. She threw us badly. At dinner, Olivia had been mentioning a new personage almost as often as she mentioned Ravioli. "I talked to Laurie today," she would begin. "She says Ravioli is busy." Or she would be closeted with her play phone. "Who are you talking to, darling?" I would ask. "Laurie," she would say. "We're talking about Ravioli." We surmised that Laurie was, so to speak, the Linda Tripp of the Ravioli operation—the person you spoke to for consolation when the big creep was ignoring you.

But a little while later a more ominous side of Laurie's role began to appear. "Laurie, tell Ravioli I'm calling," I heard Olivia say. I pressed her about who, exactly, Laurie was. Olivia shook her head. "She works for Ravioli," she said.

And then it came to us, with sickening clarity: Laurie was not the patient friend who consoled you for Charlie's absence. Laurie was the bright-toned person who answered Ravioli's phone and told you that unfortunately Mr. Ravioli was in a meeting. "Laurie says Ravioli is too busy to play," Olivia announced sadly one morning. Things seemed to be deteriorating; now Ravioli was too busy even to say he was too busy.

I got back on the phone with my sister. "Have you ever heard of an imaginary friend with an assistant?" I asked.

She paused. "Imaginary friends don't have assistants," she said. "That's not only not in the literature. That's just . . . I mean—in California they don't have assistants."

"You think we should look into it?"

"I think you should move," she said flatly.

Martha was of the same mind. "An imaginary playmate shouldn't have an assistant," she said miserably. "An imaginary playmate shouldn't have an agent. An imaginary playmate shouldn't have a publicist or a personal trainer or a caterer—an imaginary playmate shouldn't have . . . *people.* An imaginary playmate should just *play.* With the child who imagined it." She started leaving on my pillow real-estate brochures picturing quaint houses in New Jersey and Connecticut, unhaunted by busy invisible friends and their entourages.

*   *   *

Not long after the appearance of Laurie, though, something remarkable happened. Olivia would begin to tell us tales of her frustrations with Charlie Ravioli, and, after telling us, again, that he was too busy to play, she would tell us what she had done instead. Astounding and paracosmic tall tales poured out of her: she had been to a chess tournament and brought home a trophy; she had gone to a circus and told jokes. Searching for Charlie Ravioli, she had "saved all the animals in the zoo"; heading home in a taxi after a quick coffee with Ravioli, she took over the steering wheel and "got all the moneys." From the stalemate of daily life emerged the fantasy of victory. She had dreamed of a normal life with a few close friends, and had to settle for world-wide fame and the front page of the tabloids. The existence of an imaginary friend had liberated her into a paracosm, but it was a curiously New York paracosm—it was the unobtainable world outside her window. Charlie Ravioli, prince of busyness, was not an end but a means: a way out onto the street in her head, a declaration of potential independence.

Busyness is our art form, our civic ritual, our way of being us. Many friends have said to me that they love New York now in a way they never did before, and their love, I've noticed, takes for its object all the things that used to exasperate them—the curious combination of freedom, self-made fences, and paralyzing preoccupation that the city provides. "How did you spend the day?" Martha and I now ask each other, and then, instead of listing her incidents, she says merely, "Oh, you know . . . just . . . bumping into Charlie Ravioli," meaning, just bouncing from obligation to electronic entreaty, just spotting a friend and snatching a sandwich, just being busy, just living in New York. If everything we've learned in the past year could be summed up in a phrase, it's that we want to go on bumping into Charlie Ravioli for as long as we can.

Olivia still hopes to have him to herself someday. As I work late at night in the "study" (an old hallway, an Aalto screen) I keep near the "nursery" (an ancient pantry, a glass-brick wall), I can hear her shift into pre-sleep, still muttering to herself. She is still trying to reach her closest friend. "Ravioli? Ravioli?" she moans as she turns over into her pillow and clutches her blanket, and then she whispers, almost to herself, "Tell him call me. Tell him call me when he comes home."

Reading Comprehension—Points of Engagement

1. On page 119 Adam Gopnik describes talking with his sister on the phone about his daughter's too-busy imaginary friend. Gopnik's sister responds, "That sounds completely New York." What does she mean? Point to specific passages in Gopnik's essay that help you answer.

2. What does Gopnik mean when he refers to "perpetually suspended communication" (121)? What are the two "grids of busyness [that] remain dominant" in New York? Why are they important to Gopnik?

3. What is a "paracosm"? Describe it in your own words and using quotations from Gopnik's essay. How does this idea help explain Olivia's invention of Mr. Ravioli? How does it help Gopnik to understand his daughter?

4. Why does Gopnik write, "We want to go on bumping into Mr. Ravioli as long as we can" (124)? What kind of human longing is he describing? Do you think it's a healthy or unhealthy longing? Why?

Assignment Questions—Points of Departure

1. What does Adam Gopnik learn about himself and fellow New Yorkers by observing his 3-year-old daughter so closely? Think about how his perspective changes when viewing his own New York experience through the eyes of his child. Then consider the following question: What can we learn about the world and ourselves by considering both through someone else's eyes? Your project for this paper is to answer this question using Gopnik and insights from essays by Paul Davies, Malcolm Gladwell, Jane Goodall, Lenore Look, V.S. Naipaul, or Michael Pollan.

2. Mr. Ravioli may be an imaginary friend created by his daughter Olivia, but Adam Gopnik recognizes him in the adult world of New York. What is the relationship between daily life and our imaginations? Does the world around us limit our imaginations, or does the world around us show us the expansiveness of our imaginations? How and in what ways? Your project for this paper is to answer these questions using Gopnik and one of the following authors: Susan Blackmore, Alain de Botton, David Brooks, Paul Davies, Jane Goodall, Jack Hitt, Fenton Johnson, Steven Pinker, Francine Prose, Lauren Slater, or Jeanette Winterson.

3. Adam Gopnik's essay "Bumping Into Mr. Ravioli" provides a look at a specific modern American lifestyle, the life of the New Yorker. Does the essay reveal anything broader about contemporary American ideals, values, or interests? Consider the kinds of lifestyles described in essays by David Brooks, Jack Hitt, Arlie Russell Hochschild, Francine Prose, Alain de Botton, Jeanette Winterson, or John Waterbury. Use Gopnik and one of these texts to explore this notion of contemporary American values—what they are, where they come from, where they take us, how they are perceived—and most importantly, whether they are exclusively "American." Keep in

mind that Gopnik is writing specifically about New York City. Also keep in mind that Alain de Botton and Jeanette Winterson are describing English culture, and John Waterbury is describing how American culture intersects with Middle Eastern culture through education.

4. Adam Gopnik refers to the "grid[s] of busyness" that help shape life in New York City. Alain de Botton, in "On Habit," refers to the "grid of interests" he has imposed on his local street. Draw on both pieces to discuss these ideas. How do these kinds of grids work? Are they a part of our environment, or a product of thought or perception? Are they fundamentally positive, negative, or benign? Could we use this concept to change the way we live? How?

Dinosaur Dreams
Reading the bones of America's psychic mascot
Jack Hitt

Points of Access

1. When you go to a natural history museum, where are the dinosaurs located? How are they displayed? Describe them. Which dinosaurs get the most prominent placement? Why do you think museums display certain dinosaurs in some ways, and not others? What do these displays reveal about the museum curators? What do they reveal about the museum visitors?

2. Did you ever have a 'dinosaur phase' when growing up? If so, why did you find them so fascinating or intriguing? Which dinosaurs were your favorites? Why? Write as much as you can remember about when and why you were attracted to dinosaurs, and when and why you stopped being so interested in them. If you never went through a dinosaur phase as a kid, go to *Points of Access* question #4.

3. Have you seen any of the Jurassic Park movies? If so, what do you make of the dinosaurs in these movies? Do they seem realistic? Do they seem like pure entertainment? Somewhere in between real and imaginary? What's the difference between going to a natural history museum to learn about dinosaurs and watching one of these movies? Is there a difference? Why or why not? If you've never seen a Jurassic Park movie, go to *Points of Access* question #4.

4. What is paleontology? If you don't know, look it up in a college dictionary or online and provide a definition for it *in your own words*. What is popular culture? If you can't find it in a dictionary, hazard a definition of your own. Give a few examples of what you think of as popular culture. Do you see any connections between paleontology and popular culture? Why or why not? Try to write a full paragraph response. If you see no connections at all, then write about how paleontology and popular culture are different. You may make lists.

Sixty-five million years ago, conservatively speaking, the last dinosaurs lay down and died—on the ground, beside rivers, in tar pits. Then, about a hundred years ago, they got back up and have been pretty busy ever since. Hardly a week goes by that they don't make the news, because of a new theory about either how they lived or how they died. There might be word of a new prime-time TV deal, another revelry (Dinofest V is planned for next year), a new exhibit, the goings-on of paleontological hunk Paul Sereno, a Spielberg script, a hot toy, a legal dispute about some bones, an egg.

In America, where dinosaurs do most of their work (and always have), they periodically disappear from view and then resurface, like John Travolta or Democrats, capturing and losing our cycling interest. Dinosaurs are distinctly American, not only because our scholars have so often been at the forefront of fossil discoveries and paleontological theory but because the popular dinosaur is a wholly owned projection of the nationalist psyche of the United States. Their periodic rebirth in pop culture neatly signals deep tectonic shifts in our sense of ourself as a country. Even glancing appearances can be telling. After Newt Gingrich rampaged through the House of Representatives and seized power in 1994, he placed a skull of T. rex in his office. When the current resident of the White House got a new dog, he called him, strangely, "Barney"—a name most closely associated with a phony dinosaur who masks his cheerful dimness with sticky compassion.

It's been almost exactly a century since the first one stood up in New York City amid a Miramaxian media circus, and, bookending nicely, we seem to be in the clutches of another rage. One recent estimate asserts that there are probably more dinosaurs on the earth now than there were in the Mesozoic Era. The current rate of finding new species is one every seven weeks. Half of all the known dinosaurs have been discovered in the last few decades. What really marks our era are the new tools—amino-acid mapping, the CAT scan, treadmill-energetics studies—that permit us once again to read meaning in the bones and to imagine the world that was when they held up flesh.

Determining the causes of America's periodic obsession with dinosaurs is tricky. They have done a lot of heavy lifting, culturewise. Besides in children's narratives (where dinosaurs still rule the world), they have served as political totems, deranged kitsch, icons of domesticated terror, cultural mules for Darwin's (still) troubling theory, and environmental Cassandras resurrected to act out her famous final words, "I will endure to die."

In the pop-culture chaos that is uniquely our own and that swirls around paleontology's quiet drudgery, certain dinosaurs burble up to the top of our celebrity-oriented mass-media-marketplace mosh pit to float about in plain view, gazed upon by everyone. And we the people elevate them out of that frenzy as surely and by the same circuitously collective route as we do Ricky Martin, Stone Phillips, Cameron Diaz, or

Tom Wolfe. Going in and out of fashion, these giants are creations of our own making as much as the paleontologists', perhaps more so. In demanding to see them, we sculpt their meaning; like outsized Schrödinger's cats, their existence depends on whether or not we have decided to look at them.

None of these gargantuans has been more gawked at than *Tyrannosaurus rex,* the Mick Jagger of dinosaurs. And yet he's been absent on the national stage lately (as if he were off in rehab plotting his comeback tour), and there's a reason. Controversial scholarship has turned up a new interpretation of how the great meat-eater lived, and it is so at odds with T. rex's public persona that even scholars hate to talk about him anymore. In a sense, the scientific reality of the King of the Tyrant Lizards has laid bare our symbolic uses of him. So T. is in hiding.

Developed by the self-credentialed iconoclast Jack Horner, the theory holds that T. was not the great predator who marauded through primordial landscapes but rather a slow, putzy scavenger that poked around the Cretaceous countryside in search of maggoty carrion.

Horner can mount a great deal of technical evidence to prove that T. was no hunter, and I have seen him turn an audience completely around in an hour. T. had densely muscled legs with calves the length of his thighs, which are good for walking but lousy for pouncing. T. had poor eyesight, not a great trait, since hunters typically track prey at twilight. CAT scans of T.'s skulls have revealed massively dominant olfactories; he could smell from as far away as fifty to seventy miles, a handy adaptation if the meat you're looking for is malodorously ripe.

Famous predators, like lions or velociraptors, have powerful forearms to catch their lunch or to hold their prey while they rip fresh muscle from the bone with their backlegs. T.'s arms were thalidomidal, about as helpful as having two fussy little hands growing out of your nipples. "T. rex couldn't even clap," Horner points out.

T. didn't walk the way every comic book and *National Geographic* magazine used to show—upright, head raised, front claws poised—rampant, as heraldic buffs say. None of the preserved trackways showing the footprints of theropods (T.'s family) have an impression of a dragging tail between them. Rather T. probably waddled, like the ten-ton vulture he was, tail straight out, body parallel to the ground like a . . . I believe the heraldic term is wuss.

Horner has nothing but critics, and they resist his logic with the willful stubbornness of biblical creationists weighing the merits of evolutionary theory. They will admit that T. ambulated like a monstrous sandpiper, but they insist he was still a predator, dammit. Even though many museums have reset T. in his new posture, they typically turn the head and open the jaws, as if he were just glancing at you while racing by en route to some old-fashioned predatory mayhem.[1] Unlike Cretaceous Era dinosaurs, twentieth-century ones do not die easily.

If you ask Horner why early curators first set T. in a predator's stance, he'll tell you it was because the "ceilings in museums were too high and they had to fill the space." To prove his point, he'll betray an embarrassing secret: the early curators had to smash and whittle T. rex's bones and then remove vertebrae to assemble him into that fighting posture. "There was more Barnum than science in those earliest displays," Horner says. "The curators realized it was a spectacle for the nation, and that's why T. rex looked the way he did. It was what the country wanted to see."

* * *

Dinosaurs had been discovered long before modern America took up the cause, but they were easily incorporated into nearby myth. Native Americans assumed the large bones belonged to the "father of buffaloes." In England a 1677 discovery was identified as a "human thigh bone of one of the giants mentioned in the Bible." A fossilized track-way in Connecticut of a giant three-toed creature had long been thought by locals to be that of the avian god Thunderbird until more advanced colonials corrected them to understand that it was the footprint of the "raven of Noah."

It was an English scientist who first announced in 1841 that these giant bone discoveries belonged to some new order of creature he decided to call "dinosauria." And the first full dinosaur, the iguanodon, was an entirely British discovery. But those early dinosaurs say more about the Old World's pinched imagination than about its paleontology. Iguanodon refers to a reptile's tooth, and the image the English conjured from those bones was nothing more than an obese crocodile on four piano legs. Such are the rhinocerine quadrupeds that populate the first dino narrative, Sir Arthur Conan Doyle's *The Lost World.* Until Darwin, one wasn't able, intellectually, to describe a world that didn't already exist. The geological *Weltanschauung* was biblical and stagnant, yet almost immediately it was clear that we had discovered a potent new metaphor.

---

1. In Tim Haines's best-selling book, *Walking with Dinosaurs,* the author tries his hand at sustaining T.'s ebbing machismo by using a tactic of contemporary memoir publishing, the sexually explicit detail. In Haines's imagination, here are two T.s doing the nasty: "She raises her tail and he approaches quickly from behind. When he attempts to mount her, he uses his tiny forelimbs to steady himself by hooking into the thick hide of her back. The coupling is brief, but it is the first of many. . . . By staying close, he . . . increases his chances of fertilizing her by mating repeatedly. . . ." That's our boy.

The first big show of dinosaurs opened in England in 1854. To inaugurate the spectacle, the officials risibly set the dinner table inside the reconstructed body of an iguanodon. Later a famous French feast to celebrate the arrival of an American dinosaur included "*hors d'oeuvres paleontologiques*" and "*potage bisque aux Eryon jurassiclues.*" We eat dinosaurs and they eat us. We partake of their dinosaurness, they partake of our humanness. From the beginning there was a commingling, something vaguely divine. As with Christian communion, we acknowledged our desire to become them by dining on them while being consumed by them. Theophagy is not a notion that casually erupts in a culture, even kitschily.

Yet the full promise of those early dinosaurs would require New World vision. In 1858 a professor of anatomy at the University of Pennsylvania named Joseph Leidy examined an early hadrosaurus discovered in New Jersey and came to the revolutionary insight that this monster didn't tread the ground like some brute from the bestiary but stood up. Leidy was an early pioneer of the new American field "natural history"— the very phrase overturning the biblical view of the earth as static with a rather New World ideal of looking at nature as an unfolding story, a "history."

Dinomania's great awakening came at the end of the nineteenth century, and it ultimately took the form of a competition—the Bone Wars—between Professor O.C. Marsh of Yale and Edward Cope of the Philadelphia Academy of Natural Sciences. They competed in getting bigger grants to mount large-scale expeditions to increasingly more remote outbacks—in order to bribe locals and hire minions (and eventually spies) to find ever bigger bones and inscribe more and more names in the permanent book of Latinate taxonyms.

These two created an inner tension in paleontology that continues today. Marsh was an establishment figure who easily ascended into the aerie of academe by becoming a professor at Yale. (His rich uncle George Peabody donated the nest egg for the New Haven museum that still carries his name and houses many of the most famous dinosaur skeletons.) Cope, on the other hand, was a self-educated man who bankrupted himself to finance his excursions. A volatile, excitable, roaming character, Cope was never comfortable with the institutional positions offered him. In the end, his suspicions of the highly connected world in which Marsh thrived drove him to James Gordon Bennett's *New York Herald,* where he initiated one of the most vicious personal attacks in history. He accused Marsh of destroying bones in order to shore up his reputation, of plagiarizing Cope's intellectual work, and of stealing and lying.

It may almost be slapstick legend at this point, but the feud was said to have begun early on in their careers when Marsh publicly noted that Cope had placed the head of a plesiosaur on—is there any nice way to tell somebody this?—the wrong end. (Given the contingent and fragmentary nature of the field, getting the bones wrong is naturally a frequent charge and almost always correct.) From that time on, dinosaurology has been populated by both Marshite establishmentarians, who strain to lend the discipline the donnish solemnity of the Old World trivium, and Copean renegades, who invigorate it with the improvisational air of the American hobbyist.

Today's Marshites are institutionalists like John Ostrom of Yale or even general paleontologists such as Stephen Jay Gould of Harvard. Copeans (often feeling aggrieved and carrying their flamboyant reputations to faraway institutes) range from autodidact Jack Horner (with the Museum of the Rockies in Montana) to the now deceased ex-maintenance-man-cum-world-renowned eggshell-expert Karl Hirsch to the well-publicized crank Robert Bakker, a ponytailed paleontologist with a penchant for gaudy Stetsons who was once "unpaid adjunct curator" at the University of Colorado Museum.

The Marshites and the Copeans need each other, though—the former for legitimizing a discipline populated by weekend enthusiasts and the latter for bringing adventure and creativity to a field that could easily settle into its own self-contented dust. These two characters are themselves deeply American types—the fugitive genius at the frontier goddamning all tradition and the starchy conformist trying to reconcile a voluble present with a soothing knowable past. It's what gives the stately field its inescapably puerile nature. Although "paleontology" is a word of scientific distinction, the taxon "dinosauria" means "terrible lizard," a phrase straight from the imagination of a five-year-old boy.

*   *   *

The first dinosaur bone ever identified was a huge double ball joint discovered in England in 1677. When it was illustrated in 1763, the artist Richard Brookes noted its resemblance to a monstrous pair of testicles. Brookes may have thought it belonged to a well-endowed biblical giant, but he may just have been goofing around when he named it. Marshites don't like to tell this story. But, as W.J.T. Mitchell argues in *The Last Dinosaur Book*, since it is the first bone ever identified, "by the strictest rules of biological nomenclature, *Scrotum humanum* is the true name of the dinosaur."

Scrotum humanum. Dinosaurology has never been able to quite shake its Jim Carreyness, which may explain why the field attracts so many kids and amateurs. Dinosaur theorists don't need advanced degrees in organic chemistry or technical prowess with superaccelerators—just a willingness to master the quite knowable bank of dinosaur findings, a chore that often begins just before first grade. The professional work can begin shortly thereafter. Three years ago, a dinosaur expert in New Mexico discovered a new creature in the Moreno hills and wrote an award-winning book about it—*Zuniceratops christopheri,* named for Christopher Wolfe, who was eight years old at the time.

Because just what is the intellectual task of paleontologists young and old? To take a few toylike objects—really big, really cool bones—and to imagine an entire world. It's a kind of intellectual play that is never troubled by comparison with any rigorous empirical reality. The only competition is some other imagined world that seems that much more neato.

In the first decade of the twentieth century, people everywhere were hungry to see the first inhabitants of this world as they emerged from the mythic frontier of the American West. Unlike England's, America's dinosaurs were easy to find. The nonacidic prairie soils of the West coupled with constant wind erosions and mild rains meant that at those early dinosaur digs, like Como Bluff and Bone Cabin Quarry, skeletons were often just lying exposed on the ground. The first dinosaur to go on tour was a plaster cast of a diplodocus, one of the long-necked sauropods that would eventually become world famous by the name of brontosaurus. For those willing to look closely, the connection between emerging American power and the vigor extant in the skeleton was apparent. That traveling dinosaur and a subsequent discovery were known, scientifically, as *Diplodocus carnegii* and *Apatosaurus louisae,* after their patrons, Andrew and Louise Carnegie.

New York's American Museum of Natural History unveiled the first permanent display: a brontosaurus in 1905, paired in 1910 with a T. rex. Figuring out how to hold up, say, T. rex's 2,000-pound pelvis was a chore. But as luck would have it, the industrial revolution was outfitting every American home with the newfangled marvel of indoor plumbing. And that's what the curators chose—the same L joints, sink traps, U brackets, and threaded pipes that forged the infrastructure of America's emerging empire also cantilevered the spines, jaws, breastplates, and hipbones of those two great beasts.[2] It was certainly as much a celebration of our new power as it was of the

---

2. Those two dinosaurs continue to reside at the American Museum of Natural History. In a 1995 redesign of the museum's expanded collection, the original duo were set aside in a separate room—the dinosaur of dinosaur exhibits. The original armature still holds up those bones, and that old blackened plumbing is easily as beautiful as the fossils themselves. The great dinosaurs had lain down 65 million years ago, and what put them once again on their feet? The tensile strength of Pittsburgh steel.

dinosaurs, and right away they assumed oddly familiar personalities. The brontosaurus was a long-necked galoot—a cud-chewing, vegetarian, gentle giant. Then just across the aisle, the psychic opposite: T. rex, frenzied carnivorous killer. An interesting pair those two, and it is no coincidence that their erection occurred just before we entered World War I, revealing to the world the character of a new global species—the American: A big, dumb rube, until provoked—then berserker rage.

It is difficult to imagine the effect those first displays must have had on the minds of our great-grandparents. But consider: You had to make a big trip to New York to see them. Newspaper descriptions and the occasional picture only stoked the desire to go. Meanwhile, all around you, a greatness was coming together—electrical wiring, indoor plumbing, the plane, the car, the movie—and it was being assembled around, over, and through you into a colossus larger than anything since Rome. The emotion that surged when you tilted back your head to look at those early dinosaurs was awe, for sure, but it was also a suffused patriotism. The skeletons gave substance and turgor to a novel feeling of giantness that citizens must have felt as they sensed their own inexorable participation in a new American project of pure immensity, an awareness that something dinosaurian in scope was rising up in the world: The first modern superpower.

When the Roaring Twenties were in full swing, adventurer/dino hunter Roy Chapman Andrews of the American Museum of Natural History (said to be the model for Indiana Jones) set off for the Gobi Desert in search of bones. His expedition deployed America's newest projection of twentieth-century power, a fleet of cars. It's not altogether clear that Chapman was being ironic when he announced that the purpose of his trip (paid for by the new Dodge Motor Company) was "the new conquest of Central Asia."

With the rise of Nazism, our biggest dinosaur skeletons were considered matters of—and never has this phrase sounded so vulnerable—national security. As a precaution, New York's T. rex was clandestinely removed to a safe location: Pittsburgh, a place where even victorious Nazis might never go.

No sooner had the boys come home in 1945 than our Mesozoic doppelgänger began shouldering a new burden, the A-bomb. American power suddenly seemed "terrible" in the "dino" sense—indiscriminate, Oppenheimerish, annihilating. In Japan the pure destructive power of Hiroshima arose chthonically as the incarnation of American evil. Godzilla: T. rex with a foreign policy (and big forearms). In Hollywood, though, the postwar dinosaur was a means to explore science's limits. It all began with *The Beast from 20,000 Fathoms,* which begat *King Dinosaur, The Beast of Hollow Mountain, The Land Unknown, Gorgo,* and *The Lost World,* among others.

In *20,000 Fathoms* an atomic test at the North Pole revives a hybridized T. rex (again, big forearms) hellbent on returning to the place of his birth, the Hudson River valley—a.k.a. New York City (a story line more deeply true than Hollywood would ever know). At last the authorities trap the monster at Coney Island, foreshadowing by half a century *Jurassic Park's* melding of dinosaur and entertainment. As the monster ravages his way through the Tilt-a-Whirl ride, a sharpshooter hits him in the heart with a bullet packed with "radioactive isotope"—the very substance that revived him and now destroys him. The message of all these movies was clear: We can re-animate the monsters or restore them to the fossil bed. Hiroshima was terrible but containable. Behold, all ye who tremble, the majesty of American might and the righteousness of her restraint.

In the 1950s, as GIs took brides and settled into Levittowns everywhere, the dinosaur, too, was dramatically domesticated. How? One word, Benjamin: plastics. With the invention of this new pliable material, anyone could mold a dinosaur into any imaginable position. Plastic re-animated the dinosaur by putting a kind of flesh back onto those big immobile bones and giving each of them a smooth synthetic flexibility. This dinosaur stood up nearly lifesize at every Sinclair gas station, and miniatures populated the toy sections of the department stores. Severing its umbilical connection to the sober conservatism of paleontology, the dinosaur now entered pop culture as a free agent. This was one for the people, the masses—the democrasaurus. The late fifties saw the earliest dinosaur trading cards, the first dinosaur stamp, an explosion of comic books, and welcomed the sixties with *The Flintstones.*

Plastic was also the unique innovation of postindustrial America, ultimately replacing Mr. Carnegie's steel in our infrastructure and ushering in our technological revolution. Today, scarcely an item on the planet doesn't contain some. If dinosaurs ruled the earth once, plastic comes close to making that claim today. And what is plastic made from? The resurrection couldn't get more literal.

* * *

Like everybody else, dinosaurs turned off and dropped out in the sixties and seventies. There were some minor shifts. It was in this era that Horner developed his other controversial theory: that dinosaurs parented. Horner is almost single-handedly responsible for getting dinosaurs in touch with their feminine side. He had discovered some dinosaur eggs and hatchlings surrounded by fossilized "regurgitated food" and adult dung—the detritus of a mother animal caring for its helpless nest-bound offspring. Dinosaurs had come a long way from the macho "terrible lizards" that erupted *ab ovo,* ready to begin their rampages. One of Homer's discoveries was *Maiasaura* (the first use of the feminine "a" ending versus the masculine "us"), meaning "good mother lizard." Around this time, in case you don't recall, the hottest talk-show host was Phil Donahue and the president was Jimmy Carter.

Dinosaurs' next epic pop-cultural leap in the national consciousness was the movie *Jurassic Park.* Like every curator before him, Spielberg sensed it was once again time to rearrange the Rorschachian bones. The star of that movie was the velociraptor. The brontosaurus and the T. rex make almost cameo appearances, like Robert Mitchum in the *Cape Fear* remake—an insider's nod to the grizzled original. The brontosaurus has only one significant scene, sneezing a few gallons of dino snot all over the kids. Still the goofball, after all these aeons. T. rex assumes his familiar role as enraged killer, but he's still a patriot, arriving at the end to save the day, like the cavalry.

And just who was the velociraptor in this 1993 movie? For a dinosaur, he was small, human-sized, and warm-blooded. The scientist in the film noted its jugular instincts ("lethal at eight months"), cunning ("problem-solving intelligence"), and strategic adaptability ("they remember"). At a time when the Japanese seemed to be taking over the world, we gazed upon a new beast—the global-business warrior, physically downsized, entrepreneurially fleet, rapaciously alert, ready for the dissolution of the nation-state. If the Pacific Rim was poised to take over the world, then this dinosaur was our response; an image that reflected how we conceived of our enemy as much as how we conceived of our new selves. The old-economy capitalist (T. rex) is there but sidelined, yielding to the distinctive features of the new-economy capitalist—lean, mean, smart, fast, and fatal. Many of the incidental descriptions of *Jurassic Park's* velociraptor could easily be dropped into a *Fortune* magazine profile of Henry Kravis, "Chainsaw" Al Dunlop, or Larry Ellison, without any editing. Even its Latinate name eerily foreshadowed its future metaphorical role. "Velociraptor" means fast-footed thief.

After *Jurassic Park's* success, the American Museum of Natural History shook up the bones once again and then, in 1995, tossed them out into a new display that received widespread praise. What the visitor sees is very much a new world, fully reimagined as a time of environmental balance. These dinos are shown in familial clusters, in mini-dioramas under glass. Many are small and seem as approachable in their outsized terrariums as gerbils in a suburban den. They are poised not to kill but to mate and to remind us, as the Disney movies do, of the Great Circle of Life. One display comes across like an intact family brimming with centrist heterosexual values—a mom and pop psittacosauri, plus three little hatchling psitts, gathered together, possibly on their way to church. A rare dinosaur fetus is also on display. The sum total points toward a very Al Gore-like dinosaur—the ecosaur.

At least, I think that's what it means. In these tenuous epistemological days, the museum adopts an unnerving tone. Each display states a bit of current dino theory and then mercilessly undercuts itself. One glass case explains the latest nasal theory regarding duckbills, but then beside the text a yellow warning label reads: "These are all intriguing hypotheses, but the fossils do not give us enough evidence to test whether any of them are correct. The mystery remains unresolved." That's a bit too much postmodern uncertainty to hang at the eye level of a ten-year-old, don't you think?

When I asked a museum official what he thought the entirety of such an exhibit added up to, he said, "Dinosaurs were the most successful life form that ever lived on this planet, and they became extinct. Extinction is a real part of life, and it's not so bad. When the dinosaur died out, the world went on and other species were created. One of those species was the human form. I think that, in all likelihood, our species will become extinct, and when that happens, that's probably not a bad thing."

So let me get this straight. We don't know anything and we're doomed. What a distance we've traveled since we looked at that first *Scrotum humanum* and saw our own lusty selves. Ecosaur doesn't begin to capture the sagging confidence and fear of empire-wide failure embodied here. Let's upgrade. Apocalyptosaurus.

Fortunately, it wasn't long before the osteo-reply to apocalyptosaurus arrived. In the winter of 1999, the National Geographic Society announced a "feathered dinosaur" exhibit with fresh specimens from China. The entire display represented a Tony Bennett-like revival for Yale paleontologist John Ostrom, whose brilliant hypothesis about the fate of dinosaurs had gotten obscured in the last two decades of fervent debate about extinction.

Among dozens of theories about the dinosaurs' fate—including global warming, subterranean-gas leaks, magnetic fields, trans-species miscegenation, and, of course, the meteor from outer space—Ostrom's idea suggests that some dinosaurs may have just evolved. Their streamlined progeny got leaner, faster, and feathered before taking to the air. Right now they are pecking seed from the feeder dangling outside my window. Simple, elegant—parsimonious, as paleontologists like to say—and yet from a nationalist view you can understand why it was ignored. Dinosaurs evolving into the larger family of life instead of going down in a blaze of intergalactic holocaust? No way.

But there was another side to this revival. At the time, America's status as superpower, as well as keeper of dinosaurs, was beginning to be challenged by China. Amid reports about China's theft of nuclear secrets, clandestine arms sales, and independent space exploration, word came that China was building the world's largest dinosaur park in Chuanjie province. Authorities there had discovered two skeletons of dinosaurs fossilized in mid-battle—an extremely rare find of obvious commercial appeal.

"Chuanjie has now passed Utah in the United States," Chinese papers continually boast (quoting an American expert) "to become the largest burial ground of dinosaurs in the world." A staggering announcement, given China's previous clumsy attempts to enter the paleontological major league. A 1983 China find, for instance, was named *Gongbusaurus,* literally. "Ministry of Public Works-osaurus."

And now a truly brilliant Chinese breakthrough—the discovery of a feathered dinosaur, and possible proof of Ostrom's theory—was visiting America. In the exhibit, these specimens were not mere bones but taxidermically dressed up, as if stuffed after a recent hunt, feathered from head to toe in harvest colors of sedge brown, crimson red, and dark yellow, all posed in the most aggressive postures possible: raised claws, open teeth, wings volant. They looked like enraged fanged turkeys. And hidden right there in the taxonomic name was their true significance: *Sinornithosaurus millenii*—"Chinese bird-reptile of the new millennium." Freshly discovered, freshly minted—a brand-new, slimmed-down dinosaur metaphor had sprouted wings and flown off to Asia. Maybe, it seemed, America was bowing out of the game.

But then maybe not. A few weeks after the exhibit arrived in Washington (Chinese dinosaurs in the bosom of our capital—the horror, the horror!), paleo-patriots could breathe easier. Scandal erupted when it was charged that one of the exhibits was a fake. Under headlines "Piltdown Bird" and "Buyer Beware," articles wallowed in new information that Chinese peasants were cobbling together different fossils, often with glue and paint, to feed the international market. The implication was clear. Like videocassettes in a free-trade dispute, Chinese fossils were just more cheap pirated fakes being dumped in the lucrative American marketplace.

Scarcely a few weeks later came an announcement from Hollywood, Florida. A philanthropist named Michael Feinberg had purchased a fossil for a museum there, and it had been closely reexamined. In the words of a breathless AP reporter, it was "a 75-million-year-old creature with a roadrunner's body, arms that resembled clawed wings and hair-like feathers." You want feathers? America's got your feathers right here. "A dinosaur Rosetta stone," said a museum associate, just in case anyone underestimated its significance. The Linnaean name of America's new proof of birdness was as rich in meaning as *Sinornithosaurus millenii.* In its own moist and Disneyesque way, the new find reincarnated that old blend of the bront's amiability with T. rex's dormant ferocity: *Bambiraptor.*

Our Mona Lisa, as Ostrom described it. A sentimentalized dinosaur for a sentimentalized time. In the tradition begun with *Diplodocus carnegii* a century ago, the full name of the latest celebrity dinosaur is *Bambiraptor feinbergi.*

Driving a stake through the heart of the Chinese bird-dinosaur has since become a seasonal blood sport. Last year, China announced a true birdlike dinosaur discovery. They called it *Protopteryx* (meaning "first feather"). As if. Professor Alan Feduccia of the University of North Carolina at Chapel Hill looked at the evidence and immediately laughed it off as "dino-fuzz."

But feathers hardly matter anymore because paleontologists are still cooing over the latest proof of dinosaur warm-bloodedness. This confirmation, found last year, derives from the discovery of the first intact dinosaur organ—a heart—that had miraculously survived fossilization. Described as a grapefruit-sized, reddish-brown stone, it was found in the heart of the heart of the country: South Dakota. True dino-land. America—where modern dinosaurs first stirred and where they still thrive. Reddish brown, the description reads, as if the blood were still in it, almost beating. That's how it goes with dinosaurs. We're always getting closer to the true dinosaur, the next dinosaur, the best dinosaur. It's America's task. There is always another one on the way. With only a fourth of the dinosaur fossils estimated to have been found, the empire has a ways to go.

Each subsequent discovery will conceal new messages in its bones, hints of our superpower's new place in this world and our hearts. The new bones will stand up and the old ones will lie down. The theories will wax and wane. But no matter what we may think the newest dinosaur means for that month, or that decade, it will really be about what every dinosaur has always been about—not extinction but the other, deeper dream of this nation: the big comeback, the perpetual *novus ordo* of America, the unexpected feat of resurrection.

Reading Comprehension—Points of Engagement

1. Why does Jack Hitt write that "dinosaurs are distinctly American"? (128). Look to the sentences around where this quotation appears, and refer to them directly in your answer.

2. Name one of the paleontologists in Jack Hitt's essay. What does your figure believe about dinosaurs? What is his theory, his contribution to paleontology? Be as specific as you can. Then explain why he is important to Jack Hitt. What does that figure do for Hitt's essay?

3. Jack Hitt's essay tracks the changes in how dinosaurs have been represented over time, and proposes that these changes reflect American culture as much as science. Choose two different decades, and describe the dinosaur that Hitt associates with each decade. Why these particular dinosaurs? What qualities in them reflect the cultural reality of that time and why? Your answer should be 1-2 full paragraphs.

4. Who were Professor O.C. Marsh and Edward Cope? What were the "Bone-Wars" and how were these scientists involved in them? When did the Bone-Wars occur? What do the Bone Wars and Marsh and Cope's competition reveal today about the science of paleontology? What do they reveal about us as people? As Americans? Cite two passages from Hitt's essay that support your answer.

5. Who is John Ostrom? What is his theory about dinosaurs? Why does Jack Hitt find it interesting and important? Look on pages 137–138 for your answer.

Assignment Questions—Points of Departure

1. Dinosaur Dreams: Human Dreams? Part of our dream of dinosaurs is that "we're always getting closer to the true dinosaur, the next dinosaur, the best dinosaur. It's America's task. There is always another one on the way" (139). How does this idea of always looking forward to some new discovery play out in essays by Lisa Belkin, David Brooks, Paul Davies, Adam Gopnik, Arlie Russell Hochschild, Fenton Johnson, Michael Kamber, Lewis Lapham, or Jeanette Winterson? Your project for this paper is to explore Hitt's idea of the "deeper dream of this nation: the big comeback, the perpetual *novus ordo* of America, the unexpected feat of resurrection" (139) in conversation with one of these authors. How do Hitt's ideas represent more than just "dinosaur dreams" but also "human dreams"?

2. Looking at America through our representations of dinosaurs, Jack Hitt sees a connection between entertainment in popular culture—movies, the traveling circus, popular fiction—and the sciences of paleontology and natural history. How do other authors in this reader depict this relationship between popular culture and academic knowledge? Your project in this paper is to describe that relationship and to answer the following questions: Do you see a clear distinction between the imagined reality of entertainment culture and the reality of science? Do the authors you've chosen to address see any distinction? How do you know? Refer to Jack Hitt's "Dinosaur Dreams" and essays by David Brooks, Paul Davies, Arlie Russell Hochschild, Steven Johnson or Francine Prose.

3. Jack Hitt describes two "American types" in his essay: "the fugitive genius at the frontier goddamning all tradition and the starchy conformist trying to reconcile a voluble present with a soothing knowable past" (132). Do you think these are distinctly "American" types or do you think they exist in other national identities? What else marks our "national" identity and how does that affect us as individuals? Write a paper in which you answer these questions using "Dinosaur Dreams" and an essay by one of the following authors: David Brooks, Franklin Foer, Lewis Lapham, Lenore Look, V.S. Naipaul, Lauren Slater, John Waterbury, or Jeanette Winterson. Be aware of which authors are Americans addressing American identity or ideals, and which authors are concerned with other national identities. Choose your second essay carefully, based on whether you believe these types are distinctly American or not. Keep in mind that the best papers are often those that question the simplest and most obvious interpretations.

From the Frying Pan into the Fire
Arlie Russell Hochschild

Points of Access

1. Do you think that shopping—shopping at the mall, shopping for groceries, etc.—has a closer connection with your leisure time, and the time you spend with friends and family, or with your work life? Are there different kinds of shopping? What makes them different? What aspects of your attitude toward shopping make you associate it with leisure, or with work?

2. In your own words, what is capitalism? What is it for? What does it do? Do you think it affects your life in any direct way? Look up capitalism in your dictionary or online after you've thought about your own ideas concerning what it is, and see how the two match up. Did you see anything unexpected in the definition? What?

3. Unlike many other countries, the United States has very few public holidays, designated by the state as times for work to stop, and time to be given instead to family and community. Thanksgiving and Memorial Day are two of only a few weekday holidays. Consider how you would feel if you had a holiday like Thanksgiving or Memorial Day every couple of months, where every store shut, all services were at their minimal level—in fact, the whole country took the day off. How would that affect you? At all? Why would this kind of regular, state-sanctioned vacation time be a good idea? Why would it be bad, or inconvenient? Think also, about which you look forward to the most: Thanksgiving itself with your family, the long weekend away from work or school, or the shopping day in between?

An advertisement for Quaker Oats cereal in an issue of *Working Mother* magazine provides a small window on the interplay between consumption and the application of the idea of efficiency to private time in modern America.[1] In the ad, a mother, dressed in a business suit, affectionately hugs her smiling son. Beneath the image, we read: "Instant Quaker Oatmeal, for moms who have a lot of love but not a lot of time."

---

[1] See Hochschild 1997a.

The ad continues with a short story: "Nicky is a very picky eater. With Instant Quaker Oatmeal, I can give him a terrific hot breakfast in just 90 seconds. And I don't have to spend any time coaxing him to eat it!"

The ad then presents "facts" about mother and child: "Sherry Greenberg, with Nicky, age four and a half, Hometown: New York City, New York, Occupation: Music teacher, Favorite Flavor: Apples and Cinnamon." The designers of this ad, we could imagine, want us to feel we've been let in on an ordinary moment in a middle-class American morning. In this ordinary moment, Sherry Greenberg is living according to a closely scheduled, rapidly paced "adult" time, while Nicky is living according to a more dawdling, slowly paced "child" time. So the mother faces a dilemma. To meet her work deadline, she must get Nicky on "adult" time. But to be a good mother it is desirable to give her child a hot breakfast—"hot" being associated with devotion and love. To cook the hot breakfast, though, Sherry needs *time*. The ad suggests that it is the cereal itself that solves the problem. It conveys love because it is hot, but it permits efficiency because it's quickly made. The cereal would seem to reconcile an image of American motherhood of the 1950s with the female work role of 2000 and beyond.

The cereal also allows Sherry to avoid the unpleasant task of struggling with her child over scarce time. In the ad, Nicky's slow pace is implicitly attributed to his character ("Nicky is a very picky eater") and not to the fact that he is being harnessed to an accelerating pace of adult work time or protesting an adult speed-up by staging a "slowdown." By permitting the mother to avoid a fight with her son over time, the ad brilliantly evokes a common problem and proposes a commodity as a solution.

Attached to the culture of time shown in the ad is a key but hidden social logic. This modern working mother is portrayed as resembling Frederick Taylor, the famed efficiency expert of modern industry. The principle of efficiency is not located, here, at work in the person of the owner, the foreman, or the worker. It is located in the worker-as-mother. We do not see a boss pressing the worker for more efficiency at the office. Instead, we see a mother pressing her son to eat more efficiently at home. This efficiency-seeking is transferred from man to woman, from workplace to home, and from adult to child. Nicky becomes his own task master, quickly gobbling his breakfast himself because it is so delicious. Frederick Taylor has leapt the fence from factory to home, adult to child, and jumped, it seems, into the cereal box itself. Frederick Taylor has become a commodity. *It* provides efficiency. Thus, the market reinforces the idea of efficiency twice—once at a locus of production, where the worker is pressed to work efficiently, and again, as a supplier of consumer goods, where it promises to deliver the very efficiency it also demands.

Quaker Oats cereal may be a paradigm for a growing variety of goods and services—frozen dinners, computer shopping services, cell phones,[2] and the like—that claim to save time for busy working parents. They often save time at home. But the ethic of "saving time" raises the question of what we want to save time for.[3] In the case above, the photo of the happy mother and child suggests that the mother is rushing her son through breakfast, not to race out to an all-absorbing job at a dot-com company, but to teach a few piano lessons. The picture doesn't challenge our idea of the primacy, even sacredness, of Nicky's home. So we don't much notice the sly insinuation of Frederick Taylor into the scene.

Conventional versus Unconventional Wisdom

If, through modern Western eyes, the Greenbergs of this ad were a normal family, we could imagine them feeling that family life superseded all other aspects of life. That is, according to modern conventional wisdom, a happy family life is an end in itself. Earning and spending money are the means for achieving this end. Home and community are primary; workplace and mall are secondary. When we go out to work, it's to put bread on the table for the family. When we shop at the mall, it's often to buy a Christmas, birthday, or house present "for the family." Put in other terms, we often see the home and the community as sacred, and the workplace and the mall as profane. We are who we are at home and in our communities. We do what we do at work and buy what we buy at the mall.

To be sure, we make exceptions for the odd workaholic here or shopaholic there, but, as the terms imply, an overconcern with the profane realms of work and mall are, given this way of seeing things, off moral limits. Sherry Greenberg fits right in. She is

---

[2] Cell phones, home fax machines, car dictating machines, and similar gadgets are marketed, purchased, and used on the premise that these machines, like the cereal, will "save time"so that the consumer can then enjoy more leisure. In practice, though, such technology often becomes a delivery system for pressure to do more paid work. Along with new technology come new norms. Electronic mail, for example, once hailed as a way of "saving time" has escalated expectations shortening the period of time one has before one is considered rude or inattentive not to reply.

[3] Among affluent Americans, time-saving goods and services also force parents to define parenthood less in terms of production and more in terms of consumption. For example, a "good mother" in the American middle class is often seen as one who prepares her child's birthday, bakes the cake, blows up the balloons, invites her child's friends to a party. Increasingly, the busy working mother is tempted to buy the cake; in addition, new birthday services are available in American cities to help organize the party, send out the invitations, buy the gifts, blow up the balloons, and set up the food. The definition of a "good mother" moves from production to consumption. The "good mother" is now one who enjoys the party with the child. The gift is one of derationalized time.

in her kitchen feeding her son. She has what one imagines to be a manageable job. It's just that she's wanting to hurry things along a bit.

Implicit in this conventional view of family life is the idea that our use of time is like a language. We speak through it. By either what we say we want to spend time doing or what we actually spend time doing, we say what it is we hold sacred. Maybe we don't think of it just this way, but we assume that each "spending time" or each statement of feeling about time ("I wish I could spend time") is a bow from the waist to what we hold dear. It is a form of worship. Again, Sherry Greenberg is symbolizing the importance of family. It's just that she's slightly on the edge of that conventional picture because she's in a hurry to get out of it. The Quaker Oats ad both appeals to this family-comes-first picture of life and subtly challenges it, by taking sides with her desire to feed Nicky "efficiently."

The subtle challenge of the ad points, I believe, to a larger contradiction underlying stories like that of the Greenbergs. Reflecting on my research on the Fortune 500 company I call Amerco, I'll try to explore it. Increasingly, our belief that family comes first conflicts with the emotional draw of both workplace and mall. Indeed, I would argue that a constellation of pressures is pushing men and women further into the world of workplace and mall. And television—a pipeline, after all, to the mall—is keeping them there. Family and community life have meanwhile become less central as places to talk and relate, and less the object of collective rituals.

Many of us respond to these twin trends, however, not by turning away from family and community, but by actually elevating them in moral importance. Family and community are not a realm in decline, as David Popenoe argues about the family and Robert Putnam argues for the community. To many people, both have become even more important morally. We encapsulate the idea of the cherished family.[4] We separate ideal from practice. We separate the idea of "spending time with X" from the idea of "believing in the importance of X." We don't link what we think with what we do. Or as one Amerco employee put it, using company language, "I don't walk the talk at home." This encapsulation of our family ideal allows us to accommodate to what is both a pragmatic necessity and a competing source of meaning—the religion of capitalism. I say pragmatic necessity, because most Americans, men and women alike, have to work for food and rent.

At the same time, a new cultural story is unfolding. It is not that capitalism is an unambiguous object of worship. After all, American capitalism is, in reality, a highly complex, internally diverse economic system for making, advertising, and selling

---

[4] See Gillis 1994; also Popenoe 1989 and Putnam 2000.

things. But, without overstating the case, it seems true that capitalism is a cultural as well as an economic system and that the symbols and rituals of this cultural system compete with, however much they seem to serve, the symbols and rituals of community and family. This means that working long hours and spending a lot of money—instead of spending time together—have increasingly become *how* we say "I love you" at home. As Juliet Schor argues in *The Overspent American*, over the last twenty years, Americans have raised the bar on what feels like enough money to get along. In 1975, according to a Roper poll, 10 percent of people mentioned a second color TV as part of "the good life," and 28 percent did in 1991. A 1995 Merck Family Fund poll showed that 27 percent of people who earned $100,000 or more agreed with the statement, "I cannot afford to buy everything I really need." At the same time, between 1975 and 1991, the role of family in people's idea of "the good life" declined while the importance of having money increased. The importance of having a happy marriage to "the good life" declined from 84 percent in 1975 to 77 percent in 1991. Meanwhile having "a lot of money" went from 38 percent in 1975 to 55 percent in 1991.[5]

How much of a stretch is it, I wonder, to go from the trends Schor points out to Harvey Cox's daring thesis: that capitalism has become a religion? As Cox puts it:

> Just as a truly global market has emerged for the first time in human history, that market is functioning without moral guideposts and restraints, and it has become the most powerful institution of our age. Even nation-states can often do little to restrain or regulate it. More and more, the idea of "the market" is construed, not as a creation of culture ("made by human hands," as the Bible says about idols), but as the "natural" way things happen. For this reason, the "religion" the market generates often escapes criticism and evaluation or even notice. It becomes as invisible to those who live by it as was the religion of the preliterate Australians whom Durkheim studied, who described it as just "the way things are."[6]

Capitalism has, Cox suggests, its myth of origin, its legends of the fall, its doctrine of sin and redemption, its notion of sacrifice (state belt-tightening), and its hope of salvation through the free market system. Indeed, if in the Middle Ages the church provided people with a basic orientation to life, the multinational corporation's workplace, with its "mission statements," its urgent deadlines, its demands for peak performance and total quality, does so today. Paradoxically, what would seem like the most secular of systems (capitalism), organized around the most profane of activities (making a living, shopping), provides a sense of the sacred. So what began as a *means* to an end—

---

[5] Schor 1998, pp. 16–17.

[6] Cox 2001, p. 124.

capitalism the means, a good living as the end—has become an *end* itself. It's a case of mission drift writ large. The cathedrals of capitalism dominate our cities. Its ideology dominates our airwaves. It calls for sacrifice, through long hours of work, and offers its blessings, through commodities. When the terrorists struck the twin towers on 9/11, they were, perhaps, aiming at what they conceived of as a more powerful rival temple, another religion. Heartless as they were, they were correct to see capitalism, and the twin towers as its symbol, as a serious rival religion.

Like older religions, capitalism partly creates the anxieties to which it poses itself as a necessary answer. Like the fire-and-brimstone sermon that begins with "Man, the lowly sinner," and ends with "Only this church can redeem you," so the market ethos defines the poor or unemployed as "unworthy slackers" and offers work and a higher standard of living as a form of salvation. Capitalism is not, then, simply a system in the *service of* family and community; it *competes* with the family. When we separate our fantasy of family life, our ideas of being a "good mother and father" from our daily expressions of parenthood, our ideals live timelessly on while we worship at the biggest altar in town, with ten-hour days and long trips to the mall.

A constellation of forces seems to be pressing in the direction of the religion of capitalism. And while no one wants to go back to the "frying pan" of patriarchy, we need to look sharp about the fire of market individualism under capitalism. It is in the spirit of looking at that fire that we can examine several conditions that exacerbate the tendency to apply the principle of efficiency to private life.

The first factor is the inevitable—and on the whole I think beneficial—movement of women into the paid workforce.[7] Exacerbating this squeeze on time is the overall absence of government or workplace policies that foster the use of parental leave or shorter, more flexible hours. Over the last twenty years, workers have also been squeezed by a lengthening workweek. According to a recent International Labor Organization report on working hours, Americans are putting in longer hours than workers of any other industrialized nation. We now work two weeks longer each year than our counterparts in Japan, the vaunted long-work-hour capital of the world.[8] American married couples and single-par-

---

[7] Some commentators blame women's movement into paid work for the strains experienced at home—including the high divorce rate. But I would argue that it is not women's paid work per se, but work in the absence of the necessary social adjustments in the structure of care—male sharing of care at home, family-friendly workplace policies, and social honor associated with care—that make the difference.

[8] Doohan 1999. The 600-page ILO report compared hours of work in 240 countries. Useem (2000) cites 751 time-management titles listed on Amazon.com, including *Eating on the Run,* and *Please Hold: 102 Things to Do While You Wait on the Phone.*

ent families are also putting in more hours in the day and more weeks in the year than they did thirty years ago. Counting overtime and commuting time, a 1992 national sample of men averaged 48.8 hours of work, and women, 41.7.[9] Work patterns vary by social class, ethnicity, race, and the number and ages of children, of course. But, overall, between 1969 and 1996 the increase in American mothers' paid work combined with a shift toward single-parent families has led to an average decrease of 22 hours a week of parental time available (outside of paid work) to spend with children.[10] And the emotional draw of a work culture is sometimes strong enough to out-compete a weaker family culture (see "Emotional Geography and the Flight Plan of Capitalism," Chapter 15).

The Other Side of the Market Religion: Not Walking the Talk at Home

If capitalism began as a means but became an end in itself, then families and local communities must daily face a competing urgency system and a rival conception of time. Company deadlines compete with school plays. Holiday sales at the mall vie with hanging out at home. The company's schedule and rules have come, for workers, to define those of families. For the managers and production workers at Amerco, the company I studied for the *Time Bind,* the debut of a certain kind of product and its "product life cycle" came to prevail over personal anniversaries and school holidays. When family events did take precedence, they did so on company terms. As one woman explained, "My mother died and I went back to arrange for the funeral and all. I went for four days. The company gives us that for bereavement, and so that's the time I spent." In the early industrial period in Europe, whole workforces disappeared at festival time, or workers put an iron bar in the machinery, stopped the assembly line, and took a break. Company time did not always rule.

---

[9] Galinsky, Bond, and Friedman 1993, p. 9.

[10] "Families and the Labor Market, 1969–1999: Analyzing the Time Crunch," May 1999, Report by the Council of Economic Advisors, Washington, D.C. Also a 2000 report found that 46 percent of workers work 41 hours or longer, 18 percent of them 51 hours or longer (see Center for Survey Research and Analysis, University of Connecticut, "2000 Report on U.S. Working Time"). Another recent study found that elementary school teachers—those in what is often thought to be a "woman's" job—reported working ten-hour days (see Drago et al. 1999). Less time away from work means less time for children. Nationwide, half of children wish they could see their fathers more, and a third wish they could see their mothers more (Coolsen, Seligson, and Garbino 1985; Hewlett 1991, p. 105). A growing number of commentators draw links, often carelessly, between this decline in family time and a host of problems, including school failure and alcohol and drug abuse (Hewlett 1991).

In response to the challenge of this competing urgency system, I've argued, many families separate their ideal of themselves as "a close family" from a life that in reality is more hurried, fragmented, crowded, and individualized than they would like. They develop the idea of a hypothetical family, the family they would be if only they had time. And then they deal with life in a contrary fashion.

Many Amerco employees came home from a long workday to fit many necessary activities into a limited amount of time. Although there were important exceptions, many workers tried to go through domestic chores rapidly if for no other reason than to clear some space in which to go slowly. They used many strategies to save time—they planned, delegated, did several things simultaneously. They packed one activity close up against the next, eliminating the framing around each event, periods of looking forward to or back upon an event, which might have heightened its emotional impact. A 2:00 to 2:45 play date, 2:45 to 3:15 shopping trip, 3:15 to 4:45 visit to Grandma, and so on. As one mother, a sales manager, said with satisfaction, "What makes me a good employee at work is what makes me able to do all I do at home; I'm a multitasker, but [with a laugh] at work I get paid for it."

With all these activities, family time could be called "hurried" or "crowded." But in fact many working parents took a sporting "have fun" attitude toward their hurried lives: "Let's see how fast we can do this! Come on, kids, let's go!" They brought their image of the family closer to the reality of it by saying, in effect, "We like it this way." They saw hassle as challenge. In other families, parents seemed to encourage children to develop schedules parallel to and as hectic as their own. For example, the average annual vacation time both at Amerco—and in the United States as a whole—is twelve days, while schoolchildren typically have summer holidays of three months. So one Amerco mother placed her eight-year-old son in a nearby summer program and explained to him, in a you're-going-to-love-this way, "You have your job to go to, too." She talked about her schedule as she might have talked about a strenuous hike. She was having fun roughing it with multitasking and chopped-up time.

Another way of resolving the contradiction between ideal and reality was to critique the fun ethic and say, in effect, "Family life isn't supposed to be fun. It's supposed to be a hassle, but we're in the hassle together, and why isn't that okay?" This often carried families over long stretches of time, but it prevented family members from giving full attention to each other. Time was hurried (not enough time allotted for an activity—15-minute baths, 20-minute dinners, for example). Or time was crowded (one or more people were doing more than one thing at a time). Or it was uncoordinated. Only two out of four people could make it to dinner, the ball game, the reunion. If there was not some chronic avoidance of a deep tension, families usually also took another approach. They *deferred* having a good time. Instead of saying, "This hassle is fun," they said, in effect, "This hassle isn't fun. But we'll have fun *later*." They waited for the weekend, for their vacation, for "quality time."

But the more a family deferred the chance for relaxed communication, the more anxious they sometimes became about it. One man told me: "My wife and I hadn't had time together for a long time, so we decided to take some 'marital quality time' by going out to a restaurant to eat dinner together. We had a nice dinner and afterwards went for a walk. We passed a toy store and my wife wanted to shop for a toy for our child. But I told her, 'No, you have a different quality time with our child. This is *our* quality time.' So we spent the rest of the evening arguing about whose quality time it was we were spending."

Another long-hours Amerco executive seemed to take this strategy of deferral to an extreme. When I asked him whether he wished he'd spent more time with his three daughters when they were growing up, he answered, "Put it this way, I'm pleased with how they turned out." This father loved his daughters, but he loved them as results. Or rather, his feeling was "I want my wife to enjoy the process of raising them. I'll enjoy that vicariously. What I will enjoy directly is the result, the young adults." So he didn't think family life should or shouldn't be fun while the kids were small and adolescent. That was his wife's specialty. He was deferring his real enjoyment until his daughters had grown up. Even Amerco parents who spent far more time with their children occasionally justified this time in terms of future results. They were pleased at how "old for their age" their children were, how "ahead," given a limited expenditure of parental time. Perhaps, most parents held a double perspective on their children—they cared about the child as he or she was growing up and about the child as he or she emerged in adulthood. Most oriented toward the family as a source of intrinsic pleasure were women and workers in the middle or lower ranks of the company; least oriented in this way were upper management or professional men—the congregation and the priests.

From the top to the bottom of the Amerco workforce, workers were forced to answer the challenge of capitalism—not simply as a system that gave them jobs, money, and stuff, but as a system that offered them a sense of purpose and guidance in a confusing time. They had to deal with the religion of capitalism, its grip on honor and sense of worth, its subtraction from—or absorption of—family and community life. We've emerged from an era in which most women had little or no paid work to a era in which most do. Are women jumping from the frying pan of patriarchy into the fire of capitalism? Just as the early industrial workforces took off at festival time, because they were not yet "disciplined" to capitalism, maybe postindustrial ones will work out their own way of living a balanced life. There could be a balance not just between the role of piano teacher, say, and mother, but between the unpaid *world* of home and community and the money *world* of work and mall. That may be the deeper issue underlying the ad for Quaker Oats cereal. For, our cultural soil is surreptitiously prepared for ads, like that for Quaker Oats cereal, that make you spend time buying one more thing that promises to save time—which increasingly we spend earning and buying.

Reading Comprehension—Points of Engagement

1. Consider Hochschild's title, "From the Frying Pan into the Fire." What is the "frying pan" she is talking about? What is the fire? Quote from her text in support of your answer. Why are these two metaphors useful to her? What other significance is there to her using this expression?

2. Hochschild describes a "constellation of pressures [that are] pushing men and women further into the world of workplace and mall" (146).Why does Hochschild group "workplace and mall" together in this context? What pressures does she identify? List them from the text. How does she suggest we might deal with or lessen these pressures? Do you find her suggestions realistic? Why or why not?

3. Why does Hochschild treat capitalism as a religion? Give reasons from the text. What do you think of these reasons? Has Hochschild taken the comparison too far, or do you think she represents American society accurately?

Assignment Questions—Points of Departure

1. All the families in Hochschild's essay seem very busy. David Brooks and Adam Gopnik also observe this aspect of American life. How do these three authors approach the phenomenon of our busy lives as they affect our own futures and our relationships with other people? What's the main project of each author? What kinds of critiques are they each offering? Do they take the same position on the causes and effects of "busyness"? Write a paper in which you engage with Hochschild, and either Brooks or Gopnik on the role of "busyness" in our lives, and offer your own assessment of their observations.

2. According to Hochschild, "the emotional draw of a work culture is sometimes strong enough to out-compete a weaker family culture" (149). In her essay,

Hochschild shows, as it were, a worst-case scenario for the American family. But it seems that the Look family in "Facing the Village" is, in a way, using capitalism to serve the family. How are they able to do this? How is the Look family similar to the Greenbergs and the Amerco families? How are they different? Why is the difference decisive, or not decisive? How do the Looks balance the moral importance of consumerism, the moral importance of family and community, and what does this balance say about Hochschild's project in her essay?

3. Consider the following quotation from Hochschild's essay: "So what began as a *means* to an end—capitalism the means, good living as the end—has become an *end* in itself" (147–148). Hochschild makes the above observation about the effects of capitalism, mostly directing her attention to middle-class American society. In Michael Kamber's "Toil and Temptation," we see a case where American capitalism draws people from other nations in. Do the Mexican workers whom Kamber discusses bear out Hochschild's observation? How, or how not? How are the workers he talks about the same as middle-class Americans, such as those at Amerco discussed by Hochschild? How are they different? Does the pervasiveness of capitalism as an end in itself threaten more than just leisure time?

Wedded to an Illusion

Fenton Johnson

Points of Access

1. What is marriage for? Is it necessary? Why or why not? What are the primary influences on your beliefs about marriage? Why do you feel the way you do about it? Freewrite for 15 minutes.

2. The title of this essay by Fenton Johnson is "Wedded to An Illusion." One of his central claims is that what we think of as marriage is really an *ideal* we aspire to, rather than the *reality* of what marriage is. Before reading the article, what do you think about this idea, that marriage as we wish it to be is an illusion? What do you think the ideal of marriage is? Do you think that the reality, for the majority of married people, lives up to this ideal? Why, or why not?

3. The United States is currently very divided on whether same-sex couples should be allowed to marry legally. As a reflection of this division, the federal government and many states have proposed or passed legislation forbidding same-sex marriage, while others have permitted either civil unions or marriage licenses to gay couples. It is reasonable to suspect that this debate will continue to divide the country for many years. How should government respond to such division? What do you think?

L ast summer, when American politicians underwent yet another of their periodic convulsions over the status of gays and lesbians, I found myself pondering the evolving history of marriage. In response to the possible recognition of same-gender marriages by the state of Hawaii, Congress overwhelmingly passed the Defense of Marriage Act, which reserves federal benefits and rights for male-female couples and permits states not to recognize same-gender marriages performed in other states. Sponsored in the House of Representatives by Bob Barr (three marriages) and endorsed by then Senator Bob Dole (two marriages), the bill was called "gay baiting" by the White House and "unnecessary" by President Clinton (he of the colorful personal life), who signed it nonetheless in late September. The law might appear to be only so much election-year positioning and counter-positioning, but long after this year's political season is forgotten, we will be agonizing over the questions implicit in the legislation. As a married, straight friend cracked to me, "If marriage needs Congress to defend it, then we know we're in trouble."

Marriage. What does it mean these days? Peau de sole, illusion veil, old, new, borrowed, blue? Can it mean the same thing to a heterosexual couple, raised to consider it the pinnacle of emotional fulfillment, as to a same-gender couple, the most conventional of whom must find the label "married" awkward? Can it mean the same thing to a young lesbian—out since her teens, occasionally bisexual, wanting a child, planning a career—as to me, a forty-plus shell-shocked AIDS widower? And in an era of no-fault divorce, can it mean to any of us what it meant to our parents?

*   *   *

The unacceptability of gay marriages may have bloomed with sudden propitiousness on the agendas of Clinton and Dole, but the issue has been steadily moving into the legal conversation across the last twenty-five years. In 1991 three Hawaiian couples—two lesbian, one gay-male—sued the state over the denial of their applications for marriage licenses; on principle, a heterosexual ACLU attorney took the case. Two years later, to everyone's amazement, the Hawaii Supreme Court ruled, in *Baehr v. Lewin,* that the state's denial of licenses violated the Hawaii constitution's equal-rights protections. The court took care to note that the sexual orientation of the plaintiffs was irrelevant. At issue instead was discrimination based on gender: the state discriminates by offering benefits (including income tax, worker's compensation, retirement, welfare, and spousal support) to married men and women that it denies to exclusively male or female couples.

This is no minor point. What the court ruled on in Hawaii was not gay marriage but simply marriage: whether the union of two people of the same gender qualifies for the benefits the state offers to mixed-gender couples, no matter if the spouses marry for love or children or Social Security benefits, no matter if they are gay or straight or celibate—in other words, all those reasons, good and bad, for which men and women now marry.

The Hawaii justices remanded the case to a lower court, challenging the attorney general to justify gender discrimination in marriage benefits. The plaintiffs' attorneys currently expect the State Supreme Court to allow the issuance of marriage licenses to same-gender couples by late 1997, though more litigation seems as likely, given the determination and financing of the opposition. If the state court acts as the plaintiffs anticipate, the matter will surely reach the federal level. Contrary to widespread reporting and rhetoric, Article IV of the U.S. Constitution does not necessarily require states to recognize marriages performed in other states; interstate recognition of marriage remains largely unexplored legal terrain.[1] If a couple marries in Hawaii, then moves to New York or Georgia, can those states refuse to recognize the marriage? Under the Defense of Marriage Act, the answer is yes, though some legal experts argue that states already have this right, while other experts contend that the act is unconstitutional. Either way the issue invokes a resonant precedent: as recently as 1967, sixteen states refused to recognize mixed-race marriages legally performed elsewhere. Those antimiscegenation laws were struck down that same year by the U.S. Supreme Court in *Loving v. Virginia,* a landmark case that the Hawaii court cited at length in *Baehr v. Lewin.*

At stake first and foremost are the rights of gays and lesbians to assume the state-conferred benefits of marriage. The assumption of these rights is controversial enough, but Baehr has still larger implications for an institution that has historically served as the foundation of a male-dominated society. It's instructive to recall that in the late 1970s Phyllis Schlafly and her anti-Equal Rights Amendment (ERA) allies predicted that the codification of the equality of women and men, as embodied in a federal ERA, would lead to gay marriage, presumably because they felt that to codify the equality of women and men would undermine the values upon which traditional marriage rests. The federal amendment failed, but Hawaii (along with several other states) adopted its own ERA, and here we are, just as Schlafly predicted—right in the place, I argue, where we ought to be. For this is the profound and scary and exhilarating fact: to assume the equality of women and men is to demand rethinking the institution that more than any other defines how men and women relate.

*   *   *

Marriage has always been an evolving institution, bent and shaped by the historical moment and the needs and demands of its participants. The Romans recognized the phenomenon we call "falling in love," but they considered it a hindrance to the establishment of stable households. Marriages certified by the state had their foundations not in religion or romance but in pragmatics—e.g., the joining of socially prominent

---

1. States have always established their own standards for the recognition of marriage; no consistent, nationwide definition of marriage has ever existed. Currently, a few states (e.g., Pennsylvania) still recognize common-law marriages, though for such marriages to be recognized in a non-common-law state, participants must usually submit to some official procedure. Some states allow first cousins to marry, some do not and the minimum age for legal marriage varies from state to state, as does the recognition of such contracts across state lines.

households. Divorce was acceptable, and women were generally powerless to influence its outcome; the early Catholic Church restricted divorce partly as a means of protecting women and children from easy abandonment.

At the beginning of the thirteenth century, facing schisms and heresies, and seeking to consolidate its power, the Catholic Church institutionalized marriage, confirming it as a sacrament and requiring that a priest officiate—a crucial step in the intrusion of organized religion into what had previously been a private transaction. Several centuries later, the conception of "family" began to be transformed from an extended feudal unit that often included cousins, servants, and even neighbors to a tightly knit nuclear unit composed of parents and children and headed by a man. With marriage as its cornerstone, this idealized unit forms the foundation for virtually all American legislation concerning the family.

Throughout these developments, one aspect of marriage remained consistent: even as women were idealized, they were widely regarded as chattel—part of the husband's personal property; marriage was state certification of that ownership. With the women's suffrage movement came a growing acceptance of the equality of women and men, along with the principle that the individual's happiness is of equal or greater importance than the honoring of social norms, including the marriage contract. Divorce became both common and accepted, to the point that even the woman who marries into wealth gains little economic security (absent a good lawyer or a prenuptial agreement).

Women have arguably gotten the worst of both worlds: Men may more easily leave their wives, but women are nowhere near achieving earning parity, so that now they must cope with economic insecurity as well as the fear of being dumped. For every woman who revels in freedom and the income from a fulfilling career, many more face supporting themselves and often their children on welfare or at a low salary with few benefits and no job security, dependent on child support or alimony often in arrears. No wonder that almost a third of babies are now born out of wedlock, a figure that has risen consistently since the 1950s. Some of these mothers (more than a few of them lesbians) are building matriarchal families, but many are giving birth to unplanned and probably unwanted children. Whether by design or by happenstance, these unmarried women are the primary force in changing the profile of the family; any discussion about contemporary marriage that excludes them is pointless.

Both our culture and its couples are searching for some new thinking, informed by the understanding that what is at stake is our perception of the marriage contract and women's role in defining it. Understandably, advocates of same-gender marriage have shied away from territory so daunting, focusing on the narrower civil-rights issues—

the need to extend, as required by our American commitment to equal treatment before the law, the invitation to another class of people to participate in the same troubled ritual, with one tangible result being a bonanza for attorneys specializing in gay divorce.

That fight is important, but in the long run the exclusive focus on civil rights minimizes the positive implications of the social transformation lesbians and gays are helping to bring about. For centuries gay and lesbian couples, along with significant numbers of unmarried heterosexuals, have formed and maintained relationships outside legislative and social approval that have endured persecution and duress for this simple reason: love. This is not to downplay the importance of the marriage license, which comes with rights and responsibilities without which gays and lesbians will never be considered full signatories to the social contract; nor is it to imply that these relationships are perfect. It is rather to point out the nature of gay couples' particular gift, the reward of those lucky enough to be given the wits and courage to survive in the face of adversity. Many of us know as much or more about partnering than those who have fallen into it as a given, who may live unaware of the degree to which their partnerships depend on the support of conventions—including the woman's acceptance of the man's primacy.

Baehr v. Lewin represents the logical culmination of generations of challenge, by feminists joined later by gay and lesbian activists, to an institution once almost exclusively shaped by gender roles and organized religion. As such, it presents an historic opportunity to reexamine the performance and practice of the institution on which so many of our hopes, rituals, and assumptions are based; to reconsider what we are institutionalizing and why.

* * *

Seeking to provide a legally defensible justification for limiting benefits to mixed-gender marriages, the Hawaii attorney general after years of research, has thus far only confirmed this insurmountable reality: if one subscribes to the principles that government should not serve specific religious agendas and that it should not discriminate on the basis of gender, there is no logical reason to limit marriage benefits to mixed-gender couples. Opponents of same-gender marriage argue that it contradicts the essential purpose of the institution, which is procreation; but the state does not ask prospective mixed-gender spouses if they intend to have children, and the law grants a childless married couple the same rights and benefits as their most prolific married neighbors. Invoking the nation's Judeo-Christian heritage is no help; even if one believes that Christians and Jews should dictate government policy, a few of the more liberal denominations have already endorsed same-gender marriage, and the issue is under serious debate in mainstream churches.[2] How may the state take sides in a theological debate, especially when the parties to the debate are so internally divided? In 1978, the Supreme Court established in *Zablocki v. Redhail* that a citizen's right to marry is so fundamental that it cannot be denied even to individuals who have demonstrated that they are inadequate to the task. Given that the law guarantees the right of deadbeat dads and most prison inmates to marry, what could be the logic for denying that right to two men or two women who are maintaining a stable, responsible household?

The strongest argument against same-gender marriage is not logical but arbitrary: society must have unambiguous definitions to which it turns when faced with conflicts between the desires of its citizens and the interests of its larger community. Marriage is a union between a man and a woman because that is how most people define the word, however unjust this may be for same-gender couples who wish to avail themselves of its rights.

Advocates of same-gender marriage respond that "the interests of the larger community" is an evolving concept. That an institution embodies social norms does not render it immune to change—slavery was once socially accepted, just as mixed-race marriages were widely forbidden and divorce an irreparable stigma. The rebuttal is accurate, but it evades the question of where the state draws the line in balancing individual needs and desires against the maintenance of community norms. Why should the state endorse same-gender couples but not (as opponents of same-gender marriage argue will result) polygamists or child spouses? The question is now more pressing because of the prevailing sense of accelerated cultural breakdown, wherein nothing seems secure, not even the definition of . . . well, marriage.

Surely the triumph of Reaganomics and corporate bottom-line thinking is more responsible for this breakdown of the social contract than the efforts of an ostracized minority to stabilize its communities. In any case marriage and the family began their transformation long before the gay civil-rights movement. By 1975, only six years after the Stonewall rebellion that marked the first widespread public emergence of lesbians and gays, half of all marriages ended in divorce. But in uncertain times people search for scapegoats, and unless gays and lesbians can make a convincing case for the positive impact of our relationships, we are not likely to persuade any but the already converted.

---

2. Many gay Protestant congregations, Reform Jews, Unitarians, and a number of Quaker congregations have endorsed and/or performed same-gender marriage. Presbyterians recently passed a resolution urging the national office to explore the feasibility of filing friend-of-the-court briefs "in favor of giving civil rights to same-sex partners," and the Episcopal Church is studying the blessing of same-sex unions. In addition, Hawaii's Buddhist bishops have announced their support of same-gender marriage.

*   *   *

Tellingly enough, male writers have been more passionate than women in their attachment to traditional marriage forms. Among gay male writers, Andrew Sullivan (*Virtually Normal*) and William Eskridge Jr. (*The Case for Same-Sex Marriage*) have written excellent supporting arguments.[3] Both consider legalization of same-gender marriage a means toward encouraging same-gender couples to model themselves on heterosexual marriage.

Sullivan makes an eloquent case for gay marriage but gives only a nod to the high failure rate of heterosexual marriages. Eskridge is sensitive to the women's issues inherent in marriage, but like Sullivan he endorses the institution as it exists, albeit alongside other options for partnering. Along the way he endorses the myth that marriage conveys the means to control extramarital sexual behavior to men (or women) otherwise unlikely to achieve such control, as well as the myth that gay men are more promiscuous than their straight counterparts.[4] More discouraging is Eskridge's acceptance of the assumption that sexual desire is the beast lurking in our social jungle, whose containment is a prerequisite for a moral civilization (he subtitles his book *From Sexual Liberty to Civilized Commitment,* epitomizing in a phrase the puritanical impulse to make bachelorhood equivalent to moral lassitude, where all sexual expression outside wedlock is morally tainted).

That sexuality and morality are intimately linked I take as a given; one loses sight of this connection at the risk of one's self-respect and, by extension, one's ability to love others. We are surrounded by evidence of that loss of respect, particularly in television and advertising, whose relentless promotion of amoral heterosexual sex is surely the greatest factor in breaking down public and private morality. But to presume that morality follows on marriage is to ignore centuries of evidence that each is very much possible without the other.

Among heterosexual male writers, even the most intelligent dwell in fantasy logic; when they arrive at a difficult point they invoke God (an unanswering authority), or homophobic bombast, or both. James Q. Wilson, management and public policy pro-

---

3. By contrast, *Virtual Equality,* lesbian activist Urvashi Vaid's 440-page treatment of gay and lesbian civil rights, mentions same-gender marriage only glancingly by way of offering a generalized endorsement.

4. Since great numbers of gay men remain partly or wholly in the closet, there's no accurate way to measure or compare gay male and straight male experiences. But generalizations about gay male life based on behavior in bars and sex clubs are surely no more accurate than generalizations about heterosexual male behavior drawn from visiting America's red-light districts.

fessor at UCLA, is among the more reasonable, but even he attacks (with no apparent irony) the "overeducated," whom he accuses of "mounting a utilitarian assault on the family." As the ninth of nine children of a rural, blue-collar family whose parents (married forty-seven years) sacrificed a great deal to educate their children, I note that the only "overeducated" people I have met are those who take as gospel the rules they have been taught rather than open their eyes to the reality in which they live, who witness love and yet deny its full expression.

*   *   *

Not all men and women fall into marriage unconscious of role models, of course. But it's hard work to avoid a form shouted at all of us daily in a million ways, whereas for same-gender partnerships to fall into that form requires deliberate denial. For same-gender relationships to endure, the partners have to figure out that we are required to make them up as we go along. This does not mean that we are always adequate to the task, which is why my friend Frederick Hertz, an Oakland attorney specializing in same-gender partnerships, originally opposed same-gender marriage. "Marriage as it exists imposes a legal partnership on people that is seldom in sync with how they think about their relationship," he tells me. "Marriage is designed to take care of dependent spouses, people who stay home to take care of the children, as well as to compensate for economic inequalities between genders. The idea of supporting a spouse for the rest of his or her life is totally contrary to the way most people nowadays think." Hertz (a partner in a fourteen-year relationship) resists the "couple-ism" that he perceives arising among gays and lesbians because he believes it imitates a heterosexual world in which women whose partners die or abandon them are left with almost no social support. "I talk to straight divorced women in their forties and fifties," he says. "They have a lack of self-worth that's devastating. My single gay friends have a hard enough time—imagine what things would be like for them if marriage were the norm."

Then the realities of working with gay and lesbian couples struggling without social approval brought Hertz to an uneasy support of the battle for same-gender marriage rights. Unlike most advocates, however, he qualifies his endorsement by adding that "while we're working for gay-marriage rights we should also be talking about issues of economic and emotional dependency among couples . . . . A partner can contribute emotional support to a relationship that is as valuable to its sustenance as an economic contribution. We need to find legal ways to protect those dependent spouses." To that end Hertz argues for a variety of state-endorsed domestic-partnership arrangements in addition to marriage, noting that although such categories may create a kind of second-class relationship, they're a step toward the state offering options that reflect contemporary life. "I want to go to the marriage bureau and have options among ways of getting married," he says. "I want the social acceptance of marriage but with options that are more appropriate for the range of couples' experiences—including same-gender childless couples."

In other words, rather than attempt to conform same-gender couplings to an institution so deeply rooted in sexism, why not consider ways of incorporating stability and egalitarianism into new models of marriage? Rather than consider the control of sexual behavior as a primary goal of marriage, why not leave issues of monogamy to the individuals and focus instead on marriage as the primary (though not the only) means whereby two people help each other and their dependents through life?

Invoking the feminist writer Martha Fineman, American University law professor Nancy Polikoff argues that organizing society around sexually connected people is wrong; the more central units are dependents and their caretakers. Extrapolating from this thinking, one can imagine the state requiring that couples, regardless of gender, take steps toward attaining the benefits currently attached to marriage. Under this model the state might restrict the most significant of marriage's current benefits to those couples who demonstrate stability. The government might then get out of the marriage-certification business altogether; Hawaii governor Ben Cayetano, among others, has suggested as much. Government conferred benefits currently reserved for married couples would instead be allocated as rewards for behavior that contributes to social stability. Tax breaks would be awarded, regardless of marital status, to stable lower- and middle-income households financially responsible for children, the elderly, or the handicapped. Other state- or federally conferred privileges—such as residency for foreign spouses, veteran's benefits, tax-free transfer of property, and the right to joint adoption—would be reserved for couples who had demonstrated the ability to sustain a household over two to five years. The decision to assume the label "marriage" would be left to the individuals involved, who might or might not seek ratification of their decision by a priest or minister or rabbi. The motivation behind such changes would be not to eliminate marriage but to encourage and sustain stable households, while leaving the definition and sustenance of marriage to the partners involved, along with their community of relatives, friends, and—if they so choose—churches.

*   *   *

In the most profound relationship I have known, my partner and I followed a pattern typical of an enduring gay male relationship. We wrangled over monogamy, ultimately deciding to permit safe sex outside the relationship. In fact, he never acted on that permission; I acted on it exactly once, in an incident we discussed the next day. We were bound not by sexual exclusivity but by trust, mutual support, and fidelity—in a word, love, only one manifestation of which is monogamy.

Polikoff tells of another model, unconventional by the standards of the larger culture but common among gay and lesbian communities: A friend died of breast cancer; her blood family arrived for the funeral. "They were astounded to discover that their daughter had a group of people who were a family—somebody had organized a schedule, somebody brought food every night," she says. "In some ways it was the absence of marriage as a dominant institution that created space for the development of a family defined in much broader ways." I find it difficult to imagine either of these relationships—mine or that described by Polikoff—developing in the presence of marriage as practiced by most of our forebears; easier to imagine our experiences influencing the evolution of marriage to a more encompassing, compassionate place.

Earlier I called myself an "AIDS widower," but I was playing fast and loose with words; I can't be a widower, since my partner and I were never married. He was the only child of Holocaust survivors, and he taught me, an HIV-negative man preoccupied with the future, the lessons his parents had taught him: the value of living fully in the present and the power of love.

He fell ill while we were traveling in France, during what we knew would be our last vacation. After checking him into a Paris hospital, I had to sneak past the staff to be at his side; each time they ordered me out, until finally they told me they would call the police. Faced with the threat of violence, I left the room. He died alone as I paced the hall outside his door, frantic to be at his side but with no recourse—I was, after all, only his friend.

*   *   *

At a dinner party not long ago I asked a mix of gay and heterosexual guests to name ways society might better support the survival of gay and lesbian relationships. A beat of silence followed, then someone piped up: "You mean, the survival of any relationships." Everyone agreed that all relationships are under stress, that their dissolution had become an accepted, possibly assumed part of the status quo.

The question is not, as opponents would have us believe, will marriage survive the legalization of same-gender partnerships? Instead, the questions are how do society and the state support stable households in a world where the composition of families is changing, and how might same-gender relationships contribute to that end?

Denied access to marriage, lesbians and gays inevitably idealize it, but given the abuse the dominant culture has heaped on the institution, maybe it could use a little glamour. In my more hopeful moments, I think gays and lesbians might help revitalize and reconceptualize marriage by popularizing the concept of rich, whole, productive couplings based less on the regulation of sexual behavior and the maintenance of gender roles than on the formation of mutually respectful partnerships. *Baehr v. Lewin* presents us with a chance to conceive of a different way of coupling, but only if we recognize and act on its implications. Otherwise the extension (if achieved) to same-gender couples of the marital status quo will represent a landmark civil-rights victory but a subcultural defeat in its failure to incorporate into the culture at large lessons learned by generations of women and men—lesbian or gay or straight—who built and sustained and fought for partnerships outside the bounds of conventional gender roles.

*   *   *

In *Word Is Out,* a 1977 documentary portraying lesbian and gay lives, comedienne Pat Bond described butch and femme role-playing among lesbians in the 1950s, roles as unvarying as those of Ozzie and Harriet. "Relationships that lasted twenty or thirty years were role-playing," she says. "At least in that role-playing you knew the rules, you at least knew your mother and father and you knew what they did and you tried to do the same thing. . . . Now you say, 'Okay, I'm not butch or femme, I'm just me.' Well, who the hell is me? What do I do? How am I to behave?"

To heterosexuals who feel as if the marriage debate is pulling the rug of certainty from beneath them, I say, Welcome to the club. Gays' and lesbians' construction of community—which is to say, identity—is the logical culmination of the American democratic experiment, which provides its citizens with an open playing field on which each of us has a responsibility to define and then respect his or her boundaries and rules. Human nature being what it is, the American scene abounds with stories of people unable, unwilling, or uninterested in meeting that challenge—people who fare better within a package of predetermined rules and boundaries. For those people (so long as they are straight), traditional marriage and roles remain. But for the questioning mind and heart, the debate surrounding marriage is only the latest intrusion of ambiguity into the artificially ordered world of Western thinking.

And Western culture has never tolerated ambiguity. The Romans placed their faith in the state; the Christians, in God; the rationalists, in reason and science. But in marked contrast to Eastern religions and philosophy, all have in common their search for a constant governing structure, a kind of unified field theory for the workings of the heart. The emergence of gays and lesbians from the closet (a movement born of Western religious and rationalist thinking) is only one among many developments that reveal the futility of that search—how it inevitably arrives at the enigma that lies at the heart of being.

But the rules are so comforting and comfortable! And it is easier to oppress some so that others might live in certainty, ignoring the reality that the mystery of love and life and death is really grander and more glorious than human beings can grasp, much less legislate.

Reading Comprehension—Points of Engagement

1. According to Fenton Johnson, how does the assumption of equality between men and women directly affect the discussion about same-sex marriages in America? Point to two specific passages in Johnson that support your response.

2. Consider the events that Johnson cites in Hawaii, specifically the court case which provoked the creation of the Defense of Marriage Act discussed in the first paragraph. What was the ruling made in Hawaii? What particular kind of marriage does it concern? Why, according to Johnson, was this ruling important? Refer to the text in your answer.

3. Near the end of his article, Johnson quotes a guest from one of his dinner parties. In response to Johnson's question about how "society might better support the survival of gay and lesbian relationships," a guest replied, "You mean, the survival of any relationships." According to what you have read in Johnson's article, why might we consider relationships in general to be under threat? Where do these threats come from, and what forms do they take? Does Johnson offer any answers to his own question? What are these answers? And if you can't find any, why can't you?

Assignment Questions—Points of Departure

1. Fenton Johnson, Lewis Lapham, and Katha Pollitt are all concerned with how differences between and among people are perpetuated. What benefits are to be gained by a state or community by encoding difference in law or social practice, or making it a central part of how a society is defined? Are the results always positive, always negative, or a mixture between the two? What aspects of difference do you think should be recognized in law and in social practice, and to which ones should a blind eye be turned? Why? What is the result of doing either? Your project is to

answer these questions using Johnson and either Pollitt or Lapham, and to express your own views on how difference functions in American culture.

2. In "Wedded To An Illusion," Fenton Johnson discusses reasons for and against same-sex marriage, suggesting that most objections are due to convention rather than to logic. Michael Pollan, in "An Animal's Place," similarly suggests that those who argue for placing human rights over animal rights are doing so based on emotion and habit, rather than reason. For this assignment, write an essay which considers how much of what we believe to be right and moral is dictated by tradition and habit, rather than by any logical truth. How do we draw the line between these two things, in law? Is it possible at all, or must there always be room for emotion and tradition, as well as justice and reason, in our laws and legal systems?

3. Michael Kamber's essay, *Toil and Temptation,* paints a picture of Mexicans living in New York City, outside the protection of the U.S. government because they are in this country illegally. In Fenton Johnson's essay, a significant part of American society is shown to be excluded from legal and social benefits accorded to other people in the same kinds of relationships, because the two members of the relationship are of the same sex. What should be done to protect the rights of both these groups? Should they be subject to different consideration, different 'rules'? What rules should they be governed by? Why?

4. In his essay, Fenton Johnson proposes that some aspects of marriage in America are more "ideal" than "real." Consider how his critique of marriage as an institution fits into the current obsession with reality TV, which you could also argue is more ideal than real. In this paper, your project is to propose a way to understand marriage that encompasses the views of both Fenton Johnson and Francine Prose on the overlap between ideals and reality. Be sure to address their main projects as you assert your own position on whether the institution of marriage is, in fact, more ideal or more real, and for whom.

Control Artist
Steven Johnson

Points of Access

1. Do you play video games? If so, what kinds? What makes them interesting to you? If you don't play video games, why not? Was there a time when you did play? Why did you stop?

2. Have you ever watched a flock of birds take off together all at once? How do you think they know how to do that? Why don't they run into one another? Would you describe the group of birds as more organized or more chaotic? Why? What do you think allows them, or compels them, to stay as a group?

3. Do you prefer to work in collaboration with people as equals improvising as you go, or do you prefer a clear line of authority with explicit directions to follow? What are the advantages of each? Which one is more appealing to you personally? Why?

4. Why do human beings create rules to follow? What do they do for us? And why do we have a tendency to break them sometimes? What happens when we break rules? Are the consequences always and only negative? Or can you think of times when breaking rules results in a positive outcome?

On the screen, the pixels dance: bright red dots with faint trails of green, scurrying across a black background, like fireflies set against the sky of a summer night. For a few seconds, the movement on-screen looks utterly random: pixels darting back and forth, colliding, and moving on. And then suddenly a small pocket of red dots gather together in a pulsing, erratic circle, ringed by a strip of green. The circle grows as more red pixels collide with it; the green belt expands. Seconds later, another lopsided circle appears in the corner of the screen, followed by three more. The circles are unlike any geometric shape you've ever seen. They seem more like a life-form—a digital blob—pulsing haphazardly, swelling and contracting. Two blobs slowly creep toward each other, then merge, forming a single unit. After a few minutes, seven large blobs dominate, with only a few remaining free-floating red pixels ambling across the screen.

Welcome to the world of Mitch Resnick's tool for visualizing self-organizing systems, StarLogo. A descendant of Seymour Papert's legendary turtle-based programming language, Logo, StarLogo allows you to model emergent behavior using simple, English-like commands—and it displays that behavior in vivid, real-time animations. If decentralized systems can sometimes seem counterintuitive or abstract, difficult to describe in words, StarLogo makes them come to life with dynamic graphics that are uniquely suited for the Nintendo generation. If a calendar is a tool for helping us think about the flow of time, and a pie chart is a tool for thinking about statistical distributions, StarLogo is a tool for thinking about bottom-up systems. And, in fact, those lifelike blobs on the screen take us back to the very beginnings of our story: they are digital slime molds, cells aggregating into larger clusters without any "pacemaker" cell leading the way.

"Those red pixels are the individual slime mold cells," Resnick says, pointing at the screen, sitting in his Cambridge office. "They're programmed to wander aimlessly around the screen space, and as they wander, they 'emit' the green color, which quickly fades away. That color is the equivalent of the c-AMP chemical that the molds use to coordinate their behavior. I've programmed the red cells to 'sniff' the green color and follow the gradient in the color. 'Smelling' the green pixels leads the cells toward each other."

Like Gordon's ant colonies, Resnick's slime mold simulation is sensitive to population density. "Let's start with only a hundred slime mold cells," he says, adjusting a slider on the screen that alters the number of cells in the simulation. He presses a start button, and a hundred red pixels begin their frenetic dance—only this time, no clusters appear. There are momentary flashes of green as a few cells collide, but no larger shapes emerge at all.

"With a hundred cells, there isn't enough contact for the aggregates to form. But triple the population like so," he says, pulling the slider farther to the right, "and you increase the contact between cells. At three hundred cells, you'll usually get one cluster after a few minutes, and sometimes two." We wait for thirty seconds or so, and after a few false starts, a cluster takes shape near the center of the screen. "Once they come together, the slime molds are extremely difficult to break apart, even though they can be very fickle about aggregating in the first place."

Resnick then triples the population and starts the simulation over again. It's a completely different system this time around: there's a flash of red-celled activity, then almost immediately ten clusters form, nearly filling the screen with pulsing watermelon shapes. Only a handful of lonely red cells remain, drifting aimlessly between the clusters. More is *very* different. "The interesting thing is," Resnick says with a chuckle, "you wouldn't have necessarily predicted that behavior in advance, just from looking at the instructions. You might have said, the slime mold cells will all immediately form a giant cluster, or they'll form clusters that keep breaking up. In fact, neither is the case, and the whole system turns out to be much more sensitive to initial conditions. At a hundred cells, there are no clusters at all; at three hundred, you'll probably get one, but it'll be pretty much permanent; and at nine hundred cells, you'll immediately get ten clusters, but they'll bounce around a little more." But you couldn't tell any of that just by looking at the original instruction set. You have to make it *live* before you can understand how it works.

*   *   *

StarLogo may look like a video game at first glance, but Resnick's work is really more in the tradition of Friedrich Froebel, the German educator who invented kindergarten, and who spent much of his career in the early nineteenth century devising ingenious toys that would both amuse and entertain toddlers. "When Froebel designed the first kindergarten," Resnick tells me, "he developed a set of toys they called Froebel's gifts, and he carefully designed them with the assumption that the object he'd put in the hands of kids would make a big difference in what they learned and how they learned. We see the same thing carried through today. We see some of our new technology as the latter-day versions of Froebel's gifts, trying to put new sorts of materials and new types of toys in the hands of kids that will change what they think about—and the *way* they think about it."

StarLogo, of course, is designed to help kids—and grown-ups, for that matter—think about a specific type of phenomenon, but it is by no means limited to slime molds. There are StarLogo programs that simulate ant foraging, forest fires, epidemics, traffic jams—even programs that generate more traditional Euclidean shapes using bottom-up techniques. (Resnick calls this "turtle geometry," after the nickname used to describe the individual agents in a StarLogo program, a term that is itself borrowed from the original Logo language, which Papert designed to teach children about traditional programming techniques.) This knack for shape-shifting is one of the language's great virtues. "StarLogo is a type of modeling environment where kids can build models of certain phenomena that they might observe in the world," Resnick says. "Specifically, it enables them to build models of phenomena where lots of things interact with each other. So they might model cars on a highway, or they might model something like a bird flock, where the kids design behavior for lots of individual birds and then see the patterns that form through all the interactions.

"One reason that we're especially interested in building a tool like this is that these phenomena are common in the everyday world," he continues. "We see bird flocks and traffic jams all of the time. On the other hand, people have a lot of trouble understanding these types of phenomena. When people see a flock of birds, they assume the bird in the front is the leader and the others are just following. But that's not the way the real birds form flocks. In fact, each bird just follows simple rules and they end up together as a group."

At its core, StarLogo is optimized for modeling emergent systems like the ones we've seen in the previous chapters, and so the building blocks for any StarLogo program are familiar ones: local interactions between large numbers of agents, governed by simple rules of mutual feedback. StarLogo is a kind of thinking prosthetic, a tool that lets the mind wrap itself around a concept that it's not naturally equipped to grasp. We need StarLogo to help us understand emergent behavior for the same reason we need X-ray machines or calculators: our perceptual and cognitive faculties can't do the work on their own.

It's a limitation that can be surprisingly hard to overcome. Consider the story that Resnick tells of artificial-intelligence guru Marvin Minsky encountering the slime mold simulation for the first time. "One day shortly after I developed the first working prototype of StarLogo, Minsky wandered into my office. On the computer screen he saw an early version of my StarLogo slime mold program. There were several green blobs on the screen (representing a chemical pheromone), with a cluster of turtles moving around inside each blob. A few turtles wandered randomly in the empty space between the blobs. Whenever one of these turtles wandered close enough to a blob, he joined the cluster of turtles inside."

Minsky scanned the screen for a few seconds, then asked Resnick what he was working on. "I explained that I was experimenting with some self-organizing systems. Minsky looked at the screen for a while, then said, 'But those creatures aren't self-organizing. They're just moving toward the green food.'"

"Minsky had assumed that the green blobs were pieces of food, placed throughout the turtles' world. In fact, the green blobs were created by the turtles themselves. But Minsky didn't see it that way. Instead of seeing creatures organizing themselves, he saw the creatures organized around some preexisting pieces of food. He assumed that the pattern of aggregation was determined by the placement of food. And he stuck with that interpretation—at least for a while—even after I told him that the program involved self-organization."

Minsky had fallen for the myth of the ant queen: the assumption that collective behavior implied some kind of centralized authority—in this case, that the food was dictating the behavior of the slime mold cells. Minsky assumed that you could predict where the clusters would form by looking at where the food was placed when the simulation began. But there wasn't any food. Nor was there anything dictating that clusters should form in specific locations. The slime mold cells were self-organizing, albeit within parameters that Resnick had initially defined.

"Minsky has thought more—and more deeply—about self-organization and decentralized systems than almost anyone else," Resnick writes. "When I explained the rules underlying the slime mold program to him, he understood immediately what was happening. But his initial assumption was revealing. The fact that even *Marvin Minsky* had this reaction is an indication of the powerful attraction of centralized explanations."

Of course, on the most fundamental level, StarLogo is itself a centralized system: it obeys rules laid down by a single authority—the programmer. But the route from Resnick's code to those slime mold clusters is indirect. You don't program the slime mold cells to form clusters; you program them to follow patterns in the trails left behind by their neighbors. If you have enough cells, and if the trails last long enough, you'll get clusters, but they're not something you can control directly. And predicting the number of clusters—or their longevity—is almost impossible without extensive trial-and-error experimentation with the system. Kevin Kelly called his groundbreaking book on decentralized behavior *Out of Control,* but the phrase doesn't quite do justice to emergent systems—or at least the ones that we've deliberately set out to create on the computer screen. Systems like StarLogo are not utter anarchies: they obey rules that we define in advance, but those rules only govern the micromotives. The macrobehavior is another matter. You don't control that directly. All you can do is set up the conditions that you think will make that behavior possible. Then you press play and see what happens.

That kind of oblique control is a funny thing to encounter in the world of software, but it is becoming increasingly common. Programming used to be thought of as a domain of pure control: you told the computer what to do, and the computer had no choice but to obey your orders. If the computer failed to do your bidding, it inevitably had to do with a bug in your code, and not the machine's autonomy. The best programmers were the ones who had the most control of the system, the ones who could compel the machines to do the work with the least amount of code. It's no accident that Norbert Wiener derived the term *cybernetics* from the Greek word for "steersman": the art of software has from the beginning been about control systems and how best to drive them.

But that control paradigm is slowly giving way to a more oblique form of programming: software that you "grow" instead of engineer, software that learns to solve problems autonomously, the way Oliver Selfridge envisioned with his Pandemonium model. The new paradigm borrows heavily from the playbook of natural selection, breeding new programs out of a varied gene pool. The first few decades of software were essentially creationist in philosophy—an almighty power wills the program into being. But the next generation is profoundly Darwinian.

*   *   *

Consider the program for number sorting devised several years ago by supercomputing legend Danny Hillis, a program that undermines all of our conventional assumptions about how software should be produced. For years, number sorting has served as one of the benchmark tests for ingenious programmers, like chess-playing applications. Throw a hundred random numbers at a program and see how many steps it takes to sort the digits into the correct order. Using traditional programming techniques, the record for number sorting stood at sixty steps when Hillis decided to try his hand. But Hillis didn't just sit down to write a number-sorting application. What Hillis created was a recipe for learning, a program for creating another program. In other words, he didn't teach the computer how to sort numbers. He taught the computer to figure out how to sort numbers *on its own.*

Hillis pulled off this sleight of hand by connecting the formidable powers of natural selection to a massively parallel supercomputer—the Connection Machine that he himself had helped design. Instead of authoring a number-sorting program himself—writing out lines of code and debugging—Hillis instructed the computer to generate thousands of miniprograms, each composed of random combinations of instructions, creating a kind of digital gene pool. Each program was confronted with a disorderly sequence of numbers, and each tried its hand at putting them in the correct order. The first batch of programs were, as you might imagine, utterly inept at number sorting. (In fact, the overwhelming majority of the programs were good for nothing at all.) But some programs were better than others, and because Hillis had established a quantifiable goal for the experiment—numbers arranged in the correct order—the computer could select the few programs that were in the ballpark. Those programs became the basis for the next iteration, only Hillis would also mutate *their* code slightly and crossbreed them with the other promising programs. And then the whole process would repeat itself: the most successful programs of the new generation would be chosen, then subjected to the same transformations. Mix, mutate, evaluate, repeat.

After only a few minutes—and thousands of cycles—this evolutionary process resulted in a powerful number-sorting program, capable of arranging a string of random numbers in seventy-five steps. Not a record breaker, by any means, but impressive nonetheless. The problem, though, was that the digital gene pool was maxing out at the seventy-five-step mark. Each time Hillis ran the sequence, the computer would quickly evolve a powerful and efficient number sorter, but it would run out of steam at around seventy-five steps. After enough experimentation, Hillis recognized that his system had encountered a hurdle often discussed by evolutionary theorists: the software had stumbled across a local maximum in the fitness landscape.

Imagine the space of all possible number-sorting programs spread out like a physical landscape, with more successful programs residing at higher elevations, and less successful programs lurking in the valleys. Evolutionary software is a way of blindly probing that space, looking for gradients that lead to higher elevations. Think of an early stage in Hillis's cycle: one evolved routine sorts a few steps faster than its "parent" and so it survives into the next round. That survival is the equivalent of climbing up one notch on the fitness landscape. If its "descendant" sorts even more efficiently, its "genes" are passed on to the next generation, and it climbs another notch higher.

The problem with this approach is that there are false peaks in the fitness landscape. There are countless ways to program a computer to sort numbers with tolerable efficiency, but only a few ways to sort numbers if you're intent on setting a world record. And those different programs vary dramatically in the way they tackle the problem. Think of those different approaches as peaks on the fitness landscape: there are thousands of small ridges, but only a few isolated Everests. If a program evolves using one approach, its descendants may never find their way to another approach—because Hillis's system only rewarded generations that *improved* on the work done by their ancestors. Once the software climbs all the way to the top of a ridge, there's no reward in descending and looking for another, higher peak, because a less successful program—one that drops down a notch on the fitness landscape—would instantly be eliminated from the gene pool. Hillis's software was settling in at the seventy-five-step ridges because the penalty for searching out the higher points was too severe.

Hillis's stroke of genius was to force his miniprograms out of the ridges by introducing predators into the mix. Just as in real-world ecosystems, predators effectively raised the bar for evolved programs that became lazy because of their success. Before the introduction of predators, a miniprogram that had reached a seventy-five-step ridge knew that its offspring had a chance of surviving if it stayed at that local maximum, but faced almost certain death if it descended to search out higher ground. But the predators changed all that. They hunted down ridge dwellers and forced them to improvise: if a miniprogram settled into the seventy-five-step range, it could be destroyed by predator programs. Once the predators appeared on the scene, it became more productive to descend to lower altitudes to search out a new peak than to stay put at a local maximum.

Hillis structured the predator-prey relationship as an arms race: the higher the sorting programs climbed, the more challenging the predators became. If the system stumbled across a seventy-step peak then predators were introduced that hunted down seventy-step programs. Anytime the software climbers decided to rest on their laurels, a predator appeared to scatter them off to find higher elevations.

After only thirty minutes of this new system, the computer had evolved a batch of programs that could sort numbers in sixty-two steps, just two shy of the all-time record. Hillis's system functioned, in biological terms, more like an environment than an organism: it created a space where intelligent programs could grow and adapt, exceeding the capacities of all but the most brilliant flesh-and-blood programmers. "One of the interesting things about the sorting programs that evolved in my experiment is that I do not understand how they work," Hillis writes in his book *The Pattern on the Stone.* "I have carefully examined their instruction sequences, but I do not understand them: I have no simpler explanation of how the programs work than the instruction sequences themselves. It may be that the programs are not understandable."

Proponents of emergent software have made some ambitious claims for their field, including scenarios where a kind of digital Darwinism leads to a simulated intelligence, capable of open-ended learning and complex interaction with the outside world. (Most advocates don't think that such an intelligence will necessarily resemble *human* smarts, but that's another matter, one that we'll examine in the conclusion.) In the short term, though, emergent software promises to transform the way that we think about creating code: in the next decade, we may well see a shift from top-down, designed programs to bottom-up, evolved versions, like Hillis's number-sorting applet—"less like engineering a machine," Hillis says, "than baking a cake, or growing a garden."

That transformation may be revolutionary for the programmers, but if it does its job, it won't necessarily make much of a difference for the end users. We might notice our spreadsheets recalculating a little faster and our grammar checker finally working, but we'll be dealing with the end results of emergent software, not the process itself. (The organisms, in Darwinian terms, and not the environment that nurtured them.) But will ordinary computer-users get a chance to experiment with emergent software first-hand, a chance to experiment with its more oblique control systems? Will growing gardens of code ever become a mainstream activity?

In fact, we can get our hands dirty already. And we can do it just by playing a game.

*   *   *

It's probably fair to say that digital media has been wrestling with "control issues" from its very origins. The question of control, after all, lies at the heart of the interactive revolution, since making something interactive entails a shift in control, from the technology—or the puppeteers behind the technology—to the user. Most recurring issues in interactive design hover above the same underlying question: Who's driving here, human or machine? Programmer or user? These may seem like esoteric questions, but they have implications that extend far beyond design-theory seminars or cybercafé philosophizing. I suspect that we're only now beginning to understand how complicated these issues are, as we acclimate to the strange indirection of emergent software.

In a way, we've been getting our sea legs for this new environment for the past few years now. Some of the most interesting interactive art and games of the late nineties explicitly challenged our sense of control or made us work to establish it. Some of these designs belonged to the world of avant-garde or academic experimentation, while others had more mainstream appeal. But in all these designs, the feeling of wrestling with or exploring the possibilities of the software—the process of mastering the system—was transformed from a kind of prelude to the core experience of the design. It went from a bug to a feature.

There are different ways to go about challenging our sense of control. Some programs, such as the ingenious Tap, Type, Write—created by MIT's John Maeda—make it immediately clear that the user is driving. The screen starts off with an array of letters; hitting a specific key triggers a sudden shift in the letterforms presented on-screen. The overall effect is like a fireworks show sponsored by Alphabet Soup. Press a key, and the screen explodes, ripples, reorders itself. It's hypnotic, but also a little mystifying. What algorithm governs this interaction? Something happens on-screen when you type, but it takes a while to figure out what rules of transformation are at work here. You know you're doing something, you just don't know what it is.

The OSS code, created by the European avant-punk group Jodi.org, messes with our sense of control on a more profound—some would say annoying—level. A mix of anarchic screen-test patterns and eclectic viral programming, the Jodi software is best described as the digital equivalent of an aneurysm. Download the software and the desktop overflows with meaningless digits; launch one of the applications, and your screen descends instantly into an unstable mix of static and structure. Move the mouse in one direction, or double click, and there's a fleeting sense of something changing. Did the flicker rate shift? Did those interlaced patterns reverse themselves? At hard-to-predict moments, the whole picture show shuts down—invariably after a few frantic keystrokes and command clicks—and you're left wondering, Did I do that?

No doubt many users are put off by the dislocations of Tap, Type, Write and OSS, and many walk away from the programs feeling as though they never got them to work quite right, precisely because their sense of control remained so elusive. For me, I find these programs strangely empowering; they challenge the mind in the same way distortion challenged the ear thirty-five years ago when the Beatles and the Velvet Underground first began overloading their amps. We find ourselves reaching around the noise—the lack of structure—for some sort of clarity, only to realize that it's the reaching that makes the noise redemptive. Video games remind us that messing with our control expectations can be fun, even addictive, as long as the audience has recognized that the confusion is part of the show. For a generation raised on MTV's degraded images, that recognition comes easily. The Nintendo generation, in other words, has been well prepared for the mediated control of emergent software.

Take as example one of the most successful rides from the Nintendo64 platform, Shigeru Miyamoto's Zelda: Ocarina of Time. Zelda embodies the uneven development of late-nineties interactive entertainment. The plot belongs squarely to the archaic world of fairy tales—a young boy armed with magic spells sets off to rescue the princess. As a control system, though, Zelda is an incredibly complex structure, with hundreds of interrelated goals and puzzles dispersed throughout the game's massive virtual world. Moving your character around is simple enough, but figuring out what you're supposed to do with him takes hours of exploration and trial and error. By traditional usability standards, Zelda is a complete mess: you need a hundred-page guidebook just to establish what the rules are. But if you see that opacity as part of the art—like John Cale's distorted viola—then the whole experience changes: you're exploring the world of the game and the rules of the game at the same time.

Think about the ten-year-olds who willingly immerse themselves in Zelda's world. For them, the struggle for mastery over the system doesn't feel like a struggle. They've been decoding the landscape on the screen—guessing at causal relations between actions and results, building working hypotheses about the system's underlying rules—since before they learned how to read. The conventional wisdom about these kids is that they're more nimble at puzzle solving and more manually dexterous than the TV generation, and while there's certainly some truth to that, I think we lose something important in stressing how talented this generation is with their joysticks. I think they have developed another skill, one that almost looks like patience: they are more tolerant of being out of control, more tolerant of that exploratory phase where the rules don't all make sense, and where few goals have been clearly defined. In other words, they are uniquely equipped to embrace the more oblique control system of emergent software. The hard work of tomorrow's interactive design will be exploring the tolerance—that suspension of control—in ways that enlighten us, in ways that move beyond the insulting residue of princesses and magic spells.

*   *   *

With these new types of games, a new type of game designer has arisen as well. The first generation of video games may have indirectly influenced a generation of artists, and a handful were adopted as genuine objets d'art, albeit in a distinctly campy fashion. (Table-top Ms. Pac-Man games started to appear at downtown Manhattan clubs in the early nineties, around the time the Museum of the Moving Image created its permanent game collection.) But artists themselves rarely ventured directly into the game-design industry. Games were for kids, after all. No self-respecting artist would immerse himself in that world with a straight face.

But all this has changed in recent years, and a new kind of hybrid has appeared—a fusion of artist, programmer, and complexity theorist—creating interactive projects that challenge the mind and the thumb at the same time. And while Tap, Type, Write and Zelda were not, strictly speaking, emergent systems, the new generation of game designers and artists have begun explicitly describing their work using the language of self-organization. This too brings to mind the historical trajectory of the rock music genre. For the first fifteen or twenty years, the charts are dominated by lowest-common-denominator titles, rarely venturing far from the established conventions or addressing issues that would be beyond the reach of a thirteen-year-old. And then a few mainstream acts begin to push at the edges—the Beatles or the Stones in the music world, Miyamoto and Peter Molyneux in the gaming community—and the expectations about what constitutes a pop song or a video game start to change. And that transformation catches the attention of the avant-garde—the Velvet Underground, say, or the emergent-game designers—who suddenly start thinking of pop music or video games as a legitimate channel for self-expression. Instead of writing beat poetry or staging art happenings, they pick up a guitar—or a joystick.

By this standard, Eric Zimmerman is the Lou Reed of the new gaming culture. A stocky thirty-year-old, with short, club-kid hair and oversize Buddy Holly glasses, Zimmerman has carved out a career for himself that would have been unthinkable even a decide ago: bouncing between academia (he teaches at NYU's influential Interactive Telecommunications Program), the international art scene (he's done installations for museums in Geneva, Amsterdam, and New York), and the video-game world. Unlike John Maeda and/or Jodi.org, Zimmerman doesn't "reference" the iconography of gaming in his work—he openly embraces that tradition, to the extent that you have to think of Zimmerman's projects as games first and art second. They can be fiendishly fun to play and usually involve spirited competition between players. But they are also self-consciously designed as emergent systems.

"One of the pleasures of what I do," Zimmerman tells me, over coffee near the NYU campus, "is that you get to see a player take what you've designed and use it in completely unexpected ways." The designer, in other words, controls the micromotives of the player's actions. But the way those micromotives are exploited—and the macrobehavior that they generate—are out of the designer's control. They have a life of their own.

Take Zimmerman's game Gearheads, which he designed during a brief sojourn at Phillips Interactive in 1996. Gearheads is a pure-bred emergent system: a meshwork of autonomous agents following simple rules and mutually influencing each other's behavior. It is a close relative of StarLogo or Gordon's harvester ants, but it's ingeniously dressed up to look like a modern video game. Instead of spare colored pixels, Zimmerman populated the Gearhead world with an eclectic assortment of children's toys that march across the screen like a motley band of animated soldiers.

"There are twelve windup toys," Zimmerman explains. "You design a box of toys by choosing four of them. You wind up your toy and release it from the edges of the game board, and the goal of the game is to get as many toys as possible across your opponent's side of the screen. Each of the toys has a unique set of behaviors that affect the behavior of other toys." A skull toy, for instance, "frightens" toys that it encounters, causing them to reverse direction, while an animated hand winds up other toys, allowing them to march across the screen for a longer duration. As with the harvester ants or the slime mold cells, when one agent encounters another agent, both agents may launch into a new pattern of behavior. Stumble across your hundredth forager of the afternoon, and you'll switch over to midden duty; stumble across Zimmerman's skull toy and you'll turn around and go the other way.

"The key thing is that once you've released your toys, they're autonomous. You're only affecting the system from the margins," Zimmerman says. "It's a little chaos machine: unexpected things happen, and you only control it from the edges." As Zimmerman tested Gearheads in early 1996, he found that this oblique control system resulted in behavior that Zimmerman hadn't deliberately programmed, behavior that emerged out of the local interactions of the toys, despite the overall simplicity of the game.

"Two toys reverse the direction of other toys—the skull, and the Santa toy, who's called Krush Kringle," Zimmerman says. "He walks for a few steps and then he pounds the ground, and all the toys near him reverse direction. During our testing, we found a combination where you could release one Krush Kringle out there, then the walking hand that winds up toys, then another Krush Kringle. The hand would run out and wind up the first Krush, and then the Krush would pound the floor, reversing the direction of the hand, and sending it back to the second Krush, which it would wind up. Then the second Krush would stomp on the ground, and the hand would turn around and wind up the first Krush. And so the little system of these three toys would march together across the screen, like a small flock of birds. The first time we saw it happen, we were astonished."

These unexpected behaviors may not seem like much at first glance, particularly in a climate that places so much emphasis on photo-realistic, 3-D worlds and blood-spattering combat. Zimmerman's toys are kept deliberately simple; they don't simulate intelligence, and they don't trigger symphonies of surround sound through your computer speakers. A snapshot of Resnick's slime molds looks like something you might have seen on a first-generation Atari console. But I'll put my money on the slime molds and Krush Kringles nonetheless. Those watermelon clusters and autowinding flocks strike me as the very beginning of what will someday form an enormously powerful cultural lineage. Watching these patterns emerge spontaneously on the screen is a little like watching two single-celled organisms decide to share resources for the first time. It doesn't look like much, but the same logic carried through a thousand generations, or a hundred thousand—like Hillis growing his gardens of code—can end up changing the world. You just have to think about it on the right scale.

*   *   *

Most game players, alas, live on something close to day-trader time, at least when they're in the middle of a game—thinking more about their next move than their next meal, and usually blissfully oblivious to the ten- or twenty-year trajectory of software development. No one wants to play with a toy that's going to be fun after a few decades of tinkering—the toys have to be engaging *now,* or kids will find other toys. And one of the things that make all games so engaging to us is that they have rules. In traditional games like Monopoly or go or chess, the fun of the game—the play—is what happens when you explore the space of possibilities defined by the rules. Without rules, you have something closer to pure improv theater, where anything can happen at any time. Rules give games their structure, and without that structure, there's no game: every move is a checkmate, and every toss of the dice lands you on Park Place.

This emphasis on rules might seem like the antithesis of the open-ended, organic systems we've examined over the preceding chapters, but nothing could be further from the truth. Emergent systems too are rule-governed systems: their capacity for learning and growth and experimentation derives from their adherence to low-level rules: ants choosing to forage or not, based on patterns in their encounters with other ants; the Alexa software making connections based on patterns in the clickstream. If any of these systems—or, to put it more precisely, the agents that make up these systems—suddenly started following their own rules, or doing away with rules altogether, the system would stop working: there'd be no global intelligence, just a teeming anarchy of isolated agents, a swarm without logic. Emergent behaviors, like games, are all about living within the boundaries defined by rules, but also using that space to create something greater than the sum of its parts.

Understanding emergence should be a great boon for the video-game industry. But some serious challenges face the designers of games that attempt to harness the power and adaptability of self-organization and channel it into a game aimed at a mass audience. And those challenges all revolve around the same phenomenon: the capacity of emergent systems to suddenly start behaving in unpredictable ways, sorcerer's-apprentice style—like Zimmerman's flock of Krush Kringles.

Consider the case of Evolva, a widely hyped game released in mid-2000 by a British software company called Computer Artworks. The product stood as something of a change for CA, which was last seen marketing a trippy screen-saver called Organic Art that allowed you to replace your desktop with a menagerie of alien-looking life-forms. That program came bundled with a set of prepackaged images, but more adventurous users could also grow their own, "breeding" new creatures with the company's A-Life technology. While the Organic Art series was a success, it quickly became clear to the CA team that *interacting* with your creatures would be much more entertaining than simply gazing at snapshots of them. Who wants to look at Polaroids of Sea-Monkeys when you can play with the adorable little critters yourself?

And so Computer Artworks turned itself into a video-game company. Evolva was their first fully interactive product to draw upon the original artificial-life software, integrating its mutation and interbreeding routines into a game world that might otherwise be mistaken for a hybrid of Myth and Quake. The plot was standard-issue video-game fare: Earth has been invaded by an alien parasite that threatens world destruction; as a last defense, the humans send out packs of fearless "genohunters" to save the planet. Users control teams of genohunters, occupying the point of view of one while issuing commands to the others. A product of biological engineering themselves, genohunters are capable of analyzing the DNA of any creature they kill and absorbing useful strands into their own genetic code. Once you've absorbed enough DNA, you can pop over to the "mutation" screen and tinker with your genetic makeup—adding new genes and mutating your existing ones, expanding your character's skills in the process. It's like suddenly learning how to program in C++, only you have to eat the guy from tech support to see the benefits.

That appetite for DNA gives the A-Life software its entrée into the gameplay. "As the player advances through the game, new genes are collected and added to the available gene pool," lead programmer Rik Heywood explained to me in an e-mail conversation. "When the player wants to modify one of their creations, they can go to the mutation screen. Starting from the current set of DNA, two new generations can be created by combining the DNA from the existing genohunter with the DNA in the collected gene pool and some slight random mutations. The new sets of DNA are used to morph the skin, grow appendages all over the body, and develop new abilities, such as breathing fire or running faster."

The promotional material for Evolva makes a great deal of noise about this open-endedness. Some 14 billion distinct characters can be generated using the mutation screen, which means that unless Computer Artists strikes a licensing deal with other galaxies, players who venture several levels deep in the game will be playing with genetically unique genohunters. For the most part, those mutations result in relatively superficial external changes, more like a new paint job than an engine overhaul. The more sophisticated alterations to the genohunters' behavior—fire-breathing, laser-shooting, long-distance jumping, among others—are largely discrete skills programmed directly by the CA team. You won't see any genohunters spontaneously learning how to play the cello or use sonar. The bodies of your genohunters may end up looking dramatically different from where they started, but those bodies won't let their hosts adopt radically new skills.

These limitations may well make the game more enjoyable. For a sixteen-year-old Quake player who's just trying to kill as many parasites as possible on his way to the next level, suddenly learning how to read braille is only going to be a distraction. Anyone who has spent time playing a puzzle-based narrative game like Myst knows nothing is more frustrating than spending two hours trying to solve a puzzle that you don't yet have the tools to solve, because you haven't stumbled across them in your explorations of the game space. Imagine how much more frustrating to get stumped by a puzzle because you haven't evolved gills or lock-picking skills yet. In a purely open-ended system—where the tools may or may not evolve depending on the whims of natural selection—that frustration would quickly override any gee-whiz appeal of growing your own characters. And so Heywood and his team have planted DNA for complex skills near puzzles or hurdles that require those skills. "For example, if we wanted to be sure that the player had developed the ability to breath fire by a particular point in the game," he explains, "we would block the path with some flammable plants and place some creatures with a fire-breathing ability nearby."

The blind watchmaker of Evolva's mutation engine turns out to have some sight after all. Heywood's solution might be the smartest short-term move for the gamers, but it's worth pointing out that it also runs headlong against the principles of Darwinism. Not only are you playing God by deliberately selecting certain traits over others, but the DNA for those traits is planted near the appropriate obstacles. It's like some strange twist on Lamarckian evolution: the giraffe neck grows longer each generation, but only because the genes for longer necks happen to sprout next to the banana trees. The space of possibility unleashed by an open-ended Darwinian engine was simply too large for the rule-space of the game itself. A game where anything can happen is by definition not a game.

* * *

Is there a way to reconcile the unpredictable creativity of emergence with the directed flow of gaming? The answer, I think, will turn out to be a resounding yes, but it's going to take some trial and error. One way involves focusing on traditional emergent systems—such as flocks and dusters—and less on the more open-ended landscape of natural selection. Evolva is actually a great example of the virtues of this sort of approach. Behind the scenes, each creature in the Evolva world is endowed with sensory inputs and emotive states: fear, pain, aggression, and so on. Creatures also possess memories that link those feelings with other characters, places, or actions—and they are capable of sharing those associations with their comrades. As the web of associations becomes more complex, and more interconnected, new patterns of collective behavior can evolve, creating a lifelike range of potential interactions between creatures in the world.

"Say you encounter a lone creature," Heywood explains. "When you first meet it, it is maybe feeling very aggressive and runs in to attack your team. However, you have it outnumbered and start causing it some serious pain. Eventually fear will become the dominant emotion, causing the creature to run away. It runs around a corner and meets a large group of friends. It communicates with these other creatures, informing them of the last place it saw you. Being in a large group of friends brings its fear back down, and the whole group launches a new attack on the player." The *group* behavior can evolve in unpredictable ways, based on external events and each creature's emotional state, even if the virtual DNA of those creatures remains unchanged. There is something strangely comforting in this image, particularly for anyone who thinks social patterns influence our behavior as readily as our genes do. Heywood had to restrict the artificial-life engine because the powers of natural selection are too unpredictable for the rules-governed universe of a video game. But building an emergent system to simulate collective behavior among characters actually improved the game-play, made it more lifelike without making it impossible. Emergence trumps "descent with modification": you may not be able to use Evolva's mutation engine to grow wings, but your creatures can still learn new ways to flock.

There is a more radical solution to this problem, though, and it's most evident in the god-games genre. Classic games like SimCity—or 1999's best-selling semi-sequel The Sims, which lets game players interact with simulated personalities living in a small neighborhood—have dealt with the unpredictability of emergent software by eliminating predefined objectives altogether. You define your own goals in these games; you're not likely to get stuck on a level because you haven't figured out how to "grow" a certain resource, for the simple reason that there are no preordained levels to follow. You define your own hurdles as you play. In SimCity, you decide whether to build a megalopolis or a farming community, whether to build an environmentally correct new urbanist village or a digital Coketown. Of course, you may find it hard to achieve those goals as you build the city, but because those goals aren't part of the game's official rules, you don't feel stuck in the same way that you might feel stuck in Evolva, staring across the canyon without the genes for jumping.

There's a catch here, though. "The challenge is, the more autonomous the system, the more autonomous the virtual creatures, the more irrelevant the player is," Zimmerman explains. "The problem with a lot of the 'god games' is that it's difficult to feel like you're having a meaningful impact on the system. It's like you're wearing these big, fuzzy gloves and you're trying to manipulate these tiny little objects." Although it can be magical to watch a Will Wright simulation take on a life of its own, it can also be uniquely frustrating—when that one neighborhood can't seem to shake off its crime problem, or your Sims refuse to fall in love. For better or worse, we control these games from the edges. The task of the game designer is to determine just how far off the edge the player should be.

Nowhere is this principle more apparent than in the control panel that Will Wright built for The Sims. Roll your cursor along the bottom of the screen while surveying your virtual neighborhood, and a status window appears, with the latest info on your characters' emotional and physical needs: you'll see in an instant whether they've showered today, or whether they're pining for some companionship. A click away from that status window is a control panel screen, where you can adjust various game attributes. A "settings" screen is by now a standard accoutrement of any off-the-shelf game: you visit the screen to adjust the sound quality or the graphics resolution, or to switch difficulty levels. At first glance, the control panel for The Sims looks like any of these other settings screens: there's a button that changes whether the window scrolls automatically as you move the mouse, and another that turns off the background music. But alongside these prosaic options, there is a toggle switch that says, in unabashed Cartesian terms, "Free will."

If you leave "Free will" off, The Sims quickly disintegrates into a nightmare of round-the-clock maintenance, requiring the kind of constant attention you'd expect in a nursery or a home for Alzheimer's patients. Without free will, your Sims simply sit around, waiting for you to tell them what to do. They may be starving, but unless you direct them to the fridge, they'll just sit out their craving for food like a gang of suburban hunger artists. Even the neatest of the Sims will tolerate piles of rotting garbage until you specifically order them to take out the trash. Without a helpful push toward the toilet, they'll even relieve themselves right in the middle of the living room.

Playing The Sims without free will selected is a great reminder that too much control can be a disastrous thing. But the opposite can be even worse. Early in the design of The Sims, Wright recognized that his virtual people would need a certain amount of autonomy for the game to be fun, and so he and his team began developing a set of artificial-intelligence routines that would allow the Sims to think for themselves. That AI became the basis for the character's "free will," but after a year of work, the designers found that they'd been a little too successful in bringing the Sims to life.

"One of our biggest problems here was that our AI was too smart," Wright says now. "The characters chose whichever action would maximize their happiness at any given moment. The problem is that they're usually much better at this than the player." The fun of The Sims comes from the incomplete information that you have about the overall system: you don't know exactly what combination of actions will lead to a maximum amount of happiness for your characters—but the software behind the AI can easily make those calculations, because the happiness quota is built out of the game's rules. In Wright's early incarnations of the game, once you turned on free will, your characters would go about maximizing their happiness in perfectly rational ways. The effect was not unlike hiring Deep Blue to play a game of chess for you—the results were undeniably good ones, but where was the fun?

And so Wright had to dumb down his digital creations. "We did it in two ways," he says. "First, we made them focus on immediate gratification rather than long-term goals—they'd rather sit in front of the TV and be couch potatoes than study for a job promotion. Second, we gave their personality a very heavy weight on their decisions, to an almost pathological degree. A very neat Sim will spend way too much time picking up—even after other Sims—while a sloppy Sim will never do this. These two things were enough to ensure that the player was a sorely needed component—ambition? balance?—of their world." In other words, Wright made their decisions local ones and made the rules that governed their behavior more intransigent. For the emergent system of the game to work, Wright had to make the Sims more like ants than people.

I think there is something profound, and embryonic, in that "free will" button, and in Wright's battle with the autonomy of his creations—something both like and unlike the traditional talents that we expect from our great storytellers. Narrative has always been about the mix of invention and repetition; stories seem like stories because they follow rules that we've learned to recognize, but the stories that we most love are ones that surprise us in some way, that break rules in the telling. They are a mix of the familiar and the strange: too much of the former, and they seem stale, formulaic; too much of the latter, and they cease to be stories. We love narrative genres—detective, romance, action-adventure—but the word *generic* is almost always used as a pejorative.

It misses the point to think of what Will Wright does as storytelling—it doesn't do justice to the novelty of the form, and its own peculiar charms. But that battle over control that underlies any work of emergent software, particularly a work that aims to entertain us, runs parallel to the clash between repetition and invention in the art of the storyteller. A good yarn surprises us, but not too much. A game like The Sims gives its on-screen creatures some autonomy, but not too much. Emergent systems are not stories, and in many ways they live by very different rules, for both creator and consumer. (For one, emergent systems make that distinction a lot blurrier.) But the art of the storyteller can be enlightening in this context, because we already accept the premise that storytelling *is* an art, and we have a mature vocabulary to describe the gifts of its practitioners. We are only just now developing such a language to describe the art of emergence. But here's a start: great designers like Wright or Resnick or Zimmerman are *control* artists—they have a feel for that middle ground between free will and the nursing home, for the thin line between too much order and too little. They have a feel for the edges.

Reading Comprehension—Points of Engagement

1. What is an emergent system? Johnson doesn't actually define the word in this chapter of his book, but he gives you enough information to understand what it might be in the context of his essay. Using his *context and examples*, explain the term in your own words and using quotations from his text. First take notes on what you find in his essay, and then fashion a well-written paragraph response.

2. What is the relationship between emergent systems and natural selection? Take notes on each from Johnson's essay, and then fashion a paragraph defining both in relation to one another. You may use an example—one of the games described in Johnson's essay—to help you.

3. Who are the "control artists" of the title? Why does Johnson describe them as control artists? Answer in your own words and using quotations from Johnson's essay.

4. Define the following terms in your own words: self-organization, centralized system, decentralized system, micromotives, macromotives, oblique control, and fitness landscape. Make sure that you can point to passages in the essay that support your definitions. You may use a dictionary to help you, but make sure your definitions make sense in the context of Johnson's essay.

Assignment Questions—Points of Departure

1. One of the hallmarks of emergent systems is that they occur in nature. According to Steven Johnson, emergent systems function as "local interactions between large numbers of agents, governed by simple rules of mutual feedback" (172). Johnson's essay shows how these natural systems can be replicated in computer programming, specifically in gaming. Your project for this paper is to use Johnson's ideas in "Control Artist" to explore the possibilities of emergent systems in essays by Susan Blackmore, Malcolm Gladwell, Arlie Russell Hochschild, Barbara Kingsolver, Steven Pinker, or Francine Prose. To do this effectively you will have to define emergent systems fully using Johnson's text, and then propose ways in which those systems might operate in these other contexts

2. Consider the following quotation from Steven Johnson's essay: "As the web of associations becomes more complex, and more interconnected, new patterns of collective behavior can evolve, creating a lifelike range of potential interactions

between creatures in the world" (184). This quote describes a computer program, but you could also say it describes how people and/or animals function together in the world. How can the computer programs in Johnson's essay enlighten us about the ways in which we are "interconnected" with other creatures in the world? What does his essay reveal to us about the possibilities and limitations that human beings cultivate among the creatures around us? Use Johnson's essay and another by one of the following authors: Alain de Botton, David Brooks, Paul Davies, Franklin Foer, Jane Goodall, Arlie Russell Hochschild, V.S. Naipaul, Michael Pollan, or John Waterbury.

3. *The Game of Life?* Consider Johnson's observation that "emergent behaviors, like games, are all about living within the boundaries defined by rules, but also using that space to create something greater than the sum of its parts" (182). Consider, too, that "a game where anything can happen is by definition not a game" (184). How different are games from real life? How are they similar? How do these differences and similarities affect how we choose to live? Are we choosing? Or are we just responding to one another in a vast emergent system? Using Johnson's theory of emergent behavior in computer gaming, reconsider how another author's life experiences *are or are not* a kind of "game" in Johnson's terms. In other words, reconsider the essays by Lisa Belkin, Franklin Foer, Jane Goodall, Fenton Johnson, Michael Kamber, or Lewis Lapham in light of the kinds of living games that Johnson describes in "Control Artist." Use the following terms from Johnson to help you: emergent software, oblique control, free will, autonomy, unpredictability, god-games, and playing from the edges.

4. What can computer gaming teach us about rules, our tendencies to break them, and the various consequences of not following them? Are there times when we *should* break the rules? Use Johnson's essay to help you rethink why we create rules, why we break them, and what happens when we do. Consider the following quotation from Johnson as a starting point: "Narrative has always been about the mix of invention and repetition; stories seem like stories because they follow rules that we've learned to recognize, but the stories that we most love are ones that surprise us in some way, that break rules in the telling" (187). Your paper should address Steven Johnson's essay and one other by Lisa Belkin, Alain de Botton, Paul Davies, Fenton Johnson, Barbara Kingsolver, V.S. Naipaul, Francine Prose, Lauren Slater, or Jeanette Winterson.

5. Consider the following quotation from Steven Johnson's essay:

> It's probably fair to say that digital media has been wrestling with "control issues" from its very origins. The question of control, after all, lies at the heart of the interactive revolution, since making something interactive entails a shift in control, from the technology—or the puppeteers behind the technology—to the user. Most recurring issues in interactive design hover above the same underlying question: Who's driving here, human or machine? Programmer or user? (Johnson 177).

What is Johnson's position in response to these final questions? What is your position? Your project for this paper is to propose answers to these questions by engaging with essays by Steven Johnson and one of the following authors: Susan Blackmore, Malcolm Gladwell, Arlie Russell Hochschild, Barbara Kingsolver, Steven Pinker, Francine Prose, Lauren Slater, or Andrew Sullivan. In your opinion and those of the single author you've chosen, "Who's driving here, human or machine? Programmer or user?" And if neither human nor machine, programmer nor user, then *what* is in control?

Toil and Temptation
Michael Kamber

Points of Access

1. What is your initial reaction when you hear the phrase "illegal immigrant"? What attitudes toward illegal immigration are you aware of? From the news? From people you know? How do you feel about it?

2. What type of work would you be willing to do for $3.75 an hour? What types of jobs would you be unwilling to do? If you were in a foreign country would your opinion be different?

3. How would you describe this country to someone who wanted to move here for a "better life"?

For seven days after his arrival from Mexico in mid-January, Antonio Gonzalez spent his time alone in the apartment, watching Spanish-language soaps and game shows, occasionally looking out the window at the snowy Bronx streets or gazing at the 6 train as it clattered by on the el. Two years earlier, his older brother, Juan Carlos, had learned the neighborhood by each day venturing a block farther from the apartment, then returning home. When he had mastered the surrounding streets, he traveled a stop on the subway—then two, then three. But Antonio saw the police cars passing by on the streets, and fearing deportation, he stayed inside. On the eighth day, the skies cleared, and he went to work at the car wash with his brother.

Antonio and Juan Carlos left before dawn, walking north along Westchester Avenue, past the candy store, restaurant, pizza parlor, real estate office, and bodega, each business owned by immigrants: Indians, Dominicans, Italians, Guyanese, and Puerto Ricans, respectively. Antonio smiled as he passed the pizza parlor. A 15-year-old acquaintance from Zapotitlán, Antonio's village of 4500 in southern Mexico, had vanished a year earlier, and a few nights ago Antonio had gone to buy a slice and found the young man there, sweeping bits of crusts and garlic salt from the floor.

At Westchester Square, the two brothers caught the X31 bus along Tremont and Williamsbridge Avenues to Eastchester, a north Bronx neighborhood remarkable for its dreary nondescriptness: block upon block of squat one-story brick buildings, stores selling auto parts and laminated furniture, a KFC, a Dunkin Donuts, some gas stations.

At the car wash, no one tells Antonio how much he is being paid, and he does not ask. In lieu of training, he is handed a towel and told to join a dozen others—all compact, brown-skinned men like himself—who stand in the mist at the foot of the wash tunnel, eyes sandy from sleep, waiting for the cars to roll out. The men regard him coolly, saying nothing, but shout to one another in Spanish over the roar of the machinery—the blowers, spray jets, and huge flopping strands of soapy cloth that make sucking noises as they slap against the cars.

At 7 a.m., a sedan rolls out of the tunnel, and six men swarm the vehicle, quickly burnishing the exterior and wiping clean the windows from the inside. Thirty seconds later another vehicle is spit out, and Antonio joins the second group, trying to walk alongside the still-rolling car as the others do, wiping as they move.

The former slaughterhouse worker left school at 13. He has been a laborer for five years, frequently averaging 70 or more hours a week at jobs in Mexico. He has assumed that rubbing a car dry will be easy work, easy money. He is wrong. The teenager stoops, bends, and reaches for the elusive water droplets; an hour later his legs and back ache, and pain rockets through his arm as he drags the waterlogged towel over the cars for the thousandth time. The areas that he wipes are still damp, and the others take up his slack and grumble about the poor job he's doing. He is nervous and afraid to disappoint his brother, who has paid $1600 for Antonio's illegal passage to New York. He sees the boss watching him from inside the glass booth, motionless and grim-faced.

Another worker shows Antonio how to fold his towel to get better coverage, but Antonio repeatedly drops the towel as he tries to double it. Behind him, the cars are piling up in the tunnel, and he works quickly, just short of frantic. He has 11 hours and 500 cars to go. Before the day is over, he is thinking that his journey to New York is a mistake. He is thinking that he will return home soon, to Zapotitlán, his village in the state of Puebla, where the majority of New York's Mexicans come from.

If Antonio does return, he will be a man very nearly alone, in the company of young children and the elderly. Fully one third of Antonio's village—including nearly all of the working-age males and 20 percent of the women—is in New York City. Firm figures are hard to come by for a community that is largely illegal, but in the last decade, New York City's Mexican population has grown between 300 and 600 percent—depending on which experts are consulted—to a total of at least 300,000. Dr. Robert Smith, a Barnard College expert on Mexican immigration, calls the growth "astounding—the fastest of any group in the city." (So many Mexicans have left Puebla that they are called the Puebla York, in much the same way that New York City's Puerto Ricans are referred to as Nuyoricans, and Manhattan-based channel 47 hosts *Hechos Puebla*, a weekly show on Puebla current events.)

Like Antonio, nearly all the newly arrived Mexicans have traded one life of labor and poverty for another. They are young men and women who, in their homeland, have run up against the walls created by class, lack of education, and the detritus of 70-plus years of one-party rule. In Mexico, there is no future; in New York, there might be.

The residents of Zapotitlán began arriving in New York 18 years ago. A two-month investigation into the community reveals a clear majority who have fallen into a semi-permanent underclass: men and women here illegally, who trade 70-hour workweeks for a handful of cash. A small but growing number of young men have drifted into drugs and gangs. But many others—maybe one in five—have found some degree of prosperity in New York, settling into comfortable middle-class lives and easing ties to their homeland. Still others have created a dual existence, maintaining families and even businesses in Zapotitlán. They fly home a few times a year, then travel back like thieves in the night, slipping past the Border Patrol, into the Arizona desert. Of New York City's Mexican population as a whole, 75 percent are not upwardly mobile, as many as nine in 10 are "illegal," and fully half the teens are not in school.

April 15 is opening day for the Liga Mexicana de Beisból, made up of 16 teams, each representing a town in Puebla. (The baseball-crazy city of Tulcingo is fielding four separate teams.) Zapotitlán's team is making its league debut; they have new white uniforms, ordered from Mexico, bearing a cactus logo and the words *Club Zapotitlán*. On Sunday morning the players gather early at City Island and win an error-filled first game, 8-4, using a pitcher who was chased through the Arizona desert by the Border Patrol scant weeks ago. His 19-year-old son, also here illegally, works in a Dominican bodega on Tremont Avenue; the pitcher has come to help make money to pay for the son's house, under construction in Zapotitlán. He has come, he says, because he wants his son home soon, "before he becomes Americanized."

In years past, Zapotitlán's players were dispersed throughout other clubs in the league, yet a hundred or more Zapotecos would show up for a game if they heard a few of their *paisanos* were playing. "We love baseball," explains Angel Flores, one of Club Zapotitlán's founders. "But really we put the team together because the people from Zapotitlán need a place to gather." Hundreds of people from the village are expected to show up for games this year, which will be followed by barbecues and socializing.

Angel has spent 12 and a half of the last 13 years in New York working as a laborer. For several years, he has worked as a painter for an Irish contractor in Yonkers. He has watched as the man has gone from a rented house and car to an ornate home, three rental properties, and three new cars. "There is a network," Angel explains. "My boss gets all his contracts from other Irishmen."

Yet Angel is not envious of the Irishman's success; Angel makes $130 a day, tax free, a princely sum by the standards of illegal Mexicans in New York. And he has his own network; he has managed to stack the work crew with five others from Zapotitlán—including the pitcher, who is his cousin. Angel's father was a miner in Mexico, and he brags softly about his siblings there: a nurse, a lawyer, an engineer. He is not envious of them, either; he put each through college with money he earned in New York. He is an uneducated laborer, they are professionals, yet he has enabled their social mobility. His one complaint about New York? "The people from Zapotitlán, I don't see some of them for years," he says. From the Bronx, they are slowly dispersing into Queens and Brooklyn, like water seeping into the earth after the rains.

Luis Garcia, the first resident of Zapotitlán to arrive in New York, in 1983, settled near Willis Avenue, in the Bronx, down the block from where the 6 train stops under the 40th Precinct. Within a few years, dozens of friends and relatives were arriving with little more than his phone number, and they slept on his couch or on mattresses lined up on the floor. Gradually the community grew and relocated; some went out to Queens, a few moved south to the burgeoning Mexican community in Sunset Park, Brooklyn. Most, however, stayed near the 6 train, following the el north along Westchester Avenue to Soundview and Castle Hill in the Bronx. They are there today, perhaps a thousand strong; at just one building, 690 Allerton Avenue, at the corner of White Plains Road, there are an estimated 50 families from Zapotitlán. (One of the few remaining Puerto Ricans in the building says, "You're looking for Mexicans? You came to the right place, and it's getting worse!") They find each other work, baby-sit one another's children. In a strange land, they take comfort in neighbors they have known since childhood.

And sometimes, in their insular community, they find love. In 1996, Alma Rosa, a tall, graceful teenager, placed second in the local beauty pageant in San Antonio, Mexico, a nearby village that makes Zapotitlán seem like a metropolis. Alfonso, the second oldest son of a middle-class family in Zapotitlán, found her there at the pageant, and the two began to date. Yet the young girl's family strongly disapproved of Alfonso, and they sent their 19-year-old daughter away, to San Bernardino, California, where there is a small colony of townspeople. Alfonso followed and searched northern California in vain for several weeks, eventually losing hope, assuming she would be married if he ever found her. He left for New York to seek work. The following spring, at a gathering of people from Zapotitlán, he heard two men speak of her. She too had come to New York, and he called her that evening. The couple live today in a building full of Mexicans on Dean Street, in downtown Brooklyn, with their two small children and three of Alfonso's brothers.

About one-fifth of the immigrants from Zapotitlán are women, and the percentage is growing steadily. In the Mexican community as a whole, the number of women arriving in New York is higher, probably approaching 40 percent. They are working in factories, cleaning houses, and having children. The birth rate among Mexican woman rose 232 percent between 1989 and 1996; they now rank third among immigrant groups in New York City—higher than Chinese, South Asians, or Haitians. "Most of these [Mexican] women are very young, and they have a high fertility rate; it's a double whammy," says Peter Lobo of the New York City Department of Planning. "This is going to have a huge impact on New York City."

Lessons In Money and Skin Color

At the car wash, a week has passed. The pain in Antonio's body has lessened, he has learned how to handle the towel, how to flip the car doors open, wipe the seals with one quick motion, then snap the towel over his shoulder and quickly wipe the windows with a softer blue rag. His coworkers are not so intimidating now; the other Mexicans see that he will work and begin to talk and joke with him—the Salvadorans also, though they speak differently and seem harder men, having been through a war that Antonio knows nothing about. And then there are the tall, dark-skinned men, men unlike any he has seen in Mexico, who he has assumed are *morenos*, African Americans, but turn out to be Africans, and at first he is confused by the distinction ("In the dark of the tunnel, you can see just their eyes," he says with some wonderment). Because they are African, they are very proud, he is told, and dislike taking orders. With the exception of a garrulous Nigerian who has learned to speak Spanish, the Africans are given jobs where they work alone.

Spend 72 hours a week wiping other people's cars, and resentment is a constant companion. Until recently, Antonio has known only Mexicans. Lunch and downtime at the car wash are filled with talk of money and race. Eastchester is a working-to middle-class neighborhood of West Indian and African American civil servants, secretaries, teachers, construction workers. Most work hard, many favor nice cars, and the line at the car wash is a parade of conspicuous consumption—Cadillacs, Lexuses, late-model SUVs. They come here because it is nearby, and because the "Super," which includes hot wax, polish, and wheels Armoralled, costs $9, a savings of $3 over the other car wash, a half-mile down Baychester Avenue, where the white people go.

But the black people—especially the young black men—don't appreciate paying hard-earned money to have a bunch of illegals leave drops of water on their cars. If they feel they are not getting their money's worth, they wave their hands in the air and shout at the workers and then mock them: "No speek eengleesh." Antonio quickly learns the phrase "Yo, yo, yo" and an utterance that sounds to him like "fock" or "focking," which he believes to be a mean word. And noise is of particular concern. Antonio and Juan Carlos are soft-spoken and courteous. They would never raise their voices unless they were ready to fight. These black men raise their voices all the time.

The tips left by the black clientele run to silver and copper, with some dollar bills thrown in. At the end of a 12-hour shift, Antonio takes home maybe $5 in tips. Down the hill, *los blancos* leave $5 bills, and rumor has it the workers average $30 a day in tips. Times six days, that's good money. But here Antonio is stuck with the cheap *morenos* who shout at him, wear their clothes baggy, and lounge against the wall. "Where do they get their money?" he wants to know. To him, and to the other Mexicans, the young black men seem lazy and dangerous.

The first week there are days when it rains and there is no work, but soon Antonio is averaging 72 hours a week. His hourly rate remains a mystery to him. He is simply handed an envelope with $270 in cash at week's end, which he accepts without complaint. Juan Carlos is the senior laborer at the car wash. With a year and a half of experience, he makes $4 an hour. The others, he believes, make $3.75 an hour. It is straight time—nothing extra after 40 hours. A laborer working at the legal minimum wage, plus overtime, would be paid $497. The car wash has approximately 20 employees. By using workers without green cards, the owner, a Portuguese immigrant, is saving nearly a quarter of a million dollars a year.

Twenty years ago, Mexican workers had the second-highest per capita income among Hispanics. Today they have the lowest. Their average earning power has dropped 50 percent, a result of the flood of illegal laborers like Antonio who are readily exploited by tens of thousands of small businesses throughout the city—restaurants, delis, small factories, and building contractors who rely on their sub-minimum-wage labor to turn a profit.

But to Antonio, $300 a week is about $270 more than most men make in Mexico, where the minimum wage is $4 a day. After work one evening in mid-February, the two brothers walk down to the Western Union near Castle Hill Avenue. There, they send a money order for $300 to their mother in Mexico. It is their combined savings from three weeks of work. Theirs is a drop in the bucket: In 1996, the last year for which figures are available, $5.6 billion was sent home by Mexicans in the U.S., making *remesas* the third largest factor in the Mexican economy.

Of Antonio's townspeople here in New York, there is a shoe-store owner in Queens who is building a gas station in the village; a busboy at a restaurant on Madison who is part-owner of construction vehicles that are rented out in Zapotitlán for $2000 a month; a 17-year-old bodega worker on Tremont who makes $1200 a month and sends $1000 home to his mother—eating free food at his job and staying inside on his day off, lest he be tempted to spend money. They say that those who suffer the most in New York, live the best when they return to Mexico.

When he left Zapotitlán for New York, Antonio's stated dream was to build a kitchen for his mother. Upon receiving her son's money, she hires a local contractor to begin work on the addition, then abandons the project, to be completed another time. A few weeks later, Antonio sends more money and the mother of nine—who cannot read or write, but adds complex sums with lightning speed—buys several hundred dollars' worth of food and soda, and opens a small store in the front room of her house.

Life As An 'Illegal'

By late February, Antonio has begun to feel secure in the Bronx. There is solace in the daily routine; he is no longer afraid of the police that pass by, the dollar bills and coins are less confusing. Yet the frustration starts early each morning. At work, vacuum cleaner in hand, Antonio has learned to say, "Open the trunk." But the patrons frequently respond with a torrent of words, and he stands and listens helplessly. Buying coffee at the bodega is an ordeal; he gets nervous, procrastinates. What if the Puerto Rican woman is not working today? The other counter workers ask him questions that he does not understand. The customers stare as he grows flustered.

And Antonio begins to see the long-term limitations as well. The two brothers are living doubled-up, and being gouged on the rent, but cannot move; landlords won't rent to "illegals" with no credit history. Juan Carlos has a friend working at a midtown parking lot—a union job, $20 an hour, and they're hiring. But between Antonio and Juan Carlos, they have only one fake green card from Texas, with someone else's name on it.

It will never do. So they stay at the car wash, surrounded by opulence and possibilities, caged by their illegal status and lack of English. A friend suggests English classes and Antonio laughs. "We leave the house before six in the morning and get home after eight at night—some nights we work until 10. When do we take the classes?" A week later he says, "We could just stay right here, buy from the Puerto Ricans, work with the Mexicans, stay right here." He means literally and figuratively, and he shakes his head. Right here is not going to be good enough.

Success Stories

For the first generation who arrived from Zapotitlán, in the 1980s, right here wasn't good enough either. Lupe Gonzalez came across in 1987, in the trunk of a car with holes cut in the floor. The coyotes gave him a straw through which he sucked fresh air as he bounced over the roads near San Diego. The 18-year-old entered the work force as a messenger in midtown Manhattan—$100 a week plus tips. Yet the job suited him no more than the conservative lifestyle of his hometown. "I used to dress up in my sister's clothes and play with dolls when I was a child," explains Lupe. In 1991, he found a job as a hairdresser at a shop on a Bronx side street, near the Morrison Avenue stop on the 6 train. He slowly built up his clientele in the Hispanic neighborhood, and became best friends with two Puerto Rican stylists, who were also gay. "They taught me how to do my makeup, how to wear fake *tetas* and high heels. They took me to the gay clubs and balls," he says, explaining his entry into New York's gay community.

Eight years ago, he put down $5000, bought the shop he worked in, and renamed it Versace; in February of 2001, he opened a second, larger location, Style 2000. He now has five employees. On a recent April evening, the tall hairdresser with the lipstick and long hair formed elaborate curls with a hot comb in the crowded salon, the air filled with hair spray and merengue blasting from overhead speakers. The four chairs were full, and a crowd of people—Dominicans, Puerto Ricans, Mexicans, one Chinese woman—waited near the door for their hair to be cut.

As an openly gay man, a successful business person, a legal resident of the U.S., and a fluent English speaker, Lupe is clearly an anomaly in the Mexican community, whose biggest holiday is December 12, the birthday of the Virgin of Guadalupe. One expects to hear painful stories of his exclusion among his fellow immigrants from Zapotitlán: There are none. "They wave at me on the street," he says. "They know that

I'm one of the 12 sons and daughters of Delfino Gonzalez, from Zapotitlán. That's all that matters."

One Saturday night in late March, Los Tigres del Norte, a hugely popular Mexican *norteño* band, comes to New York. Antonio and Juan Carlos are there, and as the band takes the stage, the audience erupts, waves of adulation washing over the musicians. They launch into a set of ballads about being from Mexico, having nothing there—no profession or future—and risking your life to cross the border illegally; about grueling workweeks and a life that is nothing more than "from home to work, from work to home." In the crowd there is a wave of emotion that Antonio has never felt before, a current very nearly electric. He is surrounded by thousands of cheering, nearly hysterical countrymen who share his life, his pain, his frustration. Grown men—macho Mexican men—are weeping all around him.

The following Saturday night, the 18-year-old's destination is the notorious Chicano Club. Three thousand miles away, in small Mexican villages, women speak of this Bronx nightspot in hushed tones. Men speak of it with smiles on their faces. They speak of the Dominican and Puerto Rican women in high heels, skin-tight pants, and halter tops. You can hold them as close as you want—at least as long as the song is playing. You're paying for it: $2 a dance. Antonio, Juan Carlos, and two friends sit at a table, drinking rounds of Corona and watching the women in the smoke-filled room. A live band is pounding out *bachatas*, *cumbias*, and covers of hits by Los Tigres. The music and bodies and laughter begin to run together. Money that could have been saved and sent to Mexico is spent on women and beer. It is the cost of feeling alive for a night. Antonio gets home about 4 a.m., sleeps for an hour, and leaves for work, exhausted, hung over, smelling of perfume and feeling good.

Mexicans say that teenagers like Antonio lose their money and their innocence at the Chicano, but it is New York that takes these things. In Sunset Park, Brooklyn, Ignacio, a 22-year-old man from Zapotitlán, knows the Chicano well—but he cannot go there, because it is in the Bronx, and people will kill him if they find him. A strikingly handsome, muscular man, he sits in a dreary apartment, roaches blazing trails over pin-ups of naked women on the walls. He sends $500 a month to his wife and three children in Zapotitlán. They live in a house overlooking the desert and the forests of giant saguaro cactus, in a place where, in the middle of the day, one hears total silence. His family is waiting patiently for his return. He is never going back. He cannot. He is addicted to New York.

Ignacio made his first trip to New York when he was 17. He worked delivering pizzas for an Italian place on the Grand Concourse, in the Bronx. One day the teenager made the mistake of looking inside the pizza box. "When you come from Mexico, your eyes are closed," he says of his early days in the city. "Now my eyes are open." His is a complex story involving drug deliveries, vendettas, betrayals, attempted murders. The details do not matter. What matters is that he stands at night on Brooklyn street corners in a tight T-shirt and baggy pants. He has a gold chain, a .25 automatic, and some bags of coke. Much of the profit goes up his nose, and he works a day job washing dishes to support his habit and his children. His life in New York is a secret he keeps from his family. "They have this dream of who I am, why ruin that?" he asks. He's made a couple of trips back, gotten his wife pregnant twice more. But he could not stay around the friendly, trusting people of his hometown. "Their eyes are closed," he repeats dismissively.

Becoming a New Yorker

Living in New York is costing more than Antonio expected, much more. Rent, food, and transit take up over half of the $1200 a month that he earns. Then there are clothes to be bought, weekly phone calls to Mexico, haircuts, nights out, Laundromats, a large fake gold watch from Canal Street: It has been more than a month since he sent money home. Juan Carlos commiserates: "I've been here two and a half years," he says. "All I have to show for it is a pizza oven in Mexico." Though he doesn't say so, he has also purchased the building materials for his family's new concrete house, and now Antonio has helped pay for the kitchen and for his mother's new store, modest though it may be. But it is true, for themselves, they have nothing. Juan Carlos's dream of the two brothers opening a *taqueria* in Mexico seems to be years away. It is mid-April, however. Spring has come to the Bronx, and Antonio does not seem as fixated on his brother's dream as he once was. A Puerto Rican girl smiles at Antonio on a subway platform, he boldly asks for her number, and they talk on the phone. And there are more nights ahead at the Chicano Club, and at the nightspots that he has discovered along Roosevelt Avenue in Queens, where he danced for several hours one night with a pretty Peruvian woman.

At the car wash, his boss has seen that Antonio is good with his hands, and is training him to compound paint, which entails running a large buffing wheel gently over the car's surface. Antonio has heard there is good money in this, that paint shops pay $500 or more a week for a good compound man. And he has heard that the boss may open another car wash, and that Juan Carlos will be manager if he can learn English. "Really, life in New York is pretty good," Antonio says one night, sitting on a park bench, Juan Carlos at his side. "All you need is a little money." Then he and his brother begin to discuss their latest plan, which is to save enough to bring their 16-year-old brother, Fernando, to the Bronx. He has already told them he wants to come.

Reading Comprehension—Points of Engagement

1. Michael Kamber's article is entitled "Toil and Temptation." What does "temptation" refer to? Refer to specific examples in the text. Why do you think Kamber chose that word to help him describe the lives of the people he writes about?

2. Why, according to Kamber, have "nearly all the newly arrived Mexicans traded one life of labor and poverty for another"? Discuss two reasons and refer to the places in the text that show how you know.

3. Try to predict what the future might hold for Antonio and other immigrants just arriving in this country. Where could they be in ten years? Twenty years? Use evidence from the article to support your answer.

Assignment Questions—Points of Departure

1. "Toil and Temptation" shows the economic realities of illegal immigration, for the Mexicans living in the Bronx, their employer, and the society at large—a scenario made possible by capitalism. But Kamber's article also reveals the human and social realities that accompany this economic arrangement. Use what you see in "Toil and Temptation" to consider another text that explores the impacts of American capitalism on individuals, such as David Brooks, "Our Sprawling, Supersize Utopia," Adam Gopnik's "Bumping Into Mr. Ravioli," Francine Prose's "Voting Democracy Off the Island" or Arlie Russell Hochschild's "From the Frying Pan into the Fire." Use the texts to discuss how capitalism works, the economic benefits as well as the other ways it shapes people's lives, communities, and societies.

2. In his essay, Michael Kamber describes the daily lives of a group of Mexican immigrants to New York City. His title, "Toil and Temptation," suggests a very particular kind of lifestyle involving long hours of busy-ness, and hard labor. In "Bumping Into Mr. Ravioli" Adam Gopnik describes the daily lives of a very different set of busy New Yorkers. What do these two lifestyles have in common? How are they different? Why? Be specific in your analysis. Your project for this

paper is to use Kamber's essay to reconsider Gopnik's observations about New York City life.

3. The Mexicans in "Toil and Temptation" lead lives in New York that are very different from their lives in Mexico. In "Facing the Village" Lenore Look discovers that life in her father's childhood village is quite different from her family's life in the United States. Use both texts to explore the reality of living in two different cultures. What are the challenges and benefits? How might living a bicultural life shape a person?

4. The people Kamber portrays in "Toil and Temptation" move back and forth between the United States and Mexico, bringing aspects of their lives with them from place to place. V.S. Naipaul writes in "East Indian" about colonial immigrants who carry aspects of Indian culture from the "Motherland" to his native homeland of Trinidad. He says that "it is the play of a people who have been cut off. To be an Indian from Trinidad, then, is to be unlikely and exotic. It is also to be a little fraudulent. But so all immigrants become" (246). Consider this quotation from Naipaul carefully. How much of this experience of being "cut off" is true of the Mexicans in Kamber's essay? Are they as "unlikely," "exotic," or "fraudulent" as the East Indians from Trinidad? Why or why not? Use both texts to explore the relationship between a "home" country and an "adopted" country. What do we learn about both places, and about the people who travel back and forth between them?

A Fist in the Eye of God
Barbara Kingsolver

Points of Access

1. How far would you go to remove world hunger? Do you think that goal justifies any and all actions? Where would you draw the line, if any?

2. How do you feel about scientific experimentation with *plants*? Does it differ from treating animals as experimental subjects? Why or why not?

3. Was Darwinian evolution taught in your high school? Did you learn the theory of "survival of the fittest" and that humankind evolved from other species? Do you see any ethical or religious problems with teaching evolution as science?

In the slender shoulders of the myrtle tree outside my kitchen window, a humming-bird built her nest. It was in April, the sexiest month, season of bud-burst and courtship displays, though I was at the sink washing breakfast dishes and missing the party, or so you might think. Then my eye caught a flicker of motion outside, and there she was, hovering uncertainly. She held in the tip of her beak a wisp of wadded spider-web so tiny I wasn't even sure it was there, until she carefully smoodged it onto the branch. She vanished then, but in less than a minute she was back with another tiny white tuft that she stuck on top of the first. For more than an hour she returned again and again, increasingly confident of her mission, building up by infinitesimal degrees a whitish lump on the branch—and leaving me plumb in awe of the supply of spiderweb-bing on the face of the land.

I stayed at my post, washing everything I could find, while my friend did her own housework out there. When the lump had grown big enough—when some genetic trig-ger in her small brain said, "Now, that will do"—she stopped gathering and sat down on her little tuffet, waggling her wings and tiny rounded underbelly to shape the blob into a cup that would easily have fit inside my cupped hand. Then she hovered up to inspect it from this side and that, settled and waddled with greater fervor, hovered and appraised some more, and dashed off again. She began now to return with fine fila-ments of shredded bark, which she wove into the webbing along with some dry leaflets and a slap-dab or two of lichen pressed onto the outside for curb appeal. When she had made of all this a perfect, symmetrical cup, she did the most surprising thing of all: She sat on it, stretched herself forward, extended the unbelievable length of her tongue, and *licked* her new nest in a long upward stroke from bottom to rim. Then she rotated herself a minute degree, leaned forward, and licked again. I watched her go all the way around, licking the entire nest in a slow rotation that took ten minutes to complete and ended precisely back at her starting point. Passed down from hummingbird great-grandmothers immemorial, a spectacular genetic map in her mind had instructed her at every step, from snipping out with her beak the first spiderweb tuft to laying down whatever salivary secretion was needed to accrete and finalize her essential creation. Then, suddenly, that was that. Her busy urgency vanished, and she settled in for the long stillness of laying and incubation.

If you had been standing with me at my kitchen sink to witness all this, you would likely have breathed softly, as I did, "My God." The spectacular perfection of that nest, that tiny tongue, that beak calibrated perfectly to the length of the tubular red flowers from which she sucks nectar and takes away pollen to commit the essential act of copulation for the plant that feeds her—every piece of this thing and all of it, my God. You might be expressing your reverence for the details of a world created in seven days, 4,004 years ago (according to some biblical calculations), by a divine being approximately human in shape. Or you might be revering the details of a world created by a billion years of natural selection acting utterly without fail on every single life-form, one life at a time. For my money the latter is the greatest show on earth, and a church service to end all. I have never understood how anyone could have the slightest trouble blending religious awe with a full comprehension of the workings of life's creation.

Charles Darwin himself was a religious man, blessed with an extraordinary patience for observing nature's details, as well as the longevity and brilliance to put it all together. In his years of studying animate life he noticed four things, which any of us could notice today if we looked hard enough. They are:

1. Every organism produces more seeds or offspring than will actually survive to adulthood.
2. There is variation among these seeds or offspring.
3. Traits are passed down from one generation to the next.
4. In each generation the survivors succeed—that is, they survive—because they possess some advantage over the ones that don't succeed, and *because* they survive, they will pass that advantage on to the next generation. Over time, therefore, the incidence of that trait will increase in the population.

Bingo: the greatest, simplest, most elegant logical construct ever to dawn across our curiosity about the workings of natural life. It is inarguable, and it explains everything.

Most people have no idea that this, in total, is Darwin's theory of evolution. Furthermore, parents who tell their children not to listen to such talk because "it's just a theory" are ignorant of what that word means. A theory, in science, is a coherent set of principles used to explain and predict a class of phenomena. Thus, gravitational theory explains why objects fall when you drop them, even though it, too, is "just a theory." Darwin's has proven to be the most robust unifying explanation ever devised in biological science. It's stunning that he could have been so right—scientists of Darwin's time knew absolutely nothing about genetics—but he was. After a century and a half, during which time knowledge expanded boundlessly in genetics, geology, paleontology, and all areas of natural science, his simple logical construct continues to explain and predict perfectly the existence and behavior of every earthly life form we have ever studied. As the unifying principle of natural sciences, it is no more doubted among modern biologists than gravity is questioned by physicists. Nevertheless, in a bizarre recent trend, a number of states have limited or even outright banned the teaching of evolution in high schools, and many textbooks for the whole country, in turn, have wimped out on the subject. As a consequence, an entire generation of students is arriving in college unprepared to comprehend or pursue good science. Many science teachers I know are nostalgic for at least one aspect of the Cold War days, when *Sputnik* riveted us to the serious business of training our kids to real science, instead of allowing it to be diluted or tossed out to assuage the insecurities of certain ideologues.

We dilute and toss at our peril. Scientific illiteracy in our population is leaving too many of us unprepared to discuss or understand much of the damage we are wreaking on our atmosphere, our habitat, and even the food that enters our mouths. Friends of mine who opted in school for English lit instead of microbiology (an option I myself could easily have taken) sometimes come to me and ask, "In two hundred words or less, can you explain to me why I should be nervous about genetic engineering?" I tell them, "Sit down, I'll make you a cup of tea, and then get ready for more than two hundred words."

A sound-bite culture can't discuss science very well. Exactly what we're losing when we reduce biodiversity, the causes and consequences of global warming—these traumas can't be adequately summarized in an evening news wrap-up. Arguments *in favor* of genetically engineered food, in contrast, are dangerously simple: A magazine ad for an agribusiness touts its benevolent plan to "feed the world's hungry with our vitamin-engineered rice!" To which I could add in reply my own snappy motto: "If you thought that first free hit of heroin was a good idea. . . ." But before you can really decide whether or not you agree, you may need the five hundred words above and a few thousand more. If so, then sit down, have a cup of tea, and bear with me. This is important.

At the root of everything, Darwin said, is that wonder of wonders, genetic diversity. You're unlike your sister, a litter of pups is its own small Rainbow Coalition, and every grain of wheat in a field holds inside its germ a slightly separate destiny. You can't see the differences until you cast the seeds on the ground and grow them out, but sure enough, some will grow into taller plants and some shorter, some tougher, some sweeter. In a good year all or most of them will thrive and give you wheat. But in a bad year a spate of high winds may take down the tallest stalks and leave standing at harvest time only, say, the 10 percent of the crop that had a "shortness" gene. And if that wheat comprises your winter's supply of bread, plus the only seed you'll have for next year's crop, then you'll be almighty glad to have that small, short harvest. Genetic diversity, in domestic populations as well as wild ones, is nature's sole insurance policy. Environments change: Wet years are followed by droughts, lakes dry up, volcanoes rumble, ice ages dawn. It's a big, bad world out there for a little strand of DNA. But a population will persist over time if, deep within the scattered genetics of its ranks, it is literally prepared for anything. When the windy years persist for a decade, the wheat population will be overtaken by a preponderance of shortness, but if the crop maintains its diversity, there will always be recessive aspirations for height hiding in there somewhere, waiting to have their day.

How is the diversity maintained? That old black magic called sex. Every seed has two parents. Plants throw their sex to the wind, to a hummingbird's tongue, to the knees of a bee—in April you are *inhaling* sex, and sneezing—and in the process, each two parents put their scrambled genes into offspring that represent whole new genetic combinations never before seen on Earth. Every new outfit will be ready for *something,* and together—in a large enough population—the whole crowd will be ready for *anything.* Individuals will die, not at random but because of some fatal misfit between what an organism *has* and what's *required.* But the population will live on, moving always in the direction of fitness (however "fitness" is at the moment defined), not because anyone has a master plan but simply because survival carries fitness forward, and death doesn't.

People have railed at this reality, left and right, since the evening when a British ambassador's wife declared to her husband, "Oh dear, let us hope Mr. Darwin isn't right, and if he is, let us hope no one finds out about it!" Fundamentalist Christians seem disturbed by a scenario in which individual will is so irrelevant. They might be surprised to learn that Stalin tried to ban the study of genetics and evolution in Soviet universities for the opposite reason, attacking the idea of natural selection—which acts only at the level of the individual—for being anti-Communist. Through it all, the little engines of evolution have kept on turning as they have done for millennia, delivering us here and passing on, untouched by politics or what anybody thinks.

*   *   *

Nikolai Vavilov was an astounding man of science, and probably the greatest plant explorer who has ever lived. He spoke seven languages and could recite books by Pushkin from memory. In his travels through sixty-four countries between 1916 and 1940, he saw more crop diversity than anyone had known existed, and founded the world's largest seed collection.

As he combed continents looking for primitive crop varieties, Vavilov noticed a pattern: Genetic variation was not evenly distributed. In a small region of Ethiopia he found hundreds of kinds of ancient wheat known only to that place. A single New World plateau is astonishingly rich in corn varieties, while another one is rolling in different kinds of potatoes. Vavilov mapped the distribution of what he found and theorized that the degree of diversity of a crop indicated how long it had been grown in a given region, as farmers saved their seeds through hundreds and thousands of seasons. They also saved more *types* of seed for different benefits; thus popcorn, tortilla corn, roasting corn, and varieties of corn with particular colors and textures were all derived, over centuries, from one original strain. Within each crop type, the generations of selection would also yield a breadth of resistance to all types of pest and weather problems encountered through the years. By looking through his lens of genetics, Vavilov began to pinpoint the places in the world where human agriculture had originated. More modern genetic research has largely borne out his hypothesis that agriculture emerged independently in the places where the most diverse and ancient crop types, known as land races, are to be found: in the Near East, northern China, Mesoamerica, and Ethiopia.

The industrialized world depends entirely on crops and cultivation practices imported from what we now call the Third World (though evidently it was actually First). In an important departure from older traditions, the crops we now grow in the United States are extremely uniform genetically, due to the fact that our agriculture is controlled primarily by a few large agricultural corporations that sell relatively few varieties of seeds. Those who know the seed business are well aware that our shallow gene bank is highly vulnerable; when a crop strain succumbs all at once to a new disease, all across the country (as happened with our corn in 1970), researchers must return to the more diverse original strains for help. So we still rely on the gigantic insurance policy provided by the genetic variability in the land races, which continue to be hand-sown and harvested, year in and year out, by farmers in those mostly poor places from which our crops arose.

Unbelievably, we are now engaged in a serious effort to cancel that insurance policy.

It happens like this. Let's say you are an Ethiopian farmer growing a land race of wheat—a wildly variable, husky mongrel crop that has been in your family for hundreds of years. You always lose some to wind and weather, but the rest still comes through every year. Lately, though, you've been hearing about a kind of Magic Wheat that grows six times bigger than your crop, is easier to harvest, and contains vitamins that aren't found in ordinary wheat. And amazingly enough, by special arrangement with the government, it's free.

Readers who have even the slightest acquaintance with fairy tales will already know there is trouble ahead in this story. The Magic Wheat grows well the first year, but its rapid, overly green growth attracts a startling number of pests. You see insects on this crop that never ate wheat before, in the whole of your family's history. You watch, you worry. You realize that you're going to have to spray a pesticide to get this crop through to harvest. You're not so surprised to learn that by special arrangement with the government, the same company that gave you the seed for free can sell you the pesticide you need. It's a good pesticide, they use it all the time in America, but it costs money you don't have, so you'll have to borrow against next year's crop.

The second year, you will be visited by a terrible drought, and your crop will not survive to harvest at all; every stalk dies. Magic Wheat from America doesn't know beans about Ethiopian drought. The end.

Actually, if the drought arrived in year two and the end came that quickly, in this real-life fairy tale you'd be very lucky, because chances are good you'd still have some of your family-line seed around. It would be much more disastrous if the drought waited until the eighth or ninth year to wipe you out, for then you'd have no wheat left at all, Magic or otherwise. Seed banks, even if they're eleven thousand years old, can't survive for more than a few years on the shelf. If they aren't grown out as crops year after year, they die—or else get ground into flour and baked and eaten—and then this product of a thousand hands and careful selection is just gone, once and for all.

This is no joke. The infamous potato famine or Southern Corn Leaf Blight catastrophe could happen again any day now, in any place where people are once again foolish enough, or poor enough to be coerced (as was the case in Ireland), to plant an entire country in a single genetic strain of a food crop.

While agricultural companies have purchased, stored, and patented certain genetic materials from old crops, they cannot engineer a crop, ever, that will have the resilience of land races under a wide variety of conditions of moisture, predation, and temperature. Genetic engineering is the antithesis of variability because it removes the wild card—that beautiful thing called sex—from the equation.

This is our new magic bullet: We can move single genes around in a genome to render a specific trait that nature can't put there, such as ultrarapid growth or vitamin A in rice. Literally, we could put a wolf in sheep's clothing. But solving agricultural problems this way turns out to be far less broadly effective than the old-fashioned multigenic solutions derived through programs of selection and breeding. Crop predators evolve in quick and mysterious ways, while gene splicing tries one simple tack after another, approaching its goal the way Wile E. Coyote tries out each new gizmo from Acme only once, whereupon the roadrunner outwits it and Wile E. goes crestfallen back to the drawing board.

Wendell Berry, with his reliable wit, wrote that genetic manipulation in general and cloning in particular: ". . . besides being a new method of sheep-stealing, is only a pathetic attempt to make sheep predictable. But this is an affront to reality. As any shepherd would know, the scientist who thinks he has made sheep predictable has only made himself eligible to be outsmarted."

I've heard less knowledgeable people comfort themselves on the issue of genetic engineering by recalling that humans have been pushing genes around for centuries, through selective breeding of livestock and crops. I even read one howler of a quote that began, "Ever since Mendel spliced those first genes. . . ." These people aren't getting it, but I don't blame them—I blame the religious fanatics who kept basic biology out of their grade-school textbooks. Mendel did not *splice* genes, he didn't actually control anything at all; he simply watched peas to learn how their natural system of genetic recombination worked. The farmers who select their best sheep or grains to mother the next year's crop are working with the evolutionary force of selection, pushing it in the direction of their choosing. Anything produced in this way will still work within its natural evolutionary context of variability, predators, disease resistance, and so forth. But tampering with genes outside of the checks and balances you might call the rules of God's laboratory is an entirely different process. It's turning out to have unforeseen consequences, sometimes stunning ones.

To choose one example among many, genetic engineers have spliced a bacterium into a corn plant. It was arguably a good idea. The bacterium was *Bacillus thuringensis,* a germ that causes caterpillars' stomachs to explode. It doesn't harm humans, birds, or even ladybugs or bees, so it's one of the most useful pesticides we've ever discovered. Organic farmers have worked for years to expedite the path of the naturally occurring

"Bt" spores from the soil, where the bacterium lives, onto their plants. You can buy this germ in a can at the nursery and shake it onto your tomato plants, where it makes caterpillars croak before sliding back into the soil it came from. Farmers have always used nature to their own ends, employing relatively slow methods circumscribed by the context of natural laws. But genetic engineering took a giant step and spliced part of the bacterium's DNA into a corn plant's DNA chain, so that as the corn grew, each of its cells would contain the bacterial function of caterpillar killing. When it produced pollen, each grain would have a secret weapon against the corn worms that like to crawl down the silks to ravage the crop. So far, so good.

But when the so-called Bt corn sheds its pollen and casts it to the wind, as corn has always done (it's pollinated by wind, not by bees), it dusts a fine layer of Bt pollen onto every tree and bush in the neighborhood of every farm that grows it—which is rapidly, for this popular crop, becoming the territory known as the United States. There it may explode the stomach of any butterfly larva in its path. The populations of monarch butterflies, those bold little pilgrims who migrate all the way to Mexico and back on wings the consistency of pastry crust, are plummeting fast. While there are many reasons for this (for example, their winter forests in Mexico are being burned), no reasonable person can argue that dusting them with a stomach explosive is going to help matters. So, too, go other butterflies more obscure, and more endangered. And if that doesn't happen to break your heart, just wait awhile, because something that pollinates your food and builds the soil underneath it may also be slated for extinction. And there's another practical problem: The massive exposure to Bt, now contained in every cell of this corn, is killing off all crop predators except those few that have mutated a resistance to this long-useful pesticide. As a result, those superresistant mutants are taking over, in exactly the same way that overexposure to antibiotics is facilitating the evolution of antibiotic-resistant diseases in humans.

In this context of phenomenal environmental upsets, with even larger ones just offstage awaiting their cue, it's a bit surprising that the objections to genetic engineering we hear most about are the human health effects. It is absolutely true that new combinations of DNA can create proteins we aren't prepared to swallow; notably, gene manipulations in corn unexpectedly created some antigens to which some humans are allergic. The potential human ills caused by ingestion of engineered foods remain an open category—which is scary enough in itself, and I don't mean to minimize it. But there are so many ways for gene manipulation to work from the inside to destroy our habitat and our food systems that the environmental challenges loom as something on the order of a cancer that might well make personal allergies look like a sneeze. If genetically reordered organisms escape into natural populations, they may rapidly change the genetics of an entire species in a way that could seal its doom. One such scenario is the "monster salmon" with genes for hugely rapid growth, which are currently poised for accidental release into open ocean. Another scenario, less cinematic but dangerously omnipresent, is the pollen escaping from crops, creating new weeds that we cannot hope to remove from the earth's face. Engineered genes don't play by the rules that have organized life for three billion years (or, if you prefer, 4,004). And in this case, winning means loser takes all.

Huge political question marks surround these issues: What will it mean for a handful of agribusinesses to control the world's ever-narrowing seed banks? What about the chemical dependencies they're creating for farmers in developing countries, where government deals with multinational corporations are inducing them to grow these engineered crops? What about the business of patenting and owning genes? Can there be any good in this for the flat-out concern of people trying to feed themselves? Does it seem *safe,* with the world now being what it is, to give up self-sustaining food systems in favor of dependency on the global marketplace? And finally, would *you* trust a guy in a suit who's never given away a nickel in his life, but who now tells you he's made you some *free* Magic Wheat? Most people know by now that corporations can do only what's best for their quarterly bottom line. And anyone who still believes governments ultimately do what's best for their people should be advised that the great crop geneticist Nikolai Vavilov died in a Soviet prison camp.

These are not questions to take lightly, as we stand here in the epicenter of corporate agribusiness and look around at the world asking, "Why on earth would they hate us?" The general ignorance of U.S. populations about who controls global agriculture reflects our trust in an assured food supply. Elsewhere, in places where people grow more food, watch less TV, and generally encounter a greater risk of hunger than we do, they mostly know what's going on. In India, farmers have persisted in burning to the ground trial crops of transgenic cotton, and they forced their government to ban Monsanto's "terminator technology," which causes plants to kill their own embryos so no viable seeds will survive for a farmer to replant in the next generation (meaning he'd have to buy new ones, of course). Much of the world has already refused to import genetically engineered foods or seeds from the United States. But because of the power and momentum of the World Trade Organization, fewer and fewer countries have the clout to resist the reconstruction of their food supply around the scariest New Deal ever.

Even standing apart from the moral and political questions—if a scientist *can* stand anywhere without stepping on the politics of what's about to be discovered—

there are question marks enough in the science of the matter. There are consequences in it that no one knew how to anticipate. When the widely publicized Human Genome Project completed its mapping of human chromosomes, it offered an unsettling, not-so-widely-publicized conclusion: Instead of the 100,000 or more genes that had been expected, based on the number of proteins we must synthesize to be what we are, we have only about 30,000—about the same number as a mustard plant. This evidence undermined the central dogma of how genes work; that is, the assumption of a clear-cut chain of processes leading from a single gene to the appearance of the trait it controls. Instead, the mechanism of gene expression appears vastly more complicated than had been assumed since Watson and Crick discovered the structure of DNA in 1953. The expression of a gene may be altered by its context, such as the presence of other genes on the chromosome near it. Yet, genetic engineering operates on assumptions based on the simpler model. Thus, single transplanted genes often behave in startling ways in an engineered organism, often proving lethal to themselves, or, sometimes, neighboring organisms. In light of newer findings, geneticists increasingly concede that gene-tinkering is to some extent shooting in the dark. Barry Commoner, senior scientist at the Center for the Biology of Natural Systems at Queens College, laments that while the public's concerns are often derided by industry scientists as irrational and uneducated, the biotechnology industry is—ironically—conveniently ignoring the latest results in the field "which show that there are strong reasons to fear the potential consequences of transferring a DNA gene between species."

Recently I heard Joan Dye Gussow, who studies and writes about the energetics, economics, and irrationalities of global food production, discussing some of these problems in a radio interview. She mentioned the alarming fact that pollen from genetically engineered corn is so rapidly contaminating all other corn that we may soon have no naturally bred corn left in the United States. "This is a fist in the eye of God," she said, adding with a sad little laugh, "and I'm not even all that religious." Whatever you believe in—whether God for you is the watchmaker who put together the intricate workings of this world in seven days or seven hundred billion days—you'd be wise to believe the part about the fist.

Religion has no place in the science classroom, where it may abridge students' opportunities to learn the methods, discoveries, and explanatory hypotheses of science. Rather, its place is in the hearts of the men and women who study and then practice scientific exploration. Ethics can't influence the outcome of an experiment, but they can serve as a useful adjunct to the questions that get asked in the first place, and to the applications thereafter. (One must wonder what chair God occupied, if any, in the Manhattan Project.) In the halls of science there is often an unspoken sense that morals and objectivity can't occupy the same place. That is balderdash—they always have cohabited. Social norms and judgments regarding gender, race, the common good, cooperation, competition, material gain, and countless other issues reside in every active human mind, so they were hovering somewhere in the vicinity of any experiment ever conducted by a human. That is precisely why science invented the double-blind experiment, in which, for example, experimental subjects don't know whether they're taking the drug or the placebo, and neither does the scientist recording their responses, so as to avoid psychological bias in the results. But it's not possible to double-blind the scientist's approach to the task in the first place, or to the way results will be used. It is probably more scientifically constructive to acknowledge our larger agenda than to pretend it doesn't exist. Where genetic engineering is concerned, I would rather have ethics than profitability driving the program.

I was trained as a biologist, and I can appreciate the challenge and the technical mastery involved in isolating, understanding, and manipulating genes. I can think of fascinating things I'd like to do as a genetic engineer. But I only have to stand still for a minute and watch the outcome of thirty million years' worth of hummingbird evolution transubstantiated before my eyes into nest and egg to get knocked down to size. I have held in my hand the germ of a plant engineered to grow, yield its crop, and then murder its own embryos, and there I glimpsed the malevolence that can lie in the heart of a profiteering enterprise. There once was a time when Thoreau wrote, "I have great faith in a seed. Convince me that you have a seed there, and I am prepared to expect wonders." By the power vested in everything living, let us keep to that faith. I'm a scientist who thinks it wise to enter the doors of creation not with a lion tamer's whip and chair, but with the reverence humankind has traditionally summoned for entering places of worship: a temple, a mosque, or a cathedral. A sacred grove, as ancient as time.

Reading Comprehension—Points of Engagement

1. In her essay, Kingsolver calls attention to "scientific illiteracy" and claims that it leaves "too many of us unprepared to discuss and understand" biotechnology (205). What does she mean scientific illiteracy? What are the causes of this illiteracy?

2. What can make a wheat plant "Magic," and what specific problems may that cause for the plant and its environment? Are these the same problems that corn plants spliced with Bt suffer and produce?

3. Why is biotechnology a "fist," specifically, in the "eye of God"? Where does the phrase come from, and why does it fit so well?

Assignment Questions—Points of Departure

1. Are humans obligated to aid one another via technology even if that technology poses a threat to other living beings? Does it make any difference whether those other living beings are humans, animals, or plants? Are humans obligated to a certain ethical code when manipulating life—any kind of life—or do technological advances demand that we continually revise our ethical positions in order to maximize our quality of life? Who should make these decisions? On what authority? And for what reasons? Using the essays by Kingsolver, and Belkin and/or Pollan, provide answers to these questions, and propose realistic answers of your own.

2. What roles should politics, ethics, culture, and/or religion take in scientific inquiry and experimentation? Consider the following quotation from Kingsolver's essay: "Even standing apart from the moral and political questions—if a scientist *can* stand anywhere without stepping on the politics of what's about to be discovered— there are question marks enough in the science of the matter" (211–212). What does Kingsolver mean by this statement? How does it relate to her essay, "A Fist in the Eye of God"? For this paper your project is to answer these questions—focusing on politics, ethics, culture, *or* religion—then consider the implications of these questions and answers in essays by Belkin, Davies, Goodall, Hitt, Slater, or Sullivan.

3. In her essay, Kingsolver warns of a global threat to the genetic diversity of agriculture. She is not the only author in this collection interested in the effects of globalization on our quality of life—here in the United States and elsewhere in the world. Is increased globalization likely to enhance our lives in the future, or put our lives at greater risk? Write a paper in which you answer these questions by considering the effects of globalization as discussed by Kingsolver and either Franklin Foer or John Waterbury. Keep in mind that these authors may take very different positions on the benefits and risks of globalization. Part of your project is to determine *their* positions on this complex issue, even as you assert your own.

Who and What Is American?
The things we continue to hold in common
Lewis Lapham

Points of Access

1. What are your answers to the questions in Lewis Lapham's title: Who is American? What is American? Make a list of the defining characteristics of being American, as you see it. What characteristics do you use to identify yourself—either as an American or a non-American? How do you think your description fits in with the prevailing descriptions available in popular culture of what it really is to be American or to adopt an American identity?

2. Lapham describes the "false constructions of American purpose and identity" which are perpetuated by certain segments of American society. What do you think he means by "false constructions" of what it is to be American? Offer a few popular, but false, conceptions of what it is to be American. Why are they false?

3. What is patriotism for? Is it an instinctive reaction, or is it something that is manufactured and, as such, can be directed in different ways? Think about the most patriotic person, and the most patriotic act, that you can, and see if you can define what it is that makes them so. What is something that you have done, or that you think you could do, that would be a truly patriotic act? Why?

> There may not be an American character, but there is the emotion of being American. It has many resemblances to the emotion of being Russian—that feeling of nostalgia for some undetermined future when man will have improved himself beyond recognition and when all will be well.
>
> V. S. Pritchett

Were I to believe what I read in the papers, I would find it easy to think that I no longer can identify myself simply as an American. The noun apparently means nothing unless it is dressed up with at least one modifying adjective. As a plain American I have neither voice nor authentic proofs of existence. I acquire a presence only as an old American, a female American, a white American, a rich American, a black American, a gay American, a poor American, a native American, a dead American. The subordination of the noun to the adjectives makes a mockery of both the American premise and the democratic spirit, but it serves the purposes of the politicians as well as the news media, and throughout the rest of this election year I expect the political campaigns to pitch their tents and slogans on the frontiers of race and class. For every benign us, the candidates will find a malignant them; for every neighboring we (no matter how eccentric or small in number), a distant and devouring they. The strategies of division sell newspapers and summon votes, and to the man who would be king (or president or governor) the popular hatred of government matters less than the atmosphere of resentment in which the people fear and distrust one another.

Democratic politics trades in only two markets—the market in expectation and the market in blame. A collapse in the former engenders a boom in the latter. Something goes wrong in the news—a bank swindle of genuinely spectacular size, a series of killings in Milwaukee, another disastrous assessment of the nation's schools—and suddenly the air is loud with questions about the paradox of the American character or the Puritan subtexts of the American soul. The questions arise from every quarter of the political compass—from English professors and political consultants as well as from actors, corporate vice presidents, and advertising salesmen—and the conversation is seldom polite. Too many of the people present no longer can pay the bills, and a stray remark about acid rain or a third-grade textbook can escalate within a matter of minutes into an exchange of insults. Somebody calls Jesse Helms a fascist, and somebody else says that he is sick and tired of paying ransom money to a lot of welfare criminals. People drink too much and stay too late, their voices choked with anecdote and rage, their lexicons of historical reference so passionately confused that both Jefferson and Lincoln find themselves doing thirty-second commercials for racial quotas, a capital gains tax, and the Persian Gulf War.

The failures in the nation's economy have marked up the prices for obvious villains, and if I had a talent for merchandising I would go into the business of making dolls (black dolls, white dolls, red-necked dolls, feminist dolls, congressional dolls) that each of the candidates could distribute at fund-raising events with a supply of color-coordinated pins. Trying out their invective in the pre-season campaigns, the politicians as early as last October were attributing the cause of all our sorrows to any faction, interest, or minority that could excite in its audiences the passions of a beloved prejudice. David Duke in Louisiana denounced the subsidized beggars (i.e., black people) who had robbed the state of its birthright. At a partisan theatrical staged by the Democratic Party in New Hampshire, Senator Tom Harkin reviled the conspiracy of

Republican money. President Bush went to Houston, Texas, to point a trembling and petulant finger at the United States Congress. If the country's domestic affairs had been left to him, the President said, everybody would be as prosperous and smug as Senator Phil Gramm, but the liberals in Congress (blind as mollusks and selfish as eels) had wrecked the voyage of boundless opportunity.

The politicians follow the trends, and apparently they have been told by their handlers to practice the arts of the demagogue. Certainly I cannot remember an election year in which the political discourse—among newspaper editorialists and the single-issue lobbies as well as the candidates—relied so unashamedly on pitting rich against poor, black against white, male against female, city against suburb, young against old. Every public event in New York City—whether academic appointment, traffic delay, or homicide—lends itself to both a black and a white interpretation of the news. The arguments in the arenas of cultural opinion echo the same bitter refrain. The ceaseless quarrels about the canon of preferred texts (about Columbus the Bad and Columbus the Good, about the chosen company of the politically correct, about the ice people and the sun people) pick at the scab of the same questions. Who and what is an American? How and where do we find an identity that is something other than a fright mask? When using the collective national pronoun ("we the people" "we happy few," etc.) whom do we invite into the club of the we?

Maybe the confusion is a corollary to the end of the Cold War. The image of the Soviet Union as monolithic evil held in place the image of the United States as monolithic virtue. Break the circuit of energy transferred between negative and positive poles, and the two empires dissolve into the waving of sectional or nationalist flags. Lacking the reassurance of a foreign demon, we search our own neighborhoods for fiends of convincing malevolence and size.

The search is a boon for the bearers of false witness and the builders of prisons. Because it's so easy to dwell on our differences, even a child of nine can write a Sunday newspaper sermon about the centrifugal forces that drive the society apart. The more difficult and urgent questions have to do with the centripetal forces that bind us together. What traits of character or temperament do we hold in common? Why is it that I can meet a black man in a street or a Hispanic woman on a train and imagine that he and I, or she and I, share an allied hope and a joint purpose? That last question is as American as it is rhetorical, and a Belgian would think it the work of a dreaming imbecile.

What we share is a unified field of emotion, but if we mistake the sources of our energy and courage (i.e., if we think that our uniqueness as Americans rests with the adjectives instead of the noun) then we can be rounded up in categories and sold the slogan of the week for the fear of the month. Political campaigns deal in the commodity of votes, and from now until November I expect that all of them will divide the American promise into its lesser but more marketable properties. For reasons of their own convenience, the sponsors of political campaigns (Democratic, environmental, racial, Republican, sexual, or military-industrial) promote more or less the same false constructions of the American purpose and identity. As follows:

That the American achieves visible and specific meaning only by reason of his or her association with the political guilds of race, gender, age, ancestry, or social class.

The assumption is as elitist as the view that only a woman endowed with an income of $1 million a year can truly appreciate the beauty of money and the music of Cole Porter. Comparable theories of grace encourage the belief that only black people can know or teach black history, that no white man can play jazz piano, that blonds have a better time, and that Jews can't play basketball.

America was founded on precisely the opposite premise. We were always about becoming, not being; about the prospects for the future, not about the inheritance of the past. The man who rests his case on his color, like the woman who defines herself as a bright cloud of sensibility beyond the understanding of merely mortal men, makes a claim to special privilege not unlike the divine right of kings. The pretensions might buttress the cathedrals of our self-esteem, but they run counter to the lessons of our history.

We are a nation of parvenus, all bound to the hopes of tomorrow, or next week, or next year. John Quincy Adams put it plainly in a letter to a German correspondent in the 1820s who had written on behalf of several prospective émigrés to ask about the requirements for their success in the New World. "They must cast off the European skin, never to resume it," Adams said. "They must look forward to their posterity rather than backward to their ancestors."

We were always a mixed and piebald company, even on the seventeenth-century colonial seaboard, and we accepted our racial or cultural differences as the odds that we were obliged to overcome or correct. When John Charles Frémont (a.k.a. The Pathfinder) first descended into California from the East in 1843, he remarked on the polyglot character of the expedition accompanying him south into the San Joaquin Valley:

> Our cavalcade made a strange and grotesque appearance, and it was impossible to avoid reflecting upon our position and composition in this remote solitude . . . still forced on south by a desert on one hand and a mountain range on the other; guided by a civilized Indian, attended by two wild ones from the Sierra; a Chinook from the Columbia; and our

own mixture of American, French, German—all armed; four or five languages heard at once; above a hundred horses and mules, half-wild; American, Spanish, and Indian dresses and equipments intermingled—such was our composition.

The theme of metamorphosis recurs throughout the whole chronicle of American biography. Men and women start out in one place and end up in another, never quite knowing how they got there, perpetually expecting the unexpected, drifting across the ocean or the plains until they lodge against a marriage, a land deal, a public office, or a jail. Speaking to the improvised character of the American experience, Daniel Boorstin, the historian and former Librarian of Congress, also summed up the case against the arithmetic of the political pollsters' zip codes: "No prudent man dared to be too certain of exactly who he was or what he was about; everyone had to be prepared to become someone else. To be ready for such perilous transmigrations was to become an American."

That the American people aspire to become more nearly alike.

The hope is that of the ad salesman and the prison warden, but it has become depressingly familiar among the managers of political campaigns. Apparently they think that no matter how different the native songs and dances in different parts of the country, all the tribes and factions want the same beads, the same trinkets, the same prizes. As I listen to operatives from Washington talk about their prospects in the Iowa or New Hampshire primary, I understand that they have in mind the figure of a perfect or ideal American whom everybody in the country would wish to resemble if only everybody could afford to dress like the dummies in the windows of Bloomingdale's or Saks Fifth Avenue. The public opinion polls frame questions in the alphabet of name recognitions and standard brands. The simplicity of the results supports the belief that the American citizen or the American family can be construed as a product, and that with only a little more time and a little more money for research and development all of us will conform to the preferred images seen in a commercial for Miller beer.

The apologists for the theory of the uniform American success sometimes present the example of Abraham Lincoln, and as I listen to their sentimental after-dinner speeches about the poor country grown to greatness, I often wonder what they would say if they had met the man instead of the statue. Throughout most of his life Lincoln displayed the character of a man destined for failure—a man who drank too much and told too many jokes (most of them in bad taste), who was habitually late for meetings and always borrowing money, who never seized a business opportunity and missed his own wedding.

The spirit of liberty is never far from anarchy, and the ur-American is apt to look a good deal more like one of the contestants on *Let's Make a Deal* (i.e., somebody dressed like Madonna, or Wyatt Earp, or a giant iguana) than any of the yachtsmen standing around on the dock at Kennebunkport. If America is about nothing else, it is about the invention of the self. Because we have little use for history, and because we refuse the comforts of a society established on the blueprint of class privilege, we find ourselves set adrift at birth in an existential void, inheriting nothing except the obligation to construct a plausible self, to build a raft of identity on which (with a few grains of luck and a cheap bank loan) maybe we can float south to Memphis or the imaginary islands of the blessed. We set ourselves the tasks of making and remaking our destinies with whatever lumber we happen to find lying around on the banks of the Snake or Pecos River.

Who else is the American hero if not a wandering pilgrim who goes forth on a perpetual quest? Melville sent Ahab across the world's oceans in search of a fabulous beast, and Thoreau followed the unicorn of his conscience into the silence of the Maine woods. Between them they marked out the trail of American literature as well as the lines of speculation in American real estate. To a greater or a lesser extent, we are all confidence men, actors playing the characters of our own invention and hoping that the audience—fortunately consisting of impostors as fanciful or synthetic as ourselves— will accept the performance at par value and suspend the judgments of ridicule.

The settled peoples of the earth seldom recognize the American as both a chronic revolutionary and a born pilgrim. The American is always on the way to someplace else (i.e., toward some undetermined future in which all will be well), and when he meets a stranger on the road he begins at once to recite the summary of the story so far—his youth and early sorrows, the sequence of his exits and entrances, his last divorce and his next marriage, the point of his financial departure and the estimated time of his spiritual arrival, the bad news noted and accounted for, the good news still to come. Invariably it is a pilgrim's tale, and the narrator, being American, assumes that he is addressing a fellow pilgrim. He means to exchange notes and compare maps. His newfound companion might be bound toward a completely different dream of Eden (a boat marina in Naples, Florida, instead of a garden in Vermont; a career as a Broadway dancer as opposed to the vice presidency of the Wells Fargo bank), but the destination doesn't matter as much as the common hope of coming safely home to the land of the heart's desire. For the time being, and until something better turns up, we find ourselves embarked on the same voyage, gazing west into the same blue distance.

That the American people share a common code of moral behavior and subscribe to identical theories of the true, the good, and the beautiful.

Senator Jesse Helms would like to think so, and so would the enforcers of ideological discipline on the vocabulary of the doctrinaire left. The country swarms with people making rules about what we can say or read or study or smoke, and they imagine that we should be grateful for the moral guidelines (market-tested and government-inspected) imposed (for our own good) by a centralized bureau of temporal health and spiritual safety. The would-be reformers of the national character confuse the American sense of equality with the rule of conformity that governs a police state. It isn't that we believe that every American is as perceptive or as accomplished as any other, but we insist on the preservation of a decent and mutual respect across the lines of age, race, gender, and social class. No citizen is allowed to use another citizen as if he or she were a means to an end; no master can treat his servant as if he or she were only a servant; no government can deal with the governed as if they were nothing more than a mob of votes. The American loathing for the arrogant or self-important man follows from the belief that all present have bet their fortunes (some of them bigger than others, and some of them counterfeit or stolen) on the same hypothesis.

The American premise is an existential one, and our moral code is political, its object being to allow for the widest horizons of sight and the broadest range of expression. We protect the other person's liberty in the interest of protecting our own, and our virtues conform to the terms and conditions of an arduous and speculative journey. If we look into even so coarse a mirror as the one held up to us by the situation comedies on primetime television, we see that we value the companionable virtues—helpfulness, forgiveness, kindliness, and, above all, tolerance.

The passenger standing next to me at the rail might be balancing a parrot on his head, but that doesn't mean that he has invented a theory of the self any less implausible than the one I ordered from a department-store catalogue or assembled with the tag lines of a two-year college course on the great books of Western civilization. If the traveler at the port rail can balance a parrot on his head, then I can continue my discussion with Madame Bovary and Mr. Pickwick, and the two gentlemen standing aft of the rum barrels can get on with the business of rigging the price of rifles or barbed wire. The American equation rests on the habit of holding our fellow citizens in thoughtful regard not because they are exceptional (or famous, or beautiful, or rich) but simply because they are our fellow citizens. If we abandon the sense of mutual respect, we abandon the premise as well as the machinery of the American enterprise.

That the triumph of America corresponds to its prowess as a nation-state.

The pretension serves the purposes of the people who talk about "the national security" and "the vital interest of the American people" when what they mean is the power and privilege of government. The oligarchy resident in Washington assumes that all Americans own the same property instead of taking part in the same idea, that we share a joint geopolitical program instead of a common temperament and habit of mind. Even so faithful a servant of the monied interests as Daniel Webster understood the distinction: "The public happiness is to be the aggregate of individuals. Our system begins with the individual man."

The Constitution was made for the uses of the individual (an implement on the order of a plow, an ax, or a surveyor's plumb line), and the institutions of American government were meant to support the liberties of the people, not the ambitions of the state. Given any ambiguity about the order of priority or precedence, it was the law that had to give way to the citizen's freedom of thought and action, not the citizen's freedom of thought and action that had to give way to the law. The Bill of Rights stresses the distinction in the two final amendments, the ninth ("The enumeration in the Constitution, of certain rights, shall not be construed to deny or disparage others retained by the people") and the tenth ("The powers not delegated to the United States by the Constitution, nor prohibited by it to the States, are reserved to the States, respectively, or to the people").

What joins the Americans one to another is not a common nationality, language, race, or ancestry (all of which testify to the burdens of the past) but rather their complicity in a shared work of the imagination. My love of country follows from my love of its freedoms, not from my pride in its fleets or its armies or its gross national product. Construed as a means and not an end, the Constitution stands as the premise for a narrative rather than a plan for an invasion or a monument. The narrative was always plural. Not one story but many stories.

That it is easy to be an American.

I can understand why the politicians like to pretend that America is mostly about going shopping, but I never know why anybody believes the ad copy. Grant the existential terms and conditions of the American enterprise (i.e., that we are all bound to invent ourselves), and the position is both solitary and probably lost. I know a good many people who would rather be British or Nigerian or Swiss.

Lately I've been reading the accounts of the nineteenth-century adventurers and pioneers who traveled west from Missouri under circumstances almost always adverse. Most of them didn't find whatever it was they expected to find behind the next range of mountains or around the next bend in the river. They were looking for a garden in a country that was mostly desert, and the record of their passage is largely one of sorrow and failure. Travelers making their way across the Great Plains in the 1850s reported great numbers of dead horses and abandoned wagons on the trail, the echo of the hopes that so recently preceded them lingering in an empty chair or in the scent of flowers on a new grave.

Reading the diaries and letters, especially those of the women in the caravans, I think of the would-be settlers lost in an immense wilderness, looking into the mirrors of their loneliness and measuring their capacity for self-knowledge against the vastness of the wide and indifferent sky.

Too often we forget the proofs of our courage. If we wish to live in the state of freedom that allows us to make and think and build, then we must accustom ourselves to the shadows on the walls and the wind in trees. The climate of anxiety is the cost of doing business. Just as a monarchy places far fewer burdens on its subjects than a democracy places on its citizens, so also bigotry is easier than tolerance. When something goes wrong with the currency or the schools, it's always comforting to know that the faults can be easily found in something as obvious as a color, or a number, or the sound of a strange language. The multiple adjectives qualifying the American noun enrich the vocabulary of blame, and if the election year continues as it has begun I expect that by next summer we will discover that it is not only middle-aged Protestant males who have been making a wreck of the culture but also (operating secretly and sometimes in disguise) adolescent, sallow, Buddhist females.

Among all the American political virtues, candor is probably the one most necessary to the success of our mutual enterprise. Unless we try to tell each other the truth about what we know and think and see (i.e., the story so far as it appears to the travelers on the voyage out) we might as well amuse ourselves (for as long as somebody else allows us to do so) with fairy tales. The vitality of the American democracy always has rested on the capacity of its citizens to speak and think without cant. As long ago as 1838, addressing the topic of *The American Democrat,* James Fenimore Cooper argued that the word "American" was synonymous with the habit of telling the truth:

> By candor we are not to understand trifling and uncalled for expositions of truth; but a sentiment that proves a conviction of the necessity of speaking truth, when speaking at all; a contempt for all designing evasions of our real opinions.
>
> In all the general concerns, the public has a right to be treated with candor. Without this manly and truly republican quality . . . the institutions are converted into a stupendous fraud.

If we indulge ourselves with evasions and the pleasure of telling lies, we speak to our fears and our weaknesses instead of to our courage and our strength. We can speak plainly about our differences only if we know and value what we hold in common. Like the weather and third-rate journalism, bigotry in all its declensions is likely to be with us for a long time (certainly as long as the next hundred years), but unless we can draw distinctions and make jokes about our racial or cultural baggage, the work of our shared imagination must vanish in the mist of lies. The lies might win elections (or sell newspapers and economic theories) but they bind us to the theaters of wish and dream. If I must like or admire a fellow citizen for his or her costume of modifying adjectives (because he or she is black or gay or rich), then I might as well believe that the lost continent of Atlantis will rise next summer from the sea and that the Japanese will continue to make the payments—now and forever, world without end—on all our mortgages and battleships.

Among all the nations of the earth, America is the one that has come most triumphantly to terms with the mixtures of blood and caste, and maybe it is another of history's ironic jokes that we should wish to repudiate our talent for assimilation at precisely the moment in time when so many other nations in the world (in Africa and Western Europe as well as the Soviet Union) look to the promise of the American example. The jumble of confused or mistaken identities that was the story of nineteenth-century America has become the story of a late-twentieth-century world defined by a vast migration of peoples across seven continents and as many oceans. Why, then, do we lose confidence in ourselves and grow fearful of our mongrel freedoms?

The politician who would lift us to a more courageous understanding of ourselves might begin by saying that we are all, each and every one of us, as much at fault as anybody else, that no matter whom we blame for our troubles (whether George Bush, or Al Sharpton, or David Duke) or how pleasant the invective (racist, sexist, imperialist pig), we still have to rebuild our cities and revise our laws. We can do the work together, or we can stand around making strong statements about each other's clothes.

Reading Comprehension—Points of Engagement

1. Consider this passage from Lapham's essay: "If America is about nothing else, it is about the invention of the self" (220). Provide two examples from Lapham that support this perspective, and two that contradict it. What kind of people support the view that America is defined by the invention of the self? Who, according to Lapham, supports the opposing perspective?

2. How does Lapham define the "American hero." How does this compare with the general conception of what it is to be an American hero? Where do the differences and similarities lie? Be specific.

3. What does Lapham mean when he says "our racial and cultural differences [were] the odds that we were obliged to overcome or correct" (218). What strategies does he suggest were used in the past to accomplish this? Offer three of them from the text.

Assignment Questions—Points of Departure

1. How can dissent make a stronger nation? How can questioning the government be a patriotic act? In your opinion, can it? Using Lapham, and Katha Pollitt, Francine Prose, or John Waterbury, offer answers to these questions. Your project will be to assert your own perspective while addressing with integrity the positions of each author.

2. Consider the following claim about American identity made by Lewis Lapham: "If America is about nothing else, it is about the invention of the self" (220). How does this claim regarding the "self" square with Susan Blackmore's ideas in "Strange Creatures" and/or "The Ultimate Memeplex"? What role might memes play in a discussion of these authors' ideas? Are the positions of these two authors compatible or incompatible? In what ways? How do you know? Your project in this paper is to put forward your own theory about the "invention of the self" using the ideas of both Lapham and Blackmore.

3. In "Who or What is American?" Lapham contrasts the policies and campaign strategies of politicians today with the beliefs and actions that the founders of the United States followed when building this nation. Lapham gives a detailed picture of an ideal to look up to, made up not of images of conformity and complacence, but of constant change, and recognition and overcoming of difference. Where does the debate over same-sex marriage, as presented by Fenton Johnson in "Wedded to an Illusion," fit into the picture painted by Lapham? Would laws that allow same-sex marriage live up to the model of American-ness that Lapham describes in his essay, or would they fall short of that model? Would that be a bad thing? Why, or why not?

4. Is it possible for American identity—the character of America—to be exported? Why or why not? Consider Lewis Lapham's essay, "Who and what is an American?" What aspects of the American mindset, as outlined by Lewis Lapham, are discernable in essays by V.S. Naipaul or John Waterbury? Keep in mind that Naipaul is East Indian, and Waterbury writes about both America and the Middle East. What do your answers to the questions above reveal about American identity as adopted by non-Americans?

Facing the Village
Lenore Look

Points of Access

1. Imagine that you have not been home for forty years. How would you feel to be going back? What if you were going back to your parents' home instead of your own? Would you feel any links to it that were your own? Would you want to go back at all?

2. Why do you think Lenore Look's article is called "Facing the Village"? Why is going home sometimes hard?

3. Does economic prosperity always open doors, or does it sometimes close them? Can you think of any situations where it may be better to be poorer than richer—or at least *seem* not to be wealthy. What advantages does the latter gain for you, if any?

> To leave home very young and to return very old,
> With accent unchanged, but hair grown thin,
> They see but know me not,
>   the smiling children who inquire:
> "And from where do you come, Honored Guest?"
> —He Zhi-zhang (T'ang poet, A.D. 659?–744?)

On the morning of Tuesday, February 3, 1998, during the first hours of the Year of the Tiger, my father abruptly stopped our chauffeur-driven minivan just short of his childhood village in China. It was the end of an anxiety-ridden journey for him, one that he felt he had been dragged into by my mother and me: I was on a search for my roots, and Mother was fulfilling a lifelong dream of returning home. In the stubborn, juvenile way that he resorts to whenever the women in his life get their way and he is all but flailing helplessly, my father was making one last desperate attempt to abort our trip, thwart our schemes, and show us that he was in charge. We had come halfway around the world—my husband and I from New Jersey, and they from Seattle—to the threshold of reunion and discovery, and my father was still determined to turn us back.

"See," Father said in his what-did-I-tell-you tone, "nobody's home."

Father was impatient. He had been irritated by a mob of drivers at Guanghai, the Taishan port on the South China Sea, where we arrived after a four-hour hydrofoil ride from Hong Kong. Each desperate for our fare, the dozen or so drivers had singled out my father as the tribal chief of our party, swarmed him in the dusty parking lot after we had gone through Customs, and fallen into an angry shouting match and tug-of-war over the day's catch of overseas Chinese.

"I'll take you for one hundred *renmingbii!*" one man screamed upon seeing us. His shirt, shiny from wear and moist with perspiration, opened between the buttons as he pushed himself against my father.

"No, ninety here!" another man yelled, spitting white foam from between his brown teeth. A million droplets landed on my father's face. He grabbed the suitcase my father was holding and started to pull. Already, our journey to the village was worse than Father had predicted. He had feared that our presence as overseas Chinese in this area of deep poverty and lawlessness might tempt even an otherwise honest driver to take us into a remote field and rob us, but his darkest scenarios did not include stepping into an ambush at the start. It was a terrible omen.

"Don't listen to him!" seethed another, pulling my father's other arm in the opposite direction. "Eighty will do."

"Eighty!" Four or five others joined in, waving arms and fists at my father, who looked like a condemned man facing his executioners.

"Seventy!" another spat, anger pulsing through a blue, hose-sized vein in his neck. A round of "Seventy!" rose up, quick and vengeful.

Crushed on all sides, Father looked frantically for help from the two armed guards standing on the edge of the parking lot. Catching my father's eye, the guards, who had been watching with unguarded amusement, turned as though they were being summoned from their favorite TV program and retreated into the Customs building. Left to divide their spoil, the drivers began to tear at the suitcases in our hands and to pull each of us in a different direction.

Then my father spoke. He demanded to see their cars. The man tugging at my bag let go. Suddenly game-show hosts, the men made exaggerated sweeping gestures toward their prizes. To no one's surprise, these were of the booby variety: heaps of rusting scrap metal that might be mistaken for cars in working condition if one were heavily drugged or intoxicated. But there was one exception: a white, late-model Toyota mini-van. The driver, with his combed hair and tweed sports jacket, emerged like a shining redeemer. He quickly settled for sixty *renmingbii* (about $7.50) for the hour-long ride to

Tai Cheng, the provincial capital of Taishan County, where we expected to find hotel accommodations.

We rode nervously to Tai Cheng. My mother kept trying to make small talk with the driver, a thin, laconic man who had large, bloodshot eyes and protruding cheekbones and who seemed uncomfortable with her prying questions. She extracted from him his surname, Moy, and told him that her mother was a Moy. They must be from the same village, she said, meaning, You wouldn't rob your relations, would you? It turned out they were from the same place. The driver then speculated on our *ho sai gai* (good fortune) at being North American Chinese, by which he meant, I hit the jackpot! My father quickly responded with a tale of hardship, indicating to the driver that we were not worth robbing. Father explained that he had toiled most of his life in the hot kitchens of Chinese restaurants, where there was no money to be made. We are *ho kuung* (very poor), he added. It was true. My mother had recently confided to me that she earned no more than ten thousand dollars last year, sewing at the same garment factory she joined nearly thirty years ago. My father, still a cook at age sixty-eight, has reduced his hours to three days a week, undoubtedly earning much less. For all of my parents' working lives, their income has hovered around the U.S. poverty line, tethered there by their lack of education and language skills and perhaps their self-imposed isolation in a foreign, and often racist, environment. But how do you explain this to someone whose income is even lower than theirs?

While watching the driver's eyes in the rearview mirror, I discreetly removed my jewelry and lipstick, both signs of affluence, and prayed he did not know the cost of airfare. What I thought was Father's paranoia was now a sickening possibility. We were driving through nothing but remote fields on a two-lane highway that held no other traffic. In an area where a family earning the equivalent of fifty dollars a month is considered affluent, we were probably the only ones with cash in our pockets, coveted American passports, and who knows what other items that might enable a poor family to cover medical costs and other basic needs. If the driver were to rob us, there was no better place than right there. Thick and thicker cataracts of suspicion clouded our eyes, and I began to see us as a truckload of fat chickens about to be plucked. We drove on and on into nowhere.

To our inestimable relief, we finally arrived at the Taishan Garden Hotel. Our driver promptly asked if we were intending to *fan heang haa* (return to the village). He was practiced in this. Only overseas Chinese directed him to the town's fanciest hotel, which cost the equivalent of thirty dollars a night. My parents, unnerved by this stranger's foreknowledge of our itinerary, began to say that we had other plans. Sightseeing, they said.

The driver was not convinced. Tai Cheng has no tourist attractions, no shopping—nothing. The only visitors are pilgrims. Miserly with conversation earlier, Mr. Moy was now mouthy, even aggressive. He pressed further, offering to drive us to the villages of our choice for another pittance: three hundred *renmingbii*—nearly forty dollars—for the entire day. There were no other cars to hire unless we were to return to the knot of drivers at Guanghai. Reluctantly, my father negotiated again with the man all of us now suspected would eventually rob us.

*   *   *

The Taishan countryside, birthplace of Chinese immigration and the ancestral home of most North American Chinese, is flat as a frying pan. Meaning "elevated mountain" and known locally as "Hoisan," Taishan refers to a small mountain range that appears in the distance. Located just south of the Tropic of Cancer, in southern China's Guangdong Province, it is covered with a patchwork of rice paddies and taro fields, which benefit from the sun's high elevation, even in winter. Elevated dirt roads flanked by ditches four feet deep run between the paddies. These roads are wide enough for one car and one water buffalo. Lone houses, some large and ornately decorated with Victorian gingerbread or Greek Revival motifs, such as Corinthian columns, stand in an area uncharacterized by excess of any sort. Located in the western part of the Pearl River delta region, Taishan is on the margin of the highly commercialized zone centering around Hong Kong and Guangzhou. Too remote to have benefited from the trade with European merchants that began in the early nineteenth century, Taishan continues to sleep on the fringe of commerce, subsisting on a farming economy. But unlike any other part of China, it receives remittances from its native sons and daughters who have left and, with these, has built homes, schools, and roads.

My father's village was not what I had expected. Children's-book illustrations, movie scenes of walled Chinese courtyards decorated with swinging red lanterns, fish ponds, and filigree balustrades were what had filled my mind. Perhaps I was also expecting to hear the airy notes of a bamboo flute and the cries of children clad in silk pajamas and playing in leafy bamboo groves. Instead, in front of us was a cluster of low, two-story concrete buildings, gray and darkened by age. Looking like tree branches, cracks ran merciless fingers all over the walls. Windows were boarded. Not a stalk of bamboo anywhere.

The last of Father's immediate family and close relatives had immigrated to the United States in the 1960s, leaving Gnin On, the Look family village, mostly uninhabited. My great-grandfather, Look Ah Lung (Ah Lung, meaning "Big Dragon," was a name he took for himself), was the first of the Look clan to leave his centuries-old village for America. In 1889, seven years after the first Chinese Exclusion Act was passed in the States, thirteen-year-old Ah Lung, fearing starvation, became a stowaway on a ship leaving Hong Kong Harbor for Port Townsend, Washington. A waiflike youth who had a queue when he landed on American soil, he grew into a handsome and affable man who displayed a Western panache in subsequent passport photographs. He made friends quickly in the Seattle laundry where he worked and by 1903 had obtained sworn testimony from white friends that he was a native-born United States citizen, thus assuring himself and those he claimed as children a place in the Land of the Flowery Flag. His remittances and those of kinsmen whom he subsequently brought to the States were what built the concrete-block homes that stood before us. A wealthy man by village standards, Ah Lung died in the village in 1951, two years after he helped his first grandson, my father, make his way to Seattle. His widow, my great-grandmother, was the last to emigrate, doing so in 1968, at the tender age of ninety.

Father expected no reception at the village. He'd sent no advance word of our visit, certain that those who had had no means of leaving several decades ago surely would have found their way by now to Guangzhou, about two hundred miles east. There they would have found work. This remote village was quiet except for our idling car and the song of thrushes in early spring.

Father directed us to stay in the car. He opened his door and stepped out, his shoes crunching the gravel and dirt that he had not touched in fifty years. The last time he had walked that path, he was nineteen. It was a hot, tropical day in monsoon season, and he was leaving his village with an older cousin to seek his fortune in America. He had one hundred Hong Kong dollars hidden in small sums throughout the pockets of his thin cotton shirt and pants and tucked into his socks. A short time later, gun-brandishing thugs would hold up their bus, and Father would lose one-tenth of his wealth—having been told by his cousin, who had traveled before, to have the sum ready in a convenient pocket. Father wore cotton shoes on his feet, and on one shoulder had a drawstring bag that contained the rest of his wardrobe and worldly possessions: two extra shirts. His mother had not even packed him a lunch because, as he remembered it, "there was nothing left to eat."

It was 1949. There were rumors that Mao Tse-tung and his army were coming their way. Father's village was familiar with armies, having dodged Japanese soldiers for years: they hid in caves in the nearby mountains during the day and went back to their homes at night, when the enemy would return to camp. Then there was the advancement of Chiang Kai-shek's Nationalist troops, who forced out the Japanese but demanded rice, pigs, and chickens from the villagers. Another army would mean further trouble, so it was arranged for Father, the eldest son, to join his father in America. From this tiny dirt path, the two young men walked out to the larger road, where they hitched a ride on an ox cart that took them into Tai Cheng. Father had attended boarding school there, a privilege reserved for boys from families who received foreign remittances. From Tai Cheng, they took a bus to the seaport of Guanghai, where they squeezed into a jam-packed boat to begin a sixteen-hour tow by dinghy to Hong Kong. In Hong Kong, my father and his cousin boarded a plane for Seattle, where my grandfather resided and where they would resume their lives of toil and hardship, but in a new place.

*   *   *

Father ground his right foot in the dirt as though putting out a cigarette, a habit he had picked up in the village but long since given up. Then I saw him stop, as though caught by something long forgotten. There was an almost imperceptible change in his breathing. Perhaps his toes curled around the shape of a stone, or something about the road felt familiar, or his feet found something he didn't know he was looking for.

"I'll see if anyone's home," he continued in Taishanese, the rural area's patois that I grew up speaking. His tone softened slightly as his curiosity increased.

My father had good reason for resisting a return to his birthplace. As meaningful as such a visit might be, he felt the health risks were too great. As he entered his sixties, he was diagnosed with hepatitis B, a common and sometimes deadly malady among Southeast Asians born under unclean village conditions. For two years, he fought back with the aid of experimental drugs, but these left his body wasted and his spirit despondent. Finally he regained normal liver functions and had enough energy to do more than sleep away his golden years. He was afraid that any contact with the village would trigger a relapse. He fussed about this incessantly. And I bought into it, failing to see until now that it concealed a deeper resistance that he had no words for. He spoke of this only once, many years ago, almost unwittingly, letting it slip out in a conversation about something that has long since run out of memory's sieve. A few years after Father's departure, the Communist Red Guards marched into his village and paraded his mother and grandmother into the grassy area near the common well. The crazed teenagers accused them of being bourgeois pigs, for having built three houses with foreign remittances and sending husbands and sons abroad, and then they whipped them until the women fainted. No one in the village dared come forward in their defense. My grandmother, to her dying day, vowed never to return to the village and admonished each of her children and grandchildren against ever stepping foot in China. She hated her native country with a rancorous vehemence that left no room for further betrayal. But my mother would not return to China without my father; as for myself, I had every confidence that I would have found their ancestral homes on my own, though I now know I was wrong. Without my parents' childhood memory of where things were in the landscape and of the shape of their village rooftops against the sky, it would have been a futile search through a countryside of unmarked dirt roads and people so provincial that no one was certain of the names of neighboring villages.

In my mind, I have written several dozen essays, a book of poems, a jaunty travel narrative, and a voluminous family biography—all based on what happened next: the moment my father turned to walk toward his village, and the few steps that followed. But in reality, I have created these large things only in my head. None of the many pieces that I've begun have I been able to finish, and each abandoned project has taken me further from the place I need to be in order to begin. As the Year of the Rabbit commenced, marking the first anniversary of our trip, most of my other writing projects stalled or failed as well. Now—strangely and to my chagrin—my inability to tell the tale has become part of the tale.

How hard could it be to write about a simple trip to a poor village? How long should it take to describe the house where my father was born—its wooden door secured with a twist of dried grass for more than thirty years? How is it that I have not been able to describe a place so spare that it did not have electricity or running water?

Setting my own foot in the place that has been my source of myth was supposed to give me a sense of reality and purpose with which to better understand myself and my life. This enlightenment would, of course, cause me to write marvelous things. But, instead, this place has extracted from me more than I could take from it. I've come away with what I could not even dare admit I feared: an overwhelmingly unproductive year and a terrible knowledge of my limitations as a writer. The task, I've taken this long to realize, is not an accounting of details, but the cherishing of events; not the rendering of exactitudes that I have so long mistaken for truth, but a need for remembering the striking and poetic side of things—and accepting that I will never be able to fit the contents of my heart onto a page.

"Ai yaaaaahhh!" a man's voice cried deeply across the stubbled fields. The cry startled those of us in the minivan. Birds scattered into the chalky sky. I was transfixed by

what happened next. A man had emerged from the village and was striding quickly toward my father, who froze in his tracks as if he were an actor who had stepped into the wrong play. From a distance, the man looked as old as tree bark, his skin tanned and leathery. He wore Western clothes: a striped knit shirt under a thin polyester jacket, belted trousers, and black cotton shoes. His shoulders were slightly stooped, sloping gently like melted snow toward the earth, but his thick, dark hair was windswept in a youthful way. I needed to get out of the car, and fast. I knew with an insect's certainty that something big was about to pour out of the sky—the signs were everywhere—and this was what I'd come for. Yet I could not anticipate it, did not know I was looking for it. With one hand I struggled to unfasten my seat belt and with the other to hold on to my camera.

"Hoiiii Lauuuuu!" the man cried, unfurling my father's milk name like a banner across the sky and calling the birds back from their flight. His voice filled the earth, coating every brown blade of grass and stubble, every stone and pebble between us and the distant blue mountains. It was a name, as ancient and powerful as the newborn, that I had heard only my grandparents use for him.

Now it was the sound of remembering.

The thunder of resurrection.

The sound of the earth rearranging herself for his steps.

My father stumbled forward as though pushed abruptly from a long dream and immediately extended his arms in a way I'd never seen him do, like a child who wants to be picked up, held, and loved. The long decades of Father's life merged into a few brief hours, and I knew he had not really been gone from there for fifty years but only a short afternoon. Hadn't he simply gone up the path to investigate a rumor of frogs, or into the fields to tie praying mantises onto his fingers as pets, and wasn't he just now returning home after a euphoric afternoon? And wasn't his mother about to put *chaai* (kindling sticks) into the oven and begin preparing the evening rice?

I felt it: joy filling my father all at once, complete and overflowing. In a slow, peaceful moment, like the one preceding a car crash, Father floated above his difficult world, looking unfamiliar, like a stranger. Then I realized I'd never before seen him happy. He was proud, maybe, when I graduated from Princeton and approving, per-haps, when I got married, but even on those occasions, the realities of his difficult life were still reflected in his tired eyes. But here in this village, he was happy—so happy I cannot describe it. *Resplendent* perhaps comes closest. My father was *resplendent*. I had never in my life seen anything more wonderful.

Suddenly, I felt this place was familiar to me, as familiar as my own house. I was the baby being pushed into the world, I was the bride being carried down the path, I was the dead entering the earth. I was the departing emigrant seeking a future and the foreign-born daughter searching for her history. This is heritage, and the many layers of mine unfolded and embraced me in a single cry.

By the time I finally escaped from the car, the men had pulled away from their embrace. However, Father's fingertips kept touching—no, kept bouncing lightly on—the back of the man's hand, and up and down the sleeve of the man's thin jacket, as though he could not trust his eyes to believe what was before him.

The man was Father's fourth cousin, Yik Fu, who was either two years older or two years younger—neither man able to remember which. They had been constant companions in their boyhood, but had not seen or heard from each other in the half century since Father's departure.

"How did you know it was me?" Father finally stuttered when he found his voice, looking dazed yet seeming more wide awake than he'd ever been. His eyes darted wildly. In the photographs that I took of him, Father's lips are folded in at this moment, as though he is making a Herculean effort not to cry. In fact, he is wearing the same expression in each photograph I took of him on this visit.

"What do you mean how did I know?" Yik Fu replied, sounding insulted. "How can I remember? Tell me, how can I forget?"

Father folded in his lips even more, looking like a dried-apple granny. Standing next to his cousin, who was lean from a lifetime of farm work and eating only the fruit of his labor, Father looked well fed, even overfed. Father's hair was much grayer than his cousin's, but due to a life lived indoors, his face was as pale and smooth and oiled as a wealthy man's. By then, an old woman and a few children were standing nearby, watching us with curiosity. Father held on to his cousin's hand; they were again boys about to go out to play.

"Is my house still here?" Father asked tentatively, his face lit with wonder.

"Of course," his cousin said, surprised at the question.

The old woman came close to me and slipped her arm in mine. Gaunt and sun-browned, she resembled a mummy. I patted her leathery hand and smiled uneasily.

"You his daughter?" she asked through her toothless grin.

"*Haaile,*" I nodded.

"You come from far?" she asked.

"The Beautiful Country," I said, using a vernacular I thought she'd understand. But she didn't at first. Her eyes drew a blank.

"*Aiyaah,*" she said and then exclaimed, "you speak our language!" Her eyes flashed with knowledge. She understood that my father had been gone an afternoon and that I'd come back with him, a daughter he'd found among the grasses, among the frogs, among the happy times clinging to the cool underside of leaves in the nearby fields. Someone from any further away would not speak her dialect.

Taishanese closely resembles Cantonese, but suggests that the speaker is so ill bred that whenever I used it in Hong Kong and Guangzhou, I would always get the same reaction: laughter. Then feigned horror. Using the dialect made me an instant outcast, a vagrant baring a mouth of diseased teeth. Even in the United States, the dialect's associations with peasantry have not disappeared. Although Chinese dialects vary only in spoken form, not in the written, Chinese-language programs are almost always in Mandarin, the dialect of the northern scholars and now the PRC's official language. While I was growing up in Seattle, where nearly every Chinese family was of Taishan origin and spoke Taishanese at home, Chinese school offered only Cantonese, the urban and urbane dialect. But here, on the soil of my parents' home, my uneducated southern accent, deep from the muddy river delta, gushed pearls. The old woman clutched my arm tighter and looked so earnestly into my eyes that I knew she saw clearly to the bottom of them.

"Come inside for tea," she said as though we had strolled arm-in-arm every day for centuries. The children, barefoot or in plastic slippers and dressed in varying vintages of sweatshirts and sweat pants and sagging sweaters, shuffled a little closer. A woman about my age who had been gnawing on a sugar cane the size of a broom handle suddenly appeared at my side and offered me a similar treat. Instantly, I felt ashamed. I was ashamed of possessing so many sugar canes in a world so far from hers and not bringing a single one. I had come without gifts and had even talked my mother out of bringing hers.

"They'll laugh you out of the village," I had replied when Mother told me she had packed three, sixty-pound bags of her old clothing to take to the villages. She had secretly squirreled away nearly every piece of clothing she had worn since her arrival in the States in 1960, hoping someday to distribute them in her village. For weeks prior to our departure, we argued about her intended offering. Once, I pointed to a *National Geographic* article on the fashion conscious in Shanghai and then recounted numerous newspaper reports on China's new middle class. She insisted that her carefully curated collection was an appropriate gift. In the end, I triumphed. She left her used clothing at home. It sounded plausible to her, too, that there had been some changes in China in the forty years that had elapsed since she left.

But how naive could I be? Where there are no jobs, there is no money, no modernization, not even toilets. Except for the many boarded-up houses, Father's village, which now consists of only four or five families, was the same as when he left it a half century before. The Looks eat what they grow. Without refrigeration, they line up their cauliflower heads and the other *tyoi* that they've harvested from their fields along their cool kitchen floors. Their homes are swept and neat. Each house has the same floor plan, the central area being an atrium that holds the family altar, the main piece of furniture. Every day they wear the same clothes. The youngest children go around barefoot and bottomless. The oldest children were fourteen-year-old girls, who had completed middle school two years before and come to the end of their education. When asked what they'd do next, they shyly replied that they didn't know about "next."

Growing up, I knew my parents sent money to their villages. It was another one of those terrible arguments my parents had over how little money they had. But always the check would be cut, the envelope sealed and mailed. And still we ate, never missing a meal, and heated our home, though not too warmly, and marked the beginning of the school year with new clothes that Mother had sewn from inexpensive remnants. My parents never spoke to me or my brothers about the remittances, so it never occurred to me that there were beneficiaries like myself, whom they helped feed and clothe despite their own meager means. Now those children had grown, and we were meeting their children.

Speaking to me now are the faces and voices of these young women, who share my name, and others whom I met later in my mother's village. The young women are mirrors of whom I could have been, and I am a mirror of whom they could become and yet should not hope to be. I am a grown woman, the mother of two daughters, a wife, the owner of two automobiles and a house filled with as much comfort as my heart desires. I have never known hunger or cold. I collect things I do not need; I discard things that are still good. I have to exercise to stay slender. I am college educated. I read for pleasure, I attend the opera, I visit museums, I vacation in Europe. I enjoy the benefits of modern medicine. I have all my teeth. I belong to the first generation of my parents' families born outside the village. Growing up, I erased as much of my Chineseness as I could. When my parents spoke to me in Taishanese, I'd reply in English. I refused to attend Chinese school, eat with chopsticks, wear red for luck, refrain from washing my hair on holidays and birthdays. Although I made a concession to my parents to study Chinese (Mandarin) in college and found myself loving the language, I was in complete denial of any deeper links to China. In a society where remaking oneself is nearly a national religion, I was well on my way to being what I wanted to be: white. China was a disembodied foreign entity somewhere far away—interesting to study and analyze and form opinions about, as white people do, but not to be taken too seriously. I belong to the first generation to not send remittances.

Father quietly pressed two hundred *renmingbii* into his cousin's hand before we left. "Spread it around," he instructed. His cousin nodded, teary and quiet, closing his fist around a poor substitute for my father. The next day, Father repeated the gesture, pressing a fold of bills into our driver's hand, who, instead of robbing us as we had suspected he would, insisted on taking us, without charge, to where we could catch the bus to Guangzhou. The giving of money is very Chinese, and for the first time I saw the usefulness of it—and the uselessness of what I had become.

Ironically, it was my arrogance that had brought me to the village: I came looking for what I could take from it. Details for a novel in progress. But somewhere between my desire and the fulfillment of it, I fell into an abyss. Like my father, I heard my name called in that place—audible only to my ears perhaps, but maybe not—and I tumbled headlong after him into that strong morning light, undeserving. In that place full of beginnings and endings and everything in between, I knew that I, too, had come home. Here was the home that I sought. I cannot turn from it—it is more than I deserve, and it is enough.

Reading Comprehension—Points of Engagement

1. What reasons does Lenore Look give for her father not wanting to return to his village in China. Do you think his reluctance was justified? Provide evidence for your answer.

2. How is the Look family different from those they visit in China? Is it just money, or are there other differences? Do her parents still fit in?

3. Who is the trip that the Look family takes *for?* Look at all of the reasons that Lenore Look gives for taking this trip as a family. Which of the reasons do you think come closest to being fulfilled? Is anyone disappointed?

Assignment Questions—Points of Departure

1. How much is too much to give up in order to provide a better life for someone else? Consider the parent-child relationships in Lisa Belkin's "Made-to-Order Savior" and Lenore Look's essay. What have the parents in both essays sacrificed for the children? What have they lost, or gained themselves by doing what they have done?

2. Lenore Look, V.S. Naipaul, and Jeanette Winterson show how ties to home can be a burden and an inspiration all at once. How can you reconcile the negatives of a homeland with the benefits it has to offer? What benefit does having close emotional ties with your home confer? What difficult choices is it necessary to make in order to come to terms with your past, and the past as it relates to the place you come from? Why are they difficult, if at all? Your project for this paper is to consider the complicated notion of homeland as presented in Look and either Naipaul's "East Indian" or Winterson's "The World and Other Places."

3. How can money bring people together? How can it drive them apart? Do communities really benefit from the introduction of outside wealth? And what is the price that they pay, if they pay one at all? Write a paper in which you propose your own answers to these questions using the insights provided in Lenore Look's "Facing the Village" and either Franklin Foer's "Soccer vs. McWorld" or Michael Kamber's "Toil and Temptation."

East Indian

V.S. Naipaul

Points of Access

1. On a map of the world, locate the following places: England, the United States, Holland, China, Portugal, India, Malaysia, Trinidad, and Surinam. How many of these places were familiar to you before looking them up? How long did it take for you to find them on the map? Have you any ideas about what connects these places across the globe?

2. What do you think it means to be an immigrant? Is it the same thing as being a colonial? What associations do you have with each word? Why do you have those associations?

3. What nationality are you? What ethnicity are you? What do you consider your 'home country'? For each answer, make a list of the qualities that you most close associate with each of these categories of identity. For example, if I say that my home country is the United States, my list might include that I believe in democracy, that I grew up in Illinois, and that I live in New Jersey. For nationality, I might say, I'm American and my list would include that I am open, energetic, ambitious, etcetera. Make your own lists as personalized as you can. What do your lists reveal to you about the relationship you experience between nationality, ethnicity, and home?

4. What do you think of when you hear the words "New World?" Does this have just one meaning to you? Multiple meanings? Freewrite for 10 minutes writing everything you know or think about the idea of the New World.

It was about thirteen or fourteen years ago. In those days Air France used to run an Epicurean Service between London and Paris. The advertisements taunted me. Poverty makes for recklessness, and one idle day in the long summer vacation I booked. The following morning I went with nervous expectation to the Kensington air terminal. There was another Indian in the lounge. He was about fifty and very small, neat with homburg and gold-rimmed spectacles, and looking packaged in a three-piece suit. He was pure buttoned-up joy: he too was an Epicurean traveller.

"You are coming from—?"

I had met enough Indians from India to know that this was less a serious inquiry than a greeting, in a distant land, from one Indian to another.

"Trinidad," I said. "In the West Indies. And you?"

He ignored my question. "But you look Indian."

"I am."

"Red Indian?" He suppressed a nervous little giggle.

"East Indian. From the West Indies."

He looked offended and wandered off to the bookstall. From this distance he eyed me assessingly. In the end curiosity overcame misgiving. He sat next to me on the bus to the airport. He sat next to me in the plane.

"Your first trip to Paris?" he asked.

"Yes."

"My fourth. I am a newspaperman. America, the United States of America, have you been there?"

"I once spent twelve hours in New York."

"I have been to the United States of America three times. I also know the Dominion of Canada. I don't like this aeroplane. I don't like the way it is wibrating. What sort do you think it is? I'll ask the steward."

He pressed the buzzer. The steward didn't come.

"At first I thought it was a Dakota. Now I feel it is a Wiking."

The steward bustled past, dropping white disembarkation cards into laps. The Indian seized the steward's soiled white jacket.

"Steward, is this aircraft a Wiking?"

"No, sir. Not a Viking. It's a Languedoc, a French plane, sir."

"Languedoc. Of course. That is one thing journalism teaches you. Always get to the bottom of everything."

We filled in our disembarkation cards. The Indian studied my passport.

"Trinidad, Trinidad," he said, as though searching for a face or a name.

Before he could find anything the Epicurean meal began. The harassed steward pulled out trays from the back of seats, slapped down monogrammed glasses and liquor miniatures. It was a short flight, which perhaps he had already made more than once that day, and he behaved like a man with problems at the other end.

"Indian," the Indian said reprovingly, "and you are drinking?"

"I am drinking."

"At home," he said, sipping his aperitif, "I *never* drink."

The steward was back, with a clutch of half-bottles of champagne.

"Champagne!" the Indian cried, as though about to clap his tiny hands. "Champagne!" Corks were popping all over the aircraft. The trays of food came.

I grabbed the steward's dirty jacket.

"I am sorry," I said. "I should have told them. But I don't eat meat."

Holding two trays in one hand, he said, "I am sorry, sir. There is nothing else. The meals are not prepared on the plane."

"But you must have an egg or some fish or something."

"We have some cheese."

"But this is an Epicurean Service. You can't just give me a piece of cheese."

"I am sorry, sir."

I drank champagne with my bread and cheese.

"So you are not eating?"

"I am not eating."

"I enwy you." The Indian was champing through meats of various colours, sipping champagne and crying out for more. "I enwy you your wegetarianism. At home I am *strict* wegetarian. No one has even boiled an egg in my house."

The steward took away the remains of my bread and cheese, and gave me coffee, brandy, and a choice of liqueurs.

The Indian experimented swiftly. He sipped, he gulped. The flight was drawing to a close; we were already fastening our seat belts. His eyes were red and watery behind his spectacles. He stuck his hat on at comic angles and made faces at me. He nudged me in the ribs and cuffed me on the shoulder and giggled. He chucked me under the chin and sang: *"Wege-wege-wegetarian! Hin-du wege-tar-ian!"*

He was in some distress when we landed. His hat was still at a comic angle, but his flushed little face had a bottled-up solemnity. He was in for a hard afternoon. Even so, he composed himself for a farewell speech.

"My dear sir, I am a journalist and I have travelled. I hope you will permit me to say how much I appreciate it that, although separated by many generations and many thousands of miles of sea and ocean from the Motherland, you still keep up the customs and traditions of our religion. I *do* appreciate it. Allow me to congratulate you."

I was hungry, and my head was heavy. "No, no, my dear sir. Allow me to congratulate you."

*   *   *

To be a colonial is to be a little ridiculous and unlikely, especially in the eyes of someone from the metropolitan country. All immigrants and their descendants are colonials of one sort or another, and between the colonial and what one might call the metropolitan there always exists a muted mutual distrust. In England the image of the American is fixed. In Spain, where imperial glory has been dead for so long, they still whisper to you, an impartial outsider, about the loudness of *americanos*—to them people from Argentina and Uruguay. In an Athens hotel you can distinguish the Greek Americans, *back for a holiday* (special words in the vocabulary of immigrants), from the natives. The visitors speak with loud, exaggerated American accents, occasionally slightly flawed; the stances of the women are daring and self-conscious. The natives, overdoing the quiet culture and feminine modesty, appear to cringe with offence.

Yet to be Latin American or Greek American is to be known, to be a type, and therefore in some way to be established. To be an Indian or East Indian from the West Indies is to be a perpetual surprise to people outside the region. When you think of the West Indies you think of Columbus and the Spanish galleons, slavery and the naval rivalries of the eighteenth century. You might, more probably, think of calypsos and the Trinidad carnival and expensive sun and sand. When you think of the East you think of the Taj Mahal at the end of a cypress-lined vista and you think of holy men. You don't go to Trinidad, then, expecting to find Hindu pundits scuttling about country roads on motor-cycles; to see pennants with ancient devices fluttering from temples; to see mosques cool and white and rhetorical against the usual Caribbean buildings of concrete and corrugated iron; to find India celebrated in the street names of one whole district of Port of Spain; to see the Hindu festival of lights or the Muslim mourning ceremony for Husein, the Prophet's descendant, killed at the Battle of Kerbela in Arabia thirteen hundred years ago.

To be an Indian from Trinidad is to be unlikely. It is, in addition to everything else, to be the embodiment of an old verbal ambiguity. For this word "Indian" has been abused as no other word in the language; almost every time it is used it has to be qualified. There was a time in Europe when everything Oriental or everything a little unusual was judged to come from Turkey or India. So Indian ink is really Chinese ink and India paper first came from China. When in 1492 Columbus landed on the island of Guanahani he thought he had got to Cathay. He ought therefore to have called the people Chinese. But East was East. He called them Indians, and Indians they remained, walking Indian file through the Indian corn. And so, too, that American bird which to English-speaking people is the turkey is to the French *le dindon,* the bird of India.

* * *

So long as the real Indians remained on the other side of the world, there was little confusion. But when in 1845 these Indians began coming over to some of the islands

Columbus had called the Indies, confusion became total. Slavery had been abolished in the British islands; the negroes refused to work for a master, and many plantations were faced with ruin. Indentured labourers were brought in from China, Portugal and India. The Indians fitted. More and more came. They were good agriculturalists and were encouraged to settle after their indentures had expired. Instead of a passage home they could take land. Many did. The indenture system lasted, with breaks, from 1845 until 1917, and in Trinidad alone the descendants of those immigrants who stayed number over a quarter of a million.

But what were these immigrants to be called? Their name had been appropriated three hundred and fifty years before. "Hindu" was a useful word, but it had religious connotations and would have offended the many Muslims among the immigrants. In the British territories the immigrants were called East Indians. In this way they were distinguished from the two other types of Indians in the islands: the American Indians and the West Indians. After a generation or two, the East Indians were regarded as settled inhabitants of the West Indies and were thought of as West Indian East Indians. Then a national feeling grew up. There was a cry for integration, and the West Indian East Indians became East Indian West Indians.

This didn't suit the Dutch. They had a colony called Surinam, or Dutch Guiana, on the north coast of South America. They also owned a good deal of the East Indies, and to them an East Indian was someone who came from the East Indies and was of Malay stock. (When you go to an Indian restaurant in Holland you don't go to an Indian restaurant; you go to an East Indian or Javanese restaurant.) In Surinam there were many genuine East Indians from the East Indies. So another name had to be found for the Indians from India who came to Surinam. The Dutch called them British Indians. Then, with the Indian nationalist agitation in India, the British Indians began to resent being called British Indians. The Dutch compromised by calling them Hindustanis.

East Indians, British Indians, Hindustanis. But the West Indies are part of the New World and these Indians of Trinidad are no longer of Asia. The temples and mosques exist and appear genuine. But the languages that came with them have decayed. The rituals have altered. Since open-air cremation is forbidden by the health authorities, Hindus are buried, not cremated. Their ashes are not taken down holy rivers into the ocean to become again part of the Absolute. There is no Ganges at hand, only a muddy stream called the Caroni. And the water that the Hindu priest sprinkles with a mango leaf around the sacrificial fire is not Ganges water but simple tap water. The holy city of Benares is far away, but the young Hindu at his initiation ceremony in Port of Spain will still take up his staff and beggar's bowl and say that he is off to Benares to study.

His relatives will plead with him, and in the end he will lay down his staff, and there will be a ritual expression of relief.*

* * *

IT is the play of a people who have been cut off. To be an Indian from Trinidad, then, is to be unlikely and exotic. It is also to be a little fraudulent. But so all immigrants become. In India itself there is the energetic community of Parsis. They fled from Persia to escape Muslim religious persecution. But over the years the very religion which they sought to preserve has become a matter of forms and especially of burial forms: in Bombay their dead are taken to the frighteningly named Towers of Silence and there exposed to vultures. They have adopted the language of the sheltering country and their own language has become a secret gibberish. Immigrants are people on their own. They cannot be judged by the standards of their older culture. Culture is like language, ever developing. There is no right and wrong, no purity from which there is decline. Usage sanctions everything.

And these Indians from Trinidad, despite their temples and rituals, so startling to the visitors, belong to the New World. They are immigrants; they have the drive and restlessness of immigrants. To them India is a word. In moments of self-distrust this word might suggest the Taj Mahal and an ancient civilization. But more usually it suggests other words, fearfully visualized, "famine," "teeming millions." And to many, India is no more than the memory of a depressed rural existence that survived in Trinidad until only the other day. Occasionally in the interior of the island a village of thatched roofs and mud-and-bamboo walls still recalls Bengal.

* * *

In Bengal lay the great port of Calcutta. There, from the vast depressed hinterland of eastern India, the emigrants assembled for the journey by sail, often lasting four months, to the West Indies. The majority came from the provinces of Bihar and eastern Uttar Pradesh; and even today—although heavy industry has come to Bihar—these areas are known for their poverty and backwardness. It is a dismal, dusty land, made sadder by ruins and place names that speak of ancient glory. For here was the land of the Buddha; here are the cities mentioned in the Hindu epics of three thousand years

---

* Cremation is now permitted; ashes are scattered in the Caroni; and Ganges water is now imported.

ago—like Ayodhya, from which my father's family came, today a ramshackle town of wholly contemporary squalor.

The land is flat, intolerably flat, with few trees to dramatize it. The forests to which reference is often made in the epics have disappeared. The winters are brief, and in the fierce summers the fields are white with dust. You are never out of sight of low mud-walled or brick-walled villages, and there are people everywhere. An impression of tininess in vastness: tiny houses, tiny poor fields, thin, stunted people, a land scratched into dust by an ever-growing population. It is a land of famine and apathy, and yet a land of rigid caste order. Everyone has his place. Effort is futile. His field is small, his time unlimited, but the peasant still scatters his seed broadcast. He lives from hand to mouth. The attitude is understandable. In this more than feudal society of India, every-thing once belonged to the king, and later to the landlord: it was unwise to be prosper-ous. A man is therefore defined and placed by his caste alone. To the peasant on this over-populated plain, all of India, all the world, has been narrowed to a plot of ground and a few relationships.

Travel is still not easy in those parts, and from there a hundred years ago the West Indies must have seemed like the end of the world. Yet so many left, taking every-thing—beds, brass vessels, musical instruments, images, holy books, sandalwood sticks, astrological almanacs. It was less an uprooting than it appears. They were taking India with them. With their blinkered view of the world they were able to re-create eastern Uttar Pradesh or Bihar wherever they went. They had been able to ignore the vastness of India; so now they ignored the strangeness in which they had been set. To leave India's sacred soil, to cross the "black water," was considered an act of self-defilement. So completely did these migrants re-create India in Trinidad that they imposed a similar restriction on those who wished to leave Trinidad.

In a more energetic society they would have been lost. But Trinidad was stagnant in the nineteenth century. The Indians endured and prospered. The India they re-created was allowed to survive. It was an India in which a revolution had occurred. It was an India in isolation, unsupported; an India without caste or the overwhelming pressures towards caste. Effort had a meaning, and soon India could be seen to be no more than a habit, a self-imposed psychological restraint, wearing thinner with the years. At the first blast from the New World—the Second World War, the coming of Americans to the islands—India fell away, and a new people seemed all at once to have been created. The colonial, of whatever society, is a product of revolution; and the revolution takes place in the mind.

Certain things remain: the temples, the food, the rites, the names, though these become steadily more Anglicised and less recognizable to Indians; or it might be a distaste for meat, derived from a Hindu background and surviving even an Epicurean flight between London and Paris. Certainly it was odd, when I was in India two years ago, to find that often, listening to a language I thought I had forgotten, I was understanding. Just a word or two, but they seemed to recall a past life and fleetingly they gave that sensation of an experience that has been lived before. But fleetingly, since for the colonial there can be no true return.

*   *   *

In a Delhi club I met an Indian from Trinidad. I had last seen him fifteen years before. He was an adventurer. Now he was a little sad. He was an exile in the Motherland, and fifteen years had definitely taken him past youth; for him there were to be no more adventures. He was quiet and subdued. Then a worried, inquiring look came into his eyes.

"Tell me. I think we are way ahead of this bunch, don't you think?"

"But there's no question," I said.

He brightened; he looked relieved. He smiled; he laughed. "I'm *so* glad you think so. It's what I *always* tell them. Come, have a drink."

We drank. We became loud, colonials together.

1965

Reading Comprehension—Points of Engagement

1. Reread the first section of Naipaul's essay, from pages 241–243 stopping at the paragraph break, and then answer the following question with as many details as you can glean from these pages: What does it mean to be "Indian"? Focus on both the author's words as he writes and speaks them, and on the dialogue he attributes to his traveling companion.

2. What has caused there to be confusion about Indian identity, according to Naipaul? He suggests answers to this question on pages 244–246. Summarize his answers in a single paragraph written *in your own words*. You may quote from his essay once in your response.

3. On page 245, Naipaul begins his discussion of "naming" the new Indian immigrants in Trinidad. Read this passage carefully, and then think about why "naming" is so important. Freewrite for 15 minutes about "what's in a name" and provide a few examples from Naipaul's essay to support your thoughts.

4. Get into 6 small groups of 3-4 students. For each group, take one section of Naipaul, close-read it individually, and then talk about it as a group. What is going on in your section? How is it written? Why do you think Naipaul includes this section at this point in his essay? Prepare a coherent group presentation for the class. Your presentation should involve all the members of your group, should answer all of the questions above, and should include an explanation of how you think your section contributes to the overall essay.

Assignment Questions—Points of Departure

1. What does it mean to be a colonial, according to V.S. Naipaul? What does it mean to be an immigrant? What is the difference between being a colonial and being an immigrant? What do these two identities have in common? How do these identities affect a person's individual sense of themselves as a resident of their adopted or home country? Your project for this paper is to propose answers to these questions using essays by V.S. Naipaul and Lewis Lapham, Lenore Look, or Michael Kamber.

2. Think about the various rituals that you've participated in or observed in your life: graduations, weddings, funerals, church, even rituals like brushing your teeth every morning, or calling your parents every Sunday afternoon. What do these rituals *do* for you? Why do people have rituals? What happens when people lose touch with rituals? For this paper, your project is to propose answers to these questions by engaging with essays by V.S. Naipaul and one of the following authors: Alain de Botton, Jane Goodall, Fenton Johnson, or Jeanette Winterson.

3. In his essay, V.S. Naipaul describes what it means to him to be East Indian by referring to the history of his home country, Trinidad, and his own personal experience of traveling abroad. For this paper, consider how Naipaul's narrative reflects his sense of "homeland." What keeps us connected to home? What does it mean to leave home? What does it mean to take home with us? What does it mean to go back home? Is it possible to do so? Why or why not? Answer these questions using the essay by V.S. Naipaul and either Jane Goodall, Michael Kamber, Lenore Look, or Jeanette Winterson.

4. V.S. Naipaul writes that in Trinidad in the 19th century, "India could be seen to be no more than a habit, a self-imposed psychological restraint, wearing thinner with the years . . . The colonial, of whatever society, is a product of revolution; and the

revolution takes place in the mind" (247). Note carefully the terms Naipaul uses in these sentences: habit, psychological restraint, colonial, revolution, and mind. Alain de Botton, author of "On Habit," is also very interested in the relationship between "habit" and what he calls a "travelling mindset." Write a paper in which you use de Botton's ideas to reconsider Naipaul's experience as a colonial. Are their experiences different? In what ways? Why? Your project will be to explore the terms used by both authors—especially the ideas of *habit*, *revolution*, and the *travelling mindset*—and to use each essay to inform your understanding of the other one.

An Instinct to Acquire an Art

Steven Pinker

Points of Access

1. How did you learn the language that you speak at home? Was it more like the way you learned to walk, or the way that you learned to do math? Do you think that the way you learned these things is significant for showing you how your brain works? Why or why not?

2. How do animals other than humans communicate? Is it the same as the way humans communicate? What are the similarities and differences between human communication and animal communication? Why do you think these differences exist?

3. Does the fact that humans have language show that humans are more intelligent than other animals? Why or why not? What about different groups of humans? What differences are there in how different people use language? Can anyone speak (not write, but *speak*) his or her native language better than another native speaker? Which speakers are you more proficient than? Why do you think that is?

As you are reading these words, you are taking part in one of the wonders of the natural world. For you and I belong to a species with a remarkable ability: we can shape events in each other's brains with exquisite precision. I am not referring to telepathy or mind control or the other obsessions of fringe science; even in the depictions of believers these are blunt instruments compared to an ability that is uncontroversially present in every one of us. That ability is language. Simply by making noises with our mouths, we can reliably cause precise new combinations of ideas to arise in each other's minds. The ability comes so naturally that we are apt to forget what a miracle it is. So let me remind you with some simple demonstrations. Asking you only to surrender your imagination to my words for a few moments, I can cause you to think some very specific thoughts:

> When a male octopus spots a female, his normally grayish body suddenly becomes striped. He swims above the female and begins caressing her with seven of his arms. If she allows this, he will quickly reach toward her and slip his eighth arm into her breathing tube. A

series of sperm packets moves slowly through a groove in his arm, finally to slip into the mantle cavity of the female.

Cherries jubilee on a white suit? Wine on an altar cloth? Apply club soda immediately. It works beautifully to remove the stains from fabrics.

When Dixie opens the door to Tad, she is stunned, because she thought he was dead. She slams it in his face and then tries to escape. However, when Tad says, "I love you," she lets him in. Tad comforts her, and they become passionate. When Brian interrupts, Dixie tells a stunned Tad that she and Brian were married earlier that day. With much difficulty, Dixie informs Brian that things are nowhere near finished between her and Tad. Then she spills the news that Jamie is Tad's son. "My what?" says a shocked Tad.

Think about what these words have done. I did not simply remind you of octopuses; in the unlikely event that you ever see one develop stripes, you now know what will happen next. Perhaps the next time you are in a supermarket you will look for club soda, one out of the tens of thousands of items available, and then not touch it until months later when a particular substance and a particular object accidentally come together. You now share with millions of other people the secrets of protagonists in a world that is the product of some stranger's imagination, the daytime drama *All My Children*. True, my demonstrations depended on our ability to read and write, and this makes our communication even more impressive by bridging gaps of time, space, and acquaintanceship. But writing is clearly an optional accessory; the real engine of verbal communication is the spoken language we acquired as children.

In any natural history of the human species, language would stand out as the preeminent trait. To be sure, a solitary human is an impressive problem-solver and engineer. But a race of Robinson Crusoes would not give an extraterrestrial observer all that much to remark on. What is truly arresting about our kind is better captured in the story of the Tower of Babel, in which humanity, speaking a single language, came so close to reaching heaven that God himself felt threatened. A common language connects the members of a community into an information-sharing network with formidable collective powers. Anyone can benefit from the strokes of genius, lucky accidents, and trial-and-error wisdom accumulated by anyone else, present or past. And people can work in teams, their efforts coordinated by negotiated agreements. As a result, *Homo sapiens* is a species, like blue-green algae and earthworms, that has wrought far-reaching changes on the planet. Archeologists have discovered the bones of ten thousand wild horses at the bottom of a cliff in France, the remains of herds stampeded over the clifftop by groups of paleolithic hunters seventeen thousand years ago. These fossils of ancient cooperation and shared ingenuity may shed light on why saber-tooth tigers, mastodons, giant woolly rhinoceroses, and dozens of other large mammals went extinct around the time that modern humans arrived in their habitats. Our ancestors, apparently, killed them off.

Language is so tightly woven in human experience that it is scarcely possible to imagine life without it. Chances are that if you find two or more people together anywhere on earth, they will soon be exchanging words. When there is no one to talk with, people talk to themselves, to their dogs, even to their plants. In our social relations, the race is not to the swift but to the verbal—the spellbinding orator, the silver-tongued seducer, the persuasive child who wins the battle of wills against a brawnier parent. Aphasia, the loss of language following brain injury, is devastating, and in severe cases family members may feel that the whole person is lost forever.

This book is about human language. Unlike most books with "language" in the title, it will not chide you about proper usage, trace the origins of idioms and slang, or divert you with palindromes, anagrams, eponyms, or those precious names for groups of animals like "exaltation of larks." For I will be writing not about the English language or any other language, but about something much more basic: the instinct to learn, speak, and understand language. For the first time in history, there is something to write about it. Some thirty-five years ago a new science was born. Now called "cognitive science," it combines tools from psychology, computer science, linguistics, philosophy, and neurobiology to explain the workings of human intelligence. The science of language, in particular, has seen spectacular advances in the years since. There are many phenomena of language that we are coming to understand nearly as well as we understand how a camera works or what the spleen is for. I hope to communicate these exciting discoveries, some of them as elegant as anything in modern science, but I have another agenda as well.

The recent illumination of linguistic abilities has revolutionary implications for our understanding of language and its role in human affairs, and for our view of humanity itself. Most educated people already have opinions about language. They know that it is man's most important cultural invention, the quintessential example of his capacity to use symbols, and a biologically unprecedented event irrevocably separating him from other animals. They know that language pervades thought, with different languages causing their speakers to construe reality in different ways. They know that children learn to talk from role models and caregivers. They know that grammatical sophistication used to be nurtured in the schools, but sagging educational standards and the debasements of popular culture have led to a frightening decline in the ability of the average person to construct a grammatical sentence. They also know that English is a zany, logic-defying tongue, in which one drives on a parkway and parks in a driveway, plays at a recital and recites at a play. They know that English spelling takes such wackiness to even greater heights—George Bernard Shaw complained that *fish* could just as sensibly be spelled *ghoti (gh* as in *toughy, o* as in *women, ti* as in *nation)*—and that only institutional inertia prevents the adoption of a more rational, spell-it-like-it-sounds system.

In the pages that follow, I will try to convince you that every one of these common opinions is wrong! And they are all wrong for a single reason. Language is not a cultural artifact that we learn the way we learn to tell time or how the federal government works. Instead, it is a distinct piece of the biological makeup of our brains. Language is a complex, specialized skill, which develops in the child spontaneously, without conscious effort or formal instruction, is deployed without awareness of its underlying logic, is qualitatively the same in every individual, and is distinct from more general abilities to process information or behave intelligently. For these reasons some cognitive scientists have described language as a psychological faculty, a mental organ, a neural system, and a computational module. But I prefer the admittedly quaint term "instinct." It conveys the idea that people know how to talk in more or less the sense that spiders know how to spin webs. Web-spinning was not invented by some unsung spider genius and does not depend on having had the right education or on having an aptitude for architecture or the construction trades. Rather, spiders spin spider webs because they have spider brains, which give them the urge to spin and the competence to succeed. Although there are differences between webs and words, I will encourage you to see language in this way, for it helps to make sense of the phenomena we will explore.

Thinking of language as an instinct inverts the popular wisdom, especially as it has been passed down in the canon of the humanities and social sciences. Language is no more a cultural invention than is upright posture. It is not a manifestation of a general capacity to use symbols: a three-year-old, we shall see, is a grammatical genius, but is quite incompetent at the visual arts, religious iconography, traffic signs, and the other staples of the semiotics curriculum. Though language is a magnificent ability unique to *Homo sapiens* among living species, it does not call for sequestering the study of humans from the domain of biology, for a magnificent ability unique to a particular living species is far from unique in the animal kingdom. Some kinds of bats home in on flying insects using Doppler sonar. Some kinds of migratory birds navigate thousands of miles by calibrating the positions of the constellations against the time of day and year. In nature's talent show we are simply a species of primate with our own act, a knack for communicating information about who did what to whom by modulating the sounds we make when we exhale.

Once you begin to look at language not as the ineffable essence of human uniqueness but as a biological adaptation to communicate information, it is no longer as tempting to see language as an insidious shaper of thought, and, we shall see, it is not. Moreover, seeing language as one of nature's engineering marvels—an organ with "that perfection of structure and co-adaptation which justly excites our admiration," in Darwin's words—gives us a new respect for your ordinary Joe and the much-maligned English language (or any language). The complexity of language, from the scientist's point of view, is part of our biological birthright; it is not something that parents teach their children or something that must be elaborated in school—as Oscar Wilde said, "Education is an admirable thing, but it is well to remember from time to time that nothing that is worth knowing can be taught." A preschooler's tacit knowledge of grammar is more sophisticated than the thickest style manual or the most state-of-the-art computer language system, and the same applies to all healthy human beings, even the notorious syntax-fracturing professional athlete and the, you know, like, inarticulate teenage skateboarder. Finally, since language is the product of a well-engineered biological instinct, we shall see that it is not the nutty barrel of monkeys that entertainer-columnists make it out to be. I will try to restore some dignity to the English vernacular, and will even have some nice things to say about its spelling system.

The conception of language as a kind of instinct was first articulated in 1871 by Darwin himself. In *The Descent of Man* he had to contend with language because its confinement to humans seemed to present a challenge to his theory. As in all matters, his observations are uncannily modern:

> As . . . one of the founders of the noble science of philology observes, language is an art, like brewing or baking; but writing would have been a better simile. It certainly is not a true instinct, for every language has to be learned. It differs, however, widely from all ordinary arts, for man has an instinctive tendency to speak, as we see in the babble of our young children; while no child has an instinctive tendency to brew, bake, or write. Moreover, no philologist now supposes that any language has been deliberately invented; it has been slowly and unconsciously developed by many steps.

Darwin concluded that language ability is "an instinctive tendency to acquire an art," a design that is not peculiar to humans but seen in other species such as song-learning birds.

A language instinct may seem jarring to those who think of language as the zenith of the human intellect and who think of instincts as brute impulses that compel furry or feathered zombies to build a dam or up and fly south. But one of Darwin's followers,

William James, noted that an instinct possessor need not act as a "fatal automaton." He argued that we have all the instincts that animals do, and many more besides; our flexible intelligence comes from the interplay of many instincts competing. Indeed, the instinctive nature of human thought is just what makes it so hard for us to see that it is an instinct:

> It takes . . . a mind debauched by learning to carry the process of making the natural seem strange, so far as to ask for the *why* of any instinctive human act. To the metaphysician alone can such questions occur as: Why do we smile, when pleased, and not scowl? Why are we unable to talk to a crowd as we talk to a single friend? Why does a particular maiden turn our wits so upside-down? The common man can only say, *"Of course* we smile, *of course* our heart palpitates at the sight of the crowd, *of course* we love the maiden, that beautiful soul clad in that perfect form, so palpably and flagrantly made for all eternity to be loved!"
>
> And so, probably, does each animal feel about the particular things it tends to do in presence of particular objects. . . . To the lion it is the lioness which is made to be loved; to the bear, the she-bear. To the broody hen the notion would probably seem monstrous that there should be a creature in the world to whom a nestful of eggs was not the utterly fascinating and precious and never-to-be-too-much-sat-upon object which it is to her.
>
> Thus we may be sure that, however mysterious some animals' instincts may appear to us, our instincts will appear no less mysterious to them. And we may conclude that, to the animal which obeys it, every impulse and every step of every instinct shines with its own sufficient light, and seems at the moment the only eternally right and proper thing to do. What voluptuous thrill may not shake a fly, when she at last discovers the one particular leaf, or carrion, or bit of dung, that out of all the world can stimulate her ovipositor to its discharge? Does not the discharge then seem to her the only fitting thing? And need she care or know anything about the future maggot and its food?

I can think of no better statement of my main goal. The workings of language are as far from our awareness as the rationale for egg-laying is from the fly's. Our thoughts come out of our mouths so effortlessly that they often embarrass us, having eluded our mental censors. When we are comprehending sentences, the stream of words is transparent; we see through to the meaning so automatically that we can forget that a movie is in a foreign language and subtitled. We think children pick up their mother tongue by imitating their mothers, but when a child says *Don't giggle me!* or *We holded the baby rabbits,* it cannot be an act of imitation. I want to debauch your mind with learning, to make these natural gifts seem strange, to get you to ask the "why" and "how" of these seemingly homely abilities. Watch an immigrant struggling with a second language or a stroke patient with a first one, or deconstruct a snatch of baby talk, or try to program a computer to understand English, and ordinary speech begins to look different. The effortlessness, the transparency, the automaticity are illusions, masking a system of great richness and beauty.

In this century, the most famous argument that language is like an instinct comes from Noam Chomsky, the linguist who first unmasked the intricacy of the system and perhaps the person most responsible for the modern revolution in language and cognitive science. In the 1950s the social sciences were dominated by behaviorism, the school of thought popularized by John Watson and B. F. Skinner. Mental terms like "know" and "think" were branded as unscientific; "mind" and "innate" were dirty words. Behavior was explained by a few laws of stimulus-response learning that could be studied with rats pressing bars and dogs salivating to tones. But Chomsky called attention to two fundamental facts about language. First, virtually every sentence that a person utters or understands is a brand new combination of words, appearing for the first time in the history of the universe. Therefore a language cannot be a repertoire of responses; the brain must contain a recipe or program that can build an unlimited set of sentences out of a finite list of words. That program may be called a mental grammar (not to be confused with pedagogical or stylistic "grammars," which are just guides to the etiquette of written prose). The second fundamental fact is that children develop these complex grammars rapidly and without formal instruction and grow up to give consistent interpretations to novel sentence constructions that they have never before encountered. Therefore, he argued, children must innately be equipped with a plan common to the grammars of all languages, a Universal Grammar, that tells them how to distill the syntactic patterns out of the speech of their parents. Chomsky put it as follows:

> It is a curious fact about the intellectual history of the past few centuries that physical and mental development have been approached in quite different ways. No one would take seriously the proposal that the human organism learns through experience to have arms rather than wings, or that the basic structure of particular organs results from accidental experience. Rather, it is taken for granted that the physical structure of the organism is genetically determined, though of course variation along such dimensions as size, rate of development, and so forth will depend in part on external factors. . . .
>
> The development of personality, behavior patterns, and cognitive structures in higher organisms has often been approached in a very different way. It is generally assumed that in these domains, social environment is the dominant factor. The structures of mind that develop over time are taken to be arbitrary and accidental; there is no "human nature" apart from what develops as a specific historical product. . . .
>
> But human cognitive systems, when seriously investigated, prove to be no less marvelous and intricate than the physical structures that develop in the life of the organism. Why, then, should we not study the acquisition of a cognitive structure such as language more or less as we study some complex bodily organ?

At first glance, the proposal may seem absurd, if only because of the great variety of human languages. But a closer consideration dispels these doubts. Even knowing very little of substance about linguistic universals, we can be quite sure that the possible variety of language is sharply limited. . . . The language each person acquires is a rich and complex construction hopelessly underdetermined by the fragmentary evidence available [to the child]. Nevertheless individuals in a speech community have developed essentially the same language. This fact can be explained only on the assumption that these individuals employ highly restrictive principles that guide the construction of grammar.

By performing painstaking technical analyses of the sentences ordinary people accept as part of their mother tongue, Chomsky and other linguists developed theories of the mental grammars underlying people's knowledge of particular languages and of the Universal Grammar underlying the particular grammars. Early on, Chomsky's work encouraged other scientists, among them Eric Lenneberg, George Miller, Roger Brown, Morris Halle, and Alvin Liberman, to open up whole new areas of language study, from child development and speech perception to neurology and genetics. By now, the community of scientists studying the questions he raised numbers in the thousands. Chomsky is currently among the ten most-cited writers in all of the humanities (beating out Hegel and Cicero and trailing only Marx, Lenin, Shakespeare, the Bible, Aristotle, Plato, and Freud) and the only living member of the top ten.

What those citations *say* is another matter. Chomsky gets people exercised. Reactions range from the awe-struck deference ordinarily reserved for gurus of weird religious cults to the withering invective that academics have developed into a high art. In part this is because Chomsky attacks what is still one of the foundations of twentieth-century intellectual life—the "Standard Social Science Model," according to which the human psyche is molded by the surrounding culture. But it is also because no thinker can afford to ignore him. As one of his severest critics, the philosopher Hilary Putnam, acknowledges,

When one reads Chomsky, one is struck by a sense of great intellectual power; one knows one is encountering an extraordinary mind. And this is as much a matter of the spell of his powerful personality as it is of his obvious intellectual virtues: originality, scorn for the faddish and the superficial; willingness to revive (and the ability to revive) positions (such as the "doctrine of innate ideas") that had seemed passé; concern with topics, such as the structure of the human mind, that are of central and perennial importance.

The story I will tell in this book has, of course, been deeply influenced by Chomsky. But it is not his story exactly, and I will not tell it as he would. Chomsky has puzzled many readers with his skepticism about whether Darwinian natural selection (as opposed to other evolutionary processes) can explain the origins of the language organ that he argues for; I think it is fruitful to consider language as an evolutionary adaptation, like the eye, its major parts designed to carry out important functions. And Chomsky's arguments about the nature of the language faculty are based on technical analyses of word and sentence structure, often couched in abstruse formalisms. His discussions of flesh-and-blood speakers are perfunctory and highly idealized. Though I happen to agree with many of his arguments, I think that a conclusion about the mind is convincing only if many kinds of evidence converge on it. So the story in this book is highly eclectic, ranging from how DNA builds brains to the pontifications of newspaper language columnists. The best place to begin is to ask why anyone should believe that human language is a part of human biology—an instinct—at all.

Reading Comprehension—Points of Engagement

1. According to Pinker, is language a human invention? If not, what is it? Where does it come from?

2. While discussing the relationship between language and instinct, Steven Pinker cites William James and James's view of the relationship between human intelligence and the instincts that we possess. Pinker writes, based on James's arguments: "Our flexible intelligence comes from the interplay of many instincts competing" (256). In your own words, what does this sentence mean? According to James, where does our intelligence stem from? What produces it? How does he describe our intelligence?

3. What, in Pinker's view, is the relationship between human language, spider web-spinning, bird-song and bat sonar? What does he use his discussion of all these things to show?

Assignment Questions—Points of Departure

1. Think about the title of Steven Pinker's essay, "An Instinct to Acquire an Art." How much of what we do as adults is instinct, and how much is art? What are the differences between the two? How do those differences affect our motivations and actions? Your project for this paper is to answer these questions by using Pinker to reconsider the ideas and experiences described by one of the following authors: Susan Blackmore, Alain de Botton, Adam Gopnik, Steven Johnson, Barbara King-

solver, or Lauren Slater. In your paper make sure you address how each author defines or deals with these ideas of "instinct" and "art." Be aware that they may use different terms to describe similar ideas. Use their terms, and the connections you make between the essays, to propose your own answers to the assignment questions above.

2. Whether we are looking on the level of our own communities, of our lives on this planet, or as living on just one planet in the whole universe, humans seem to need to define ourselves in relationship to other entities: sometimes other groups of people, sometimes other creatures or things. Write an essay in which you consider the following question: what place do humans hold in the world, and in the universe? Are we unique, or are we just part of a bigger system? And then, what place do we have in this system? Do we need to consider other entities when figuring out what we, as humans, are and are not, or are the confines of our own experience enough? Refer to essays by Steven Pinker and either Alain de Botton, Paul Davies, Franklin Foer, Malcolm Gladwell, Steven Johnson, Michael Pollan, Lauren Slater, or Jeanette Winterson.

3. How driven are humans by biological imperatives, and how much of human nature do we need to attribute to other factors such as environment, culture, or spirituality? Are there other factors? How do they affect us? What do we gain by taking the biological approach? What do we lose? In your paper, refer to essays by Steven Pinker and one of the following authors: Susan Blackmore, Jane Goodall, Arlie Russell Hochschild, Steven Johnson, Barbara Kingsolver, Katha Pollitt, Francine Prose, or Andrew Sullivan.

4. Most people work hard to build links and similarities with other people, just as they work hard to highlight and accentuate what makes them unique and different. What do these two tendencies reveal to us about our attitudes towards ourselves, and what we hold as important? What would changing our focus do to the way we function in society, or, indeed, amongst other animals? Answer these questions using essays by Steven Pinker, and one of the following authors: Malcolm Gladwell, Fenton Johnson, Lewis Lapham, Lenore Look, V.S. Naipaul, Michael Pollan, or John Waterbury.

An Animal's Place
Michael Pollan

Points of Access

1. What is morality? How would you define your morals? Where do your ideas of morality come from?

2. Do you eat meat? Why or why not? Are your reasons primarily habitual, nutritional, moral? How long have you maintained your current eating habits regarding meat? If they've changed, especially in the last few years, what prompted the change?

3. Do animals deserve respect? What does it mean to give respect to an animal? Is it the same as giving respect to a person? Why or why not?

The first time I opened Peter Singer's *Animal Liberation,* I was dining alone at the Palm, trying to enjoy a rib-eye steak cooked medium-rare. If this sounds like a good recipe for cognitive dissonance (if not indigestion), that was sort of the idea. Preposterous as it might seem, to supporters of animal rights, what I was doing was tantamount to reading *Uncle Tom's Cabin* on a plantation in the Deep South in 1852.

Singer and the swelling ranks of his followers ask us to imagine a future in which people will look back on my meal, and this steakhouse, as relics of an equally backward age. Eating animals, wearing animals, experimenting on animals, killing animals for sport: all these practices, so resolutely normal to us, will be seen as the barbarities they are, and we will come to view "speciesism"—a neologism I had encountered before only in jokes—as a form of discrimination as indefensible as racism or anti-Semitism.

Even in 1975, when *Animal Liberation* was first published, Singer, an Australian philosopher now teaching at Princeton, was confident that he had the wind of history at his back. The recent civil rights past was prologue, as one liberation movement followed on the heels of another. Slowly but surely, the white man's circle of moral consideration was expanded to admit first blacks, then women, then homosexuals. In each case, a group once thought to be so different from the prevailing "we" as to be undeserving of civil rights was, after a struggle, admitted to the club. Now it was animals' turn.

That animal liberation is the logical next step in the forward march of moral progress is no longer the fringe idea it was back in 1975. A growing and increasingly influential movement of philosophers, ethicists, law professors and activists are convinced that the great moral struggle of our time will be for the rights of animals.

So far the movement has scored some of its biggest victories in Europe. Earlier this year, Germany became the first nation to grant animals a constitutional right: the words "and animals" were added to a provision obliging the state to respect and protect the dignity of human beings. The farming of animals for fur was recently banned in England. In several European nations, sows may no longer be confined to crates nor laying hens to "battery cages"—stacked wired cages so small the birds cannot stretch their wings. The Swiss are amending their laws to change the status of animals from "things" to "beings."

Though animals are still very much "things" in the eyes of American law, change is in the air. Thirty-seven states have recently passed laws making some forms of animal cruelty a crime, 21 of them by ballot initiative. Following protests by activists, McDonald's and Burger King forced significant improvements in the way the U.S. meat industry slaughters animals. Agribusiness and the cosmetics and apparel industries are all struggling to defuse mounting public concerns over animal welfare.

Once thought of as a left-wing concern, the movement now cuts across ideological lines. Perhaps the most eloquent recent plea on behalf of animals, a new book called *Dominion,* was written by a former speechwriter for President Bush. And once outlandish ideas are finding their way into mainstream opinion. A recent Zogby poll found that 51 percent of Americans believe that *primates* are entitled to the same rights as human children.

What is going on here? A certain amount of cultural confusion, for one thing. For at the same time many people seem eager to extend the circle of our moral consideration to animals, in our factory farms and laboratories we are inflicting more suffering on more animals than at any time in history. One by one, science is dismantling our claims to uniqueness as a species, discovering that such things as culture, tool making, language and even possibly self-consciousness are not the exclusive domain of Homo sapiens. Yet most of the animals we kill lead lives organized very much in the spirit of Descartes, who famously claimed that animals were mere machines, incapable of thought or feeling. There's a schizoid quality to our relationship with animals, in which sentiment and brutality exist side by side. Half the dogs in America will receive Christmas presents this year, yet few of us pause to consider the miserable life of the pig—an animal easily as intelligent as a dog—that becomes the Christmas ham.

We tolerate this disconnect because the life of the pig has moved out of view. When's the last time you saw a pig? (Babe doesn't count.) Except for our pets, real animals—animals living and dying—no longer figure in our everyday lives. Meat comes from the grocery store, where it is cut and packaged to look as little like parts of animals as possible. The disappearance of animals from our lives has opened a space in which there's no reality check, either on the sentiment or the brutality. This is pretty much where we live now, with respect to animals, and it is a space in which the Peter Singers and Frank Perdues of the world can evidently thrive equally well.

Several years ago, the English critic John Berger wrote an essay, "Why Look at Animals?" in which he suggested that the loss of everyday contact between ourselves and animals—and specifically the loss of eye contact—has left us deeply confused about the terms of our relationship to other species. That eye contact, always slightly uncanny, had provided a vivid daily reminder that animals were at once crucially like and unlike us; in their eyes we glimpsed something unmistakably familiar (pain, fear, tenderness) and something irretrievably alien. Upon this paradox people built a relationship in which they felt they could both honor and eat animals without looking away. But that accommodation has pretty much broken down; nowadays, it seems, we either look away or become vegetarians. For my own part, neither option seemed especially appetizing. Which might explain how I found myself reading *Animal Liberation* in a steakhouse.

* * *

This is not something I'd recommend if you're determined to continue eating meat. Combining rigorous philosophical argument with journalistic description, *Animal Liberation* is one of those rare books that demand that you either defend the way you live or change it. Because Singer is so skilled in argument, for many readers it is easier to change. His book has converted countless thousands to vegetarianism, and it didn't take long for me to see why: within a few pages, he had succeeded in throwing me on the defensive.

Singer's argument is disarmingly simple and, if you accept its premises, difficult to refute. Take the premise of equality, which most people readily accept. Yet what do we really mean by it? People are not, as a matter of fact, equal at all—some are smarter than others, better looking, more gifted. "Equality is a moral idea," Singer points out, "not an assertion of fact." The moral idea is that everyone's interests ought to receive equal consideration, regardless of "what abilities they may possess." Fair enough; many philosophers have gone this far. But fewer have taken the next logical step. "If possessing a higher degree of intelligence does not entitle one human to use another for his or her own ends, how can it entitle humans to exploit nonhumans for the same purpose?"

This is the nub of Singer's argument, and right around here I began scribbling objections in the margin. *But humans differ from animals in morally significant ways.* Yes they do, Singer acknowledges, which is why we shouldn't treat pigs and children alike. Equal consideration of interests is not the same as equal treatment, he points out: children have an interest in being educated; pigs, in rooting around in the dirt. But where their interests are the same, the principle of equality demands they receive the same consideration. And the one all-important interest that we share with pigs, as with all sentient creatures, is an interest in avoiding pain.

Here Singer quotes a famous passage from Jeremy Bentham, the 18th-century utilitarian philosopher, that is the wellspring of the animal rights movement. Bentham was writing in 1789, soon after the French colonies freed black slaves, granting them fundamental rights. "The day *may* come," he speculates, "when the rest of the animal creation may acquire those rights." Bentham then asks what characteristic entitles any being to moral consideration. "Is it the faculty of reason or perhaps the faculty of discourse?" Obviously not, since "a full-grown horse or dog is beyond comparison a more rational, as well as a more conversable animal, than an infant." He concludes: "The question is not, Can they *reason?* nor, Can they *talk?* but, Can they *suffer?*"

Bentham here is playing a powerful card philosophers call the "argument from marginal cases," or A.M.C. for short. It goes like this: there are humans—infants, the severely retarded, the demented—whose mental function cannot match that of a chimpanzee. Even though these people cannot reciprocate our moral attentions, we nevertheless include them in the circle of our moral consideration. So on what basis do we exclude the chimpanzee?

Because he's a chimp, I furiously scribbled in the margin, *and they're human!* For Singer that's not good enough. To exclude the chimp from moral consideration simply because he's not human is no different from excluding the slave simply because he's not white. In the same way we'd call that exclusion racist, the animal rightist contends that it is speciesist to discriminate against the chimpanzee solely because he's not human.

But the differences between blacks and whites are trivial compared with the differences between my son and a chimp. Singer counters by asking us to imagine a hypothetical society that discriminates against people on the basis of something nontrivial—say, intelligence. If that scheme offends our sense of equality, then why is the fact that animals lack certain human characteristics any more just as a basis for discrimination? Either we do not owe any justice to the severely retarded, he concludes, or we do owe it to animals with higher capabilities.

This is where I put down my fork. If I believe in equality, and equality is based on interests rather than characteristics, then either I have to take the interests of the steer I'm eating into account or concede that I am a speciesist. For the time being, I decided to plead guilty as charged. I finished my steak.

But Singer had planted a troubling notion, and in the days afterward, it grew and grew, watered by the other animal rights thinkers I began reading: the philosophers Tom Regan and James Rachels; the legal theorist Steven M. Wise; the writers Joy Williams and Matthew Scully. I didn't *think* I minded being a speciesist, but could it be, as several of these writers suggest, that we will someday come to regard speciesism as an evil comparable to racism? Will history someday judge us as harshly as it judges the Germans who went about their ordinary lives in the shadow of Treblinka? Precisely that question was recently posed by J.M. Coetzee, the South African novelist, in a lecture delivered at Princeton; he answered it in the affirmative. If animal rightists are right, "a crime of stupefying proportions" (in Coetzee's words) is going on all around us every day, just beneath our notice.

It's an idea almost impossible to entertain seriously, much less to accept, and in the weeks following my restaurant face-off between Singer and the steak, I found myself marshaling whatever mental power I could muster to try to refute it. Yet Singer and his allies managed to trump almost all my objections.

My first line of defense was obvious. *Animals kill one another all the time. Why treat animals more ethically than they treat one another?* (Ben Franklin tried this one long before me: during a fishing trip, he wondered, "If you eat one another, I don't see why we may not eat you." He admits, however, that the rationale didn't occur to him until the fish were in the frying pan, smelling "admirably well." The advantage of being a "reasonable creature," Franklin remarks, is that you can find a reason for whatever you want to do.) To the "they do it, too" defense, the animal rightist has a devastating reply: do you really want to base your morality on the natural order? Murder and rape are natural, too. Besides, humans don't need to kill other creatures in order to survive; animals do. (Though if my cat, Otis, is any guide, animals sometimes kill for sheer pleasure.)

This suggests another defense. *Wouldn't life in the wild be worse for these farm animals?* "Defenders of slavery imposed on black Africans often made a similar point," Singer retorts. "The life of freedom is to be preferred."

But domesticated animals can't survive in the wild; in fact, without us they wouldn't exist at all. Or as one 19th-century political philosopher put it, "The pig has a stronger interest than anyone in the demand for bacon. If all the world were Jewish, there would be no pigs at all." But it turns out that this would be fine by the animal rightists: for if pigs don't exist, they can't be wronged.

Animals on factory farms have never known any other life. Singer replies that "animals feel a need to exercise, stretch their limbs or wings, groom themselves and turn around, whether or not they have ever lived in conditions that permit this." The measure of their suffering is not their prior experiences but the unremitting daily frustration of their instincts.

O.K., the suffering of animals is a legitimate problem, but the world is full of problems, and surely human problems must come first! Sounds good, and yet all the animal people are asking me to do is to stop eating meat and wearing animal furs and hides. There's no reason I can't devote myself to solving humankind's problems while being a vegetarian who wears synthetics.

But doesn't the fact that we could choose to forgo meat for moral reasons point to a crucial moral difference between animals and humans? As Kant pointed out, the human being is the only moral animal, the only one even capable of entertaining a concept of "rights." What's wrong with reserving moral consideration for those able to reciprocate it? Right here is where you run smack into the A.M.C.: the moral status of the retarded, the insane, the infant and the Alzheimer's patient. Such "marginal cases," in the detestable argot of modern moral philosophy, cannot participate in moral decision making any more than a monkey can, yet we nevertheless grant them rights.

That's right, I respond, for the simple reason that they're one of us. And all of us have been, and will probably once again be, marginal cases ourselves. What's more, these people have fathers and mothers, daughters and sons, which makes our interest in their welfare deeper than our interest in the welfare of even the most brilliant ape.

Alas, none of these arguments evade the charge of speciesism; the racist, too, claims that it's natural to give special consideration to one's own kind. A utilitarian like Singer would agree, however, that the feelings of relatives do count for something. Yet the principle of equal consideration of interests demands that, given the choice between performing a painful medical experiment on a severely retarded orphan and on a normal ape, we must sacrifice the child. Why? Because the ape has a greater capacity for pain.

Here in a nutshell is the problem with the A.M.C.: it can be used to help the animals, but just as often it winds up hurting the marginal cases. Giving up our speciesism will bring us to a moral cliff from which we may not be prepared to jump, even when logic is pushing us.

And yet this isn't the moral choice I am being asked to make. (Too bad; it would be so much easier!) In everyday life, the choice is not between babies and chimps but between the pork and the tofu. Even if we reject the "hard utilitarianism" of a Peter Singer, there remains the question of whether we owe animals that can feel pain any moral consideration, and this seems impossible to deny. And if we do owe them moral consideration, how can we justify eating them?

This is why killing animals for meat (and clothing) poses the most difficult animal rights challenge. In the case of animal testing, all but the most radical animal rightists are willing to balance the human benefit against the cost to the animals. That's because the unique qualities of human consciousness carry weight in the utilitarian calculus: human pain counts for more than that of a mouse, since our pain is amplified by emotions like dread; similarly, our deaths are worse than an animal's because we understand what death is in a way they don't. So the argument over animal testing is really in the details: is this particular procedure or test *really* necessary to save human lives? (Very often it's not, in which case we probably shouldn't do it.) But if humans no longer need to eat meat or wear skins, then what exactly are we putting on the human side of the scale to outweigh the interests of the animal?

I suspect that this is finally why the animal people managed to throw me on the defensive. It's one thing to choose between the chimp and the retarded child or to accept the sacrifice of all those pigs surgeons practiced on to develop heart-bypass surgery. But what happens when the choice is between "a lifetime of suffering for a nonhuman animal and the gastronomic preference of a human being?" You look away—or you stop eating animals. And if you don't want to do either? Then you have to try to determine if the animals you're eating have really endured "a lifetime of suffering."

* * *

Whether our interest in eating animals outweighs their interest in not being eaten (assuming for the moment that is their interest) turns on the vexed question of animal suffering. Vexed, because it is impossible to know what really goes on in the mind of a cow or a pig or even an ape. Strictly speaking, this is true of other humans, too, but since humans are all basically wired the same way, we have excellent reason to assume that other people's experience of pain feels much like our own. Can we say that about animals? Yes and no.

I have yet to find anyone who still subscribes to Descartes's belief that animals cannot feel pain because they lack a soul. The general consensus among scientists and philosophers is that when it comes to pain, the higher animals are wired much like we are for the same evolutionary reasons, so we should take the writhings of the kicked dog at face value. Indeed, the very premise of a great deal of animal testing—the reason it has value—is that animals' experience of physical and even some psychological pain closely resembles our own. Otherwise, why would cosmetics testers drip chemicals into the eyes of rabbits to see if they sting? Why would researchers study head trauma by traumatizing chimpanzee heads? Why would psychologists attempt to induce depression and "learned helplessness" in dogs by exposing them to ceaseless random patterns of electrical shock?

That said, it can be argued that human pain differs from animal pain by an order of magnitude. This qualitative difference is largely the result of our possession of language and, by virtue of language, an ability to have thoughts about thoughts and to imagine alternatives to our current reality. The philosopher Daniel C. Dennett suggests that we would do well to draw a distinction between pain, which a great many animals experience, and suffering, which depends on a degree of self-consciousness only a few animals appear to command. Suffering in this view is not just lots of pain but pain intensified by human emotions like loss, sadness, worry, regret, self-pity, shame, humiliation and dread.

Consider castration. No one would deny the procedure is painful to animals, yet animals appear to get over it in a way humans do not. (Some rhesus monkeys competing for mates will bite off a rival's testicle; the very next day the victim may be observed mating, seemingly little the worse for wear.) Surely the suffering of a man able to comprehend the full implications of castration, to anticipate the event and contemplate its aftermath, represents an agony of another order.

By the same token, however, language and all that comes with it can also make certain kinds of pain *more* bearable. A trip to the dentist would be a torment for an ape that couldn't be made to understand the purpose and duration of the procedure.

As humans contemplating the pain and suffering of animals, we do need to guard against projecting on to them what the same experience would feel like to us. Watching a steer force-marched up the ramp to the kill-floor door, as I have done, I need to remind myself that this is not Sean Penn in "Dead Man Walking," that in a bovine brain the concept of nonexistence is blissfully absent. "If we fail to find suffering in the [animal] lives we can see," Dennett writes in *Kinds of Minds,* "we can rest assured there is no invisible suffering somewhere in their brains. If we find suffering, we will recognize it without difficulty."

* * *

Which brings us—reluctantly, necessarily—to the American factory farm, the place where all such distinctions turn to dust. It's not easy to draw lines between pain and suffering in a modern egg or confinement hog operation. These are places where the subtleties of moral philosophy and animal cognition mean less than nothing, where everything we've learned about animals at least since Darwin has been simply . . . set aside. To visit a modern CAFO (Confined Animal Feeding Operation) is to enter a world that, for all its technological sophistication, is still designed according to Cartesian principles: animals are machines incapable of feeling pain. Since no thinking person can possibly believe this any more, industrial animal agriculture depends on a suspension of disbelief on the part of the people who operate it and a willingness to avert your eyes on the part of everyone else.

From everything I've read, egg and hog operations are the worst. Beef cattle in America at least still live outdoors, albeit standing ankle deep in their own waste eating a diet that makes them sick. And broiler chickens, although they do get their beaks snipped off with a hot knife to keep them from cannibalizing one another under the stress of their confinement, at least don't spend their eight-week lives in cages too small to ever stretch a wing. That fate is reserved for the American laying hen, who passes her brief span piled together with a half-dozen other hens in a wire cage whose floor a single page of this magazine could carpet. Every natural instinct of this animal is thwarted, leading to a range of behavioral "vices" that can include cannibalizing her cagemates and rubbing her body against the wire mesh until it is featherless and bleeding. Pain? Suffering? Madness? The operative suspension of disbelief depends on more neutral descriptors, like "vices" and "stress." Whatever you want to call what's going on in those cages, the 10 percent or so of hens that can't bear it and simply die is built into the cost of production. And when the output of the others begins to ebb, the hens will be "force-molted"—starved of food and water and light for several days in order to stimulate a final bout of egg laying before their life's work is done.

Simply reciting these facts, most of which are drawn from poultry-trade magazines, makes me sound like one of those animal people, doesn't it? I don't mean to, but this is what can happen when . . . you look. It certainly wasn't my intention to ruin anyone's breakfast. But now that I probably have spoiled the eggs, I do want to say one thing about the bacon, mention a single practice (by no means the worst) in modern hog production that points to the compound madness of an impeccable industrial logic.

Piglets in confinement operations are weaned from their mothers 10 days after birth (compared with 13 weeks in nature) because they gain weight faster on their hormone- and antibiotic-fortified feed. This premature weaning leaves the pigs with a lifelong craving to suck and chew, a desire they gratify in confinement by biting the tail of the animal in front of them. A normal pig would fight off his molester, but a demoralized pig has stopped caring. "Learned helplessness" is the psychological term, and it's not uncommon in confinement operations, where tens of thousands of hogs spend their entire lives ignorant of sunshine or earth or straw, crowded together beneath a metal roof upon metal slats suspended over a manure pit. So it's not surprising that an animal as sensitive and intelligent as a pig would get depressed, and a depressed pig will allow his tail to be chewed on to the point of infection. Sick pigs, being underperforming "production units," are clubbed to death on the spot. The U.S.D.A.'s recommended solution to the problem is called "tail docking." Using a pair of pliers (and no anesthetic), most but not all of the tail is snipped off. Why the little stump? Because the whole point of the exercise is not to remove the object of tail-biting so much as to render it *more* sensitive. Now, a bite on the tail is so painful that even the most demoralized pig will mount a struggle to avoid it.

Much of this description is drawn from *Dominion,* Matthew Scully's recent book in which he offers a harrowing description of a North Carolina hog operation. Scully, a Christian conservative, has no patience for lefty rights talk, arguing instead that while God did give man "dominion" over animals ("Every moving thing that liveth shall be meat for you"), he also admonished us to show them mercy. "We are called to treat them with kindness, not because they have rights or power or some claim to equality but . . . because they stand unequal and powerless before us."

Scully calls the contemporary factory farm "our own worst nightmare" and, to his credit, doesn't shrink from naming the root cause of this evil: unfettered capitalism. (Perhaps this explains why he resigned from the Bush administration just before his book's publication.) A tension has always existed between the capitalist imperative to maximize efficiency and the moral imperatives of religion or community, which have historically served as a counterweight to the moral blindness of the market. This is one of "the cultural contradictions of capitalism"—the tendency of the economic impulse to erode the moral underpinnings of society. Mercy toward animals is one such casualty.

More than any other institution, the American industrial animal farm offers a nightmarish glimpse of what capitalism can look like in the absence of moral or regulatory constraint. Here in these places life itself is redefined—as protein production—and with it suffering. *That* venerable word becomes "stress," an economic problem in search of a cost-effective solution, like tail-docking or beak-clipping or, in the industry's latest plan, by simply engineering the "stress gene" out of pigs and chickens. "Our own worst nightmare" such a place may well be; it is also real life for the billions of animals unlucky enough to have been born beneath these grim steel roofs, into the brief, pitiless life of a "production unit" in the days before the suffering gene was found.

*   *   *

Vegetarianism doesn't seem an unreasonable response to such an evil. Who would want to be made complicit in the agony of these animals by eating them? You want to throw *something* against the walls of those infernal sheds, whether it's the Bible, a new constitutional right or a whole platoon of animal rightists bent on breaking in and liberating the inmates. In the shadow of these factory farms, Coetzee's notion of a "stupefying crime" doesn't seem far-fetched at all.

But before you swear off meat entirely, let me describe a very different sort of animal farm. It is typical of nothing, and yet its very existence puts the whole moral question of animal agriculture in a different light. Polyface Farm occupies 550 acres of rolling grassland and forest in the Shenandoah Valley of Virginia. Here, Joel Salatin and his family raise six different food animals—cattle, pigs, chickens, rabbits, turkeys and sheep—in an intricate dance of symbiosis designed to allow each species, in Salatin's words, "to fully express its physiological distinctiveness."

What this means in practice is that Salatin's chickens live like chickens; his cows, like cows; pigs, pigs. As in nature, where birds tend to follow herbivores, once Salatin's cows have finished grazing a pasture, he moves them out and tows in his "eggmobile," a portable chicken coop that houses several hundred laying hens—roughly the natural size of a flock. The hens fan out over the pasture, eating the short grass and picking insect larvae out of the cowpats—all the while spreading the cow manure and eliminating the farm's parasite problem. A diet of grubs and grass makes for exceptionally tasty eggs and contented chickens, and their nitrogenous manure feeds the pasture. A few weeks later, the chickens move out, and the sheep come in, dining on the lush new growth, as well as on the weed species (nettles, nightshade) that the cattle and chickens won't touch.

Meanwhile, the pigs are in the barn turning the compost. All winter long, while the cattle were indoors, Salatin layered their manure with straw, wood chips—and corn. By March, this steaming compost layer cake stands three feet high, and the pigs, whose powerful snouts can sniff out and retrieve the fermented corn at the bottom, get to spend a few happy weeks rooting through the pile, aerating it as they work. All you can see of these pigs, intently nosing out the tasty alcoholic morsels, are their upturned pink hams and corkscrew tails churning the air. The finished compost will go to feed the grass; the grass, the cattle; the cattle, the chickens; and eventually all of these animals will feed us.

I thought a lot about vegetarianism and animal rights during the day I spent on Joel Salatin's extraordinary farm. So much of what I'd read, so much of what I'd accepted, looked very different from here. To many animal rightists, even Polyface Farm is a death camp. But to look at these animals is to see this for the sentimental conceit it is. In the same way that we can probably recognize animal suffering when we see it, animal happiness is unmistakable, too, and here I was seeing it in abundance.

For any animal, happiness seems to consist in the opportunity to express its creaturely character—its essential pigness or wolfness or chickenness. Aristotle speaks of each creature's "characteristic form of life." For domesticated species, the good life, if we can call it that, cannot be achieved apart from humans—apart from our farms and, therefore, our meat eating. This, it seems to me, is where animal rightists betray a profound ignorance about the workings of nature. To think of domestication as a form of enslavement or even exploitation is to misconstrue the whole relationship, to project a human idea of power onto what is, in fact, an instance of mutualism between species. Domestication is an evolutionary, rather than a political, development. It is certainly not a regime humans imposed on animals some 10,000 years ago.

Rather, domestication happened when a small handful of especially opportunistic species discovered through Darwinian trial and error that they were more likely to survive and prosper in an alliance with humans than on their own. Humans provided the animals with food and protection, in exchange for which the animals provided the humans their milk and eggs and—yes—their flesh. Both parties were transformed by the relationship: animals grew tame and lost their ability to fend for themselves (evolution tends to edit out unneeded traits), and the humans gave up their hunter-gatherer ways for the settled life of agriculturists. (Humans changed biologically, too, evolving such new traits as a tolerance for lactose as adults.)

From the animals' point of view, the bargain with humanity has been a great success, at least until our own time. Cows, pigs, dogs, cats and chickens have thrived, while their wild ancestors have languished. (There are 10,000 wolves in North America, 50,000,000 dogs.) Nor does their loss of autonomy seem to trouble these creatures. It is wrong, the rightists say, to treat animals as "means" rather than "ends," yet the happiness of a working animal like the dog consists precisely in serving as a "means." Liberation is the last thing such a creature wants. To say of one of Joel Salatin's caged chickens that "the life of freedom is to be preferred" betrays an ignorance about chicken preferences—which on this farm are heavily focused on not getting their heads bitten off by weasels.

But haven't these chickens simply traded one predator for another—weasels for humans? True enough, and for the chickens this is probably not a bad deal. For brief as it is, the life expectancy of a farm animal would be considerably briefer in the world beyond the pasture fence or chicken coop. A sheep farmer told me that a bear will eat a lactating ewe alive, starting with her udders. "As a rule," he explained, "animals don't get 'good deaths' surrounded by their loved ones."

The very existence of predation—animals eating animals—is the cause of much anguished hand-wringing in animal rights circles. "It must be admitted," Singer writes, "that the existence of carnivorous animals does pose one problem for the ethics of Animal Liberation, and that is whether we should do anything about it." Some animal rightists train their dogs and cats to become vegetarians. (Note: cats will require nutritional supplements to stay healthy.) Matthew Scully calls predation "the intrinsic evil in nature's design . . . among the hardest of all things to fathom." *Really?* A deep Puritan streak pervades animal rights activists, an abiding discomfort not only with our animality, but with the animals' animality too.

However it may appear to us, predation is not a matter of morality or politics; it, also, is a matter of symbiosis. Hard as the wolf may be on the deer he eats, the herd depends on him for its well-being; without predators to cull the herd, deer overrun their habitat and starve. In many places, human hunters have taken over the predator's ecological role. Chickens also depend for their continued well-being on their human predators—not individual chickens, but chickens as a species. The surest way to achieve the extinction of the chicken would be to grant chickens a "right to life."

Yet here's the rub: the animal rightist is not concerned with species, only individuals. Tom Regan, author of *The Case for Animal Rights,* bluntly asserts that because "species are not individuals . . . the rights view does not recognize the moral rights of species to anything, including survival." Singer concurs, insisting that only sentient individuals have interests. But surely a species can have interests—in its survival, say—just as a nation or community or a corporation can. The animal rights movement's exclusive concern with individual animals makes perfect sense given its roots in a culture of liberal individualism, but does it make any sense in nature?

Consider this hypothetical case: In 1611 Juan da Goma (aka Juan the Disoriented) made accidental landfall on Wrightson Island, a six-square-mile rock in the Indian Ocean. The island's sole distinction is as the only known home of the Arcania tree and the bird that nests in it, the Wrightson giant sea sparrow. Da Goma and his crew stayed a week, much of that time spent in a failed bid to recapture the ship's escaped goat—who happened to be pregnant. Nearly four centuries later, Wrightson Island is home to 380 goats that have consumed virtually every scrap of vegetation in their reach. The youngest Arcania tree on the island is more than 300 years old, and only 52 sea sparrows remain. In the animal rights view, any one of those goats have at least as much right to life as the last Wrightson sparrow on earth, and the trees, because they are not sentient, warrant no moral consideration whatsoever. (In the mid-80's a British environmental group set out to shoot the goats, but was forced to cancel the expedition after the Mammal Liberation Front bombed its offices.)

The story of Wrightson Island (recounted by the biologist David Ehrenfeld in *Beginning Again*) suggests at the very least that a human morality based on individual rights makes for an awkward fit when applied to the natural world. This should come as no surprise: morality is an artifact of human culture, devised to help us negotiate social relations. It's very good for that. But just as we recognize that nature doesn't provide an adequate guide for human social conduct, isn't it anthropocentric to assume that our moral system offers an adequate guide for nature? We may require a different set of ethics to guide our dealings with the natural world, one as well suited to the particular needs of plants and animals and habitats (where sentience counts for little) as rights suit us humans today.

*   *   *

To contemplate such questions from the vantage of a farm is to appreciate just how parochial and urban an ideology animals rights really is. It could thrive only in a world where people have lost contact with the natural world, where animals no longer pose a threat to us and human mastery of nature seems absolute. "In our normal life," Singer writes, "there is no serious clash of interests between human and nonhuman animals." Such a statement assumes a decidedly urbanized "normal life," one that certainly no farmer would recognize.

The farmer would point out that even vegans have a "serious clash of interests" with other animals. The grain that the vegan eats is harvested with a combine that shreds field mice, while the farmer's tractor crushes woodchucks in their burrows, and his pesticides drop songbirds from the sky. Steve Davis, an animal scientist at Oregon State University, has estimated that if America were to adopt a strictly vegetarian diet, the total number of animals killed every year would actually *increase,* as animal pasture gave way to row crops. Davis contends that if our goal is to kill as few animals as possible, then people should eat the largest possible animal that can live on the least intensively cultivated land: grass-fed beef for everybody. It would appear that killing animals is unavoidable no matter what we choose to eat.

When I talked to Joel Salatin about the vegetarian utopia, he pointed out that it would also condemn him and his neighbors to importing their food from distant places, since the Shenandoah Valley receives too little rainfall to grow many row crops. Much the same would hold true where I live, in New England. We get plenty of rain, but the hilliness of the land has dictated an agriculture based on animals since the time of the Pilgrims. The world is full of places where the best, if not the only, way to obtain food from the land is by grazing animals on it—especially ruminants, which alone can transform grass into protein and whose presence can actually improve the health of the land.

The vegetarian utopia would make us even more dependent than we already are on an industrialized national food chain. That food chain would in turn be even more dependent than it already is on fossil fuels and chemical fertilizer, since food would need to travel farther and manure would be in short supply. Indeed, it is doubtful that you can build a more sustainable agriculture without animals to cycle nutrients and support local food production. If our concern is for the health of nature—rather than, say, the internal consistency of our moral code or the condition of our souls—then eating animals may sometimes be the most ethical thing to do.

There is, too, the fact that we humans have been eating animals as long as we have lived on this earth. Humans may not need to eat meat in order to survive, yet doing so is part of our evolutionary heritage, reflected in the design of our teeth and the structure of our digestion. Eating meat helped make us what we are, in a social and biological sense. Under the pressure of the hunt, the human brain grew in size and complexity, and around the fire where the meat was cooked, human culture first flourished. Granting rights to animals may lift us up from the brutal world of predation, but it will entail the sacrifice of part of our identity—our own animality.

Surely this is one of the odder paradoxes of animal rights doctrine. It asks us to recognize all that we share with animals and then demands that we act toward them in a most unanimalistic way. Whether or not this is a good idea, we should at least acknowledge that our desire to eat meat is not a trivial matter, no mere "gastronomic preference." We might as well call sex—also now technically unnecessary—a mere "recreational preference." Whatever else it is, our meat eating is something very deep indeed.

*   *   *

Are any of these good enough reasons to eat animals? I'm mindful of Ben Franklin's definition of the reasonable creature as one who can come up with reasons for whatever he wants to do. So I decided I would track down Peter Singer and ask him what he thought. In an e-mail message, I described Polyface and asked him about the implications for his position of the Good Farm—one where animals got to live according to their nature and to all appearances did not suffer.

"I agree with you that it is better for these animals to have lived and died than not to have lived at all," Singer wrote back. Since the utilitarian is concerned exclusively with the sum of happiness and suffering and the slaughter of an animal that doesn't comprehend that death need not involve suffering, the Good Farm adds to the total of animal happiness, provided you replace the slaughtered animal with a new one. However, he added, this line of thinking doesn't obviate the wrongness of killing an animal that "has a sense of its own existence over time and can have preferences for its own future." In other words, it's O.K. to eat the chicken, but he's not so sure about the pig. Yet, he wrote, "I would not be sufficiently confident of my arguments to condemn someone who purchased meat from one of these farms."

Singer went on to express serious doubts that such farms could be practical on a large scale, since the pressures of the marketplace will lead their owners to cut costs and corners at the expense of the animals. He suggested, too, that killing animals is not conducive to treating them with respect. Also, since humanely raised food will be more expensive, only the well-to-do can afford morally defensible animal protein. These are important considerations, but they don't alter my essential point: what's wrong with animal agriculture—with eating animals—is the practice, not the principle.

What this suggests to me is that people who care should be working not for animal rights but animal welfare—to ensure that farm animals don't suffer and that their deaths are swift and painless. In fact, the decent-life-merciful-death line is how Jeremy Bentham justified his own meat eating. Yes, the philosophical father of animal rights was himself a carnivore. In a passage rather less frequently quoted by animal rightists, Bentham defended eating animals on the grounds that "we are the better for it, and they are never the worse. . . . The death they suffer in our hands commonly is, and always may be, a speedier and, by that means, a less painful one than that which would await them in the inevitable course of nature."

My guess is that Bentham never looked too closely at what happens in a slaughter-house, but the argument suggests that, in theory at least, a utilitarian can justify the killing of humanely treated animals—for meat or, presumably, for clothing. (Though leather and fur pose distinct moral problems. Leather is a byproduct of raising domestic animals for food, which can be done humanely. However, furs are usually made from wild animals that die brutal deaths—usually in leg-hold traps—and since most fur species aren't domesticated, raising them on farms isn't necessarily more humane.) But whether the issue is food or fur or hunting, what should concern us is the suffering, not the killing. All of which I was feeling pretty good about—until I remembered that utilitarians can also justify killing retarded orphans. Killing just isn't the problem for them that it is for other people, including me.

* * *

During my visit to Polyface Farm, I asked Salatin where his animals were slaughtered. He does the chickens and rabbits right on the farm, and would do the cattle, pigs and sheep there too if only the U.S.D.A. would let him. Salatin showed me the open-air abattoir he built behind the farmhouse—a sort of outdoor kitchen on a concrete slab, with stainless-steel sinks, scalding tanks, a feather-plucking machine and metal cones to hold the birds upside down while they're being bled. Processing chickens is not a pleasant job, but Salatin insists on doing it himself because he's convinced he can do it more humanely and cleanly than any processing plant. He slaughters every other Saturday through the summer. Anyone's welcome to watch.

I asked Salatin how he could bring himself to kill a chicken.

"People have a soul; animals don't," he said. "It's a bedrock belief of mine." Salatin is a devout Christian. "Unlike us, animals are not created in God's image, so when they die, they just die."

The notion that only in modern times have people grown uneasy about killing animals is a flattering conceit. Taking a life is momentous, and people have been working to justify the slaughter of animals for thousands of years. Religion and especially ritual has played a crucial part in helping us reckon the moral costs. Native Americans and other hunter-gathers would give thanks to their prey for giving up its life so the eater might live (sort of like saying grace). Many cultures have offered sacrificial animals to the gods, perhaps as a way to convince themselves that it was the gods' desires that demanded the slaughter, not their own. In ancient Greece, the priests responsible for the slaughter (priests!—now we entrust the job to minimum-wage workers) would sprinkle holy water on the sacrificial animal's brow. The beast would promptly shake its head, and this was taken as a sign of assent. Slaughter doesn't necessarily preclude respect. For all these people, it was the ceremony that allowed them to look, then to eat.

Apart from a few surviving religious practices, we no longer have any rituals governing the slaughter or eating of animals, which perhaps helps to explain why we find ourselves where we do, feeling that our only choice is to either look away or give up meat. Frank Perdue is happy to serve the first customer; Peter Singer, the second.

Until my visit to Polyface Farm, I had assumed these were the only two options. But on Salatin's farm, the eye contact between people and animals whose loss John Berger mourned is still a fact of life—and of death, for neither the lives nor the deaths of these animals have been secreted behind steel walls. "Food with a face," Salatin likes to call what he's selling, a slogan that probably scares off some customers. People see very different things when they look into the eyes of a pig or a chicken or a steer—a being without a soul, a "subject of a life" entitled to rights, a link in a food chain, a vessel for pain and pleasure, a tasty lunch. But figuring out what we do think, and what we can eat, might begin with the looking.

We certainly won't philosophize our way to an answer. Salatin told me the story of a man who showed up at the farm one Saturday morning. When Salatin noticed a PETA bumper sticker on the man's car, he figured he was in for it. But the man had a different agenda. He explained that after 16 years as a vegetarian, he had decided that the only way he could ever eat meat again was if he killed the animal himself. He had come to *look*.

"Ten minutes later we were in the processing shed with a chicken," Salatin recalled. "He slit the bird's throat and watched it die. He saw that the animal did not look at him accusingly, didn't do a Disney double take. The animal had been treated with respect when it was alive, and he saw that it could also have a respectful death— that it wasn't being treated as a pile of protoplasm."

Salatin's open-air abattoir is a morally powerful idea. Someone slaughtering a chicken in a place where he can be watched is apt to do it scrupulously, with consideration for the animal as well as for the eater. This is going to sound quixotic, but maybe all we need to do to redeem industrial animal agriculture in this country is to pass a law requiring that the steel and concrete walls of the CAFOs and slaughterhouses be replaced with . . . glass. If there's any new "right" we need to establish, maybe it's this one: the right to look.

No doubt the sight of some of these places would turn many people into vegetarians. Many others would look elsewhere for their meat, to farmers like Salatin. There are more of them than I would have imagined. Despite the relentless consolidation of the American meat industry, there has been a revival of small farms where animals still live their "characteristic form of life." I'm thinking of the ranches where cattle still spend their lives on grass, the poultry farms where chickens still go outside and the hog farms where pigs live as they did 50 years ago—in contact with the sun, the earth and the gaze of a farmer.

For my own part, I've discovered that if you're willing to make the effort, it's entirely possible to limit the meat you eat to nonindustrial animals. I'm tempted to think that we need a new dietary category, to go with the vegan and lactovegetarian and piscatorian. I don't have a catchy name for it yet (humanocarnivore?), but this is the only sort of meat eating I feel comfortable with these days. I've become the sort of shopper who looks for labels indicating that his meat and eggs have been humanely grown (the American Humane Association's new "Free Farmed" label seems to be catching on), who visits the farms where his chicken and pork come from and who asks kinky-sounding questions about touring slaughterhouses. I've actually found a couple of small processing plants willing to let a customer onto the kill floor, including one, in Cannon Falls, Minn., with a glass abattoir.

The industrialization—and dehumanization—of American animal farming is a relatively new, evitable and local phenomenon: no other country raises and slaughters its food animals quite as intensively or as brutally as we do. Were the walls of our meat industry to become transparent, literally or even figuratively, we would not long continue to do it this way. Tail-docking and sow crates and beak-clipping would disappear overnight, and the days of slaughtering 400 head of cattle an hour would come to an end. For who could stand the sight? Yes, meat would get more expensive. We'd probably eat less of it, too, but maybe when we did eat animals, we'd eat them with the consciousness, ceremony and respect they deserve.

Reading Comprehension—Points of Engagement

1. What does "A.M.C." (264) stand for? What does it mean? Provide an example of it in your answer.

2. What is unique about Joel Salatin's farm? Describe it in your own words (271).

3. This is a three-part exercise that will result in three well-constructed paragraphs. First, *summarize* the arguments of three authors Pollan mentions. This task should result in three separate and independently coherent paragraphs. Second, *summarize* Pollan's position in response to each of these authors. Tack these "responses" to each individual author onto the paragraphs you've already written. Third, *analyze* the relationship between the author's position and Pollan's response. Is Pollan persuaded? If so, in what ways? If not, then why not? Tack your analysis onto each of the three paragraphs following Pollan's position.

Assignment Questions—Points of Departure

1. Can humans live harmoniously with nature, or is our "natural" human reaction to attempt manipulation and control? What would it take for humans to live in a way that is beneficial to them, and to plants and animals as well? Write a paper in which you discuss the challenges of living harmoniously with nature, and propose realistic solutions. Your project should engage actively with texts by Michael Pollan and either Barbara Kingsolver, Jane Goodall, or David Brooks.

2. What are the benefits and detriments to treating living beings—plants, animals, people—as experimental subjects? Is it important to push ethical boundaries in this way? Why or why not? When do we know when we have gone too far? In addition to "An Animal's Place, consider the ideas in Lisa Belkin's "The Made-to-Order Savior," "A Fist in the Eye of God" by Barbara Kingsolver, or "Dr. Daedalus" by Lauren Slater.

3. Of what significance is the role of sight in our decision-making? Is "seeing" the effects of a decision first-hand the most useful way to evaluate the worth of that decision? *Is* seeing believing, or is sight a variable—something that changes depending on *when* it takes place? Write a paper in which you consider the importance of vision or perception in how we choose to act in essays by Pollan, and Lenore Look, Jane Goodall, Alain de Botton, or Jeanette Winterson.

Marooned on Gilligan's Island:
Are Women Morally Superior to Men?
Katha Pollitt

Points of Access

1. Do men and women have different "natural" tendencies toward aggressiveness? When you think of peace activists or humanitarians, who comes to mind? What kinds of people? Be specific in your answer.

2. In your lifetime, how have women's roles changed? To answer this, think of various locations such as your own home, places you've worked, situations at school, and randomly on the street.

3. Likewise, how have men's roles changed in the past twenty years? What are the current social, familial, and educational "standards" for men? Are they any different from when you were young?

Some years ago, I was invited by the wife of a well-known writer to sign a women's peace petition. It made the points such documents usually make: that women, as mothers, caregivers and nurturers, have a special awareness of the precariousness of human life, see through jingoism and Cold War rhetoric and would prefer nations to work out their difficulties peacefully so that the military budget could be diverted to schools and hospitals and housing. It had the literary tone such documents usually have, as well—at once superior and plaintive, as if the authors didn't know whether they were bragging or begging. We are wiser than you poor deluded menfolk, was the subtext, so will you please-please-please listen to your moms?

To sign or not to sign? Of course, I was all for peace. But was I for peace *as a woman*? I wasn't a mother then—I wasn't even an aunt. Did my lack of nurturing credentials make my grasp of the horrors of war and the folly of the arms race only theoretical, like a white person's understanding of racism? Were mothers the natural leaders of the peace movement, to whose judgment nonmothers, male and female, must defer, because after all we couldn't *know*, couldn't *feel* that tenderness toward fragile human life that a woman who had borne and raised children had experienced? On the other hand, I was indeed a woman. Was motherhood with its special wisdom somehow deep inside me, to be called upon when needed, like my uterus?

Complicating matters in a way relevant to this essay was my response to the famous writer's wife herself. Here was a woman in her fifties, her child-raising long behind her. Was motherhood the only banner under which she could gain a foothold on civic life? Perhaps so. Her only other public identity was that of a wife, and wifehood, even to a famous man, isn't much to claim credit for these days. ("To think I spent all those years ironing his underpants!" she once burst out to a mutual friend.) Motherhood was what she had in the work-and-accomplishment department, so it was understandable that she try to maximize its moral status. But I was not in her situation: I was a writer, a single woman. By sending me a petition from which I was excluded even as I was invited to add my name, perhaps she was telling me that by leading a nondomestic life I had abandoned the moral high ground, was "acting like a man," but could redeem myself by acknowledging the moral preeminence of the class of women I refused to join.

The ascription of particular virtues—compassion, patience, common sense, nonviolence—to mothers, and the tendency to conflate "mothers" with "women," has a long history in the peace movement, but it goes way beyond issues of war and peace. At present it permeates discussions of just about every field, from management training to theology. Indeed, although the media like to caricature feminism as denying the existence of sexual differences, for the women's movement and its opponents alike "difference" is where the action is. Thus, business writers wonder if women's nurturing, intuitive qualities will make them better executives. Educators suggest that female students suffer in classrooms that emphasize competition over cooperation. Women politicians tout their playground-honed negotiating skills, their egoless devotion to public service, their gender-based commitment to fairness and caring. A variety of political causes—environmentalism, animal rights, even vegetarianism—are promoted as logical extensions of women's putative peacefulness, closeness to nature, horror of aggression and concern for others' health. (Indeed, to some extent these causes are arenas in which women fight one another over definitions of femininity, which is why debates over disposable diapers and over the wearing of fur—both rather minor sources of harm, even if their opponents are right—loom so large and are so acrimonious.) In the arts, we hear a lot about what women's "real" subjects, methods and materials ought to be. Painting is male. Rhyme is male. Plot is male. Perhaps, say the Lacanian feminists, even logic and language are male. What is female? Nature. Blood. Milk. Communal gatherings. The moon. Quilts.

Haven't we been here before? Indeed we have. Woman as sharer and carer, woman as earth mother, woman as guardian of all the small rituals that knit together a family and a community, woman as beneath, above or beyond such manly concerns as law, reason, abstract ideas—these images are as old as time. Open defenders of male supremacy have always used them to declare women flatly inferior to men; covert ones use them to place women on a pedestal as too good for this naughty world. Thus, in the *Eumenides*, Aeschylus celebrated law as the defeat by males of primitive female principles of bloodguilt and vengeance, while the Ayatollah Khomeini thought women should be barred from judgeships because they were too tenderhearted. Different rationale, same outcome: Women, because of their indifference to an impersonal moral order, cannot be full participants in civic life.

There exists an equally ancient line of thought, however, that uses femininity to posit a subversive challenge to the social order: Think of Sophocles' Antigone, who resists tyranny out of love and piety, or Aristophanes' Lysistrata, the original women's-strike-for-peace-nik, or Shakespeare's unworldly, loving innocents: Desdemona, Cordelia. For reasons of power, money and persistent social structures, the vision of the morally superior woman can never overcome the dominant ethos in reality but exists alongside it as a kind of permanent wish or hope: If only powerful and powerless could change places, and the meek inherit the earth! Thus, it is perpetually being rediscovered, dressed in fashionable clothes and presented, despite its antiquity, as a radical new idea.

*   *   *

In the 1950s, which we think of as the glory days of traditional sex roles, the anthropologist Ashley Montagu argued in "The Natural Superiority of Women" that females had it all over males in every way that counted, including the possession of two X chromosomes that made them stabler, saner and healthier than men, with their X and Y. Montagu's essay, originally published in *The Saturday Review* and later expanded into a book, is witty and high-spirited and, interestingly, anticipates the current feminist challenge to male-defined categories. (He notes, for example, that while men are stronger than women in the furniture-moving sense, women are stronger than men when faced with extreme physical hardship and tests of endurance; so when we say that men are stronger than women, we are equating strength with what men have.) But the fundamental thrust of Montagu's essay was to confirm traditional gender roles while revising the way we value them. Having proved to his own satisfaction that women could scale the artistic and intellectual heights, he argued that most would (that is, should) refrain, because women's true genius was "humanness," and their real mission was to "humanize" men before men blew up the world. And that, he left no doubt, was a full-time job.

Contemporary proponents of "difference feminism" advance a variation on the same argument, without Montagu's puckish humor. Instead of his whimsical chromosomal explanation, we get, for example, the psychoanalytic one proposed by Nancy Chodorow in *The Reproduction of Mothering*: Daughters define themselves by relating to their mothers, the primary love object of all children, and are therefore empathic, relationship-oriented, nonhierarchical and interested in forging consensus; sons must separate from their mothers, and are therefore individualistic, competitive, resistant to connection with others and focused on abstract rules and rights. Chodorow's theory has become a kind of mantra of difference feminism, endlessly cited as if it explained phenomena we all agree are universal, though this is far from the case. The central question Chodorow poses—Why are women the primary caregivers of children?—could not even be asked before the advent of modern birth control, and can be answered without resorting to psychology. Historically, women have taken care of children because high fertility and lack of other options left most of them no choice. Those rich enough to avoid personally raising their children often did, as Rousseau observed to his horror.

Popularizers of Chodorow water down and sentimentalize her thesis. They embrace her proposition that traditional mothering produces "relational" women and "autonomous" men but forget her less congenial argument that it also results in sexual inequality, misogyny and hostility between mothers and daughters, who, like sons, desire independence but have a much harder time achieving it. Unlike her followers, Chodorow does not romanticize mothering: "Exclusive single parenting is bad for mother and child alike," she concludes; in a tragic paradox, female "caring," "intimacy" and "nurturance" do not soften but *produce* aggressive, competitive, hypermasculine men.

The relational woman and autonomous man described in psychoanalytic terms by Chodorow have become stock figures in other areas of social science as well. Thus, in her immensely influential book, *In a Different Voice*, the educational psychologist Carol Gilligan argues that the sexes make moral decisions according to separate criteria: Women employ an "ethic of care," men an "ethic of rights." The sociolinguist Deborah Tannen, in the best-selling *You Just Don't Understand*, analyzes male-female conversation as "cross-cultural communication" by people from different backgrounds: the single-sex world of children's play in which girls cooperate and boys compete. While these two writers differ in important ways—Tannen, writing at a more popular level, is by far the clearer thinker and the one more interested in analyzing actual human interactions in daily life, about which she is often quite shrewd—they share important liabilities, too. Both largely confine their observations to the white middle class—especially Gilligan, much of whose elaborate theory of gendered ethics rests on interviews with a handful of Harvard-Radcliffe undergraduates—and seem unaware that this limits the applicability of their data. (In their 1992 book, *Meeting at the Crossroads*, Gilligan and her coauthor, Lyn Mikel Brown, make a similar mistake. Their whole theory of "loss of relationship" as the central trauma of female adolescence rests on interviews with students at one posh single-sex private school.) Both massage their findings to fit their theories: Gilligan's male and female responses are actually quite similar to each other, as experimenters have subsequently shown by removing the names and asking subjects to try to sort the answers by gender; Tannen is quick to attribute blatant rudeness or sexism in male speech to anxiety, helplessness, fear of loss of face—to anything, indeed, but rudeness and sexism. Both look only at what people say, not what they do. For Tannen this isn't a decisive objection because speech is her subject, although it limits the extent to which her findings can be applied to other areas of behavior; for Gilligan, it is a major obstacle, unless you believe, as she apparently does, that the way people say they would resolve farfetched hypothetical dilemmas—Should a poor man steal drugs to save his dying wife?—tells us how they reason in real-life situations or, more important, how they act.

But the biggest problem with all these accounts of gender difference is that they credit the differences they find to universal features of male and female development rather than to the economic and social positions men and women hold, or to the actual power differences between individual men and women. In *The Mismeasure of Woman*, her trenchant and witty attack on contemporary theories of gender difference, Carol Tavris points out that much of what can be said about women applies as well to poor people, who also tend to focus more on family and relationships and less on work and self-advancement; to behave deferentially with those more socially powerful; and to appear to others more emotional and "intuitive" than rational and logical in their thinking. Then, too, there is the question of whether the difference theorists are measuring anything beyond their own willingness to think in stereotypes. If Chodorow is right, relational women and autonomous men should be the norm, but are they? Or is it just that women and men use different language, have different social styles, offer different explanations for similar behavior? Certainly, it is easy to find in one's own acquaintance, as well as in the world at large, men and women who don't fit the models. Difference feminists like to attribute ruthlessness, coldness and hyperrationality in successful women—Margaret Thatcher is the standard example to the fact that men control the networks of power and permit only women like themselves to rise. But I've met plenty of rigid, insensitive, aggressive women who are stay-at-home mothers and secretaries and nurses. And I know plenty of sweet, unambitious men whose main satisfactions lie in their social, domestic and romantic lives, although not all of them would admit this to an inquiring social scientist. We tend to tell strangers what we think will make us sound good. I myself, to my utter amazement, informed a telephone pollster that I exercised regularly, a barefaced lie. How much more difficult to describe truthfully one's moral and ethical values even if one knew what they were, which, as Socrates demonstrated at length, almost no one does.

So why are Gilligan and Tannen the toasts of feminist social science, endlessly cited and discussed in academia, and out of it too, in gender-sensitivity sessions in the business world and even, following the Anita Hill–Clarence Thomas hearings, in Congress? The success of the difference theorists proves yet again that social science is one part science and nine parts social. They say what people want to hear: Women really are different, in just the ways we always thought. Women embrace Gilligan and Tannen because they offer flattering accounts of traits for which they have historically been castigated. Men like them because, while they urge understanding and respect for "female" values and behaviors, they also let men off the hook: Men have power, wealth and control of social resources because women don't really want them. The pernicious tendencies of difference feminism are perfectly illustrated by the Sears sex discrimination case, in which Rosalind Rosenberg, a professor of women's history at Barnard College, testified for Sears that female employees held lower-paying salaried jobs while men worked selling big-ticket items on commission because women preferred low-risk, noncompetitive positions that did not interfere with family responsibilities. Sears won its case.

* * *

While early-childhood development is the point of departure for most of the difference feminists, it is possible to construct a theory of gendered ethics on other grounds. The most interesting attempt I've seen is by the pacifist philosopher Sara Ruddick. Although not widely known outside academic circles, her *Maternal Thinking* makes an argument that can be found in such mainstream sources as the columns of Anna Quindlen in *The New York Times*. For Ruddick it is not psychosexual development that produces the Gilliganian virtues but intimate involvement in child-raising, the hands-on work of mothering. Men too can be mothers if they do the work that women do. (And women can be Fathers—a word Ruddick uses, complete with arrogant capital letter, for distant, uninvolved authority-figure parents.) Mothers are patient, peace-loving, attentive to emotional context and so on, because those are the qualities you need to get the job done, the way accountants are precise, lawyers argumentative, writers self-centered. Thus mothers constitute a logical constituency—for pacifist and antiwar politics, and, by extension, a "caring" domestic agenda.

But what is the job of mothering? Ruddick defines "maternal practice" as meeting three demands: preservation, growth and social acceptability. She acknowledges the enormously varying manifestations of these demands, but she doesn't incorporate into her theory the qualifications, limits and contradictions she notes—perhaps because to do so would reveal these demands as so flexible as to be practically empty terms.

Almost anything mothers do can be explained under one of these rubrics, however cruel, dangerous, unfair or authoritarian—the genital mutilation of African and Arab girls, the foot-binding of prerevolutionary Chinese ones, the sacrifice of some children to increase the resources available for others, as in the killing or malnourishing of female infants in India and China today. In this country, many mothers who commit what is legally child abuse *think* they are merely disciplining their kids in the good old-fashioned way. As long as the practices are culturally acceptable (and sometimes even when they're not), the mothers who perform them think of themselves as good parents. But if all these behaviors count as mothering, how can mothering have a necessary connection with any single belief about anything, let alone how to stop war, or any single set of personality traits, let alone nonviolent ones?

We should not be surprised that motherhood does not produce uniform beliefs and behaviors: It is, after all, not a job; it has no standard of admission, and almost nobody gets fired. Motherhood is open to any woman who can have a baby or adopt one. *Not* to be a mother is a decision; becoming one requires merely that a woman accede, perhaps only for as long as it takes to get pregnant, to thousands of years of cumulative social pressure. After that, she's on her own; she can soothe her child's nightmares or let him cry in the dark. Nothing intrinsic to child-raising will tell her what is the better choice for her child (each has been the favored practice at different times). Although Ruddick starts off by looking closely at maternal practice, when that practice contradicts her own ideas about good mothering it is filed away as an exception, a distortion imposed by Fathers or poverty or some other outside force. But if you add up all the exceptions, you are left with a rather small group of people—women like Ruddick herself, enlightened, up-to-date, educated, upper-middle-class liberals.

And not even all of them. Consider the issue of physical punishment. Ruddick argues that experience teaches mothers that violence is useless; it only creates anger, deception and more violence. Negotiation is the mother's way of resolving disputes and encouraging good behavior. As Ann Crittenden put it in *The Nation* during the Gulf War: "One learns, in theory and in practice, to try to resolve conflict in ways that do not involve the sheer imposition of will or brute force. One learns that violence just doesn't work." Crittenden would have a hard time explaining all those moms in uniform who participated in Operation Desert Storm—but then she'd have a hard time explaining all those mothers screaming at their kids in the supermarket, too.

As it happens, I agree that violence is a bad way to teach, and I made a decision never, no matter what, to spank my daughter. But mothers who do not hit their children, or permit their husbands to do so, are as rare as conscientious objectors in wartime. According to one survey, 78 percent approve of an occasional "good, hard spanking"— because they think violence is an effective way of teaching, because they think that hitting children isn't really violence, because they just lose it. Even *Parenting* found that more than a third of its readers hit their kids. And *Parenting*'s audience is not only far more educated, affluent and liberal than the general population, it consists entirely of people who care what experts think about child development—and contemporary experts revile corporal punishment. Interestingly, the moms who hit tended to be the ones who fretted the most about raising their children well. Mothers who think too much?

Like old-style socialists finding "proletarian virtue" in the working class, Ruddick claims to be describing what mothers do, but all too often she is really prescribing what she thinks they ought to do. "When their children flourish, almost all mothers have a sense of well-being." Hasn't she ever heard of postpartum depression? Of mothers who belittle their children's accomplishments and resent their growing independence? "What mother wouldn't want the power to keep her children healthy . . . to create hospitals, schools, jobs, day care, and work schedules that serve her maternal work?" Notice how neatly the modest and commonsensical wish for a healthy child balloons into the hotly contested and by no means universal wish of mothers for day-care and flextime. Notice, too, how Ruddick moves from a mother's desire for social institutions that serve *her* children to an assumption that this desire translates into wanting comparable care for *all* children. But mothers feature prominently in local struggles against busing, mergers of rich and poor schools and the opening in their neighborhoods of group homes for foster children, boarder babies and the retarded. Why? The true reasons may be property values and racism, but what these mothers often say is that they are simply protecting their kids. Ruddick seems to think Maternal Thinking leads naturally to Sweden; in the United States it is equally likely to lead to Fortress Suburbia.

As Gilligan does with all women, Ruddick scrutinizes mothers for what she expects to find, and sure enough, there it is. But why look to mothers for her peaceful constituency in the first place? Why not health professionals, who spend their lives saving lives? Or historians, who know how rarely war yields a benefit remotely commensurate with its cost in human misery? Or, I don't know, gardeners, blamelessly tending their innocent flowers? You can read almost any kind of work as affirming life and conferring wisdom. Ruddick chooses mothering because she's already decided that women possess the Gilliganian virtues and she wants a non-essentialist peg to hang them on, so that men can acquire them, too. A disinterested observer scouring the world for labor that encourages humane values would never pick child-raising: It's too quirky, too embedded in repellent cultural norms, too hot.

*   *   *

Despite its intellectual flabbiness, difference feminism is deeply appealing to many women. Why? For one thing, it seems to explain some important phenomena: that women—and this is a cross-cultural truth—commit very little criminal violence compared with men; that women fill the ranks of the so-called caring professions; that women are much less likely than men to abandon their children. Difference feminists want to give women credit for these good behaviors by raising them from the level of instinct or passivity—the Camille Paglia vision of femininity—to the level of moral choice and principled decision. Who can blame women for embracing theories that tell them the sacrifices they make on behalf of domesticity and children are legitimate, moral, even noble? By stressing the mentality of nurturance—the *ethic* of caring, maternal *thinking*—Gilligan and Ruddick challenge the ancient division of humanity into rational males and irrational females. They offer women a way to argue that their views have equal status with those of men and to resist the customary marginalization of their voices in public debate. Doubtless many women have felt emboldened by Gilliganian accounts of moral difference: Speaking in a different voice is, after all, a big step up from silence.

The vision of women as sharers and carers is tempting in another way, too. Despite much media blather about the popularity of the victim position, most people want to believe they act out of free will and choice. The uncomfortable truth that women have all too little of either is a difficult hurdle for feminists. Acknowledging the systematic oppression of women seems to deprive them of existential freedom, to turn them into puppets, slaves and Stepford wives. Deny it, and you can't make change. By arguing that the traditional qualities, tasks and ways of life of women are as important, valuable and serious as those of men (if not more so), Gilligan and others let women feel that nothing needs to change except the social valuation accorded to what they are already doing. It's a rationale for the status quo, which is why men like it, and a burst of grateful applause, which is why women like it. Men keep the power, but since power is bad, so much the worse for them.

Another rather curious appeal of difference feminism is that it offers a way for women to define themselves as independent of men. In a culture that sees women almost entirely in relation to men, this is no small achievement. Sex, for example—the enormous amount of female energy, money and time spent on beauty and fashion and romance, on attracting men and keeping them, on placating male power, strategizing ways around it or making it serve one's own ends—plays a minute role in these theories. You would never guess from Gilligan or Ruddick that men, individually and collectively, are signal beneficiaries of female nurturance, much less that this goes far to explain why society encourages nurturance in women. No, it is always children whom women are described as fostering and sacrificing for, or the community, or even other women—not husbands or lovers. It's as though wives cook dinner only for their kids, leaving the husband to raid the fridge on his own. And no doubt many a woman, quietly smoldering at her mate's refusal to share domestic labor, persuades herself that she is serving only her children, or her own preferences, rather than confront the inequality of her marriage.

The peaceful mother and the relational woman are a kinder, gentler, leftish version of "family values," and both are modern versions of the separate-spheres ideology of the Victorians. In the nineteenth century, too, some women tried to turn the ideology of sexual difference on its head and expand the moral claims of motherhood to include the public realm. Middle-class women became social reformers, abolitionists, temperance advocates, settlement workers and even took paying jobs in the "helping professions"—nursing, social work, teaching—which were perceived as extensions of women's domestic role although practiced mostly by single women. These women did not deny that their sex fitted them for the home, but argued that domesticity did not end at the front door of the house, or confine itself to dusting (or telling the housemaid to dust). Even the vote could be cast as an extension of domesticity: Women, being more moral than men, would purify the government of vice and corruption, end war and make America safe for family life. (The persistence of this metaphor came home to me when I attended a Women's Action Coalition demonstration during the 1992 Democratic National Convention. There—along with WAC's funny and ferocious all-in-black drum corps and contingents of hip downtown artists brandishing Barbara Kruger posters and shouting slogans like "We're Women! We're Angry! We're Not Going Shopping!"—was a trio of street performers with housecoats and kerchiefs over black catsuits and spiky hair, pushing brooms: Women will clean up government!)

The separate-spheres ideology had obvious advantages for middle-class women in an era when they were formally barred from higher education, political power and most jobs that paid a living wage. But its defects are equally obvious. It defined all women by a single standard, and one developed by a sexist society. It offered women no way to enter jobs that could not be defined as extensions of their domestic roles—you could be a math teacher but not a mathematician, a secretary but not a sea captain—and no way to challenge any but the grossest abuses of male privilege. Difference feminists are making a similar bid for power on behalf of women today, and are caught in similar contradictions. Once again, women are defined by their family roles. Child-raising is seen as woman's glory and joy and opportunity for self-transcendence, while Dad naps on the couch. Women who do not fit the stereotype are castigated as unfeminine— nurses nurture, doctors do not—and domestic labor is romanticized and sold to women as a badge of moral worth.

*   *   *

For all the many current explanations of perceived moral difference between the sexes, one hears remarkably little about the material basis of the family. Yet the motherhood and womanhood being valorized cannot be considered apart from questions of power, privilege and money. There is a reason a non-earning woman can proudly call herself a "wife and mother" and a non-earning man is just unemployed: The traditional female role, with its attendant real or imagined traits and values, implies a male income. Middle-class women go to great lengths to separate themselves from this uncomfortable fact. One often hears married mothers defend their decision to stay at home by heaping scorn on paid employment—caricatured as making widgets or pushing papers or dressing for success—and the difference feminists, too, like to distinguish between altruistic, poorly paid female jobs and the nasty, profitable ones performed by men. In *Prisoners of Men's Dreams*, Suzanne Gordon comes close to blaming the modest status of jobs like nursing and flight attending on women's entry into jobs like medicine and piloting, as if before the women's movement those female-dominated occupations were respected and rewarded. (Nurses should be glad the field no longer has a huge captive labor pool of women: The nursing shortage has led to dramatic improvements in pay, benefits and responsibility. Now nurses earn a man-size income, and men are applying to nursing school in record numbers—exactly what Gordon wants.) It's all very well for some women to condemn others for "acting like men"—i.e., being ambitious, assertive, interested in money and position. But if their husbands did not "act like men," where would they be? Jean Bethke Elshtain, who strenuously resists the notion of gendered ethics, nevertheless bemoans the loss to their communities when women leave volunteering and informal mutual support networks for paid employment. But money must come from somewhere; if women leave to men the job of earning the family income (an option fewer and fewer families can afford), they will be economically dependent on their husbands, a situation that, besides carrying obvious risks in an age of frequent divorce, weakens their bargaining position in the family and insures that men will largely control major decisions affecting family life.

Difference theorists would like to separate out the aspects of traditional womanhood that they approve of and speak only of those. But the parts they like (caring, nurturing, intimacy) are inseparable from the parts they don't like (economic dependence and the subordination of women within the family). The difference theorists try to get around this by positing a world that contains two cultures—a female world of love and ritual and a male world of getting and spending and killing—which mysteriously share a single planet. That vision is expressed neatly in a recent pop-psychology title, *Men Are From Mars, Women Are From Venus*. It would be truer to say men are from Illinois and women are from Indiana—different, sure, but not in ways that have much ethical consequence.

The truth is, there is only one culture, and it shapes each sex in distinct but mutually dependent ways in order to reproduce itself. To the extent that the stereotypes are true, women have the "relational" domestic qualities *because* men have the "autonomous" qualities required to survive and prosper in modern capitalism. She needs a wage earner (even if she has a job, thanks to job discrimination), and he needs someone to mind his children, hold his hand and have his emotions for him. This—not, as Gordon imagines, some treason to her sex—explains why women who move into male sectors act very much like men: If they didn't, they'd find themselves back home in a jiffy. The same necessities and pressures affect them as affect the men who hold those jobs. Because we are in a transition period, in which many women were raised with modest expectations and much emphasis on the need to please others, social scientists who look for it can find traces of empathy, caring and so on in some women who have risen in the world of work and power. But when they tell us that women doctors will transform American medicine, or women executives will transform the corporate world, they are looking backward, not forward. If women really do enter the workforce on equal terms with men—if they become 50 percent of all lawyers, politicians, car dealers and prison guards—they may be less sexist (although the example of Soviet doctors, a majority of them female, is not inspiring to those who know about the brutal gynecological customs prevailing in the former U.S.S.R.). And they may bring with them a distinct set of manners, a separate social style. But they won't be, in some general way, more honest, kind, egalitarian, empathic or indifferent to profit. To argue otherwise is to believe that the reason factory owners bust unions, doctors refuse Medicaid patients and New York City school custodians don't mop the floors is because they are men.

The ultimate paradox of difference feminism is that it has come to the fore at a moment when the lives of the sexes are becoming less distinct than they ever have been in the West. Look at the decline of single-sex education (researchers may tout the benefits of all-female schools and colleges, but girls overwhelmingly choose coeducation); the growth of female athletics; the virtual abolition of virginity as a requirement for girls; the equalization of college-attendance rates of males and females; the explosion of employment for married women and mothers even of small children; the crossing of workplace gender lines by both females and males; the cultural pressure on men to be warm and active fathers, to do at least some housework, to choose mates who are their equals in education and income potential.

It's fashionable these days to talk about the backlash against equality feminism—I talk this way myself when I'm feeling blue—but equality feminism has scored amazing successes. It has transformed women's expectations in every area of their lives. However, it has not yet transformed society to meet those expectations. The workplace still discriminates. On the home front few men practice egalitarianism, although many preach it; single mothers—and given the high divorce rate, every mother is potentially a single mother—lead incredibly difficult lives.

In this social context, difference feminism is essentially a way for women both to take advantage of equality feminism's success and to accommodate themselves to its limits. It appeals to particular kinds of women—those in the "helping professions" or the home, for example, rather than those who want to be bomber pilots or neurosurgeons or electricians. At the popular level, it encourages women who feel disadvantaged or demeaned by equality to direct their anger against women who have benefited from it by thinking of them as gender traitors and of themselves as suffering for their virtue—thus the hostility of some nurses toward female doctors, and of some stay-at-home mothers toward employed mothers.

For its academic proponents, the appeal lies elsewhere: Difference feminism is a way to carve out a safe space in the face of academia's resistance to female advancement. It works much like multiculturalism, making an end run around a static and discriminatory employment structure by creating an intellectual niche that can be filled only by members of the discriminated-against group. And like other forms of multiculturalism, it looks everywhere for its explanatory force—biology, psychology, sociology, cultural identity—*except* economics. The difference feminists cannot say that the differences between men and women are the result of their relative economic positions, because to say that would be to move the whole discussion out of the realm of psychology and feel-good cultural pride and into the realm of a tough political struggle over the distribution of resources and justice and money.

Although it is couched in the language of praise, difference feminism is demeaning to women. It asks that women be admitted into public life and public discourse not because they have a right to be there but because they will improve them. Even if this were true, and not the wishful thinking I believe it to be, why should the task of moral and social transformation be laid on women's doorstep and not on everyone's—or, for that matter, on men's, by the you-broke-it-you-fix-it principle? Peace, the environment, a more humane workplace, economic justice, social support for children—these are issues that affect us all and are everyone's responsibility. By promising to assume that responsibility, difference feminists lay the groundwork for excluding women again, as soon as it becomes clear that the promise cannot be kept.

No one asks that other oppressed groups win their freedom by claiming to be extra-good. And no other oppressed group thinks it must make such a claim in order to be accommodated fully and across the board by society. For blacks and other racial minorities, it is enough to want to earn a living, exercise one's talents, get a fair hearing in the public forum. Only for women is simple justice an insufficient argument. It is as though women don't really believe they are entitled to full citizenship unless they can make a special claim to virtue. Why isn't being human enough?

In the end, I didn't sign that peace petition, although I was sorry to disappoint a woman I liked, and although I am very much for peace. I decided to wait for a petition that welcomed my signature as a person, an American, a citizen implicated, against my will, in war and the war economy. I still think I did the right thing.

Reading Comprehension—Points of Engagement

1. What are the qualities associated with "difference feminism" as Pollitt sees it? What are the elements of equality feminism? Make a list of the various theorists she cites and determine where on the feminist spectrum they fall. Then explore why Pollitt feels that the appropriate academic framework for gender issues is economics.

2. Write a paragraph or two on how "nature" gets "gendered." In other words, how does biological sex take on social meaning and conversely how are social roles traced to physiology? Consider the following passage from Pollitt as a starting

point: "Difference theorists would like to separate out the aspects of traditional womanhood that they approve of and speak only of those. But the parts they like (caring, nurturing, intimacy) are inseparable from the parts they don't like (economic dependence and subordination of women within the family). The difference theorists try to get around this by positing a world that contains two cultures—a female world of love and ritual and a male world of getting and spending and killing. . . .The truth is, there is only one culture, and it shapes each sex in distinct but mutually dependent ways in order to reproduce itself" (292).

3. How is gender both a *part of* and *apart from* nature? Once you outline an answer for that question, consider bringing your understanding of it to Gilligan's claim that "women employ an 'ethic of care', men an 'ethic of rights' " (284). In other words, how do biological details get transformed into complex social expectations?

Assignment Questions—Points of Departure

1. Reconsider this claim made by Katha Pollitt: "The truth is, there is only one culture, and it shapes each sex in distinct but mutually dependent ways in order to reproduce itself" (292). Do you think Andrew Sullivan believes in this "one culture" idea? Would he see the mutual dependency Katha Pollitt describes in the same way she does? Does he feel that one gender is morally superior in the sense that Pollitt explores? Do you? Your project in this paper is to offer your own position on these questions and to answer them by referencing Sullivan and Pollitt's essays with integrity.

2. Consider the following quotation from Lauren Slater: "Today it is not uncommon for human beings to shift belief systems several times in a lifetime and with relatively little psychological discomfort" (326). Is this statement applicable to Pollitt's own struggle with feminism? What feminist "camp" does she align herself with and is that allegiance absolute? How do Slater's ideas of having a "fundamental core" versus being "protean" play into Pollitt's discussion about difference and equality feminism?

3. What in Jane Goodall's text reveals her ethical position as a woman (according to Pollitt's theorists)? What qualities, according to difference feminism, contribute to her work as a scientist? Would the principles of difference feminism appeal to Goodall, who, according to Pollitt, is not in a "helping profession," but rather a primarily male-dominated field of primatology?

Voting Democracy Off the Island
Reality TV and the Republican Ethos
Francine Prose

Points of Access

1. Have you watched reality television? If not, why not? If so, why? What, specifically, interests you or doesn't interest you about reality TV? Freewrite for 15 minutes.

2. Describe your understanding of democracy.

3. Think about the phrase "family values." What kind of values do you imagine they are? Where does your impression of "family values" come from?

Not even Melana can believe it's real. As the "former NFL cheerleader and beauty queen looking to fall in love with the perfect guy" swans a bit dazedly through the Palm Springs mansion in which she will soon undertake the task of selecting Mr. Right from among sixteen eligible bachelors, she coos about the thrill of living a "dream come true."

It's the premiere episode of NBC's *Average Joe*, one of the extremely popular and profitable "reality-based" television shows that, in recent years, have proliferated to claim a significant share of major-network prime time. Featuring ordinary people who have agreed to be filmed in dangerous, challenging, or embarrassing situations in return for the promise of money, romance, or fame, these offerings range from *Who Wants to Marry a Millionaire?* to *Who Wants to Marry My Dad?*, from long-run hits such as *Survivor* and *The Real World* to the short-lived *Are You Hot?* and *Boy Meets Boy*.

The title *Average Joe* has evidently alerted Melana to the possibility that her bachelor pool may not be stocked with the same species of dazzling hunks, those walking miracles of body sculpting, cosmetic dentistry, and hair-gel expertise who courted "The Bachelorette." Clearly, she's expecting to meet the more routinely, unself-consciously attractive sort of guy one might spot on the street or at the water cooler.

But, as frequently happens, the audience is privy to an essential truth—or, in the argot of reality programming, a "reveal"—concealed from the hapless participants.

Now, as the cameras whisk us to the bachelors' quarters, we instantly get the visual joke that is, even by the standards of reality TV, sadistic.

The men about to compete for Melana's affections are not merely Joe Well Below Average but Joe Out of the Question. Several are obese; others have tics, dermatological or dental problems, or are short, bespectacled, balding, stooped. Racial and cultural diversity is provided by a diminutive "university professor" from Zimbabwe with a penchant for intellectual boasting and grave fashion miscalculations.

Although the sight of Melana's suitors is intended to amuse and titillate rather than to touch us, it would (to paraphrase Dickens amid this Dickensian crowd) take a heart of stone not to be moved by the moment when the men take a look at one another and realize that their inclusion in this confraternity of nerds is probably not a mistake.

Meanwhile, night has fallen on the desert, and the lovely Melana, all dressed up and as starry-eyed as a kid on Christmas morning, comes out to meet the guys. A white limousine pulls up. A male model emerges, and Melana's face brightens, only to darken seconds later when he announces that, sadly, he is not one of her bachelors.

The white limo carries the tease away. Presently a bus arrives.

The bus doors open. They send the fat guys out first. And by the time a half-dozen sorry specimens are lined up, grinning their hearts out, even Melana gets it. Her shock and dismay are genuine. The men cannot help but notice. "This is *bad*," she whispers, and we can read her lips. "Someone's messing with my head."

What lends the scene its special poignancy is that Melana knows, as do we, that what has befallen her is not some cruel accident of fate. Rather, she has brought misfortune on herself. In filling out the questionnaire that led to her being selected as the heroine of *Average Joe*, she indicated that "a good personality" mattered more to her than did appearance. And in doing so, she violated one of the cardinal rules, a basic article of faith, one of the values that this new version of reality pumps out, hour after hour, night after night, into the culture. Had Melana watched more reality-based TV, she would have learned that surface beauty (preferably in concert with a strong manipulative instinct, a cunning ability to play the game, and vast quantities of money) is all that counts. Melana has transgressed. And now, as we sit back and watch, she is about to be punished.

*   *   *

If this—a dash of casual brutality, a soupçon of voyeurism—is your recipe for entertainment, it's a taste you can satisfy, in the privacy of your living room, nearly every evening. In fact, unless you own one of those televisions that allow you to watch two programs at once, you may be forced to make some hard choices.

On a typical night—Thanksgiving Eve, November 26, 2003—you could, at eight, watch a contestant on CBS's *Survivor Pearl Islands* secure himself some sympathy by misleading his fellow tribe members into thinking that his grandmother has just died. But witnessing the "biggest lie ever told on *Survivor*" would mean missing the episode of NBC's *Queer Eye for the Straight Guy* in which a quintet of homosexual fashion and lifestyle advisers convince a balding lawyer to lose his unflattering hairpiece. At nine, you could shop along with ABC's Trista for *Trista & Ryan's Wedding*, an account of the big-ticket ceremony that would solemnize the love affair spawned, as America watched, on *The Bachelorette*. And at ten, on *Extreme Makeover*, the most literally invasive series so far, two lucky souls (chosen from more than 10,000 applicants) have their lives transformed by plastic surgery. On this night a man whose 200-pound weight loss has left him looking like a shar-pei, and a rather pretty grade-school teacher—who believes that she is only a rhinoplasty and a chin implant away from rivaling her beautiful sisters—will go under the knife.

In the event that three hours of watching your fellow humans suffer and squirm and endure surgical procedures has left you feeling uneasy about how you have spent your time, or what you have found amusing, you can be reassured—as are the network executives, it would seem—by the fact that you are not alone. In January 2003 the premiere of Fox Network's *Joe Millionaire*, in which a construction worker courted women tricked into believing that he possessed a vast personal fortune, attracted 18.6 million viewers; 40 million tuned in for its conclusion. *American Idol*, the talent show that asks fans to vote for their favorite contestants by telephone, received 110 million calls in its first season and 15.5 million calls during the final show alone. By contrast, the most popular national news program—NBC's *Nightly News*—averages around 11 million viewers per night.

Like Melana, network accountants were quick to see reality shows as a dream come true. For although production values and costs have risen, reality-based programs are still relatively cheap to produce, mostly because they avoid the expense of hiring actors whose salary demands can rise astronomically if the show becomes a hit. One consequence is that television actors have seen a radical reduction in the number and range of available roles.

Despite the fact that journalists periodically hail the death of reality TV, it has proved remarkably long-lived. MTV's *The Real World*, which sends seven attractive young strangers to spend six months turning their luxury housing into a Petri dish of sexual, racial, and interpersonal tension, has been running since 1992. Now in its eighth season, *Survivor* has airlifted a succession of warring "tribes" from the Amazon to the jungles of Thailand. During the week of November 17–23, 2003, the only shows more popular than *Survivor Pearl Islands* (which drew 19.9 million viewers) were *CSI*, *ER*, and *Friends*.

On aesthetic grounds alone, it's arguable that reality-based shows are no better or worse than *CSI*, *ER*, and *Friends*. But the most obvious difference is the most crucial one. Fans of *Friends* understand that they are watching a sitcom, cast with celebrity actors. Watching *Survivor* and *The Real World*, they believe that they are observing real men and women.

Viewers do, of course, realize that some of what they're seeing has been instigated or exacerbated by the show's producers. Yet the fact is that viewers *are* watching people who, regardless of their career ambitions or masochistic exhibitionism, are amateurs who may have been chosen *for* their fragility and instability. Many of the "Average Joes" could never get hired as character actors. And observing their response to stress and humiliation generates a gladiatorial, bread-and-circus atmosphere that simply does not exist when we see movie stars in scrubs sail a gurney down the halls of *ER*.

Reality-based TV, then, is not a scripted fiction but an improvisation, an apparently instructive improvisation that doles out consistent and frequently reinforced lessons about human nature and, yes, reality. These programs also generate a jittery, adrenalized buzz that produces a paradoxically tranquilized numbness in which our defenses relax and leave us more receptive to the "information" we are receiving. For this reason alone, even those who take pride in never looking at TV, except for the occasional peek at PBS, might want to tune in and see what reality their fellow citizens have been witnessing.

*   *   *

What might future anthropologists (or, for that matter, contemporary TV-addicted children and adults) conclude about our world if these programs constituted their primary source of information? The most obvious lesson to be drawn from reality TV, the single philosophical pole around which everything else revolves, is that the laws of natural selection are even more brutal, inflexible, and sensible than one might suppose from reading *Origin of Species*. Reality is a Darwinian battlefield on which only the fittest survive and it's not merely logical but admirable to marshal all our skills and resources to succeed in a struggle that only one person can win.

Compelling its testy, frequently neurotic castaways to operate as if they were several rungs down the evolutionary ladder, grubbing roots and berries and forced to earn such basic necessities as blankets by performing acrobatic stunts, *Survivor* is the prototype. The show urges its participants to labor for their tribe but always, ultimately, for themselves. Because at the end of the day—in this case, the final episode—only one person will walk away with a million dollars. And in case we lose sight of first principles, the show's motto, which appears in its logo, is "Outwit. Outplay. Outlast."

Survivor is the younger American cousin of the 1997 Swedish *Expedition Robinson*, a title judged too literary for the U.S. market. It's probably just as well that the series wasn't called *Expedition Robinson*. *Robinson Crusoe* and *Swiss Family Robinson* extol the virtues and advantages of fellowship and cooperation, whereas on *Survivor* such considerations are useful only to a point. *Survivor* could be Defoe's masterpiece rewritten by Ayn Rand. And for all its Darwinian trappings, the series offers a skewed view of the *purpose* of the struggle for dominance. Propagating the species is the last thing on these people's minds.

And so the steps that lead toward that goal aren't determined by physical combat or brilliant displays of plumage. Rather, contestants are eliminated by a democratic process; every few days, tribe members vote on which of their fellows will be forced to leave the island. As we watch, the loser trudges across a rope bridge or rock ledge and off to a dismal future without a million dollars.

* * *

Observant readers may already have noted that the guiding principles to which I've alluded—flinty individualism, the vision of a zero-sum society in which no one can win unless someone else loses, the conviction that altruism and compassion are signs of folly and weakness, the exaltation of solitary striving above the illusory benefits of cooperative mutual aid, the belief that certain circumstances justify secrecy and deception, the invocation of a reviled common enemy to solidify group loyalty—are the exact same themes that underlie the rhetoric we have been hearing and continue to hear from the Republican Congress and our current administration.

Of course, no sensible person would imagine that Donald Rumsfeld is sitting down with the producers of reality-based TV to discuss the possibility that watching the contestants sweat and strain to bring civilization to the jungle will help us accept the sacrificing we have been and are still being asked to make in Iraq. On the other hand, there is the unsettling precedent set by *Profiles from the Front Line*, a series that aired around the time of the war in Iraq and was produced for ABC Entertainment by Jerry Bruckheimer, whose credits include *Black Hawk Down*.

According to an advance release from the network,

> the Pentagon and the Department of Defense lent their full support and cooperation to this unique production. . . . As America prepares for a possible war with Iraq, the country continues to wage a perilous war on terrorism. ABC will transport viewers to actual battlefields in Central Asia with a six-episode series that will feature actual footage of the elite U.S. Special Operations forces apprehending possible terrorists, as well as compelling, personal stories of the U.S. military men and women who bear the burden and risks of this fighting.

Indeed, ABC News complained that—in order to film the soldiers arresting a "big-time" Taliban leader, disarming rockets, providing medical care to Afghan civilians, capturing fuel-truck hijacks, and accepting the love and gratitude of the Afghan people—the show's producers were being granted a level of access to the troops that Pentagon officials denied the network's actual reporters.

But even when the collaboration between the military, the government, and the entertainment industry is not nearly so overt, these shows continue to transmit a perpetual, low-frequency hum of agitprop. The ethics (if one can call them that) and the ideals that permeate these programs at once deflect and reinforce the basest, most mindless and ruthless aspects of the current political zeitgeist. If the interests of the corporate culture that controls our television stations are at heart the same as those that fund and support lobbyists and politicians, it stands to reason that—when network executives do meet to determine what is appropriate, entertaining, profitable, what people want and need to see—they are unlikely to flinch at portraying stylized versions of the same behavior we read about in the press, or can observe on the Senate floor.

*   *   *

Among the notions of reality that the designers of these shows appear to hold in common with the participants in the corporate strategy session—or, one presumes, the Pentagon or Cabinet meeting—is the vision of the world as a vast human-behavior laboratory. Its population of lab rats can be coolly observed by the research scientists (the market analyst, the politician, the TV viewer), who can then draw profitable lessons from their subjects' responses. Let's see how the castaways behave when they are ordered to abandon their humble camp and exiled to a new locale. Let's watch how the homely bachelors compete for the hand of the beauty, how quickly the public embraces the next revolution in junk food, and how the citizens of the Middle East deal with their altered circumstances when we change their regimes and encourage them to adopt Western values. Meanwhile, this objective, experimental mode dispels any qualms we might feel about the fact that the research subjects are humans who might have their own ideas and opinions about how they want to live.

Presumably, many of these shows' creators would be unnerved to hear that the harmless amusements they are concocting actually reflect, reinforce, and codify a specific political agenda. But it might come as less of a surprise to, say, Mark Burnett, the executive producer of *Survivor*.

At seventeen, the London-born Burnett joined the British army and became a paratrooper, a decorated member of the elite Parachute Regiment, with which he saw combat in the Falkland Islands and in Northern Ireland. In 1982 he set out for Central America, then in the throes of widespread guerrilla warfare and counterinsurgency terrorism. En route to work there as a military advisor with the British Special Air Service, he decided instead to get off the plane in Los Angeles and seek his fortune in Hollywood.

After brief stints as a nanny and a T-shirt salesman, his military background and media ambitions inspired him to enter the Raid Gauloises, an annual French race that sent teams on rugged courses through the Oman desert and the jungles of Borneo. In 1995, Burnett started his own version of the French competition, the Eco-Challenge, which (over the objections of environmentalists) took place in Utah and was filmed for the Discovery Channel. When the 1998 Eco-Challenge, staged in Morocco, received an Emmy Award, Burnett was in an ideal position to market the American rights to *Survivor*, which he had presciently acquired.

Reading Mark Burnett's résumé cannot help but make *Survivor* seem even more like a weekly dispatch from the Central American terrorist training camp to which he may have been headed when he was lured off course by the siren song of Hollywood. And our unease about the cozy relationship between the broadcasting industry and its advertisers is hardly soothed when we learn that Burnett has given "motivational, leadership and teambuilding speeches" for such clients as IBM, Citibank, Sony, USA Networks, Discovery Channel, and Ad-Week Asia. Knowing all this can only make us doubly aware, and wary, of the nuggets of motivational and guerrilla training we are receiving along with the seemingly innocent pleasure of picking sides and favorites, deciding which bachelor or bachelorette we'd choose.

The merciless individualism and bloodthirsty competition turn out to represent the noblest, most heroic aspect of this new reality. The darker, more cynical message—the lesson beneath the lesson, so to speak—is that every human being can and will do *anything* for money. Like those consciousness-altering substances that hurtled the Hashishins and certain indigenous tribes into battle, the smell of $50,000 intoxicates the contestants on *Fear Factor* enough to achieve a protracted out-of-body experience. How else to explain their ability to so suppress both instinct and free will that they don't gag over goblets of liquefied night-crawler guts, don't recoil from a helmet of rats, don't rebel when they are instructed to crawl into a pitch-black cave tunnel and retrieve as many ripe skunk carcasses as possible in a limited time?

Pragmatism is the main concern, whereas morality is a luxury or, worse, an impediment, an albatross. And given the limitlessness of what our fellow humans will do for cash, considering the folly of acting according to ethical scruples, it's only logical that everyone lies all the time. In some shows—*Joe Millionaire* had twenty-five women convinced that its protagonist was rich, and the gay hero of *Boy Meets Boy* had not been informed that several of his suitors were actually straight—the lying is institutionalized; elsewhere deception is a more spontaneous, situational response. When that *Survivor* contestant cons the privilege of going off alone with a friend from home because the friend allegedly brings news of the contestant's supposedly dead grandma, it truly does take you aback. Doesn't the guy have enough common sense to be superstitious?

The notion that everyone is, at heart, mendacious is reinforced in the parallel meta-reality outside the programs themselves—in the media coverage of the scandals that regularly erupt when contestants are exposed for not being what they appear. But why should that surprise us? We've seen the lies told on the show. One assumes that the audience was less astonished than Darva Conger, the lucky winner of *Who Wants to Marry a Millionaire?*, to learn that the finances of her rich new husband were shakier than he'd let on. Nor are we amazed to hear that an eligible bachelor is a former underwear model, or that the "university professor" on *Average Joe* has his own website advertising his skill as an actor. And why was that talented contestant kicked off *American Idol* just because of her involvement in Internet porn? The problem, apparently, is not the act of lying but rather the need to maintain strict control over who is permitted to lie, and under what circumstances.

*   *   *

The segment of TV broadcasting that is not merely "reality-based" but claims to report "reality"—the evening news and so-called news magazines such as *20/20* and *Dateline NBC*—are learning, along with the rest of us, the lessons of *Fear Factor* and *Survivor*. Having observed the public's comfort with the notion of people's willingness to do anything for money, these quasi-journalistic shows no longer hesitate to air programs such as the one, last fall, in which kidnap victim Elizabeth Smart and her family relived her horrific ordeal and, incidentally, plugged her parents' new book. Having noted how unquestioningly all the world loves a winner, the producers of the nightly news can cease worrying about their instinct to shape their coverage in support of whichever party or idea is currently leading in the polls.

If the truth is a millstone around one's neck, civility is likewise a hobble guaranteed to slow us down. And why should we be polite when rudeness is so amusing, and when we all secretly know that the spectacle of exclusion and humiliation is the highest form of entertainment? Pity the unfortunate parent trying to instruct a school-age child in the importance of kindness and empathy when that child has been watching *American Idol* and has observed that producer Simon Cowell's star rises each time he destroys—in a hiss of clipped, Brit venom—one of the poor souls guilty of singing badly while auditioning for the show's judges.

It is almost a relief to retreat to the candlelit, soft-focus world of the mating reality shows. That is, until we realize that these too are death matches of a sort, that the competing bachelors and bachelorettes will blithely mislead and betray one another in pursuit of the man or woman of their dreams. Still, part of what sets these shows apart from the rest is that, unlike the castaways and delusional music hopefuls, the suitors and love objects are meant to be not only "real" but "nice" people. One way we know this is that they continually espouse a set of fantasies, hopes, and ideals that (although the finalists are often shown making out in the Jacuzzi and shutting the bedroom door on the film crew at the culmination of decisive "private dates") would gladden the hearts of right-wing Christian proponents of old-fashioned Family Values.

You might think we lived in a society in which divorce were not an option as the bachelors and bachelorettes burble on—in show after show, series after series—about finding "the soul mate I want to spend the rest of my life with" and about the "tremendous feelings" they are developing for whichever contestant they feel capable of loving "with all my heart and soul." Contestants remind themselves and one another to "follow your heart," to "listen to your heart," as if (and despite the observable evidence to the contrary) neither the eyes, the brain, nor the genitals deserve to be consulted. Just as the purpose of *Survivor* is to outwit, outplay, and outlast, the aim of the mating shows is to get the guy or girl and *get married*. It's sexual competition as spectator sport, true, but with an earnest, conservative face. There are deeply hurt feelings (the men scowl and shake their heads, the women weep) when suitors are rejected.

Even the families get involved. *Meet My Folks* invites competitors to live in the same house with the love object's parents. The show is partly based on a popular film, starring Robert DeNiro as a paranoid, snooping, ex-CIA future father-in-law from hell. But by the time the plot reached TV, it had deftly made the leap from Hollywood high comedy to Main Street reality, to the homes of suspicious couples who subject their grown children's suitors to humiliating polygraph tests and spy on them, via hidden cameras, at play with their sons or daughters in the hot tub. In fact, the producers of these shows have gotten precisely the sort of go-ahead for which John Ashcroft has long campaigned. Plenty of eavesdropping and surveillance transpires; one Average Joe was eliminated after being secretly videotaped insulting the 400-pound "Cousin" Danielle, who was actually Melana in a fat suit. The mechanisms of surveillance—the cameras, listening devices, and polygraph tests—have been seamlessly integrated into everyday life.

Indeed, on several of these series, the last remaining suitors are taken home to meet Mom and Dad, the siblings, and best friends. And the loved ones get to weigh in on which prospective mate will fit into the family. Because what's at stake here is *marriage*. Only rarely does anyone—usually a concerned parent or friend—inquire if this is really love or something manufactured by the producers.

In case we, too, have doubts about where all this is heading, the miniseries *Trista & Ryan's Wedding* celebrates the union between a good-looking fireman and the former Miami Heat cheerleader who was a runner-up on *The Bachelor* and who was brought back as *The Bachelorette* so that this time, just to make things more equal, *she* could choose. Carrying us across the commercial breaks with hints of prenuptial jitters ("Will the wedding go on as planned?"), it's a consumer blowout, a catalogue of lavish table settings, flower arrangements, wedding gowns, and the platinum- and diamond-encrusted "most expensive bridal shoe in the history of the world." It's fitting that consumerism should be the theme of this theme wedding, not only because television is, obviously, a vehicle for advertising, or because the show's concept facilitates the product placement that's so much a part of reality programming, but also because the entire courtship has been a shopping event. A purchasing decision has been made among twenty-five suitable, competing products who labored long and hard to commodify and sell themselves.

In a nod to today's "reality," the array of suitors often includes a few nonwhite candidates, but although the contestants-of-color are rarely eliminated in the first round, no program so far has meant true love for an interracial couple. In fact, the gene pool is a shallow one. Ryan is a fireman, but he, like most male contestants, looks like a model. The women either resemble cheerleaders or are cheerleaders, perky blondes with cute bodies, pert noses, and slightly strangulated Tweetie Bird voices. Reality TV is not where you go to have your stereotypes undermined and subverted. The gay guys on *Queer Eye for the Straight Guy* tend toward the nellie hysteric with the ability to out-shop Trista and a gift for initiating the nominally heterosexual male into the taboo joys of consumer culture.

Always gently testing the limit of what the culture will put up with, careful to give the bachelorette, as well as the bachelor, a chance to choose a mate, the networks are unlikely to take a chance on an *Average Jane* in which the genders are reversed, the male model obliged to pick from twenty-six ugly bachelorettes. Perhaps it's assumed that few viewers could accept the basic premise of the male beauty falling in love with the beast, regardless of her many good qualities. And perhaps it would be rightly feared that opinion might turn against a series that evoked the old-fashioned fraternity dog-fight, those contests held to see which brother could bring the ugliest date to the party. It's worth noting that in the final episode of *Average Joe*, Melana rejected the ordinary-looking guy (who turned out to be a millionaire) in favor of one of the handsome con-testants who, in a typical reality-TV plot twist, had been introduced into the game near the end of the series. Opting out of the game if one fails to find a suitable soul mate is simply not a possibility, for in the Republican corporatocracy there are always enough goods in the display case so that no sane shopper could refuse to make a purchase.

If these shows observe a sort of mass-market correctness, even as they reinforce gen-der stereotype and cliché, they also toe a fairly traditional line when it comes to class. The producers cast these scenarios from a solidly middle-class population. The well-off fami-lies in *Meet My Folks* have the sort of houses Americans are supposed to have: houses large enough to host the team of applicants competing to take their offspring on a roman-tic vacation. And the very wealthiest segment of the population is shown to have a heart of gold, just as we've always been led to believe. *The Simple Life* dispatches Lionel Richie's daughter (and Michael Jackson's goddaughter) Nicole and socialite Paris Hilton to slouch around an Arkansas farm, get grossed out in the cow barn, pretend not to know what Wal-Mart is, and reveal an underlying, insouciant sweetness.

In theory, *The Real World* should get credit for at least addressing the issue of race. But it's demoralizing to watch the new housemates move into their luxury digs and to be able to predict, from the start, that the one who's not going to get along with the oth-ers (especially not the racist provocateur who often shows up in the group) is the angry or militant black guy. One of these, the loose cannon David, was ultimately thrown out of the house and off the show in *The Real World: Los Angeles*. When the black guy in the Seattle series, Stephen, hit a female cast member in the face, he was permitted to remain only after agreeing to take an anger-management course. And so the cautionary, conservative message is clear: If these happen to be the only African Americans you've observed at close range, you might think twice before seeking one out as a room mate or a neighbor.

* * *

The ways in which *The Real World* has evolved over its eleven-year history provides a window onto the pressures that its producers must face to keep the show's young demographic tuning in. The most recent round, *The Real World: Paris*, focused on a group of American kids, installed in a suburban château, who spent more time in strip clubs than at the Louvre. Assigned to write an article on Versailles, two housemates downloaded the information from the Internet rather than bothering to go there. Rarely has the American public's notorious lack of interest in the world beyond our borders been made to seem cuter or more inconsequential: xenophobia as a harmless symptom of youthful ennui.

But it's the penultimate series, *The Real World: Las Vegas*, that became one of the most talked-about so far and may be a more reliable index of where reality TV is going. In their sybaritic penthouse at the Palms Casino Hotel, the Las Vegas suitemates far outdistanced their predecessors in their lack of inhibition about on-camera nudity, sex, bisexual threesomes in the hot tub, and round-the-clock debauchery. This fall, a cast member on *The Real World: San Diego* filed charges alleging that she was given a date-rape drug and assaulted by the friend of a housemate. Reportedly, the producers have been less than cooperative with the police investigation, and one wonders what role this incident will play in the show, whether it will be mined to inject the aging series with a revivifying shot of drama.

If television in general and reality TV in particular are indeed drugs, the principles of pharmacology would suggest that viewers will need an increasingly powerful fix just to maintain the same high. The producers of *The Real World* are currently launching *Starting Over*, a daytime series in which six women, lodged in a group home and aided by "life coaches," are put through the equivalent of rehab and forced to confront their problems with overeating, substance abuse, and social isolation. Unlike *The Real World*, which usually includes at least a few mentally healthy housemates, the women in *Starting Over* will presumably be selected to create a veritable zoo of conflicting personality disorders. On cable pay-per-view channels, contestants on *Can You Be a Porn Star?* will compete for $100,000 and a contract with an "adult video distributor." And O. J. Simpson has reputedly been approached to star in his own reality series.

Most recently, *Survivor* producer Mark Burnett has turned his attentions from the actual jungle to the corporate jungle ("where staying alive means using both street smarts and book smarts") to create *The Apprentice*, which sends contestants to work in Donald Trump's office and be entertainingly bullied by the Manhattan real-estate tycoon. Divided into teams, the participants (the mix of "Ivy League MBA graduates and street entrepreneurs with no college education" promises to add a frisson of class war) are assigned tasks that involve "sales, marketing, promotions, charities, real estate deals, finance, advertising pitches, and facilities management." Instead of being voted off the island, losers will be fired by Trump, and the winner will be given a $250,000 job with The Trump Organization.

By the time the competitors have run this high-stakes gauntlet, skinning and cooking rodents on a tropical island will presumably seem like a day at the beach. But even if reality TV continues to explore the far frontiers of cruelty and competition, it's unnecessary for these programs to get much more sadistic or grotesque. They merely need to stay the same, and to last long enough to produce an entire generation that has grown up watching them and may consequently have some trouble distinguishing between reality TV and reality. Because what matters is not what's on television but the ghostly afterimage that lingers in our minds and clouds our vision after we turn off the television.

It's all too easy to envision a time when the White House will no longer feel compelled to sell a projected war to the American people but can merely pitch it to Jerry Bruckheimer, whose new series will show us why we need to spread our influence— preferably by force, since diplomacy is less apt to translate into compelling TV— throughout the Middle East. And it's nearly as frightening to conjure up the specter of the singles bar haunted by baffled bachelors and bachelorettes who have spent years watching cheerleaders mate with male models and are struggling to comparison-shop cool-headedly for the best available match while simultaneously following the daunting imperative to "follow your heart" and find "the soul mate" with whom you are destined to spend the rest of your life.

As a way of reaching the American public, and inculcating audiences with a highly particular and politicized system of values, reality TV has already proved far more effective than more literal-minded representations of the governmental agenda. On the night of December 18, the stylishly dressed Paris Hilton, working in the kissing booth in a rural fair, drew 800,000 more viewers than did President George W. Bush, who was being interviewed by Diane Sawyer after the capture of Saddam Hussein. Were the President and his advisers frustrated, or surprised, or were their tender feelings hurt, by their inability to compete with the skinny socialite whose sex tape had made the rounds of the Internet? More likely they were reassured. With the public's attention so firmly focused on Paris baking pies, the administration can rest assured that it may pretty much do what it wants.

*   *   *

If reality TV does turn out to be not only the present but also the future of prime-time television, it seems more than likely that a steady, high-intake, long-term diet of *Survivor* and *The Bachelorette* will subtly, or not so subtly, affect the views and values of the audiences that tune in week after week. Watching a nightly Darwinian free-for-all cannot help but have a desensitizing effect. Once you've absorbed and assimilated the idea that civility is, at best, a frill, you may find yourself less inclined to suppress an eruption of road rage or the urge to ridicule the homely Average Joe who dares to approach a pretty girl. If the lesson of reality TV is that anyone will do anything for money, that every human interaction necessarily involves the swift, calculated formation and dissolution of dishonest, amoral alliances, it seems naive to be appalled by the fact that our government has been robbing us to pay off its supporters in the pharmaceutical industry and among the corporations profiting from the rebuilding of Iraq. After you've seen a "real person" lie about his grandmother's death, you may be slightly less shocked to learn that our leaders failed to come clean about the weapons of mass destruction.

After all, it's the way the world works; it's how people behave. We can't have witnessed all that reality without having figured that out by now. How foolish it would be to object to the billing practices of companies such as Halliburton, or to the evidence that our government has been working behind the scenes to dismantle the social security system and to increase (in the guise of reducing) what the elderly will have to pay for health care. *Everybody* acts like that, given half the chance. And we all admire a winner, regardless of how the game was won.

Which is the message we get, and are meant to be getting, every time a bachelor outsmarts his rivals, every time the castaways vote a contender off the island and inch one rung up the ladder. Indeed, those weekly tribal councils at which the voting occurs, held in a cavern or cave decorated to evoke the palm-fringed exotica of the tiki lounge or the Bugs Bunny cartoon, are arguably the most disturbing and pernicious moments in the reality-TV lineup. They're a travesty of democracy so painfully familiar, so much like what our political reality is actually becoming, that it's far more unnerving than watching Donald Trump brutally fire each week's losers, or ugly single guys made to feel even more unattractive than they are.

The castaways vote, as we do, but it's a democracy that might have been conceived if the spirit of Machiavelli had briefly possessed the mind of Thomas Jefferson; indeed, the reasons behind the survivors' ballots might puzzle our Founding Fathers. Because this fun-house version of the electoral process seeks to dismantle civilization rather than to improve it; the goal is neither a common good nor the furthering of life, liberty, or the pursuit of happiness. It's a parody of democracy, robbed of its heart and soul, a democracy in which everyone always votes, for himself.

Reading Comprehension—Points of Engagement

1. First, identify three ethics or ideals that, according to Francine Prose, characterize reality television. For each, cite an example; then explain how a certain show promotes a specific value, according to Prose.

2. How, according to Prose, do the values "reflected, codified and reinforced" by reality television work to the advantage of conservative politicians?

3. What kind of democracy does Prose say a show like *Survivor* epitomizes? What do you think of her idea?

Assignment Questions—Points of Departure

1. In "Voting Democracy Off the Island" Francine Prose proposes that a particular set of American values is promoted by reality television. Consider another text that offers insight into American values such as Michael Kamber's "Toil and Temptation," Adam Gopnik's "Bumping Into Mr. Ravioli," Fenton Johnson's "Wedded to An Illusion," or John Waterbury's "Hate Your Policies, Love Your Institutions." Use both texts to create an expanded discussion of American values. How does what you see in the other text, or texts, intersect with Prose's ideas, and how do both affect your own thinking about American values?

2. Consider the following quotation from Francine Prose's essay: "Reality-based TV . . . is not a scripted fiction but an improvisation, an apparently instructive improvisation that doles out consistent and frequently reinforced lessons about human nature, and yes, reality" (300). How can Malcolm Gladwell's theory of thin-slices help us to understand Prose's observations in "Voting Democracy Off the Island"? Do viewers of reality TV use thin-slicing as they watch? Do the

people on reality TV use thin-slicing as they relate to one another on the show? Your project for this paper is to use Gladwell's theory of thin-slicing to help *you* evaluate Prose's ideas about American popular culture, reality TV, and human relationships.

3. In her essay, Prose argues that reality television offers viewers "a parody of democracy" (311). Consider what she means, then use her idea as a lens through which to view another text that discusses the American political system, such as John Waterbury's "Hate Your Policies, Love Your Institutions," or Lewis Lapham's "Who and What Is American?" What do you learn about how American democracy works?

Dr. Daedalus

Lauren Slater

Points of Access

1. Does changing how you look change who you are? Provide several examples to support your answer.

2. What does the word average mean to you? Does it seem positive or negative, for example?

3. What does it mean to "play god"? Do you consider this a positive expression or a negative expression? Explain your answer.

Part 1: Beautiful People

Joe Rosen, plastic surgeon at the renowned Dartmouth-Hitchcock Medical Center, and by any account an odd man, has a cold. But then again, he isn't sure it's a cold. "It could be anthrax," he says as he hurries to the car, beeper beeping, sleet sleeting, for it's a freezing New England midwinter day when all the world is white. Joe Rosen's nose is running, his throat is raw, and he's being called into the ER because some guy made meat out of his forefinger and a beautiful teenager split her fine forehead open on the windshield of her SUV. It seems unfair, he says, all these calls coming in on a Sunday, especially because he's sick and he isn't sure whether it's the flu or the first subtle signs of a biological attack. "Are you serious?" I say to him. Joe Rosen is smart. He graduated cum laude from Cornell and got a medical degree from Stanford in 1978. And we're in his car now, speeding toward the hospital where he reconstructs faces, appends limbs, puffs and preens the female form. "You really wonder," I say, "if your cold is a sign of a terrorist attack?"

Joe Rosen, a respected and controversial plastic surgeon, wonders a lot of things, some of them directly related to his field, others not. Joe Rosen wonders, for instance, whether Osama bin Laden introduced the West Nile virus to this country. Joe Rosen wonders how much bandwidth it would take to make virtual-reality contact lenses available for all. Joe Rosen wonders why both his ex-wife and his current wife are artists, and what that says about his deeper interests. Joe Rosen also wonders why we insist on the kinds of conservative medical restraints that prevent him from deploying some of his most creative visions: wings for human beings; cochlear implants to enhance hearing, beefing up our boring ears and giving us the range of an owl; super-duper delicate rods to jazz up our vision—binocular, beautiful—so that we could see for many miles and into depths as well. Joe Rosen has ideas: implants for this, implants for that, gadgets, gears, discs, buttons, sculpting soft cartilage that would enable us, as humans, to cross the frontiers of our own flesh and emerge as something altogether . . . what? Something other.

And we're in the car now, speeding on slick roads toward the hospital, beeper beeping, sleet sleeting, passing cute country houses with gingerbread trim, dollops of smoke hanging above bright brick chimneys; his New Hampshire town looks so sweet. We pull into the medical center. Even this has a slight country flair to it, with gingham curtains hanging in the rows of windows. We skid. Rosen says, "One time I was in my Ford Explorer with my daughter, Sam. We rolled, and the next thing I knew we were on the side of the highway, hanging upside down like bats." He laughs.

We go in. I am excited, nervous, running by his bulky side with my tape recorder to his mouth. A resident in paper boots comes up to us. He eyes the tape recorder, and Rosen beams. Rosen is a man who enjoys attention, credentials. A few days ago he boasted to me, "You shouldn't have any trouble with the PR people in this hospital. I've had three documentaries made of me here already."

"Can I see them?" I asked.

"I don't know," Rosen answered, suddenly scratching his nose very fast. "I guess I'm not sure where I put them," and something about his voice, or his nose, made me wonder whether the documentaries were just a tall tale.

Now the resident rushes up to us, peers at the tape recorder, peers at me. "They're doing a story on me," Rosen says. "For *Harper's*."

"Joe is a crazy man, a nutcase," the resident announces, but there's affection in his voice.

"Why the beeps?" Rosen asks.

"This guy, he was working in his shop, got his finger caught in an electric planer . . . The finger's hamburger," the resident says. "It's just hamburger."

We go to the carpenter's cubicle. He's a man with a burly beard and sawdust-caked boots. He lies too big for the ER bed, his dripping finger held high in the air and splinted. It does look like hamburger.

I watch Rosen approach the bed, the wound. Rosen is a largish man, with a curly head of hair, wearing a Nordstrom wool coat and a cashmere scarf. As a plastic surgeon, he thinks grand thoughts but traffics mostly in the mundane. He has had over thirty papers published, most of them with titles like "Reconstructive Flap Surgery" or "Rhinoplasty for the Adolescent." He is known among his colleagues only secondarily for his epic ideas; his respect in the field is rooted largely in his impeccable surgical skill with all the toughest cases: shotgunned faces, smashed hands.

"How ya doin'?" Rosen says now to the carpenter. The carpenter doesn't answer. He just stares at his mashed finger, held high in the splint.

Rosen speaks softy, gently. He puts his hand on the woodworker's dusty shoulder. "Looks bad," he says, and he says this with a kind of simplicity—or is it empathy?— that makes me listen. The patient nods. "I need my finger," he says, and his voice sounds tight with tears. "I need it for the work I do."

Rosen nods. His tipsiness, his grandiosity, seem to just go away. He stands close to the man. "Look," he says, "I'm not going to do anything fancy right now, okay? I'll just have my guys sew it up, and we'll try to let nature take its course. I think that's the best thing, right now. To let nature take its course."

The carpenter nods. Rosen has said nothing really reassuring but his tone is soothing, his voice rhythmic, a series of stitches that promises to knit the broken together.

We leave the carpenter. Down the hall, the teenage beauty lies in still more serious condition, the rent in her forehead so deep we can see, it seems, the barest haze of her brain.

"God," whispers Rosen as we enter the room. "I dislike foreheads. They get infected so easily."

He touches the girl. "You'll be fine," he says. "We're not going to do anything fancy here. Just sew you up and let nature take its course."

I think these are odd, certainly unexpected words coming from a man who seems so relentlessly anti-nature, so visionary and futuristic in his interests. But then again, Rosen himself is odd, a series of swerves, a topsy-turvy, upside-down, smoke-and-mirrors sort of surgeon, hanging in his curious cave, a black bat.

"I like this hospital," Rosen announces to me as we leave the girl's room. "I like its MRI machines." He pauses.

"I should show you a real marvel," he suddenly says. He looks around him. A nurse rushes by, little dots of blood on her snowy smock. "Come," Rosen says.

We ride the elevator up. The doors whisper open. Outside, the sleet has turned to snow, falling fast and furious. The floor we're on is ominously quiet, as though there are no patients here, or as though we're in a morgue. Rosen is ghoulish and I am suddenly scared. I don't know him really. I met him at a medical-ethics convention at which he discussed teaching *Frankenstein* to his residents and elaborated, with a little light in his eye, on the inherent beauty in hybrids and chimeras, if only we could learn to see them that way. "Why do we only value the average?" he'd asked the audience. "Why are plastic surgeons dedicated only to restoring our current notions of the conventional, as opposed to letting people explore, if they want, what the possibilities are?"

Rosen went on to explain other things at that conference. It was hard for me to follow his train of thought. He vacillates between speaking clearly, almost epically, to mumbling and zigzagging and scratching his nose. At this conference he kangaroo-leapt from subject to subject: the army, biowarfare, chefs with motorized fingers that could whip eggs, noses that doubled as flashlights, soldiers with sonar, the ocean, the monsters, the marvels. He is a man of breadth but not necessarily depth. "According to medieval man," Rosen said to the convention, finally coming clear, "a monster is someone born with congenital deformities. A marvel," he explained, "is a person with animal parts—say, a tail or wings." He went on to show us pictures, a turn-of-the-century newborn hand with syphilitic sores all over it, the fingers webbed in a way that might have been beautiful but not to me, the pearly skin stretched to nylon netting in the crotch of each crooked digit.

And the floor we're on now is ominously quiet, except for a hiss somewhere, maybe some snake somewhere, with a human head. We walk for what seems a long time. My tape recorder sucks up the silence.

Rosen turns, suddenly, and with a flourish parts the curtains of a cubicle. Before me, standing as though he were waiting for our arrival, is a man, a real man, with a face beyond description. "Sweeny,"* Rosen says, gesturing toward the man, "has cancer of the face. It ate through his sinus cavities, so I scraped off his face, took off his tummy fat, and made a kind of, well, a new face for him out of the stomach. Sweeny, you look good!" Rosen says.

Sweeny, his new face, or his old stomach, oozing and swollen from this recent, radical surgery, nods. He looks miserable. The belly-face sags, the lips wizened and puckered like an anus, the eyes in their hills of fat darting fast and frightened.

"What about my nose?" Sweeny says, and then I notice: Sweeny has no nose. The cancer ate that along with the cheeks, etc. This is just awful. "That comes next. We'll use what's left of your forehead." A minute later, Rosen turns to me and observes that pretty soon women will be able to use their buttocks for breast implants. "Where there's fat," Rosen says, "there are possibilities."

---

* Not his real name.

*   *   *

The coffee is hot and good. We drink it in the hospital cafeteria while we wait for the weather to clear. "You know," Rosen says, "I'm really proud of that face. I didn't follow any protocol. There's no textbook to tell you how to fashion a face eaten away by cancer. Plastic surgery is the intersection of art and science. It's the intersection of the surgeon's imagination with human flesh. And human flesh," Rosen says, "is infinitely malleable. People say cosmetic surgery is frivolous—boobs and noses. But it's so much more than that! The body is a conduit for the soul, at least historically speaking. When you change what you look like, you change who you are."

I nod. The coffee, actually, is too damn hot. The delicate lining of skin inside my mouth starts to shred. The burn-pain distracts me. I have temporarily altered my body, and thus my mind. For just one moment, I am a burned-girl, not a writer-girl. Rosen may be correct. With my tongue I flick the loose skin, picture it, pink and silky, on fire.

*   *   *

No, plastic surgery is not just boobs and noses. Its textbooks are tomes—thick, dusty, or slick, no matter—that all open up to images of striated muscle excised from its moorings, bones—white, calcium-rich—elongated by the doctor's finest tools. Plastic surgery, as a medical specialty, is very confusing. It aims, on the one hand, to restore deformities and, on the other hand, to alter the normal. Therefore, the patients are a motley crew. There is the gorgeous blonde with the high sprayed helmet of hair who wants a little tummy tuck, even though she's thin, and then there is the Apert Syndrome child, the jaw so foreshortened the teeth cannot root in their sockets. Plastic surgery—like Rosen, its premier practitioner—is flexible, high-minded, and wide-ranging, managing to be at once utterly necessary and ridiculously frivolous, all in the same breath, all in the same scalpel.

According to the American Society of Plastic Surgeons, last year more than 1.3 million people had cosmetic surgery performed by board-certified plastic surgeons, an increase of 227 percent since 1992. (These numbers do not include medically necessary or reconstructive surgeries.) The five most popular procedures were liposuction (229,588), breast augmentation (187,755), eyelid surgery (172,244), the just available Botox injections (118,452), and face lifts (70,882). Most cosmetic surgeries are performed on women, but men are catching up: the number of men receiving nose jobs— their most popular procedure—has increased 141 percent since 1997. The vast majority of patients are white, but not necessarily wealthy. A 1994 study found that 65 percent of cosmetic-surgery patients had a family income of less than $50,000, even though neither state nor private health insurance covers the cost of cosmetic surgeries. These figures alone point to the tremendous popularity and increasing acceptance of body alteration, and suggest that the slippery slope from something as bizarre as eyelid tucks to something still more bizarre, like wings, may be shorter than we think.

This medical specialty is ancient, dating back to 800 B.C., when hieroglyphics describe crude skin grafts. Rosen once explained to me that plastic surgery started as a means to blur racial differences. "A long time ago," he'd said, "Jewish slaves had clefts in their ears. And some of the first plastic surgery operations were to remove those signs of stigma."

One history book mentions the story of a doctor named Joseph Dieffenbach and a man with grave facial problems. This man had the sunken nose of syphilis, a disease widely associated with immorality. Dieffenbach, one of the fathers of plastic surgery, so the story goes, devised a gold rhinoplasty bridge for this marginal man, thus giving him, literally, a Midas nose and proving, indeed, that medicine can make criminals kings.

As a field, plastic surgery is troubled, insecure. It is a lot like psychiatry, or dentistry, in its inferior status as a subspecialty of medicine. In fact, the first plastic-surgery association, started in 1921, was an offshoot of oral practitioners. Read: teeth people. Not to digress, but the other day I woke up with a terrible toothache and rushed in to see a dentist. I said to him, just to be friendly, "What sort of training do you need for your profession?" He said, "You need A LOT of training, believe me. I trained with the same guys who cure your cancer, but I don't get the same respect."

I wonder if Rosen ever feels like my dentist, and if that's why he's so grandiose, like the little boy who is a bully. Sander Gilman, a cultural critic of plastic surgery, writes that, in this group of doctors, there are a lot of big words thrown around in an effort to cover up the sneaking suspicion that their interventions are not important. One is not ever supposed to say "nose job"; it's called rhinoplasty. Gilman writes, "The lower the perceived status of a field . . . the more complex and 'scientific' the discourse of the field becomes."

Of course, I rarely meet a doctor who doesn't like jargon and doesn't like power. Rosen may be different only in intensity. "I'm not a cosmetic surgeon," Rosen keeps repeating to me.

He says, "Really, there's no such thing as just cosmetic surgery. The skin and the soul are one." On paper, maybe, this comment seems a little overblown, but delivered orally, in a New England town when all the world is white, it has its lyrical appeal.

When Rosen cries out that he's not "just a cosmetic surgeon," he's put his finger on a real conflict in his field. Where does necessary reconstruction end and frivolous interventions begin? Are those interventions really frivolous, or are they emblematic of the huge and sometimes majestic human desire to alter, to transcend? If medicine is predicated upon the notion of making the sick well, and a plastic surgeon operates on someone who is not sick, then can the patient truly be called a patient, and the doctor a doctor? Who pays for this stuff, when, where, and how? These are the swirling questions. Over a hundred years ago Jacques Joseph, another of plastic surgery's founding fathers, wrote that beauty was a medical necessity because a person's looks can create social and economic barriers. Repairing the deformity, therefore, allows the man to function in a fully healthy way in society. Voilà. Function and form, utilitarianism and aestheticism, joined at the hip, grafted together: skin tight.

*   *   *

Perhaps we can accept Joseph's formulation. Okay, we say. Calm down. We say this to all the hopping, hooting cosmetic surgeons who want to stake out their significance. Okay, we respect you. I'd like to say this to Rosen, but I can't. Rosen's ideas and aspirations, not to mention his anthrax concerns, go beyond what I am comfortable with, though I can't quite unearth the architecture of my concerns. After all, he doesn't want to hurt anyone. Maybe it's because Rosen isn't just talking about everyday beauty and its utilitarian aspects. He is talking EXTREMES. When Rosen thinks of beauty, he thinks of the human form stretched on the red-hot rack of his imagination, which is mired in medieval texts and books on trumpeter swans. At its outermost limits, beauty becomes fantastical, perhaps absurd. Here is where Rosen rests. He dreams of making wings for human beings. He has shown me blue-prints, sketches of the scalpel scissoring into skin, stretching flaps of torso fat to fashion gliders piped with rib bone. When the arm stretches, the gliders unfold, and human floats on currents of air. Is he serious? At least partially. He gives lectures to medical students on the meaning of wings from an engineering perspective, a surgeon's perspective, and a patient's perspective. He has also thought of cochlear implants to enhance normal hearing, fins to make us fishlike, and echolocation devices so that we can better navigate the night. He does not understand the limits we place on hands. He once met a Vietnamese man with two thumbs on one hand. This man was a waiter, and his two thumbs made him highly skilled at his job. "Now," says Rosen, "if that man came to me and said, 'I want you to take off my extra thumb,' I'd be allowed, but I wouldn't be allowed to put an extra thumb on a person, and that's not fair."

We can call Rosen ridiculous, a madman, a monster, a marvel. We could dismiss him as a techno geek or a fool or just plain immature. But then there are the facts. First of all,

Rosen is an influential man, an associate professor of surgery at Dartmouth Medical School and the director of the Plastic Surgery Residency Program at the medical center. He was senior fellow at the C. Everett Koop Institute from 1997 to 1998, and he has also served on advisory panels for the navy and for NASA's Medical Care for the Mission to Mars, 2018. Rosen consults for the American Academy of Sciences committee on the role of virtual-reality technology, and he is the former director of the Department of Defense's Emerging Technology Threats workforce. In other words, this is a man taken seriously by some serious higher-ups. "Echolocation devices," Rosen explains, "implanted in a soldier's head, could do a lot to enhance our military capacity." And this isn't just about the army's fantasies of the perfect soldier. Rosen travels worldwide (he gave over a dozen presentations last year) and has had substantial impact not only scalpeling skin but influencing his colleagues' ethics in a myriad of ways. "He has been essential in helping me to conceptualize medicine outside of the box," says Charles Lucey, MD, a former colleague of Rosen's at the Dartmouth Medical School. John Harris, a medical-ethics specialist in Manchester, England, writes in *Wonderwoman and Superman* that "in the absence of an argument or the ability to point to some specific harm that might be involved in crossing species boundaries, we should regard the objections *per se* to such practices . . . as mere and gratuitous prejudice." Rosen himself says, "Believe me. Wings are not way off. It is not a bad idea. Who would have thought we'd ever agree to hold expensive, potentially dangerous radioactive devices up to our ears for hours on end, day after day, just so we could gossip. That's cell phones for you," he says. And smiles.

Rosen has a nice smile. It's, to be sure, a little boyish, but it's charming. Sometimes Rosen is shy. "I mumble a lot," he acknowledges. "I don't really like people. I don't really like the present. I am a man who lives in the past and in the future only."

Now we leave the emergency room. The snow has stopped. The roads are membraned with ice. The sun is setting in the New Hampshire sky, causing the hills to sparkle as though they're full of little lights and other electric things. We drive back to his house, slowly. The emergencies are over, the patients soothed or suffering, he has done what can be done in a day, and still his nose runs. He coughs into his fist. "Truth be told," he says to me, "I didn't start out wanting to be a surgeon, even though I always, ALWAYS, had big ideas. In kindergarten, when the other kids were making these little ditsy arts-and-crafts projects, I was building a room-size Seventh Fleet ship." He goes on. As a child he wanted to be an artist. In high school he became obsessed with Picasso's *Guarnica* and spent months trying to replicate it in the style of Van Gogh. As a freshman at Cornell, he made a robotic hand that could crack his lobster for him, and from then on it was hands, fingers, knees, and toes. His interests in the technical aspects of the body drew him away from the arts and eventually into medical school, which was, in his mind, somewhere between selling out and moving on.

We pull into his driveway. Rosen lives in a sprawling ranch-style house. He has a pet hen, who waits for us in the evergreen tree. His second wife, Stina Kohnke, is young and, yes, attractive. I'm afraid to ask how old she is; he looks to be at least fifty-three and she looks twenty-three, though maybe that's beside the point. Nevertheless, it all gets thrown into my mental stew: grandiose man, military man, medicine man, wants to make wings, young thing for a mate. Rooster and hen. Maybe there is no story here. Maybe there's just parody. All breadth, no depth. Except for this. Everyone I tell about Rosen and his wings, his *fin de siècle* mind, widens his or her eyes, leans forward, and says, "You're kidding." People want to hear more. *I* want to hear more. His ideas of altering the human form are repugnant and delicious, and that's a potent combination to unravel. And who among us has not had flying dreams, lifted high, dramatically free, a throat-catching fluidity in our otherwise aching form, above the ocean, all green, like moving marble?

* * *

Rosen and his wife have invited me for dinner. I accept. Stina is an artist. Her work is excellent. "Joe is an inspiration for me," she says. "He brings home pictures of his patients, and I sculpt their limbs from bronze." In her studio, she has a riot of red-bronze deformed hands clutching, reaching, in an agony of stiffness. She has fashioned drawer pulls from gold-plated ears. You go to open the breadbox, the medicine cabinet, the desk drawer, and you have to touch these things. It's at once creepy and very beautiful.

We sit at their stone dining-room table. Behind us is a seventy-gallon aquarium full of fish. Cacti, pink and penile, thrust their way into the odd air. Stina, homesick for her native California, has adorned the living room with paper palm trees and tiny live parakeets. We talk. Stina says, "Joe and I got married because we found in each other the same aesthetic and many moral equivalents. We found two people who could see and sculpt the potential in what others found just ugly."

"How did you two meet?" I ask.

"Oh, I knew Stina's sister, who was an art professor . . . That sort of thing," mumbles Rosen.

"I kissed him first," says Stina. She reaches across the table, picks up Rosen's hand, and wreathes her fingers through his. She holds on tightly, as if she's scared. I study Stina. She is conventionally pretty. She has a perfect Protestant nose and a lithe form, and a single black bra strap slips provocatively from beneath her blouse. Rosen, a man who claims to love the unusual, has picked a very usual beauty.

"Look!" Stina suddenly shouts. I jump, startled. "Look at her ears!" she says to Rosen.

Before I know it they are both leaning forward, peering at my ears. "Oh, my God," says Stina, "you have the most unusual ears."

Now, this is not news to me. I have bat ears, plain and simple. They stick out stupidly. In the fifth grade, I used to fasten them to the sides of my skull with pink styling tape in the hope of altering their shape. I have always disliked my ears.

Rosen uncurls his index finger and touches my left ear. He runs his finger along the bumpy, malformed rim. "You're missing the *scapha*," he says. "It's a birth defect."

"I have a birth defect?" I say. I practically shout this, being someone who desires deeply not to be defective. That's why I take Prozac every day.

"Joe," says Stina, "are those not the most amazing ears. They would be so perfect to sculpt."

"They're just a perfect example," Rosen echoes, "of the incredible, delectable proliferation of life-forms. We claim most life-forms gravitate toward the mean, but that's not true. Lots of valid life exists at the margins of the bell curve. You have beautiful ears," he says to me.

"I have nice ears?" I say. "Really?"

This is just one reason why I won't dismiss Rosen out of hand. Suddenly, I see my ears a little differently. They have a marvelous undulating ridge and an intricately whorled entrance, and they do not stick out so much as jauntily jut; they are ears with an attitude. Rosen has shifted my vision without even touching my eyes. He is, at the very least, a challenger of paradigms; he calls on your conservatism, pushes hard.

That night, I do not dream of wings. I dream of Sweeny and his oozing face. I dream he comes so close to me that I smell him. Then I wake up. Sweeny is very sick. He is going to die soon. Earlier in the day, I asked Rosen when, and Rosen said, "Oh, soon," but he said it as if he didn't really care. Death does not seem to interest Rosen. Beauty, I think, can be cold.

Part II: Monster and Marvels

Today, Rosen and I are attending a conference together in Montreal. Here, everyone speaks French and eats baguettes. The conference room is old-fashioned, wainscoted with rich mahogany, ornate carvings of creatures and angels studding the ceiling, where a single light hangs in a cream-colored orb. Around the table sit doctors, philosophers, graduate students: this is a medical-ethics meeting, and Rosen is presenting his ideas. On the white board, in bold black lines, he sketches out his wings, and then the discussion turns to a patient whose single deepest desire was to look like a lizard. He wanted a doctor to split his tongue and scale his skin, and then put horns on his head. "You wouldn't do that, would you?" a bespectacled doctor asks. "Once," says Rosen, dodging in a fashion typical of him, "there was a lady in need of breast reconstruction who wanted blue areolas. What's wrong with blue areolas? Furthermore, rhinoplasty has not reached its real potential. Why just change the nose? Why not change the gene for the nose, so that subsequent generations will benefit from the surgery? Plastic surgery, in the future, can be about more than the literal body. It can be about sculpting the genotype as well."

The bespectacled doctor raises his hand. "Would you make that man into a lizard?" the doctor asks again. "What I want to know is, if a patient came to you and said, 'I want you to give me wings,' or 'Split my tongue,' would you actually do it?"

"Look," says Rosen, "we genetically engineer food. That's an issue."

"You're not answering my question," the doctor says, growing angry. Other people are growing angry, too. "Do you see any ethical dilemmas in making people into pigs, or birds?" another attendee yells out. This attendee is eating a Yodel, peeling off the chocolate bark and biting into a swirl of cream.

Rosen darts and dodges. "There is such a thing as liberty," he says.

"Yes," someone says, "but there's such a thing as the Hippocratic oath, too."

This goes on and on. At last a professor of anthropology says, "Just tell us, clearly, please. Would you give a human being wings, if the medical-ethics board allowed it?"

Rosen puts down his black marker. He rubs his eyes. "Yes," he says, "I would. I can certainly see why we don't devote research money to it. I can see why the NIH would fund work on breast cancer over this, but I don't have any problem with altering the human form. We do it all the time. It is only our Judeo-Christian conservatism that makes us think this is wrong. Who here," he says, "doesn't try to send their children to the best schools, in the hopes of altering them? Who here objects to a Palm Pilot, a thing we clasp to our bodies, with which we receive rapid electronic signals? Who here doesn't surround themselves with a metal shell and travel at death-defying speeds? We have always altered ourselves, for beauty or for power, and so long as we are not causing harm what makes us think we should stop?"

For a group of intelligent people everyone looks baffled. What Rosen has said is very right and very wrong, but no one can quite articulate the core conflicts. After all, we seem to think it's okay to use education as a way of neuronally altering the brain, but not surgery. We take Prozac, even Ritalin, to help transform ourselves, but recoil when it comes to wings. Maybe we're not recoiling. Maybe wings are just a dumb idea. No one in his right mind would subject himself to such a superfluous and strenuous operation. Yet socialite Jocelyne Wildenstein has dedicated much of her life to turning herself into a cat, via plastic surgery. She has had her lips enlarged and her face pulled back at the eyes to simulate a feline appearance. An even more well-known case is Michael Jackson, who has whitened himself, slimmed his nose, and undergone multiple other aesthetic procedures. The essential question here is whether these people are, and forever will be, outliers, or whether they represent the cutting edge of an ever more popular trend. Carl Elliott, a bioethicist and associate professor at the University of Minnesota, recently wrote in *The Atlantic* about a strange new "trend" of perfectly healthy folks who desire nothing more than to have a limb amputated, and about the British doctor who has undertaken this surgery, believing that if he doesn't amputate the patients will do it themselves, which could lead to gangrene. Elliott wonders whether amputation obsession will morph into another psychiatric diagnosis, whether, like hysteria, it will "catch on." The metaphor of contagion is an interesting one. Multiple-personality disorder "caught on"; hysteria caught on. Why then might not an unquenchable desire for wings or fins catch on, too? In any case, we use medical/viral metaphors to explain trends, and, in the case of plastic surgery, we then use medical means to achieve the trend's demands.

Rosen himself now repeats to the conferees, "We have always altered ourselves for beauty or for power. The chieftains in a certain African tribe remove their left ears, without Novocain. Other tribes put their bodies through intense scarification processes for the sake of style. In our own culture, we risk our bodies daily to achieve status, whether it's because we're bulimic or because we let some surgeon suck fat from us, with liposuction. Wings will be here," Rosen says. "Mark my words."

He suddenly seems so confident, so clear. We should do this; beauty is marvelous and monstrous. Beauty is difference, and yet, to his patients in the ER just two weeks back, he kept saying, "Let nature take its course." Perhaps he is more ambivalent than he lets on.

*   *   *

Later that evening, over dinner, conferees gossip about Rosen. "He's a creep," someone says. "A megalomaniac," someone else adds. For a creep or a megalomaniac, though, he's certainly commanding a lot of attention. Clearly, his notions are provocative. "The problem with wings," says someone, "is that only rich people would have them, would be able to afford them. Our society might begin to see rich people as more godly than ever."

I order a glass of wine. The waitress sets it on the table, where it blazes in its goblet, bright as a tulip. With this wine, I will tweak not only my mind but all its neuronal projections as well. My reflexes will slow down and my inhibitions will lift, making it possible for me to sound either very stupid or very smart. Is this wine an ethical problem? I ask the group that.

"Wine is reversible," someone says. "Wings aren't."

"Well, suppose they *were* reversible," someone says. "Supposing a surgeon could make wings that were removable. Then would we be reacting this way?"

"It's a question of degree," a philosopher pipes up. He is bald and skinny, with bulging eyes. "Rosen is going to the nth degree. It's not fair to lump that in with necessary alterations, or even questionably necessary alterations. Without doubt, it is very clear, diagnostically, that wings are not necessary."

I think about this. I think about what Rosen might say to this. I can imagine that his answer might have something to do with the fluidity of the concept of necessary. Four years ago, cell phones weren't necessary. Now they seem to be. Furthermore, he might say, if a person wants wings, if wings won't hurt a person, if they will help a person enjoy life and feel more beautiful, and if, in turn, the winged woman or man helps us to see beauty in what was before unacceptable, as we adjust and then come to love the sight of her spreading and soaring, then isn't this excellent? Later on, in my hotel room, I stand in front of the mirror, naked. My body contains eons. Once, we were single cells, then fish, then birds, then mammals, and the genes for all these forms lie dormant on their cones of chromosomes. We are pastiches at the cellular, genetic level. This may be why I fear open spaces, blank pages, why I often dream my house opens up into endless rooms I never knew were there, and I float through them with a kind of terror. It is so easy to seep, to be boundless. We clutch our cloaks of skin.

Back in Boston, I try to ascertain clearly, logically, what so bothers people about Rosen's ideas. At first glance, it might seem fairly obvious. I mean, wings. That's playing God. We should not play God. We should not reach for the stars. Myth after myth has shown us the dangers of doing so—Icarus, the Tower of Babel; absolute power corrupts absolutely. Bill Joy, chief scientist at Sun Microsystems, says, as our technological capabilities expand, "a sequence of small, individually sensible advances leads to an accumulation of great power and, concomitantly, great danger." Rosen's response to this: "So are we supposed to stop advancing? And who says it's bad to play God? We already alter the course of God's 'will' in hundreds of ways. When we use antibiotics to combat the flu, when we figure out a way to wipe smallpox off the very face of the earth, surely we're altering the natural course of things. Who says the natural course of things is even right? Maybe God isn't good."

The second objection might have to do with our notions of categorical imperatives. Mary Douglas wrote in her influential anthropological study *Purity and Danger* that human beings have a natural aversion to crossing categories, and that when we do transgress we see it as deeply dirty. In other words, shoes in themselves are not dirty, but when you place them on the dining-room table they are. When you talk about crossing species, either at the genetic or the anatomical level, you are mucking about in long-cherished categories that reflect our fundamental sense of cleanliness and aesthetics. Rosen's response to this, when I lob it at him in our next meeting: "Who says taboos are anything but prejudice at rock bottom? Just because it feels wrong doesn't mean it is. To a lot of people, racial intermingling and miscegenation feel wrong, but to me they're fine. I'm not a racist, and I'm not a conservative."

The third objection I can come up with has to do with the idea of proteanism. Proteus, a minor mythological figure, could shape-shift at will, being alternately a tiger, a lizard, a fire, a flood. Robert Lifton, one of, I think, the truly deep thinkers of the last century, has explored in his volumes how Proteus has become a symbol for human beings in our time. Lacking traditions, supportive institutions, a set of historically rooted symbols, we have lost any sense of coherence and connection. Today it is not uncommon for a human being to shift belief systems several times in a lifetime, and with relatively little psychological discomfort. We are Catholics, Buddhists, reborn, unborn, artists, and dot-commers until the dot drops out of the com and it all comes crashing down. We move on. We remarry. Our protean abilities clearly have their upside. We are flexible and creative. But the downside is, there is no psychic stability, no substantive self, nothing really meaty and authentic. We sense this about ourselves. We know we are superficial, all breadth and no depth. Rosen's work embodies this tendency, literally. He desires to make incarnate the identity diffusion so common to our culture. Rosen is in our face making us face up to the fact that the inner and outer connections have crumbled. In our ability to be everything, are we also nothing?

For me, this hits the nail on the head. I do not object to Rosen on the basis of concerns about power, or of Mary Douglas's cross-category pollution theory. After all, who, really, would wings reasonably benefit but the window washers among us? And as for the pollution issue, protean person that I am, I could probably adjust to a little chimerical color. Rosen's ideas and aspirations are frightening to me because they are such vivid, visceral examples of a certain postmodern or perhaps, more precisely put, post-authentic sensibility we embrace and fear as we pop our Prozacs and Ritalins and decide to be Jewish and then Episcopalian and then chant with the monks on some high Himalayan mountain via a cheap plane ticket we purchased in between jobs and just before we sold our condo in a market rising so fast that when it falls it will sound like all of the precious china plates crashing down from the cabinet—a mess. What a mess!

Over and over again, from the Middle Ages on, when the theologian Pico wrote, in a direct and influential challenge to the Platonic idea of essential forms—"We have given you, Adam, no visage proper to yourself, nor endowment properly your own . . . trace for yourself the lineaments of your own nature . . . in order that you, as the free and proud shaper of your own being, fashion yourself in the form you may prefer . . . [W]ho then will not look with awe upon this our chameleon . . ." —over and over, since those words at least, we as human beings have fretted about the question of whether there is anything fixed at our core, any set of unalterable traits that make us who we were and are and always will be. Postmodernism, by which I mean the idea of multiplicity, the celebration of the pastiche, and the rejection of logical positivism and absolutism as viable stances, will never die out, despite its waning popularity in academia. Its roots are too deep and ancient. And there has been, perhaps, no field like modern medicine, with all its possibilities and technological wizardry, to bring questions of authenticity to the burning forefront of our culture. At what point, in altering ourselves, would we lose our essential humanity? Are there any traits that make us essentially human? When might we become monsters or marvels, or are we already there? I vividly remember reading a book by a woman named Martha Beck. She had given birth to a Down's syndrome child and she wrote in a few chilling sentences that because of one tiny chromosome, her child, Adam, is "as dissimilar from me as a mule is from a donkey. He is, in ways both obvious and subtle, a different beast." Is it really that simple, that small? One tiny chromosome severs us from the human species? One little wing and we're gone?

As for me, I am an obsessive. I like my categories. I check to make sure the stove is off three times before I go to bed. I have all sorts of other little rituals. At the same time, I know I am deeply disrooted. I left my family at the age of fourteen, never to return. I do not know my family tree. Like so many of us, I have no real religion, which is of course partly a good thing but partly a bad thing. In any case, last year, in some sort of desperate mood, I decided to convert from Judaism to Episcopalianism, but when it came time to put that blood and body in my mouth I couldn't go through with it. Was this because at bottom I just AM a Jew and this amness has profundity? Or was this because I don't like French bread, which is what they were using at the conversion ceremony? In any case, at the crucial moment of incorporation, I fled the church like the proverbial bride who cannot make the commitment.

I want to believe there is something essential and authentic about me, even if it's just my ears. And although my feelings of diffusion may be extreme, I am certainly not the only one who's felt she's flying too fast. Lifton writes, "Until relatively recently, no more than a single major ideological shift was likely to occur in a lifetime, and that one would be long remembered for its conflict and soul searching. But today it is not unusual for several such shifts to take place within a year or even a month, whether in the realm of politics, religion, aesthetic values, personal relationships. . . . Quite rare is the man or woman who has gone through life holding firmly to a single ideological vision. More usual is a tendency toward ideological fragments, bits and pieces of belief systems that allow for shifts, revisions, and recombinations."

What Lifton has observed in the psyche Rosen wants to make manifest in the body. I ask Rosen, "So, do you believe we are just in essence protean, that there is nothing fundamental, or core, to being human?"

He says, "Lauren, I am a scientist. My original interests were in nerves. I helped develop, in the 1980s, one of the first computer-grown nerve chips. The answer to your question may lie in how our nervous systems operate."

Part III: The Protean Brain

First, a lesson. In the 1930s, researchers, working on the brains of apes, found that the gray matter contained neural representations of all the afferent body parts. Ape ears, feet, skin, hands, were all richly represented in the ape brain in a series of neural etchings, like a map. Researchers also realized that when a person loses a limb—say, the right arm—this portion of the neural map fades away. Sometimes even stranger things happen. Sometimes amputees claimed they could feel their missing arm when, for instance, someone touched their cheek. This was because the arm map had not faded so much as morphed, joined up its circuitry with the cheek map, so it was all confused.

It was then discovered, not surprisingly, that human beings also have limb maps in their brains. Neurologists conceptualized this limb map as "a homunculus," or little man. Despite my feminist leanings, I am enchanted by the idea of a little man hunched in my head, troll-like, banging a drum, grinning from ear to ear. Of course the homunculus is not actually shaped like a human; it is, rather, a kind of human blueprint, like the drawing of the house in all its minute specificity. Touch the side of your skull. Press in. Buried, somewhere near there, is a beautiful etching of your complex human hand, rich in neural web-work and delicate, axonal tendrils designed to accommodate all the sensory possibilities of this prehensile object. Move your hand upward, press the now sealed soft spot, and you will be touching your toe map. Your eye map is somewhere in your forehead and your navel map is somewhere in your cerebellum, a creased, enfolded series of cells that recall, I imagine, ancient blue connections, a primitive love.

Today, Rosen is giving a lecture. I have come up to New Hampshire to hear him, and, unlike on the last visit, the day is beautiful and bright. Rosen explains how brains are partly plastic, which comes from the Greek root meaning to mold, to shape. When we lose a limb, the brain absorbs its map or rewires it to some other center. Similarly, Rosen explains, when we gain a limb, the brain almost immediately senses it and goes about hooking it up via neural representation. "If I were to attach a sonographically powered arm to your body," Rosen explains, "your brain would map it. If I were to attach a third thumb, your brain would map it, absolutely. Our bodies change our brains, and our brains are infinitely moldable. If I were to give you wings, you would develop, literally, a winged brain. If I were to give you an echolocation device, you would develop in part a bat-brain."

Although the idea of a brain able to incorporate changes so completely may sound strange, many neurological experiments have borne out the fact that our gray matter does reorganize according to the form and function of our appendages. Because no one has yet appended animal forms to the human body, however, no studies have been done that explore what the brain's response to what might be termed an "evolutionary insult" would be. Assuming, probably wrongly but assuming nevertheless, that human beings represent some higher form of species adaptation, at least in terms of frontal-lobe intelligence, the brain might find it odd to be rewiring itself to presumably more primitive structures, structures we shed a long time ago when we waded out of the swamps and shed our scales. Rosen's desire to meld human and animal forms, and the incarnation of this desire in people like the cat-woman and the lizard-man, raise some interesting questions about the intersection of technology and primitivism. Although we usually assume technology is somehow deepening the rift between nature and culture, it also can do the opposite. In other words, technology can be, and often is, extremely primitive, not only because it allows people a sort of id-like, limbic-driven power (i.e., nuclear weaponry) but also because it can provide the means to toggle us down the evolutionary ladder, to alter our brains, stuck in their rigid humanness, so that we are at last no longer landlocked.

All this is fascinating and, of course, unsettling to me. Our brains are essentially indiscriminate, able to morph—like the sea god Proteus himself—into fire, a flood, a dragon, a swan. I touch my brain and feel it flap. Now I understand more deeply what Rosen meant when he said, "Plastic surgery changes the soul." To the extent that we believe our souls are a part of our brains, Rosen is right. And, all social conflict about its place in the medical hierarchy aside, plastic surgery is really neurosurgery, because it clearly happens, at its most essential level, north of the neck. When a surgeon modifies your body, he modifies your oh-so-willing, bendable brain.

I get a little depressed, hearing this lecture. It seems to me proof at the neuronal level that we have the capacity to be, in fact, everything, and thus in some sense nothing. It confirms my fear that I, along with the rest of the human species, could slip-slide through life without any specificity, or "specieficity." Last year, I had my first child. I wonder what I will teach her, what beliefs about the body and the brain and the soul I really hold. I think, "I will show her pictures of her ancestors," but the truth is, I don't have any pictures. I think, "I will teach her my morals," but I don't know exactly what my morals are, or where they came from. I know I am not alone. Like Rosen, perhaps, I am just extreme. Now I feel a kind of kinship with him. We are both self-invented, winging our way through.

Rosen comes up to me. He is finished with his talk. "So do you understand what I mean," he asks, "about the limitlessness of the brain?"

"Does it ever make you sad?" I say. "Does it ever just plain and simple make you scared?"

Rosen and I look at each other for a long time. He does seem sad. I recall him telling me once that when he envisions the future fifty years out, he hopes he is gone, because, he said, "While I like it here, I don't like it that much." I have the sense, now, that he struggles with things he won't tell me. His eyes appear tired, his face drained. I wonder if he wakes in the middle of the night, frightened by his own perceptions. Strange or not, there is something constant in Rosen, and that's his intelligence, his uncanny ability to defend seemingly untenable positions with power and occasional grace. In just three weeks he will travel to a remote part of Asia to participate in a group called Interplast, made up of doctors and nurses who donate their time to help children with cleft lips and palates. I think it's important to mention this—not only Bin Laden, bandwidth, anthrax, and wings but his competing desire to minister. The way, at the dinner table, he tousles his children's hair. His avid dislike of George W. Bush. His love of plants and greenery. Call him multifaceted or simply slippery, I don't know. All I do know is that right now, when I look at his face, I think I can see the boy he once was, the Seventh Fleet ship, the wonder, all that wonder.

"Do you and Stina want to go out for dinner? We could go somewhere really fancy, to thank you," I say, "for all your time."

"Sure," says Rosen. "Give me a minute. I'll meet you in the hospital lobby," and then he zips off to who knows where, and I am alone with my singular stretched self on the third floor of the Dartmouth-Hitchcock Medical Center. I wander down the long hallways. Behind the curtained cubicles there is unspeakable suffering. Surely that cannot be changed, not ever. Behind one of these cubicles sits Sweeny, and even if we learn to see him as beautiful, the bottom-line truth is that he still suffers. Now I want to touch Sweeny's dying face. I want to put my hand right on the center of pain. I want to touch Rosen's difficult face, and my baby daughter's face as well, but she is far from me, in some home we will, migrants that our family is, move on from sometime soon. I once read that a fetus does not scar. Fetal skin repairs itself seamlessly, evidence of damage sinking back into blackness. Plastic surgery, for all its incredible advances, has not yet been able to figure out how to replicate this mysterious fetal ability in the full-born human. Plastic surgery can give us wings and maybe even let us sing like loons, but it cannot stop scarring. This is oddly comforting to me. I pause to sit on a padded bench. A very ill woman pushing an IV pole walks by. I lift up my pant leg and study the scar I got a long time ago, when I fell off a childhood bike. The scar is pink and raised and shaped like an *o*, like a hole maybe, but also like a letter, like a language, like a little piece of land that, for now, we cannot cross over.

Reading Comprehension—Points of Engagement

1. Consider Lauren Slater's main question: "Where does necessary reconstruction end and frivolous interventions begin? Are those interventions really frivolous or are they emblematic of the huge and sometimes majestic human desire to transcend?" (318–319). What's necessary and what is frivolous? What does Slater think? What do you think? What about the human desire to transcend? Look closely in that paragraph for your answer.

2. Joe Rosen tells a questioner that he would give a person wings. Explain his rationale as you understand it. Then respond. Do you agree or disagree?

3. Slater introduces the idea of proteanism on page 326. What does she mean, and what are her concerns about people adopting a protean self?

Assignment Questions—Points of Departure

1. According to Slater, Joe Rosen's advice to his patients, "let nature take its course," seems odd coming from "a man who seems so relentlessly anti-nature" (315). What's the conflict, in Slater's mind? Why might he say both things? Then keeping Rosen's dual view in mind, consider another author who also explores complicated ideas about the natural order of things, such as Michael Pollan, David Brooks, or Barbara Kingsolver. What do you learn about nature and anti-nature?

2. Consider the following passage: "At what point, in altering ourselves, would we lose our essential humanity? Are there any traits that make us essentially human? When might we become monsters or marvels, or are we already there?" (327). How does Slater answer these questions? Rosen? You? What about other authors in this collection? Lisa Belkin? Andrew Sullivan? Write a paper in which you address these questions and engage with the ideas in Slater's essay and either Belkin or Sullivan.

3. Consider the following question that Lauren Slater poses to Dr. Rosen: " 'So, do you believe we are just in essence protean, that there is nothing fundamental, or core, to being human?' " (328). What is Rosen's answer? What is Slater's answer? Yours? In your answer make sure you refer to the answers by Rosen or Slater, and keep their positions distinct. Then use those answers you've generated from Slater's text to further explore the issues of personal identity raised in another essay, such as Malcolm Gladwell's "The Theory of Thin Slices," Lenore Look's "Facing the Village," Francine Prose's "Voting Democracy Off the Island," Andrew Sullivan's "The He Hormone," or Katha Pollitt's "Marooned on Gilligan's Island."

4. Slater struggles to understand the limits of science and nature in her essay, whereas Jane Goodall feels the two are entirely attuned. Given this tension, how would either Slater or Rosen answer the following questions from Goodall, "What is our human responsibility? And what, ultimately, is our human destiny? Were we going to go on destroying God's creation, fighting each other, hurting the other creatures of His planet? Or were we going to find ways to live in greater harmony with each other and with the natural world?" (114). Use examples from Rosen's work to help answer these questions, or consider exploring Slater's own personal reflections. How does Goodall bridge the divide between science and nature and could this perspective be employed by Slater?

The He Hormone

Andrew Sullivan

Points of Access

1. Is "gender" a natural trait or a set of social rules? How is biological sex different from gender? Use examples to support your claims.

2. What qualities, behaviors, and activities are associated with femininity? Make a list. What qualities, behaviors, and activities are associated with masculinity? Make another list. Now compare them. Is there any overlap in qualities? Why, do you think, or why not? Have any of these gendered qualities changed during your lifetime? If so, how and why?

3. As social creatures, we often develop simple ways of regarding each other, usually as a mixture of truth and stereotype. Think about the way men and women are regarded, either in the United States, or in another culture. What assumptions are made about female bodies? What assumptions are made about the male physique? How much of these assumptions are based on truth and how much on stereotype? Do you participate in these assumptions consciously? In what ways?

It has a slightly golden hue, suspended in an oily substance and injected in a needle about half as thick as a telephone wire. I have never been able to jab it suddenly in my hip muscle, as the doctor told me to. Instead, after swabbing a small patch of my rump down with rubbing alcohol, I push the needle in slowly until all three inches of it are submerged. Then I squeeze the liquid in carefully, as the muscle often spasms to absorb it. My skin sticks a little to the syringe as I pull it out, and then an odd mix of oil and blackish blood usually trickles down my hip.

I am so used to it now that the novelty has worn off. But every now and again the weirdness returns. The chemical I am putting in myself is synthetic testosterone: a substance that has become such a metaphor for manhood that it is almost possible to forget that it has a physical reality. Twenty years ago, as it surged through my pubescent body, it deepened my voice, grew hair on my face and chest, strengthened my limbs, made me a man. So what, I wonder, is it doing to me now?

There are few things more challenging to the question of what the difference between men and women really is than to see the difference injected into your hip. Men and women differ biologically mainly because men produce 10 to 20 times as much testosterone as most women do, and this chemical, no one seriously disputes, profoundly affects physique, behavior, mood and self-understanding. To be sure, because human beings are also deeply socialized, the impact of this difference is refracted through the prism of our own history and culture. But biology, it is all too easy to forget, is at the root of this process. As more people use testosterone medically, as more use testosterone-based steroids in sports and recreation and as more research explores the behavioral effects of this chemical, the clearer the power of that biology is. It affects every aspect of our society, from high divorce rates and adolescent male violence to the exploding cults of bodybuilding and professional wrestling. It helps explain, perhaps better than any other single factor, why inequalities between men and women remain so frustratingly resilient in public and private life. This summer, when an easy-to-apply testosterone gel hits the market, and when more people experience the power of this chemical in their own bodies, its social importance, once merely implicit, may get even harder to ignore.

My own encounter with testosterone came about for a simple medical reason. I am H.I.V.-positive, and two years ago, after a period of extreme fatigue and weight loss, I had my testosterone levels checked. It turned out that my body was producing far less testosterone than it should have been at my age. No one quite knows why, but this is common among men with long-term H.I.V. The usual treatment is regular injection of artificial testosterone, which is when I experienced my first manhood supplement.

At that point I weighed around 165 pounds. I now weigh 185 pounds. My collar size went from a 15 to a 17 1/2 in a few months; my chest went from 40 to 44. My appetite in every sense of that word expanded beyond measure. Going from napping two hours a day, I now rarely sleep in the daytime and have enough energy for daily workouts and a hefty work schedule. I can squat more than 400 pounds. Depression, once a regular feature of my life, is now a distant memory. I feel better able to recover from life's curveballs, more persistent, more alive. These are the long-term effects. They are almost as striking as the short-term ones.

Because the testosterone is injected every two weeks, and it quickly leaves the bloodstream, I can actually feel its power on almost a daily basis. Within hours, and at most a day, I feel a deep surge of energy. It is less edgy than a double espresso, but just as powerful. My attention span shortens. In the two or three days after my shot, I find it harder to concentrate on writing and feel the need to exercise more. My wit is quicker, my mind faster, but my judgment is more impulsive. It is not unlike the kind of rush I get before talking in front of a large audience, or going on a first date, or getting on an airplane, but it suffuses me in a less abrupt and more consistent way. In a word, I feel braced. For what? It scarcely seems to matter.

And then after a few days, as the testosterone peaks and starts to decline, the feeling alters a little. I find myself less reserved than usual, and more garrulous. The same energy is there, but it seems less directed toward action than toward interaction, less toward pride than toward lust. The odd thing is that, however much experience I have with it, this lust peak still takes me unawares. It is not like feeling hungry, a feeling you recognize and satiate. It creeps up on you. It is only a few days later that I look back and realize that I spent hours of the recent past socializing in a bar or checking out every potential date who came vaguely over my horizon. You realize more acutely than before that lust is a chemical. It comes; it goes. It waxes; it wanes. You are not helpless in front of it, but you are certainly not fully in control.

Then there's anger. I have always tended to bury or redirect my rage. I once thought this an inescapable part of my personality. It turns out I was wrong. Late last year, mere hours after a T shot, my dog ran off the leash to forage for a chicken bone left in my local park. The more I chased her, the more she ran. By the time I retrieved her, the bone had been consumed, and I gave her a sharp tap on her rear end. "Don't smack your dog!" yelled a burly guy a few yards away. What I found myself yelling back at him is not printable in this magazine, but I have never used that language in public before, let alone bellow it at the top of my voice. He shouted back, and within seconds I was actually close to hitting him. He backed down and slunk off. I strutted home, chest puffed up, contrite beagle dragged sheepishly behind me. It wasn't until half an hour later that I realized I had been a complete jerk and had nearly gotten into the first public brawl of my life. I vowed to inject my testosterone at night in the future.

That was an extreme example, but other, milder ones come to mind: losing my temper in a petty argument; innumerable traffic confrontations; even the occasional slightly too prickly column or e-mail flame-out. No doubt my previous awareness of the mythology of testosterone had subtly primed me for these feelings of irritation and impatience. But when I place them in the larger context of my new testosterone-associated energy, and of what we know about what testosterone tends to do to people, then it seems plausible enough to ascribe some of this increased edginess and self-confidence to that biweekly encounter with a syringe full of manhood.

* * *

Testosterone, oddly enough, is a chemical closely related to cholesterol. It was first isolated by a Dutch scientist in 1935 from mice testicles and successfully synthesized by the German biologist Adolf Butenandt. Although testosterone is often thought of as the definition of maleness, both men and women produce it. Men produce it in their testicles; women produce it in their ovaries and adrenal glands. The male body converts some testosterone to estradiol, a female hormone, and the female body has receptors for testosterone, just as the male body does. That's why women who want to change their sex are injected with testosterone and develop male characteristics, like deeper voices, facial hair and even baldness. The central biological difference between adult men and women, then, is not that men have testosterone and women don't. It's that men produce much, much more of it than women do. An average woman has 40 to 60 nanograms of testosterone in a deciliter of blood plasma. An average man has 300 to 1,000 nanograms per deciliter.

Testosterone's effects start early—really early. At conception, every embryo is female and unless hormonally altered will remain so. You need testosterone to turn a fetus with a Y chromosome into a real boy, to masculinize his brain and body. Men experience a flood of testosterone twice in their lives: in the womb about six weeks after conception and at puberty. The first fetal burst primes the brain and the body, endowing male fetuses with the instinctual knowledge of how to respond to later testosterone surges. The second, more familiar adolescent rush—squeaky voices, facial hair and all—completes the process. Without testosterone, humans would always revert to the default sex, which is female. The Book of Genesis is therefore exactly wrong. It isn't women who are made out of men. It is men who are made out of women. Testosterone, to stretch the metaphor, is Eve's rib.

The effect of testosterone is systemic. It engenders both the brain and the body. Apart from the obvious genital distinction, other differences between men's and women's bodies reflect this: body hair, the ratio of muscle to fat, upper-body strength and so on. But testosterone leads to behavioral differences as well. Since it is unethical to experiment with human embryos by altering hormonal balances, much of the evidence for this idea is based on research conducted on animals. A Stanford research group, for example, as reported in Deborah Blum's book *Sex on the Brain*, injected newborn female rats with testosterone. Not only did the female rats develop penises from their clitorises, but they also appeared fully aware of how to use them, trying to have sex with other females with merry abandon. Male rats who had their testosterone blocked after birth, on the other hand, saw their penises wither or disappear entirely and presented themselves to the female rats in a passive, receptive way. Other scientists, theorizing that it was testosterone that enabled male zebra finches to sing, injected mute female finches with testosterone. Sure enough, the females sang. Species in which the female is typically more aggressive, like hyenas in female-run clans, show higher levels of testosterone among the females than among the males. Female sea snipes, which impregnate the males, and leave them to stay home and rear the young, have higher testosterone levels than their mates. Typical "male" behavior, in other words, corresponds to testosterone levels, whether exhibited by chromosomal males or females.

Does this apply to humans? The evidence certainly suggests that it does, though much of the "proof" is inferred from accidents. Pregnant women who were injected with progesterone (chemically similar to testosterone) in the 1950's to avoid miscarriage had daughters who later reported markedly tomboyish childhoods. Ditto girls born with a disorder that causes their adrenal glands to produce a hormone like testosterone rather than the more common cortisol. The moving story, chronicled in John Colapinto's book *As Nature Made Him,* of David Reimer, who as an infant was surgically altered after a botched circumcision to become a girl, suggests how long-lasting the effect of fetal testosterone can be. Despite a ruthless attempt to socialize David as a girl, and to give him the correct hormonal treatment to develop as one, his behavioral and psychological makeup was still ineradicably male. Eventually, with the help of more testosterone, he became a full man again. Female-to-male transsexuals report a similar transformation when injected with testosterone. One, Susan/Drew Seidman, described her experience in *The Village Voice* last November. "My sex-drive went through the roof," Seidman recalled. "I felt like I had to have sex once a day or I would die. . . . I was into porn as a girl, but now I'm really into porn." For Seidman, becoming a man was not merely physical. Thanks to testosterone, it was also psychological. "I'm not sure I can tell you what makes a man a man," Seidman averred. "But I know it's not a penis."

The behavioral traits associated with testosterone are largely the cliché-ridden ones you might expect. The Big T correlates with energy, self-confidence, competitiveness, tenacity, strength and sexual drive. When you talk to men in testosterone therapy, several themes recur. "People talk about extremes," one man in his late 30's told me. "But that's not what testosterone does for me. It makes me think more clearly. It makes me think more positively. It's my Saint Johnswort." A man in his 20's said: "Usually, I cycle up the hill to my apartment in 12th gear. In the days after my shot, I ride it easily in 16th." A 40-year-old executive who took testosterone for bodybuilding purposes told me: "I walk into a business meeting now and I just exude self-confidence. I know there are lots of other reasons for this, but my company has just exploded since my treatment. I'm on a roll. I feel capable of almost anything."

When you hear comments like these, it's no big surprise that strutting peacocks with their extravagant tails and bright colors are supercharged with testosterone and that mousy little male sparrows aren't. "It turned my life around," another man said. "I felt stronger—and not just in a physical sense. It was a deep sense of being strong, almost spiritually strong." Testosterone's antidepressive power is only marginally understood. It doesn't act in the precise way other antidepressants do, and it probably helps alleviate gloominess primarily by propelling people into greater activity and restlessness, giving them less time to think and reflect. (This may be one reason women tend to suffer more from depression than men.) Like other drugs, T can also lose potency if overused. Men who inject excessive amounts may see their own production collapse and experience shrinkage of their testicles and liver damage.

Individual effects obviously vary, and a person's internal makeup is affected by countless other factors—physical, psychological and external. But in this complex human engine, testosterone is gasoline. It revs you up. A 1997 study took testosterone samples from 125 men and 128 women and selected the 12 with the lowest levels of testosterone and the 15 with the highest. They gave them beepers, asked them to keep diaries and paged them 20 times over a four-day period to check on their actions, feelings, thoughts and whereabouts. The differences were striking. High-testosterone people "experienced more arousal and tension than those low in testosterone," according to the study. "They spent more time thinking, especially about concrete problems in the immediate present. They wanted to get things done and felt frustrated when they could not. They mentioned friends more than family or lovers."

Unlike Popeye's spinach, however, testosterone is also, in humans at least, a relatively subtle agent. It is not some kind of on-off switch by which men are constantly turned on and women off. For one thing, we all start out with different base-line levels. Some women may have remarkably high genetic T levels, some men remarkably low, although the male-female differential is so great that no single woman's T level can exceed any single man's, unless she, or he, has some kind of significant hormonal imbalance. For another, and this is where the social and political ramifications get complicated, testosterone is highly susceptible to environment. T levels can rise and fall depending on external circumstances—short term and long term. Testosterone is usually elevated in response to confrontational situations—a street fight, a marital spat, a presidential debate—or in highly charged sexual environments, like a strip bar or a pornographic website. It can also be raised permanently in continuously combative environments, like war, although it can also be suddenly lowered by stress.

Because testosterone levels can be measured in saliva as well as in blood, researchers like Alan Booth, Allan Mazur, Richard Udry and particularly James M. Dabbs, whose book *Heroes, Rogues and Lovers* will be out this fall, have compiled quite a database on these variations. A certain amount of caution is advisable in interpreting the results of these studies. There is some doubt about the validity of onetime samples to gauge underlying testosterone levels. And most of the studies of the psychological effects of testosterone take place in culturally saturated environments, so that the difference between cause and effect is often extremely hard to disentangle. Nevertheless, the sheer number and scale of the studies, especially in the last decade or so, and the strong behavioral correlations with high testosterone, suggest some conclusions about the social importance of testosterone that are increasingly hard to gainsay.

* * *

Testosterone is clearly correlated in both men and women with psychological dominance, confident physicality and high self-esteem. In most combative, competitive environments, especially physical ones, the person with the most T wins. Put any two men in a room together and the one with more testosterone will tend to dominate the interaction. Working women have higher levels of testosterone than women who stay at home, and the daughters of working women have higher levels of testosterone than the daughters of housewives. A 1996 study found that in lesbian couples in which one partner assumes the male, or "butch," role and another assumes the female, or "femme," role, the "butch" woman has higher levels of testosterone than the "femme" woman. In naval medical tests, midshipmen have been shown to have higher average levels of testosterone than plebes. Actors tend to have more testosterone than ministers, according to a 1990 study. Among 700 male prison inmates in a 1995 study, those with the highest T levels tended to be those most likely to be in trouble with the prison authorities and to engage in unprovoked violence. This is true among women as well as among men, according to a 1997 study of 87 female inmates in a maximum security prison. Although high testosterone levels often correlate with dominance in interpersonal relationships, it does not guarantee more social power. Testosterone levels are higher among blue-collar workers, for example, than among white-collar workers, according to a study of more than 4,000 former military personnel conducted in 1992. A 1998 study found that trial lawyers—with their habituation to combat, conflict and swagger—have higher levels of T than other lawyers.

The salient question, of course, is, How much of this difference in aggression and dominance is related to environment? Are trial lawyers naturally more testosteroned, and does that lead them into their profession? Or does the experience of the courtroom raise their levels? Do working women have naturally higher T levels, or does the prestige of work and power elevate their testosterone? Because of the limits of researching such a question, it is hard to tell beyond a reasonable doubt. But the social context clearly matters. It is even possible to tell who has won a tennis match not by watching the game, but by monitoring testosterone-filled saliva samples throughout. Testosterone levels rise for both players before the match. The winner of any single game sees his T production rise; the loser sees it fall. The ultimate winner experiences a postgame testosterone surge, while the loser sees a collapse. This is true even for people watching sports matches. A 1998 study found that fans backing the winning side in a college basketball game and a World Cup soccer match saw their testosterone levels rise; fans rooting for the losing teams in both games saw their own T levels fall. There is, it seems, such a thing as vicarious testosterone.

One theory to explain this sensitivity to environment is that testosterone was originally favored in human evolution to enable successful hunting and combat. It kicks in, like adrenaline, in anticipation of combat, mental or physical, and helps you prevail. But a testosterone crash can be a killer too. Toward the end of my two-week cycle, I can almost feel my spirits dragging. In the event of a just-lost battle, as Matt Ridley points out in his book *The Red Queen,* there's a good reason for this to occur. If you lose a contest with prey or a rival, it makes sense not to pick another fight immediately. So your body wisely prompts you to withdraw, filling your brain with depression and self-doubt. But if you have made a successful kill or defeated a treacherous enemy, your hormones goad you into further conquest. And people wonder why professional football players get into postgame sexual escapades and violence. Or why successful businessmen and politicians often push their sexual luck.

Similarly, testosterone levels may respond to more long-term stimuli. Studies have shown that inner-city youths, often exposed to danger in high-crime neighborhoods, may generate higher testosterone levels than unthreatened, secluded suburbanites. And so high T levels may not merely be responses to a violent environment; they may subsequently add to it in what becomes an increasingly violent, sexualized cycle. (It may be no accident that testosterone-soaked ghettos foster both high levels of crime and high levels of illegitimacy.) In the same way, declines in violence and crime may allow T levels to drop among young inner-city males, generating a virtuous trend of further reductions in crime and birth rates. This may help to explain why crime can decline precipitously, rather than drift down slowly, over time. Studies have also shown that men in long-term marriages see their testosterone levels progressively fall and their sex drives subsequently decline. It is as if their wives successfully tame them, reducing their sexual energy to a level where it is more unlikely to seek extramarital outlets. A 1993 study showed that single men tended to have higher levels of testosterone than married men and that men with high levels of testosterone turned out to be more likely to have had a failed marriage. Of course, if you start out with higher T levels, you may be more likely to fail at marriage, stay in the sexual marketplace, see your testosterone increase in response to this and so on.

None of this means, as the scientists always caution, that testosterone is directly linked to romantic failure or violence. No study has found a simple correlation, for example, between testosterone levels and crime. But there may be a complex correlation. The male-prisoner study, for example, found no general above-normal testosterone levels among inmates. But murderers and armed robbers had higher testosterone levels than mere car thieves and burglars. Why is this not surprising? One of the most remarkable, but least commented on, social statistics available is the sex differential in crime. For decades, arrest rates have shown that an overwhelmingly disproportionate number of arrestees are male. Although the sex differential has narrowed since the chivalrous 1930's, when the male-female arrest ratio was 12 to 1, it remains almost 4 to 1, a close echo of the testosterone differential between men and women. In violent crime, men make up an even bigger proportion. In 1998, 89 percent of murders in the United States, for example, were committed by men. Of course, there's a nature-nurture issue here as well, and the fact that the sex differential in crime has decreased over this century suggests that environment has played a part. Yet despite the enormous social changes of the last century, the differential is still 4 to 1, which suggests that underlying attributes may also have a great deal to do with it.

This, then, is what it comes down to: testosterone is a facilitator of risk—physical, criminal, personal. Without the influence of testosterone, the cost of these risks might seem to far outweigh the benefits. But with testosterone charging through the brain, caution is thrown to the wind. The influence of testosterone may not always lead to raw physical confrontation. In men with many options it may influence the decision to invest money in a dubious enterprise, jump into an ill-advised sexual affair or tell an egregiously big whopper. At the time, all these decisions may make some sort of testosteroned sense. The White House, anyone?

*   *   *

The effects of testosterone are not secret; neither is the fact that men have far more of it than women. But why? As we have seen, testosterone is not synonymous with gender;

in some species, it is the female who has most of it. The relatively new science of evolutionary psychology offers perhaps the best explanation for why that's not the case in humans. For neo-Darwinians, the aggressive and sexual aspects of testosterone are related to the division of labor among hunter-gatherers in our ancient but formative evolutionary past. This division—men in general hunted, women in general gathered—favored differing levels of testosterone. Women need some testosterone—for self-defense, occasional risk-taking, strength—but not as much as men. Men use it to increase their potential to defeat rivals, respond to physical threats in strange environments, maximize their physical attractiveness, prompt them to spread their genes as widely as possible and defend their home if necessary.

But the picture, as most good evolutionary psychologists point out, is more complex than this. Men who are excessively testosteroned are not that attractive to most women. Although they have the genes that turn women on—strong jaws and pronounced cheekbones, for example, are correlated with high testosterone—they can also be precisely the unstable, highly sexed creatures that childbearing, stability-seeking women want to avoid. There are two ways, evolutionary psychologists hazard, that women have successfully squared this particular circle. One is to marry the sweet class nerd and have an affair with the college quarterback: that way you get the good genes, the good sex and the stable home. The other is to find a man with variable T levels, who can be both stable and nurturing when you want him to be and yet become a muscle-bound, bristly gladiator when the need arises. The latter strategy, as Emma Bovary realized, is sadly more easily said than done.

So over millennia, men with high but variable levels of testosterone were the ones most favored by women and therefore most likely to produce offspring, and eventually us. Most men today are highly testosteroned, but not rigidly so. We don't have to live at all times with the T levels required to face down a woolly mammoth or bed half the village's young women. We can adjust so that our testosterone levels make us more suitable for co-parenting or for simply sticking around our mates when the sexual spark has dimmed. Indeed, one researcher, John Wingfield, has found a suggestive correlation in bird species between adjustable testosterone levels and males that have an active role to play in rearing their young. Male birds with consistently high testosterone levels tend to be worse fathers; males with variable levels are better dads. So there's hope for the new man yet.

From the point of view of men, after all, constantly high testosterone is a real problem, as any 15-year-old boy trying to concentrate on his homework will tell you. I missed one deadline on this article because it came three days after a testosterone shot and I couldn't bring myself to sit still long enough. And from a purely genetic point of view, men don't merely have an interest in impregnating as many women as possible; they also have an interest in seeing that their offspring are brought up successfully and their genes perpetuated. So for the male, the conflict between sex and love is resolved, as it is for the female, by a compromise between the short-term thrill of promiscuity and the long-term rewards of nurturing children. Just as the female does, he optimizes his genetic outcome by a stable marriage and occasional extramarital affairs. He is just more likely to have these affairs than a woman. Testosterone is both cause and effect of this difference.

And the difference is a real one. This is so obvious a point that we sometimes miss it. But without that difference, it would be hard to justify separate sports leagues for men and women, just as it would be hard not to suspect judicial bias behind the fact that of the 98 people executed last year in the United States, 100 percent came from a group that composes a little less than 50 percent of the population; that is, men. When the discrepancy is racial, we wring our hands. That it is sexual raises no red flags. Similarly, it is not surprising that 55 percent of everyone arrested in 1998 was under the age of 25— the years when male testosterone levels are at their natural peak.

It is also controversial yet undeniable that elevating testosterone levels can be extremely beneficial for physical and mental performance. It depends, of course, on what you're performing in. If your job is to whack home runs, capture criminals or play the market, then testosterone is a huge advantage. If you're a professional conciliator, office manager or teacher, it is probably a handicap. Major League Baseball was embarrassed that Mark McGwire's 1998 season home-run record might have been influenced by his use of androstenedione, a legal supplement that helps increase the body's own production of testosterone. But its own study into andro's effects concluded that regular use of it clearly raises T levels and so improves muscle mass and physical strength, without serious side effects. Testosterone also accelerates the rate of recovery from physical injury. Does this help make sense of McGwire's achievement? More testosterone obviously didn't give him the skill to hit 70 home runs, but it almost certainly contributed to the physical and mental endurance that helped him do so.

Since most men have at least 10 times as much T as most women, it therefore makes sense not to have coed baseball leagues. Equally, it makes sense that women will be underrepresented in a high-testosterone environment like military combat or construction. When the skills required are more cerebral or more endurance-related, the male-female gap may shrink, or even reverse itself. But otherwise, gender inequality in these fields is primarily not a function of sexism, merely of common sense. This is a highly controversial position, but it really shouldn't be. Even more unsettling is the racial gap in testosterone. Several solid studies, published in publications like *Journal of the National Cancer Institute,* show that black men have on average 3 to 19 percent more testosterone than white men. This is something to consider when we're told that black men dominate certain sports because of white racism or economic class rather than black skill. This reality may, of course, feed stereotypes about blacks being physical but not intellectual. But there's no evidence of any trade-off between the two. To say that someone is physically gifted is to say nothing about his mental abilities, as even N.F.L. die-hards have come to realize. Indeed, as Jon Entine points out in his new book, *Taboo,* even the position of quarterback, which requires a deft mix of mental and physical strength and was once predominantly white, has slowly become less white as talent has been rewarded. The percentage of blacks among N.F.L. quarterbacks is now twice the percentage of blacks in the population as a whole.

* * *

But fears of natural difference still haunt the debate about gender equality. Many feminists have made tenacious arguments about the lack of any substantive physical or mental differences between men and women as if the political equality of the sexes depended on it. But to rest the equality of women on the physical and psychological equivalence of the sexes is to rest it on sand. In the end, testosterone bites. This year, for example, Toys "R" Us announced it was planning to redesign its toy stores to group products most likely to be bought by the same types of consumers: in marketing jargon, "logical adjacencies." The results? Almost total gender separation. "Girl's World" would feature Easy-Bake Ovens and Barbies; "Boy's World," trucks and action figures. Though Toys "R" Us denied that there was any agenda behind this—its market research showed that gender differences start as young as 2 years old—such a public out-cry ensued that the store canceled its plans. Meanwhile, Fox Family Channels is about to introduce two new, separate cable channels for boys and girls, boyzChannel and girlzChannel, to attract advertisers and consumers more efficiently. Fox executives told *The Wall Street Journal* that their move is simply a reflection of what Nielsen-related research tells them about the viewing habits of boys and girls: that, "in general terms, girls are more interested in entertainment that is relationship-oriented," while boys are "more action-oriented." T anyone? After more than two decades of relentless legal, cultural and ideological attempts to negate sexual difference between boys and girls, the market has turned around and shown that very little, after all, has changed.

Advocates of a purely environmental origin for this difference between the sexes counter that gender socialization begins very early and is picked up by subtle inferences from parental interaction and peer pressure, before being reinforced by the collective culture at large. Most parents observing toddlers choosing their own toys and play patterns can best judge for themselves how true this is. But as Matt Ridley has pointed out, there is also physiological evidence of very early mental differences between the sexes, most of it to the advantage of girls. Ninety-five percent of all hyperactive kids are boys; four times as many boys are dyslexic and learning-disabled as girls. There is a greater distinction between the right and left brain among boys than girls, and worse linguistic skills. In general, boys are better at spatial and abstract tasks, girls at communication. These are generalizations, of course. There are many, many boys who are great linguists and model students, and vice versa. Some boys even prefer, when left to their own devices, to play with dolls as well as trucks. But we are talking of generalities here, and the influence of womb-given testosterone on those generalities is undeniable.

Some of that influence is a handicap. We are so used to associating testosterone with strength, masculinity and patriarchal violence that it is easy to ignore that it also makes men weaker in some respects than women. It doesn't correlate with economic power: in fact, as we have seen, blue-collar workers have more of it than white-collar workers. It gets men into trouble. For reasons no one seems to understand, testosterone may also be an immune suppressant. High levels of it can correspond, as recent studies have shown, not only with baldness but also with heart disease and a greater susceptibility to infectious diseases. Higher levels of prostate cancer among blacks, some researchers believe, may well be related to blacks' higher testosterone levels. The aggression it can foster and the risks it encourages lead men into situations that often wound or kill them. And higher levels of testosterone-driven promiscuity make men more prone to sexually transmitted diseases. This is one reason that men live shorter lives on average than women. There is something, in other words, tragic about testosterone. It can lead to a certain kind of male glory; it may lead to valor or boldness or impulsive romanticism. But it also presages a uniquely male kind of doom. The cockerel with the brightest comb is often the most attractive and the most testosteroned, but it is also the most vulnerable to parasites. It is as if it has sacrificed quantity of life for intensity of experience, and this trade-off is a deeply male one.

So it is perhaps unsurprising that those professions in which this trade-off is most pronounced—the military, contact sports, hazardous exploration, venture capitalism, politics, gambling—tend to be disproportionately male. Politics is undoubtedly the most controversial because it is such a critical arena for the dispersal of power. But consider for a moment how politics is conducted in our society. It is saturated with combat, ego, conflict and risk. An entire career can be lost in a single gaffe or an unexpected shift in the national mood. This ego-driven roulette is almost as highly biased toward the testosteroned as wrestling. So it makes some sense that after almost a century of electorates made up by as many women as men, the number of female politicians remains pathetically small in most Western democracies. This may not be endemic to politics; it may have more to do with the way our culture constructs politics. And it is not to say that women are not good at government. Those qualities associated with low testosterone—patience, risk aversion, empathy—can all lead to excellent governance. They are just lousy qualities in the crapshoot of electoral politics.

*   *   *

If you care about sexual equality, this is obviously a challenge, but it need not be as depressing as it sounds. The sports world offers one way out. Men and women do not compete directly against one another; they have separate tournaments and leagues. Their different styles of physical excellence can be appreciated in different ways. At some basic level, of course, men will always be better than women in many of these contests. Men run faster and throw harder. Women could compensate for this by injecting testosterone, but if they took enough to be truly competitive, they would become men, which would somewhat defeat the purpose.

The harder cases are in those areas in which physical strength is important but not always crucial, like military combat or manual labor. And here the compromise is more likely to be access but inequality in numbers. Finance? Business? Here, where the testosterone-driven differences may well be more subtly psychological, and where men may dominate by discrimination rather than merit, is the trickiest arena. Testosterone-induced impatience may lead to poor decision-making, but low-testosterone risk aversion may lead to an inability to seize business opportunities. Perhaps it is safest to say that unequal numbers of men and women in these spheres is not prima facie evidence of sexism. We should do everything we can to ensure equal access, but it is foolish to insist that numerical inequality is always a function of bias rather than biology. This doesn't mean we shouldn't worry about individual cases of injustice; just that we shouldn't be shocked if gender inequality endures. And we should recognize that affirmative action for women (and men) in all arenas is an inherently utopian project.

Then there is the medical option. A modest solution might be to give more women access to testosterone to improve their sex drives, aggression and risk affinity and to help redress their disadvantages in those areas as compared with men. This is already done for severely depressed women, or women with hormonal imbalances, or those lacking an adequate sex drive, especially after menopause. Why not for women who simply want to rev up their will to power? Its use needs to be carefully monitored because it can also lead to side effects, like greater susceptibility to cancer, but that's what doctors are there for. And since older men also suffer a slow drop-off in T levels, there's no reason they should be cold-shouldered either. If the natural disadvantages of gender should be countered, why not the natural disadvantages of age? In some ways, this is already happening. Among the most common drugs now available through Internet doctors and pharmacies, along with Viagra and Prozac, is testosterone. This summer, with the arrival of AndroGel, the testosterone gel created as a medical treatment for those four to five million men who suffer from low levels of testosterone, recreational demand may soar.

Or try this thought experiment: what if parents committed to gender equity opted to counteract the effect of testosterone on boys in the womb by complementing it with injections of artificial female hormones? That way, structural gender difference could be eradicated from the beginning. Such a policy would lead to "men and women with normal bodies but identical feminine brains," Matt Ridley posits. "War, rape, boxing, car racing, pornography and hamburgers and beer would soon be distant memories. A feminist paradise would have arrived." Today's conservative cultural critics might also be enraptured. Promiscuity would doubtless decline, fatherhood improve, crime drop, virtue spread. Even gay men might start behaving like lesbians, fleeing the gym and marrying for life. This is a fantasy, of course, but our increasing control and understanding of the scientific origins of our behavior, even of our culture, is fast making those fantasies things we will have to actively choose to forgo.

But fantasies also tell us something. After a feminist century, we may be in need of a new understanding of masculinity. The concepts of manliness, of gentlemanly behavior, of chivalry have been debunked. The New Age bonding of the men's movement has been outlived. What our increasing knowledge of testosterone suggests is a core understanding of what it is to be a man, for better and worse. It is about the ability to risk for good and bad; to act, to strut, to dare, to seize. It is about a kind of energy we often rue but would surely miss. It is about the foolishness that can lead to courage or destruction, the beauty that can be strength or vanity. To imagine a world without it is to see more clearly how our world is inseparable from it and how our current political pieties are too easily threatened by its reality.

And as our economy becomes less physical and more cerebral, as women slowly supplant men in many industries, as income inequalities grow and more highly testosteroned blue-collar men find themselves shunted to one side, we will have to find new ways of channeling what nature has bequeathed us. I don't think it's an accident that in the last decade there has been a growing focus on a muscular male physique in our popular culture, a boom in crass men's magazines, an explosion in violent computer games or a professional wrestler who has become governor. These are indications of a cultural displacement, of a world in which the power of testosterone is ignored or attacked, with the result that it re-emerges in cruder and less social forms. Our main task in the gender wars of the new century may not be how to bring women fully into our society, but how to keep men from seceding from it, how to reroute testosterone for constructive ends, rather than ignore it for political point-making.

For my part, I'll keep injecting the Big T. Apart from how great it makes me feel, I consider it no insult to anyone else's gender to celebrate the uniqueness of one's own. Diversity need not mean the equalization of difference. In fact, true diversity requires the acceptance of difference. A world without the unruly, vulnerable, pioneering force of testosterone would be a fairer and calmer, but far grayer and duller, place. It is certainly somewhere I would never want to live. Perhaps the fact that I write this two days after the injection of another 200 milligrams of testosterone into my bloodstream makes me more likely to settle for this colorful trade-off than others. But it seems to me no disrespect to womanhood to say that I am perfectly happy to be a man, to feel things no woman will ever feel to the degree that I feel them, to experience the world in a way no woman ever has. And to do so without apology or shame.

Reading Comprehension—Points of Engagement

1. Identify two ethical issues Sullivan raises regarding his testosterone injections. Using these two issues, both likely controversial, create one list of the advantages of using hormone supplements, and one list of the disadvantages. Which of these lists is more compelling to you? Has Sullivan succeeded in making his point? What *is* his point in your opinion?

2. How is social environment a factor when examining testosterone levels? What does Andrew Sullivan say about social pressure to conform or achieve? Does he manage to separate his own use of hormone supplements from his academic discussion of biology and gender? If so, how does he justify it? If not, do his personal examples strengthen his position? Why?

3. What assumptions does Sullivan make about men and women that weaken or contradict his own argument? Point to specific passages in his essay that support your answer. Does he see the treatment of race differently from the treatment of gender? If so, how?

Assignment Questions—Points of Departure

1. Focus on exactly how Sullivan suggests we should "channel what nature" has given us in light of Lauren Slater's musings on what is "natural" in "Dr. Daedalus." First, locate Sullivan's position on testosterone injections and consider how this would fit into Dr. Rosen's belief in letting people explore the possibilities of bodily self-transformation. Consider also, Slater's ambivalence about Rosen's project. How is altering the natural body—through plastic surgery or hormone injections—both "utterly necessary and ridiculously frivolous" (317)? What are the moral consequences of these kinds of alterations? Are plastic surgery and testosterone injections equivalent in a moral sense, or is one more justified than the other? Support your own position in response to these questions by engaging with both authors, and be sure to distinguish in your paper between Slater's position and Dr. Rosen's position.

2. In rendering one of Darwin's main tenets in "A Fist in the Eye of God," Barbara Kingsolver concludes, "In each generation the survivors succeed—that is, they survive—because they possess some advantage over the ones that don't succeed" (204). How does this statement affect what Sullivan has to say about evolutionary psychologists? What is the impact of social Darwinism on what Sullivan calls an "economy becom[ing] less physical and more cerebral" (347)?

3. How would Katha Pollitt respond to Sullivan's view of masculinity? Would Sullivan more likely side with difference feminists or equality feminists? How would the various difference feminists in Pollitt's essay consider Sullivan's argument? How would equality feminists treat his essay? Does he feel that one gender is morally superior in the sense that Pollitt discusses? How do you know? Do you agree with him? Your project is to engage with the views in both texts, and to provide answers of your own to these questions in light of those views.

Hate Your Policies, Love Your Institutions
John Waterbury

Points of Access

1. Think about the education you've received so far in your life. What kind of *educational system* have you been schooled in? Private? Public? Religious? Non-religious? Expensive? Free? Strict? Liberal? Write down everything you can about the system (or systems) in which you have been educated. Then write down how you think these educational systems have affected you, how they have shaped your opinion about education itself, and how they have influenced the ways you think about the world around you.

2. Have you ever attended a religious school? If so, where and at what grade levels? In the United States or abroad? If not, what kind of school did you attend? Do you think religion should be taught in schools? If yes, under what circumstances? If no, why not? How has your own educational experience shaped your answers to these questions?

3. What does being in college mean to you? How much of it is about getting the degree, and how much of it is about acquiring knowledge? Think about this: does it matter what you study? Or is it more important to be able to say you graduated and have a Bachelor's degree? What do you plan to do with your undergraduate degree? What do you think it will get you? What won't it get you? Finally, do you think your responses would be the same if you were not at an American college or university? Why or why not?

"Why Do They Hate Us?"

Two groups have come under examination in the "why do they hate us?" debate that has unfolded since September 11, 2001. One comprises the perpetrators of violence and terrorism—the Osama bin Ladens, the Mohammad Attas, and some suicide bombers. They are fanatics in every sense of the word. Their interpretations of politics and Islam are so extreme that they disparage the great majority of Muslim Middle Easterners as "unbelievers." They are not going to be deterred by debate, compromise, sanctions, or even the threat of death. The challenge they pose to the United States is a security issue, a matter to be dealt with through careful police work and military action. America's resources are adequate for dealing with this threat.

The vastly larger group of Muslim Middle Easterners who express anger toward the United States and evince some sympathy for bin Laden pose a far more serious challenge. This group's members are afflicted by middle-class frustrations, governed by political systems that give them no voice, and burdened by economies that offer them few opportunities. They are witnessing a conflict over land and sacred places in which they perceive the United States as applying two standards of equity and two standards of measuring violence, each in favor of Israel. That resulting frustration and anger leads to expressions of sympathy for those who resort to violence against the United States.

A Gallup poll last year asked nearly 10,000 respondents in nine predominantly Muslim countries whether they had a favorable or an unfavorable opinion of the United States. The range of unfavorable views ran from a low of 33 percent in Turkey to a high of 68 percent in Pakistan. The poll also found that respondents overwhelmingly described the United States as "ruthless, aggressive, conceited, arrogant, easily provoked, biased." But such opinions tend to be not so much about the American people or their institutions as they are about the U.S. government and its actions. For example, an even more recent poll in Lebanon showed that half of all respondents "like or love" the American people, whereas 81 percent oppose its government. In particular, there is high respect in the Middle East for U.S. institutions of higher learning, a number of which have been successfully transplanted to the region. These U.S. institutions have produced Middle Eastern leaders with whom Americans can hammer out the issues in terms and language they mutually understand and respect.

Double Standards

The conflict of interests between the United States and the Muslim Middle East is old. The antecedents of the current crisis go back at least to World War II, and the Palestinians and Israelis have been at its heart. Religion may sometimes provide its rhetoric and emotional underpinning, but it is nonetheless a conflict over real estate. The Muslim Middle East is not uniformly engaged in this question, but no part of the region is indifferent to it. Those who so vehemently deny any linkage between the Israeli-Palestinian conflict and the broader crisis must pull their heads out of the sand.

After September 11, a spate of analysis claimed that what was at stake was some sort of deep-seated hatred of America's democratic institutions, its free economy, and its wealth. That is a more comforting explanation of Muslim rage than the notion that the United States has violated its own norms, elevated conflicts of interest to crusades against evil, and dismissed entire peoples as hopelessly corrupt, violent, and mired in medieval cant.

Of course, there is a difference between the leaders of the Muslim Middle East and their peoples. With few exceptions, the leaders do not welcome democracy in any form—and the United States has in most instances endorsed authoritarianism. General Pervez Musharraf's specious popular approval by referendum in Pakistan and a similar fiasco in Tunisia are but the most recent episodes. It would seem that Washington believes that Pakistanis and Tunisians would not welcome free and fair elections.

Some American observers tried to boil the question down to the statement "They hate us for our wealth." Well, the United States is rich, but "they" also question the distribution of wealth in their own societies, not merely in ours. Muslims believe that wealth honestly acquired is good in the eyes of God so long as wealthy Muslims share their wealth with the poor. Similarly, the charge that "They hate us for our free enterprise" does not stick, either. In many parts of the Muslim Middle East, as in Europe, there is great ambivalence about open markets and unfettered enterprise. Few espouse socialism, and in many ways Islam endorses a minimalist state. But the concern for social welfare and safety nets has sustained a badly bruised faith in the state that many Americans might find peculiar or naive.

Interests or Culture?

Today's crisis is not one of values, let alone civilizations, but one of interests. Western values, to the extent that they are held in common, are widely (albeit not universally) shared and admired in the Muslim Middle East. The same goes for Western institutions. The real problem is that the various sides in the crisis do not understand the "other's" interests or the "other's" politics. Hence they have not found a way to talk intelligibly and intelligently about the nature of their conflicting interests. The only good news is that it is easier to reconcile conflicts of interest than conflicts of values.

The United States now dominates the world militarily and economically. It is obviously not the first world power to do so. Such dominance usually comes about through some form of institutional superiority in the conduct of government, economic life, and military organization. The Romans, the Ottomans, and the British enjoyed institutional superiority over the peoples they subordinated. Arguably the Soviet Union did not, and its hegemony was relatively short-lived. Peoples who bear the brunt of dominant economic and military power have almost always resented, even hated, the subordination they experience while admiring grudgingly the institutions that sustain that subordination. The resentment and anger is all the greater when the dominant power dismisses the subordinate peoples as unworthy of its institutions, perhaps seeing those peoples as so culturally flawed that they could never sustain them on their own.

By contrast, America is admired for its transparent politics, independent judiciary, adherence to due process, encouragement of entrepreneurship, linking of rewards to performance, provision of economic opportunity, and rapid social mobility. Perhaps no single institutional feature of American dominance is more admired than its system of higher education. Even radical Islamists are not shy about sending their children to be educated in the United States. This extensive admiration of American institutions therefore presents an underexploited opportunity for dealing with the current crisis.

That said, any attempt to deal with the widespread rage against Washington in the Muslim Middle East will have to proceed on multiple fronts. It certainly requires a reexamination of some of Washington's policies toward the region, particularly its passive support of regimes that are becoming more, not less, authoritarian. It also requires an aggressive public relations program to explain those U.S. policies that have been misunderstood and to highlight the real opportunities for international collaboration. But just as important, it should include an effort to build on the esteem that American institutions possess in the region, which is perhaps the strongest weapon in Washington's "soft power" arsenal.

The Failure of Higher Education

The American institution that the Muslim Middle East has the greatest familiarity with and greatest respect for is the U.S. educational system. The university of which I am president has been in business since 1866. It has been joined over the years by others such as the American University of Cairo and Roberts College in Istanbul. These institutions had already had a significant impact on higher learning in the Middle East in the first half of the twentieth century, and the end of the Cold War witnessed an explosion of "American" institutions of learning in the region: high schools, institutes, colleges, and universities. When they can, they proudly bear the adjective "American"; they all advertise their "American" content.

This enthusiasm for "American" schools stands in stark contrast to the despair that hovers around alternative local systems of education. In the Middle East today, most institutions of higher education are overcrowded and underproductive. They are overwhelmed by the rapid growth of school-age populations and undermined by sluggish economic growth, which has led to a collapse of public finance, badly strained budgets, and steadily eroding educational standards. Slow growth has also meant that few jobs are created, while available jobs do not match the poor skills of the graduates of the educational system. Even in Lebanon, which enjoys a relatively flexible and market-responsive educational system, one-third of all engineers are currently unemployed (at least as engineers). The region as a whole has too many physicians and not enough nurses, too many civil engineers and not enough foremen, too many architects and not enough electricians. In many countries, the state has effectively become the employer of last resort, loading up the public bureaucracies with students who cannot find productive work.

In the last 25 years, university enrollment in the Middle East and North Africa (excluding Turkey and Iran) has trebled to around three million students. Three-quarters of these students have been in nonscientific and nontechnical fields. Most are enrolled in vast mills for the production of government employees. Unemployment rates for those between 15 and 25 years of age, the range in which most high school and university graduates are concentrated, are over 40 percent for the entire region. Disguised unemployment is considerably higher. For many years now there has been an inverse relationship between levels of education and employment rates—that is, the less education one has, the more likely one is to be employed.

There is good evidence that the impressive increases in enrollments have come at the price of declining standards. The great cut-off is still between secondary school and the university. Two-thirds to three-quarters of high school students either fail to graduate from high school or pass their high school exams at levels too low to earn them admission to the university. In Saudi Arabia, for example, 200,000 high school graduates fight for about 40,000 university places each year. Those left behind must compete against the many, and often highly skilled, foreign workers who make up 60 percent of the Saudi labor force. Official Saudi policy is to replace foreign workers with more Saudis. Whether young Saudis will have the stomach for the work carried out by Indians, Sri Lankans, Pakistanis, Filipinos, Palestinians, Yemenis, Sudanese, and Egyptians is not at all clear, but many other Middle Eastern countries do not even have a foreign work force to displace in favor of their own youth.

The Politics of Survival

There are exceptions to this trend, but they are very rare. In only one country did the educational system really deliver on its promise to become the tool for molding a new society and inculcating the values of equality, solidarity, and national identity. In Turkey, Mustafa Kemal AtatUrk's revolution after World War I used the educational system to embed firmly the values of secularism, republicanism, and Turkish nationalism—not only in his own generation, but in every generation since then. AtatUrk arguably had the greatest intergenerational impact of any revolutionary leader of the twentieth century, and the Turkish republic's schools were critical to his success.

Other Middle Eastern states tried to emulate this achievement by nationalizing private and religious schools and bringing the religious establishment under tight state control. Egypt's president, Gamal Abdel Nasser, absorbed the ancient and revered Islamic university al-Azhar into the state educational system, and other regimes followed suit. (Some exceptions were Saudi Arabia, Pakistan, Morocco, and post-1979 Iran, where the governing establishments identified themselves as Islamic.) In the mid-1970s, when fundamentalist Islam was allowed to take root in some provincial Egyptian universities, especially in Assiut, President Anwar Sadat saw these incursions as useful counterweights to the leftist remnants of the Nasserist era. Moreover, Saudi Arabia, flush with the earnings of the post-1973 oil boom, was in a position to buy influence with regional states in fiscal crisis and promote the House of Saud's religious values. The temptation to fight the ideological left with the religious right was strong everywhere—and endorsed by the United States. But fiscal crises and the waning of revolutionary ardour neutralized the capacity of the school systems to produce the right kind of students for the right jobs. This trend was part and parcel of the general failure of state-led growth. As the revolutionary transformation petered out, beleaguered rulers had to learn merely how to survive. These regimes' drive for ideological control eventually slacked off as their embrace of expediency grew tighter.

Thus as religious activism developed momentum, several leaders tried to co-opt new religious movements by borrowing and banalizing their rhetoric. More ominously, they tried to concede to these movements ever more control over educational institutions, from primary schools to universities. Leaders who had been unable to use the schools to produce new citizens thought it generally harmless to concede such a blunt instrument to their Islamic adversaries. Even in Saudi Arabia, where the royal establishment had distanced itself from its Wahhabi roots, the guardians of the Wahhabi flame were granted strong influence over all stages of education—an idea that seemed the better part of wisdom. Only under the region's most repressive regimes, Syria and Iraq, was a tight state grip kept on the educational establishment.

Pieces of the educational infrastructure drifted under the control of assertive new religious groups just as whole pieces of the economy were ceded to the private sector. It was inevitable that fiscally strapped regimes would take the next step and allow the private sector to begin to finance education at all levels and, in many instances, for profit. There are now four private universities in Egypt, fourteen in Jordan, seven in the Palestinian territories, four in Sudan, and eight in Yemen. In Lebanon, there are almost as many private primary and secondary schools as there are public, and 20 out of the country's 21 universities are private.

In the United States too there has been a growth in the involvement of the private sector in education. But in the Middle East this trend exhibits fewer of the advantages and many more of the dangers than does its U.S. counterpart. Private institutions tend to be self-financing, able to raise funds from sectarian, ideological, or programmatic supporters, and they are generally staffed with highly motivated personnel. But it is difficult for public authorities to control the curriculum or to monitor what goes on in the classroom. In Lebanon, the Shiite group Hezbollah (designated by the State Department as a terrorist organization with global reach) now spends about $3.5 million a year to educate some 23,000 students at all levels. It has a generous financial-aid budget, allowing it to reach students in Lebanon's most deprived regions. The Islamic Association, funded by Saudi Arabia, is also active at a somewhat more modest level. In short, states in the region feel they must call on the nongovernmental sector to help save their educational systems. That gambit is very risky, for those who answer the call will range from zealots to hucksters, along with everyone in between.

Sold American

In recent years, "American" schools and universities have been established in Armenia, Azerbaijan, Bulgaria, Kazakhstan, Morocco, Jordan, and Sharjah and Dubai of the United Arab Emirates. They have long been present in Egypt, Palestine, and Lebanon, and in the latter country there has been a surge in new American institutions in recent years. Now that Syria has legalized the establishment of private schools and universities, private Syrian investors will inevitably seek partnerships with U.S. institutions. Similarly, in Saudi Arabia the private sector has been encouraged to invest in primary through university education, and there again ties with U.S. institutions are being sought. In one of the most spectacular partnerships, Qatar has contracted with Cornell's Weill School of Medicine to set up a fully accredited medical school that will graduate its first doctors in about five years.

Most of this American involvement in Middle Eastern education is highly constructive, but it has been mirrored by another trend that is potentially harmful. Many private institutions in the Middle East now claim to offer an "American education," but some of them offer only the name and not the content. Some of these new American institutions may well earn the adjective a bad reputation. They are simply marketing the name itself, offering some business and computer courses, but providing little of the real curriculum and content that makes the model distinctive. Because there are no credible national or regional accreditation bodies, almost any group of private investors can enter the market. Parents are sufficiently desperate or gullible to grab what appears to be a life buoy called "American."

The new "American" schools address an audience that by and large may have little real knowledge of what American higher education is all about. What they do know is that the U.S. system has been hugely successful and has had global impact. They know that it has not only helped make the United States the economic and military superpower that it is, but that it has produced the scientific, business, and educational leadership for many other countries. This audience also recognizes English as the key to technology and business, and as their children's ladder to success. They do not know much or care about the real keys to this success—flexibility and choice, critical thinking and problem solving, academic freedom, and broad-based, general education. But they do see that something happens at MIT or Berkeley or the American University of Beirut that does not happen in their public institutions, and they desperately want that something for their children.

This market is made up of the growing middle class composed of graduates of the public institutions established in the state-led experiments of the 1960s and 1970s. They sense the slow tectonic shift in their economies in favor of the domestic and international private sectors. They are fully aware of the technological and information revolution sweeping the world, and they do not want their children to be left behind. For this market, the word "American" is to education what "Swiss" is to watches.

No Silver Bullet

It is tempting for someone like myself to piggyback onto the war against terrorism by claiming that higher education, American and otherwise, is the universal solvent that reduces to manageable proportions the frustrations and anger of ill-trained and unemployable youth who feed into radical movements. But the evidence does not unambiguously point in that direction. In their study of Lebanon's Hezbollah, the scholars Alan Krueger and Jitka Maleckova have shown that neither relative poverty nor low levels of education correlate with the resort to violence and terror. To the contrary, the relatively well educated and the better off are more likely to embrace violence. Mohammed Atta is probably paradigmatic in this sense. It could be that these more privileged individuals are fueled by outrage at the poverty and illiteracy they see around them, but there is no solid evidence for this theory. No educator could guarantee that all students all of the time will go forth to be productive, reasonable citizens, and no rational person should expect that. It is true, however, that education provides broad pictures of deprivation and injustice because it is the obligation of higher education to help people understand broad historical trends and broad patterns in the distribution of economic and political power.

To say that some recipients of higher education may become politically extreme, professionally dishonest, or criminal obviously does not mean that education should be done away with. The probability is that all forms of education generally spread important values of work and reward for performance, broaden world views, and provide skills with which individuals can earn a decent livelihood and contribute to their societies. The few bad apples that are graduated unfortunately can have a destructive impact out of all proportion to their tiny numbers.

Higher education cannot erase clashing interests or inimical policies. But it can have a role in shaping the way conflicts are conducted, the rhetoric of the debate itself, and the analysis of what is at stake. It can promote a broader understanding of the route to certain impasses and of alternative roads past them. When conflict itself appears inevitable, people can learn to enter battle more in sorrow than in anger, to maintain a minimum respect for their opponents, and to keep at least a thread of contact with their enemies. But most of the institutions of higher education in the Muslim Middle East are not designed to play this role. They act as degree mills, not centers of analysis and debate. Students may graduate with some skills, but they tend to either keep the values they brought with them or imbibe those of the religious groups to whom university politics have been ceded.

In contrast, the American institutions in the region help provide an education that encourages the open debate of issues, the cultivation of a skeptical attitude toward received wisdom, and habits of weighing and assessing evidence in an effort to solve real problems. Those institutions do not train large numbers, but they also have a far-reaching impact because they train leaders in all walks of life. Those leaders may continue to resent U.S. policies and criticize U.S. leadership, but they want to import its institutional successes in governance, legal arrangements, and business organization.

These universities are private and relatively expensive. They are all struggling to increase financial aid to make their education available to less advantaged students from the region. Congress is now in a role to help. It has been considering a new, federally funded Middle East Partnership Initiative, which, if passed, would allocate modest funding from an initial appropriation of $20 million for scholarships to bring students from the Islamic world to American schools in the Middle East. No matter how small these initial sums are, such money would be well spent.

These American institutions are not islands; they are thoroughly enmeshed in their regions' societies through their faculty, students, staff, and trustees. But their American roots are strong and nurtured by constant contact with U.S. academia. They are points of vibrant contact and exchange between our societies. What these institutions do, one hopes, will become contagious.

Reading Comprehension—Points of Engagement

1. On pages 352–353, Waterbury provides several reasons for his question, "Why do they hate us?" List as many as you can. Then identify the one that is most compelling to Waterbury and explain why he takes that position. Take note of the section titles in your answer. They may help you narrow your list down and identify Waterbury's position.

2. Consider the following quote from Waterbury's essay: "Today's crisis is not one of values, let alone civilizations, but one of interests" (353). What does this mean? What crisis? Whose values? What civilizations? Whose interests? Look closely at the context of this quotation, then paraphrase it *in your own words* in 3-4 sentences. Be sure you explain Waterbury's important terms: crisis, conflict, values, interests, and any other terms you deem relevant to representing Waterbury's position fully and accurately.

3. According to Waterbury, what are the hallmarks of American education? Look on page 358 for your answer, and list them. Write 1-2 sentences on the significance of these hallmarks in terms of the affect, and effectiveness, of American education abroad. Next, turn to page 355 and answer the following question: How do these American institutions in the Middle East compare with local systems of education? Be as detailed as you can in 1-2 paragraphs. Incorporate at least two quotations from Waterbury in your answer.

4. Close-read the section titled "No Silver Bullet." What is Waterbury's position on the potential for education to mitigate international conflict? (Look up the word mitigate if you don't know what it means). Choose one 1-2 sentence quotation from this section that you think best represents Waterbury's position and write it down. Next choose one 1-2 sentence quotation from this section that describes the challenges facing American institutions in the Middle East. Finally, construct a full paragraph using these two quotations that incorporates your *own* response to the question: how successful can education be in mitigating international conflict?

Assignment Questions—Points of Departure

1. Is education the solution to serious conflict? What is Waterbury's position on this issue? What about the positions represented in essays by Franklin Foer, Malcolm Gladwell, or Jack Hitt? What about your position? Do you think that education, American or otherwise, can ultimately solve conflicts between individuals or groups of people? What kind, or quality, of education? If not education, then what? And under what circumstances? Refer to essays by Waterbury and at least one other author from the list above, and be clear about what *kind* of conflict each author addresses. Remember that a single author may also describe a number of different positions, some of which may belong to other people. Be sure to close-read and distinguish between your position, your authors' positions, and other positions they may represent in their essays.

2. What do you think should be the relationship between religion and government? What role should education have in this relationship? Your project for this paper is to articulate a textually-engaged response to these two difficult questions using essays by John Waterbury and one of the following authors: Lisa Belkin, Paul Davies, Jane Goodall, Arlie Russell Hochschild, Fenton Johnson, Barbara King-solver, or Lewis Lapham.

3. John Waterbury claims that the current foreign relations crisis between America and the Middle East is not one of "values" but one of "interests" (353). What does this mean? Are these conflicts of interest true only between America and the Middle East, or are they the nature of all international relations? How would V.S. Naipaul respond to this question? How would Franklin Foer respond to this question? Lewis Lapham? Lenore Look? What do these other essays reveal about the national adoption of "values" and "interests"? Write a paper in which you answer these questions using Waterbury and Naipaul, Foer, Lapham or Look.

4. Is it possible for American identity—the character of America—to be exported? Why or why not? What does Waterbury have to say about this? Lewis Lapham? Lenore Look? Michael Kamber? Write a paper in which your propose your own response to the question of whether it's possible to "export America." To help you get started, consider the following questions in the context of the essays you've chosen to address: What, about America, is so appealing to other countries? What makes the exportation of these attributes of America challenging in these countries? How do different countries value these attributes differently? Do they? And finally, is it possible to export America at all?

The World and Other Places
Jeanette Winterson

Points of Access

1. When you dream at night, or daydream during the day, how do you experience your physical surroundings? Are you more conscious of them? Less? Is the physical world more vivid or does it seem to disappear around you? How are you sitting? Lying down? Do you close your eyes when you daydream, or leave them open? Freewrite for 15 minutes about what happens to you and the world around you when you 'go someplace else' in your mind.

2. When you hear the word "romance" what do you think of? What do you regard as romantic? List as many descriptions of romance as you can. What makes these things romantic? What do these kinds of romances do for you? What do you get from them as a person?

3. Have you ever heard the expressions "I'm going to look for myself" or "I'm going off to find myself"? What do these expressions mean? How do people act on these statements? Do they literally go someplace new? Do they act differently than they normally would? Do you think they find what they're looking for? What do you think that is? What do you think they find?

When I was a boy I made model aeroplanes.

We never had the money to go anywhere, sometimes we didn't have the money to go to the shop. There were six of us at night in the living room, six people and six carpet tiles. Usually the tiles were laid two by three in a dismal rectangle, but on Saturday night, aeroplane night, we took one each and sat cross legged with the expectation of an Arabian prince. We were going to fly away, and we held on to the greasy underside of our mats, waiting for the magic word to lift us.

Bombay, Cairo, Paris, New York. We took it in turns to say the word, and the one whose word it was, took my model aeroplane and spun it where it hung from the ceiling, round and round our blow-up globe. We had saved cereal tokens for the globe and it had been punctured twice. Iceland was held together by Sellotape and Great Britain was only a rubber bicycle patch on the panoply of the world.

*   *   *

I had memorised the flight times from London Heathrow to anywhere you could guess at in the world. It was my job to announce our flying time, the aircraft data, and to wish the passengers a comfortable trip. I pointed out landmarks on the way and we would lean over the fireplace to take a look at Mont Blanc or crane our necks round the back of the settee to get a glimpse of the Rockies.

Half way through our trip, Mother, who was Chief Steward, swayed down the aisle with cups of tea and toast and Marmite. After that, Dad came forward with next week's jobs around the house scribbled on little bits of paper. We dipped into the pouch, and somebody, the lucky one, would get Duty Free on theirs, and they didn't have to do a thing.

When we reached our destination, we were glad to stand up and stretch our legs. Then my sister gave us each a blindfold. We put it on, and sat quietly, dreaming, imagining, while one of us started talking about the strange place we were visiting.

*   *   *

How hot it is getting off the plane. Hot and stale like opening the door of a tumble drier. There are no lights to show us where to go. Death will be this way; a rough passage with people we have never met and a hasty run across the tarmac to the terminal building.

Inside, in the day-for-night illumination, a group of Indians were playing cellos. Who are these orchestral refugees? Can it be part of the service? Beyond them, urchins with bare feet are leaping up and down with ragged cardboard signs, each bearing the name of someone more important than ourselves. These are the people who will be whisked away in closed cars to comfortable beds. The rest of us will search for the bus.

Luggage. Heaven or Hell in the hereafter will be luggage or the lack of it. The ones who recognised that love is enough and that possessions are borrowed pastimes, will float free through the exit sign, their arms ready to hug their friends, their toothbrush in their pocket. The ones who stayed up late, gathering and gathering like demented bees, will find that you can take it with you. The joke is that you have to carry it yourself.

*   *   *

Here comes the bus. It has three wheels, maybe four, and the only part noisier than the engine is the horn. All human life is here. I am travelling between a chicken coop and a fortune teller. The chickens peck at my legs and suddenly the fortune teller grabs my palm. She laughs in my face.

'When you grow up you will learn to fly.'

For the rest of the journey I am bitten by mosquitoes.

*   *   *

At last we have reached the Hotel Cockroach. Dusty mats cover the mud floor and the Reception Clerk has an open wound in his cheek. He tells me he was stabbed but not to worry. Then he serves me lukewarm tea and shows me my room. It has a view over the incinerator and is farthest from the bathroom. At least I will not learn to think highly of myself.

In the darkness and the silence I can hear, far below, the matter of life continuing without me. The night-shift. What are they doing, these people who come and go, cleaning, bringing food, wanting money, wanting to fight. What will they eat? Where will they sleep? Do they love someone? How many of them will see morning? Will I?

Dreams. The smell of incense and frangipani. The moon sailing on her back makes white passages on the dun floor. The moon and the white clouds at the window. How many times have I seen it? How many times do I stop and look as if I had never seen it before? Perhaps it is true that the world is made new again every day but our minds are not. The clamp that holds me will not let me go.

During the night a mouse gave birth behind the skirting board.

*   *   *

At the end of my story, my family and I swopped anecdotes and exchanged souvenirs. Later, we retired to bed with the weariness of a traveller's reunion. We had done what the astronauts do, travelled in space that did not belong to us, uncoupled ourselves from time.

That night, I knew I would get away, better myself. Not because I despised who I was, but because I did not know who I was. I was waiting to be invented. I was waiting to invent myself.

*   *   *

The pilot and I went up in the aeroplane. It was a Cessna, modern and beautiful, off white with a blue stripe right round it and a nose as finely balanced as a pedigree muzzle. I wanted to cup it in both hands and say, 'Well done boy.'

In spite of the air conditioned cockpit, overwarm and muzzy in an unexpected economy class way, the pilot had a battered flying jacket stuffed behind his seat. It was authentic, grubby sheepskin and a steel zip. I asked him why he needed it.

'Romance,' he said, grinning. 'Flying is romantic, even now, even so.'

We were under a 747 at the time, and I thought of the orange seats crammed three abreast on either side, and all the odds and ends of families struggling with their plastic trays and beach gear.

'Is that romantic?' I said, pointing upwards.

He glanced out of the reinforced glass.

'That's not flying. Thats following the road.'

For a while we travelled in silence. I watched him; strong jaw with necessary stubble. Brown eyes that never left the sky. He was pretending to be the only man in the air. His dream was the first dream, when men in plus fours and motorcycle goggles pedalled with the single mindedness of a circus chimp to get their wooden frames and canvas wings upwards and upwards and upwards. It was a solo experience even when there were two of you.

What did Amy Johnson say? 'If the whole world were flying beside me I would still be flying alone.' Rhetoric, you think, frontier talk. Then you reach your own frontier and it's not rhetoric anymore.

*   *   *

My parents were so proud of me when I joined the Air Force. I stood in our cluttered living room in my new uniform and I felt like an angel on a visit. I felt like Gabriel come to tell the shepherds the Good News.

'Soon you'll have your own wings,' said my mother.

My father had bought a bottle of Scotch.

In my bedroom, the model aeroplanes had been carefully dusted. Sopwith Camel. Spitfire. Tiger Moth. I picked them up one by one and turned over their balsa wood frames and rice paper wings. I never used a kit. What hopes they carried. More than the altar at church. More than a good school report. In the secret places, under the fuselage, stuck to the tail-fin, I had hidden my hopes.

My mother came in. 'Will you take them with you?' I shook my head. I'd be laughed at, made fun of. Yet each of us in our bunks at lights-out would be thinking of model aeroplanes and the things from home we couldn't talk about anymore.

She said, 'I gave them a wipe anyway.'

*   *   *

Bombay. Cairo. Paris. New York. I've been to those places now. The curious thing is that no matter how different they are, the people are all preoccupied with the same things, that is, the same thing; how to live. We have to eat, we want to make money, but in every pause the question returns: How shall I live?

I saw three things that made this clear to me.

*   *   *

The first was a beggar in New York. He was sitting, feet apart, head in hands, on a low wall beside a garage. As I walked by him, he whispered, 'Do you have two dollars?' I gave him the folded bills, and he said, 'Can you sit with me a minute?'

His name was Tony. He was a compulsive gambler trying to go straight. He thought he might land a job on Monday morning if only he could sleep the weekend in a hostel, get some rest, be clean. For a week he had been sleeping by the steam duct of the garage.

I gave him the hostel money and a little more for food and the clenched fist of his body unfolded. He was talkative, gentle. Already in his mind he had the job, was making a go of it, and had met a sweet woman in a snack bar. Was that the gambler in him or ordinary human hope? Already in his mind he was looking past the job and the apartment into the space that had turned him over the wall.

'Nobody used to look at me,' he said. 'Even when I had money, I was one of those guys who get looked through. It's like being a ghost. If no one can see you you're dead. What's the point of trying to live if you are already dead?'

He shook my hand and thanked me. He was going to the hostel before it closed, or maybe he was going to a dog, I can't know. I don't need to know. There's enough I need to know just for myself.

*   *   *

I said there were three things. The second was a dress designer living over her studio in Milan. She was rich, she was important. She liked airmen. I used to sit with her in the studio, she never had time for a meal or a trip somewhere, she ate like an urchin, one leg hooked round her stool, palm full of olives. She spat the stones at her models. We were talking one night and she got angry. She prodded me with the shears she kept on her work table.

'Stop thinking,' she said. 'The more you think, the faster you cut your own throat. What is there to think about? It always ends up the same way. In your mind there is a bolted door. You have to work hard not to go near that door. Parties, lovers, career, charity, babies, who cares what it is, so long as you avoid the door. There are times, when I am on my own, fixing a drink, walking upstairs, when I see the door waiting for me. I have to stop myself pulling the bolt and turning the handle. Why? On the other side of the door is a mirror, and I will have to see myself. I'm not afraid of what I am. I'm afraid I will see what I am not.'

*   *   *

I said there were three things. The third was a woman in the park with her dog. The dog was young. The woman was old. Every so often she took out a bottle of water and a little bowl and gave the dog a drink.

'Come on Sandy,' she'd say, when he'd finished, and they would both disappear into the bushes, the dog's tail bobbing behind.

She was poor, I could see that. Put us side by side and how do we look? I'm six feet tall in a smart airman's uniform and I have a strong grip and steady eyes. She's about five feet high and threadbare. I could lift her with one hand.

But when she met my gaze one day I dropped my eyes and blushed like a teenager. I was walking past her in the opposite direction and I smiled and said, 'How are you?'

She looked at me with eyes that have long since pierced through the cloud cover and as we talked, I realised she was happy. Happy. The kind of happiness that comes from a steadiness inside. This was genuine. This was not someone who had turned away from the bolted door. It was open. She was on the other side.

*   *   *

For some years, early in my Air Force days, I did not bother myself with the single simple question that is the hardest in the world. How shall I live? I was living wasn't I? I was adventure, manliness, action. That's how we define ourselves isn't it?

Then one day I awoke with the curious sensation of no longer being myself. I hadn't turned into a beetle or a werewolf and my friends treated me in the same way as before, I put on my favourite well-worn clothes, bought newspapers, took a holiday, went to Milan, walked in the park. At last I called on the doctor.

'Doctor I'm not myself anymore.'

He asked me about my sex life and prescribed a course of antidepressants.

I went to the library and borrowed books from the philosophy and psychology sections, terrified in case I should be spotted by someone who knew me. I read Jung who urged me to make myself whole, I read Lacan who wants me to accept that I'm not.

None of it helped me. All the time I thought crazily, 'If this isn't me then I must be somewhere else.'

*   *   *

That's when I started travelling so much, left the forces, bought my own plane. Mostly I teach flying now, and sometimes I take out families who have won the First Prize in a packet soup competition. It doesn't matter. I have plenty of free time and I do what I need to do, which is to look for myself.

I know that if I fly for long enough, for wide enough, for far enough, I'll catch a signal on the radar that tells me there's another aircraft on my wing. I'll glance out of the reinforced glass, and it won't be a friendly pilot that I'll see, all stubble and brown eyes. It will be me. Me in the cockpit of that other plane.

*   *   *

I went home to visit my mother and father. I flew over their village, taxied down their road and left the nose of my plane pushed up against the front door. The tail was just on the pavement and I was worried that some traffic warden might issue a ticket for obstruction, so I hung a sign on the back that said 'FLYING DOCTOR.'

I'm always nervous about going home, just as I am nervous about rereading books that have meant a lot to me.

My parents wanted me to tell them about the places I've been and what I've seen, their eyes were eager and full of life.

Bombay. Cairo. Paris. New York. We have invented them so many times that to tell the truth will be a disappointment. The blow-up globe still hangs over the mantelpiece, its plastic crinkly and torn. The countries of the Common Market are held together with red tape.

We went through my postcards one by one. I gave them presents; a sari for my mother and a Stetson for my father. They are the children now.

Time passes through the clock. It's time for me to leave. They come outside to wave me off.

'It's a lovely plane,' says my mother. 'Does it give you much trouble?'

I rev the engine and the neighbours stand in astonishment in their doorways as the plane gathers speed down our quiet road. A moment before the muzzle breaks through the apostal window in the church, I take off, rising higher and higher, and disappearing into the end stream of the sun.

Reading Comprehension—Points of Engagement

1. Consider the following quote from page 365: "That night, I knew I would get away, better myself. Not because I despised who I was, but because I did not know who I was. I was waiting to be invented. I was waiting to invent myself." What does the

narrator mean by these statements? What happens directly before this passage to influence the narrator's intentions? What happens directly after? How does the structure effect your understanding of the narrator's experiences, intentions and actions?

2. What does Winterson mean when she writes, "Rhetoric, you think, frontier talk. Then you reach your own frontier and it's not rhetoric anymore" (366)? Rewrite this idea in your own words, and expand on it, using examples both from her story and from your own experience.

3. Near the middle of the story, the narrator proclaims that wherever he goes, "people are all preoccupied with the same things, that is, the same thing: how to live" (366). What are the three things that make this clear to the narrator? Look to pages 367–368 for your answers. List them. Then provide 2-3 sentences of explanation for each about why you think these events or observations were so clarifying for the narrator in determining how to live.

4. Consider the following two passages from Winterson: "Then one day I awoke with the curious sensation of no longer being myself . . . All the time I thought crazily, 'If this isn't me then I must be somewhere else'" (368). Why does the narrator no longer feel like himself? Point to specific sentences within this section that help you answer this question.

5. Consider the following refrain in Winterson's essay: "Bombay. Cairo. Paris. New York" (363). Now read this passage in context on page 369, the last place it appears. Why is this refrain important to the narrator? What does it teach us by appearing over and over in the essay? What does it teach the narrator? How do you know?

Assignment Questions—Points of Departure

1. What are dreams and what do they do for us? Can we shape reality through our dreams? How and to what extent? Write a paper in which you answer these questions using essays by Jeanette Winterson and one of the following authors: David Brooks, Adam Gopnik, Jack Hitt, Michael Kamber, Lewis Lapham, Lenore Look, Francine Prose, or Lauren Slater.

2. What is true happiness? Do you think it is possible? How do you think it should be defined? What would it look like? Use essays by Winterson and one of the following authors to propose answers to these questions: Alain de Botton, David Brooks,

Malcolm Gladwell, Jane Goodall, Adam Gopnik, Arlie Russell Hochschild, Fenton Johnson, Michael Kamber, V.S. Naipaul, or Francine Prose.

3. Can we invent, and re-invent, ourselves? If so, how do we do it? If not, why not? What does Jeanette Winterson have to say about the possibilities of self-invention, who we are, and who we can be, as human beings? What about Lisa Belkin, Susan Blackmore, Malcom Gladwell, Adam Gopnik, Lewis Lapham, Lenore Look, Steven Pinker, Katha Pollitt, Francine Prose, Lauren Slater, and Andrew Sullivan? Write a paper in which you propose answers to these questions using Winterson and one of these other authors.

4. Consider the following quotation from Winterson's story: "Perhaps it is true that the world is made new again every day but our minds are not. The clamp that holds me will not let me go" (365). What does Winterson mean by this? Does the world around us limit our imaginations, or does the world around us show us the expansiveness of our imaginations? How and in what ways? Your project for this paper is to answer this question using Winterson and one of the following authors: Susan Blackmore, Alain de Botton, David Brooks, Paul Davies, Jane Goodall, Jack Hitt, Lenore Look, Katha Pollitt, Lauren Slater, or Andrew Sullivan.

Acknowledgments

"The Made-to-Order Savior" by Lisa Belkin. Originally published in *The New York Times Magazine;* July 1, 2001, Late Edition—Final, Section 6, Page 36, Column 1. Copyright 2001 by Lisa Belkin.

"Strange Creatures" by Susan Blackmore, from *The Meme Machine,* published by Oxford University Press, 1999, pp 1–9. Copyright 1999 by Susan Blackmore. Reprinted by permission of Oxford University Press.

"The Ultimate Memeplex" by Susan Blackmore, from *The Meme Machine,* published by Oxford University Press, 1999, pp 219–234. Copyright 1999 by Susan Blackmore. Reprinted by permission of Oxford University Press.

"On Habit" by Alain de Botton, from *The Art of Travel.* Copyright © 2002 by Alain de Botton. Reprinted by permission of the author.

"Our Sprawling Supersize Utopia." Excerpted and adapted with permission of Simon & Schuster Adult Publishing Group from *On Paradise Drive* by David Brooks. Copyright © 2004 by David Brooks.

"E.T. and God." © 2003 P.C.W. Davies , as first published in *The Atlantic Monthly.*

"Soccer vs. McWorld" by Franklin Foer. Copyright 2004 by *Foreign Policy.* Reproduced with permission of *Foreign Policy* in the format Textbook via Copyright Clearance Center.

"The Theory of Thin Slices: How a Little Bit of Knowledge Goes a Long Way" by Malcolm Gladwell, from *Blink.* Copyright © 2005 by Malcolm Gladwell. Reprinted by permission of the author.

"In the Forests of Gombe" by Jane Goodall, from *Orion,* Spring 2000. © The Jane Goodall Institute www.janegoodall.org.

"Bumping Into Mr. Ravioli." Copyright © 2002 by Adam Gopnik, as originally appeared in September 30, 2002 issue of *The New Yorker.* Reprinted with the permission of The Wylie Agency, Inc.

Contributors

Since 1995 **Lisa Belkin** has been a contributing writer, specializing in medical and social issues, for *The New York Times Magazine*, where "The Made-to-Order Savior" first appeared in 2001. Her books include *First Do No Harm*, about a hospital's ethics committee, *Show Me A Hero*, about the impact of desegregation, and *Life's Work: Confessions of an Unbalanced Mom*. She lives in Westchester County, New York.

Susan Blackmore's *The Meme Machine* has been translated into 11 languages. A visiting lecturer at the University of the West of England, Bristol, her interests include evolutionary theory, consciousness, and meditation. She writes for several magazines and newspapers and has written a number of other books, including *Beyond the Body*, *Dying to Live*, and the autobiographical *In Search of the Light*.

Alain de Botton's work has been described as "philosophy of everyday life." In *The Art of Travel*, from which "On Habit" is selected, he explores the psychology of travel. De Botton's other books include *On Love, How Proust Can Change your Life*, and *The Consolations of Philosophy*. He lives in London.

Journalist and political analyst **David Brooks** is a senior editor at *The Weekly Standard* and a contributing editor at *Newsweek*. His work appears in *The Atlantic Monthly*, and he is a commentator for National Public Radio and the NewsHour with Jim Lehrer. He is the author of *Bobos In Paradise: The New Upper Class and How They Got There* and editor of the anthology *Backward and Upward: The New Conservative Writing*. He lives in Washington, D.C.

Paul Davies's work explores such essential questions as the nature of time, the foundations of quantum mechanics, the origin of life, and the nature of consciousness. A professor of physics and natural philosophy, he has written over 25 books, including *The Edge of Infinity, Other Worlds*, and *God and the New Physics*. He contributes regularly to newspapers, journals and magazines, including *The Economist, The New York Times, Scientific American*, and *The Atlantic Monthly*, where "E.T. and God" appeared in 2003.

Franklin Foer is assistant editor of *The New Republic*. He writes about politics and the media for *U.S. News and World Report*. His work has appeared in *Slate*, *The New York Times*, *The Washington Post*, *Lingua Franca* and *Spin*. He lives in Washington, D.C.

A staff writer for *The New Yorker* since 1996, **Malcolm Gladwell** is well-known as the author of *The Tipping Point: How Little Things Can Make a Big Difference*. His latest book is *Blink: The Power of Thinking without Thinking*, in which the contribution to this collection, "The Theory of Thin Slices," originally appeared. Malcolm Gladwell was born in England, grew up in Canada, and now lives in New York City.

Jane Goodall is in her fifth decade of studying and writing about primate behavior in Gombe. She founded the Gombe Stream Research Center in Tanzania and the Jane Goodall Institute for Wildlife Research and Conservation in Silver Spring, MD. Her books include *In the Shadow of Man*, *Reason for Hope*, and two volumes of autobiographical letters.

A contributing writer to *The New Yorker* since 1986, **Adam Gopnik**'s work has also been heard on the Canadian Broadcasting Corporation. His most recent book, *Paris to the Moon,* chronicles his family's life in Paris from 1995-2000. Despite his sister's advice in "Bumping Into Mr. Ravioli," Adam Gopnik currently lives in New York City with his family.

Jack Hitt is a contributing editor to *Harper's*, *GQ*, *This American Life*, and formerly, to *Lingua Franca*. His work also often appears in the *New York Times Magazine*, *Outside Magazine* and the *LA Times*. The essay in this collection, "Dinosaur Dreams," was originally published in *Harper's Magazine*. A native of South Carolina, Jack Hitt now lives in New Haven, Connecticut.

Arlie Russell Hochschild's "From the Frying Pan into the Fire," is a chapter from her most recent book, *The Commercialization of Intimate Life: Notes from Home and Work*, which explores the changing roles of men and women. She is also the author of *The Managed Heart* and *The Time Bind*. Her work has appeared in *Harper's Magazine*, *Mother Jones*, and *Psychology Today*. She lives in San Francisco.

Fenton Johnson is the author of two award-winning novels, *Crossing the River* and *Scissors, Paper, Rock*, and a memoir, *Geography of the Heart*. A contributor to *Harper's Magazine* and *The New York Times Magazine*, he currently teaches at the University of Arizona.

Steven Johnson is the author of several books including *Interface Culture*, *Everything Bad is Good For You*, and *Emergence: The Interconnected Lives of Ants, Brains Cities, and Software*, where the chapter, "Control Artist," first appeared in print. He is also a contributing editor at *Wired Magazine*, a columnist for *Discover*, and a regular blogger. Johnson and his family live in New York City.

Michael Kamber has researched extensively the immigrant population in New York and its effect on Mexican society. A freelance writer and photographer, he has published in Wired.com, *Brooklyn Bridge*, and Mother Jones.com. The essay in this anthology, "Toil and Temptation," first appeared in the *Village Voice*, where it was part three of a series on immigration called "Crossing To The Other Side." Michael Kamber lives in New York City.

Originally a journalist and scientific writer, **Barbara Kingsolver** has emerged as one of America's prominent activist voices. Well-known as a prolific novelist, Kingsolver has also written several volumes of essays, including *Small Wonders*, where "A Fist in the Eye of God" was originally published. Kingsolver lives in Tucson, Arizona.

Lewis Lapham is editor of *Harper's Magazine* and author of a number of books including *Lapham's Rules of Influence* and *Lights, Camera, Democracy!* Before joining *Harper's*, the magazine in which "Who and What is American?" was originally published, Lapham worked as a reporter, syndicated columnist, and host of several public television series. He lives and writes in New York City.

Lenore Look has authored several children's books including *Love as Strong as Ginger* and *Henry's First Moon Birthday*. Her essay "Facing the Village" was first published in the *Mānoa*, an Asian/Pacific academic journal, and then included in *The Best American Essays* (2001). Look, a graduate of Princeton University, lives in Randolph, NJ.

Nobel laureate **V.S. Naipaul** (Sir Vidiadhar Surajprasad Naipaul) was born in Trinidad in the West Indies to parents who had emigrated from India. On receiving a scholarship to Oxford University, he moved to the United Kingdom where he lived, when not traveling, for the remainder of his life. Naipaul worked as a freelance writer and broadcaster as well as a novelist and poet, and received the Nobel Prize in Literature in 2001. "East Indian" reflects the exploration of identity and post-colonial sensibility that permeates Naipaul's writing.

Steven Pinker is an experimental psychologist whose research focuses on language acquisition and cognition. The Johnstone Professor of Psychology at Harvard University, Pinker has also written four influential and popular books about psychology, most recently *The Blank Slate*, and starting in 1992 with *The Language Instinct*, to which "An Instinct to Acquire an Art" is the introduction. In addition to his scholarly accolades, Pinker's Harvard website cites his appearance as 'stud mullet' on the mullet-lovers.com website, providing evidence not only of his distinguished career, but also of his wonderful sense of humor.

Michael Pollan is a regular contributing writer to *The New York Times Magazine*. His latest books, *A Place of My Own* and *The Botany of Desire*, and essays, "Power Steer" and "An Animal's Place," are concerned with genetic engineering, the beef industry, gardening and scientific responsibility. Pollan lives in Connecticut where he continues his work in environmental journalism.

Katha Pollitt's groundbreaking *Nation* column, "Subject to Debate," has won her acclaim for more than a decade. Her essays on politics, cultural trends, feminism, and current events have been compiled in two volumes, *Reasonable Creatures: Essays on Women and Feminism* (1994) and *Subject to Debate: Sense and Dissents on Women, Politics and Culture* (2001). She lives and writes in New York City.

As a regular contributing editor to *Harper's Magazine*, **Francine Prose** has authored more than ten works of fiction and nonfiction. Her work has been called "elegant, eloquent and compassionate" and earned her recognition and awards from Guggenheim and Fulbright. She lives in New York City where she is also a Director's Fellow at the Center for Scholars and Writers at the New York City Public Library.

Lauren Slater is an author and psychotherapist whose work has been included in *The Best American Essays* (1994 and 1997). Her creative fiction has earned her many awards including the New Letters Literary Award and the Missouri Review Award.

"Dr. Daedalus" appears courtesy of *Harper's Magazine*. Slater lives and works in Massachusetts.

As a political scientist, **Andrew Sullivan** has written for *The New Republic*, *Esquire*, *The Washington Post*, *Daily Telegraph* and the *Sunday Times of London*. He is also a well-known blogger. His often-controversial topics and three nonfiction books have earned him several awards. Sullivan's cover story on testosterone, "The He Hormone," comes from *The New York Times Magazine*.

John Waterbury has written extensively on the politics of the Middle East, as well as the political economy of public enterprise. After holding the position of Professor of Politics and International Relations at Princeton University for 20 years, Waterbury moved to Lebanon, where he has been president of the American University of Beirut since 1998.

Growing up in the North of England with Pentecostal parents who wanted her to be a missionary, **Jeanette Winterson** came to attention in the British literary world in 1985 with her first novel *Oranges Are Not The Only Fruit*. Winterson is perhaps best known for her novels, but also has written in various other modes, including the anthology of short stories to which the essay in this collection, "The World And Other Places," gives its name. She is also a regular contributor to several major English newspapers. Winterson now divides her time between Oxfordshire and London.

Thanks to:

The Rutgers students in *Basic Composition* and *Basic Composition with Reading,* for your hard work at connective thinking, and for making the possibilities in this collection of essays come alive in your papers;

The Rutgers Writing Program instructors who launched the 1st edition of *Points of Departure* and contributed to this 2nd edition, for your insight, experience, and investment in making this reader a success in your classrooms;

Dee Renfrow and Anisha Sandhu at Houghton Mifflin, for making the work of publishing such a pleasure;

Richard Miller, Kurt Spellmeyer, Ann Jurecic, and Barclay Barrios, for your continued guidance, encouragement, professional and personal support;

Heather Robinson, for being a daily inspiration at the Douglass College Writing Program, and for your absolute dependability and invaluable collaboration over the two years of developing this book;

And finally, thanks to Denise and Nolan Huizenga, for your unwavering friendship and for giving me a peaceful place to think and work; to Laura Fuerstein, for keeping my feet on the ground and my face forward; and to Lauren Butcher, for being who you are, and for being who you are to me.

This collection is dedicated to my mother and father who taught me how to read.

Michelle

Michelle J. Brazier is an Assistant Director in the Rutgers Writing Program, and the Course Coordinator of Basic Composition. A doctoral candidate in the Rutgers English Department, she is completing her dissertation on Gertrude Stein, basic writers, and the development of the writing voice. Before entering graduate school at Rutgers and serving as an instructor and administrator in the Writing Program, Ms. Brazier was an Undergraduate Admissions Officer at Yale University, where she did her undergraduate studies in English and music.